Y0-BDT-810

The
Dublin Book
Of Irish Verse
1728–1909

The Dublin Book Of Irish Verse

1728–1909

Edited by

John Cooke

Granger Index Reprint Series

BOOKS FOR LIBRARIES PRESS
FREEPORT, NEW YORK

First Published 1909
Reprinted 1971

INTERNATIONAL STANDARD BOOK NUMBER:
0-8369-6251-6

LIBRARY OF CONGRESS CATALOG CARD NUMBER:
70-152148

PRINTED IN THE UNITED STATES OF AMERICA

PREFACE

THE DUBLIN BOOK OF IRISH VERSE is modelled on the lines of 'The Oxford Book of English Verse.' The Editor has made a careful and independent examination of the work of Irish writers, and where the selections include poems contained in existing Anthologies, the excellence or particular suitability of such extracts supplies a sufficient reason for their insertion.

The aim has been to render the book a fully representative volume of Anglo-Irish Verse. Due prominence has been given to the new school of Irish writers, the rapidly increasing volume of whose verse is, perhaps, the most remarkable feature of the Irish literary revival of our time.

The system adopted in the arrangement of authors is chronological down to recent years, when an alphabetical order is substituted. Notes are supplied at the end of the volume on such passages in the text as require elucidation; and occasional footnotes are given, where considered absolutely necessary to render the meaning of words and phrases explicit.

OLIVER GOLDSMITH

1 *Stanzas: On Woman*

1728–1774

WHEN lovely Woman stoops to folly,
And finds too late that men betray,
What charm can soothe her melancholy,
What art can wash her guilt away?

The only art her guilt to cover,
To hide her shame from every eye,
To give repentance to her lover,
And wring his bosom, is—to die.

2 *Hope*

From the Oratorio of 'The Captivity'

THE wretch condemned with life to part
Still, still on hope relies;
And every pang that rends the heart
Bids expectation rise.

Hope, like the gleaming taper's light,
Adorns and cheers our way;
And still, as darker grows the night,
Emits a brighter ray.

3

Memory

From the Same

MEMORY, thou fond deceiver!
  Still importunate and vain;
To former joys recurring ever,
  And turning all the past to pain;

Though, like the world, opprest oppressing,
  Thy smiles increase the wretch's woe,
And he who wants each other blessing
  In thee must ever find a foe.

4

The Pastor

From 'The Deserted Village'

AT church, with meek and unaffected grace,
  His looks adorned the venerable place;
Truth from his lips prevailed with double sway,
And fools, who came to scoff, remained to pray.
The service past, around the pious man,
With steady zeal, each honest rustic ran;
E'en children followed with endearing wile,
And plucked his gown, to share the good man's smile.
His ready smile a parent's warmth expressed;
Their welfare pleased him, and their cares distressed:
To them his heart, his love, his griefs were given,
But all his serious thoughts had rest in heaven.
As some tall cliff that lifts its awful form,
Swells from the vale, and midway leaves the storm,
Though round its breast the rolling clouds are spread,
Eternal sunshine settles on its head.

OLIVER GOLDSMITH

5 *From 'Threnodia Augustalis'*

WITH garlands of beauty, the Queen of the May
 No more will her crook or her temples adorn ;
For who'd wear a garland when she is away,
 When she is removed and shall never return!
On the grave of Augusta these garlands be placed,
 We'll rifle the Spring of its earliest bloom ;
And there shall the cowslip and primrose be cast,
 And the new blossomed thorn shall whiten her tomb !

Chorus

On the grave of Augusta this garland be placed,
 We'll rifle the Spring of its earliest bloom ;
And there shall the cowslip and primrose be cast,
 And the tears of her country shall water her tomb !

GEORGE OGLE

6 *Mailligh Mo Stór*

1742–1814

AS down by Banna's banks I strayed,
 One evening in May,
The little birds, in blithest notes,
 Made vocal every spray ;
They sung their little notes of love,
 They sung them o'er and o'er.
Ah ! grádh mo chroîdhe, mo cailín óg,
 'Si Mailligh mo stór.[1]

[1] Gra machree, ma colleen oge, Molly asthore—Love of my heart, my dear young girl, my darling Molly.

The daisy pied, and all the sweets
  The dawn of Nature yields—
The primrose pale, and violet blue,
  Lay scattered o'er the fields ;
Such fragrance in the bosom lies
  Of her whom I adore.
Ah ! gra machree, etc.

I laid me down upon a bank,
  Bewailing my sad fate,
That doomed me thus the slave of love
  And cruel Molly's hate ;
How can she break the honest heart
  That wears her in its core ?
Ah ! gra machree, etc.

You said you loved me, Molly dear !
  Ah ! why did I believe ?
Yet who could think such tender words
  Were meant but to deceive ?
That love was all I asked on earth—
  Nay, heaven could give no more.
Ah ! gra machree, etc.

Oh ! had I all the flocks that graze
  On yonder yellow hill,
Or lowed for me the numerous herds
  That yon green pasture fill—
With her I love I'd gladly share
  My kine and fleecy store.
Ah ! gra machree, etc.

GEORGE OGLE

Two turtle-doves, above my head,
  Sat courting on a bough;
I envied them their happiness,
  To see them bill and coo.
Such fondness once for me was shewn,
  But now, alas! 'tis o'er.
Ah! gra machree, etc.

Then fare thee well, my Molly dear!
  Thy loss I e'er shall moan;
Whilst life remains in my poor heart,
  'Twill beat for thee alone:
Though thou art false, may heaven on thee
  Its choicest blessings pour.
Ah! gra machree, etc.

JOHN PHILPOT CURRAN

7 *Let us be Merry before we go*

1750-1817

IF sadly thinking, with spirits sinking,
  Could, more than drinking, my cares compose,
A cure for sorrow from sighs I'd borrow,
  And hope to-morrow would end my woes.
But as in wailing there's nought availing,
  And Death unfailing will strike the blow,
Then for that reason, and for a season,
  Let us be merry before we go.

To joy a stranger, a wayworn ranger,
  In ev'ry danger my course I've run;
Now hope all ending, and death befriending,
  His last aid lending, my cares are done.

No more a rover, or hapless lover,
   My griefs are over—my glass runs low ;
Then for that reason, and for a season,
   Let us be merry before we go.

8 *The Monks of the Screw*

WHEN St. Patrick this order established,
   He called us the 'Monks of the Screw' ;
Good rules he revealed to our Abbot
   To guide us in what we should do.
But first he replenished our fountain
   With liquor the best from on high ;
And he said, on the word of a saint,
   That the fountain should never run dry.

'Each year, when your octaves approach,
   In full chapter convened let me find you ;
And when to the convent you come,
   Leave your favourite temptation behind you.
And be not a glass in your convent—
   Unless on a festival—found ;
And, this rule to enforce, I ordain it
   One festival all the year round.

'My brethren, be chaste—till you're tempted ;
   While sober, be grave and discreet ;
And humble your bodies with fasting,
   As oft as you've nothing to eat.
Yet, in honour of fasting, one lean face
   Among you I'd always require ;
If the Abbot should please, he may wear it,
   If not, let it come to the Prior.'

Come, let each take his chalice, my brethren,
And with due devotion prepare,
With hands and with voices uplifted,
Our hymn to conclude with a prayer.
May this chapter oft joyously meet,
And this gladsome libation renew,
To the Saint, and the Founder, and Abbot,
And Prior, and Monks of the Screw!

9 *Cushla Ma Chree*[1]

DEAR Erin, how sweetly thy green bosom rises!
An emerald set in the ring of the sea!
Each blade of thy meadows my faithful heart prizes,
Thou queen of the west! the world's cushla ma chree!

Thy gates open wide to the poor and the stranger—
There smiles hospitality hearty and free;
Thy friendship is seen in the moment of danger,
And the wand'rer is welcomed with cushla ma chree.

Thy sons they are brave; but, the battle once over,
In brotherly peace with their foes they agree;
And the roseate cheeks of thy daughters discover
The soul-speaking blush that says cushla ma chree.

Then flourish for ever, my dear native Erin!
While sadly I wander an exile from thee;
And, firm as thy mountains, no injury fearing,
May heaven defend its own cushla ma chree!

[1] Darling of my heart.

RICHARD BRINSLEY SHERIDAN

10 *Here's to the Maiden*

From 'The School for Scandal'

1751-1816

HERE'S to the maiden of bashful fifteen,
Here's to the widow of fifty ;
Here's to the flaunting extravagant quean,
And here's to the housewife that's thrifty !

Chorus

Let the toast pass,
Drink to the lass,
I'll warrant she'll prove an excuse for the glass.

Here's to the charmer whose dimples we prize ;
Now to the maid who has none, sir :
Here's to the girl with a pair of blue eyes,
And here's to the nymph with but one, sir !
Let the toast pass, etc.

Here's to the maid with a bosom of snow ;
Now to her that's as brown as a berry :
Here's to the wife with a face full of woe,
And now to the damsel that's merry !
Let the toast pass, etc.

For let 'em be clumsy, or let 'em be slim,
Young or ancient, I care not a feather ;
So fill up your glasses, nay, fill to the brim,
And let us e'en toast them together.
Let the toast pass, etc.

RICHARD BRINSLEY SHERIDAN

11 *Thou canst not Boast of Fortune's Store*

From 'The Duenna'

THOU canst not boast of Fortune's store,
  My love, while me they wealthy call:
But I was glad to find thee poor,
  For with my heart I'd give thee all.
    And then the grateful youth shall own
    I loved him for himself alone.

But when his worth my hand shall gain,
  No word or look of mine shall show
That I the smallest thought retain
  Of what my bounty did bestow:
    Yet still his grateful heart shall own
    I loved him for himself alone.

12 *Dry be that Tear*

DRY be that tear, my gentlest love,
  Be hush'd that struggling sigh;
Nor seasons, day, nor fate shall prove
  More fix'd, more true than I.
Hush'd be that sigh, be dry that tear,
  Cease boding doubt; cease anxious fear—
    Dry be that tear.

RICHARD BRINSLEY SHERIDAN

Ask'st thou how long my love will stay,
 When all that's new is past?
How long? ah, Delia, can I say
 How long my life will last?
Dry be that tear, be hush'd that sigh;
 At least I'll love thee till I die—
  Hush'd be that sigh.

And does that thought affect thee too,
 The thought of Sylvio's death,
That he who only breathed for you,
 Must yield that faithful breath?
Hush'd be that sigh, be dry that tear,
 Nor let us lose our heaven here—
  Dry be that tear.

WILLIAM DRENNAN

13

Eiré[1]

1754–1820

WHEN Eiré first rose from the dark-swelling flood,
 God blessed the green island, and saw it was
  good;
The emerald of Europe, it sparkled and shone,
In the ring of the world, the most precious stone.
In her sun, in her soil, in her station thrice blest,
With her back towards Britain, her face to the west,
Eiré stands proudly insular, on her steep shore,
And strikes her high harp 'mid the ocean's deep roar.

[1] Erin.

But when its soft tones seem to mourn and to weep,
A dark chain of silence is thrown o'er the deep;
At the thought of the past the tears gush from her
eyes,
And the pulse of her heart makes her white bosom
rise.
O! sons of green Eiré, lament o'er the time
When religion was war, and our country a crime;
When man in God's image inverted His plan,
And moulded his God in the image of man.

When the interest of state wrought the general woe,
The stranger a friend, and the native a foe;
While the mother rejoiced o'er her children oppressed,
And clasped the invader more close to her breast;
When, with Pale for the body and Pale for the soul,
Church and State joined in compact to conquer the
whole;
And, as Shannon was stained with Milesian blood,
Eyed each other askance and pronounced it was
good.

By the groans that ascend from your forefathers'
grave,
For their country thus left to the brute and the slave,
Drive the demon of Bigotry home to his den,
And where Britain made brutes now let Eiré make
men.
Let my sons like the leaves of the shamrock unite,
A partition of sects from one footstalk of right,
Give each his full share of the earth and the sky,
Nor fatten the slave where the serpent would die.

Alas ! for poor Eiré, that some are still seen
Who would dye the grass red from their hatred to
Green ;
Yet, O ! when you're up and they're down, let them
live,
Then yield them that mercy which they would not
give.
Arm of Eiré, be strong ! but be gentle as brave !
And, uplifted to strike, be still ready to save !
Let no feeling of vengeance presume to defile
The cause of, or men of, the Emerald Isle.

The cause it is good, and the men they are true,
And the Green shall outlive both the Orange and
Blue !
And the triumphs of Eiré her daughters shall share,
With the full swelling chest, and the fair flowing
hair.
Their bosom heaves high for the worthy and brave,
But no coward shall rest on that soft-swelling
wave ;
Men of Eiré ! awake, and make haste to be blest,
Rise—Arch of the Ocean, and Queen of the West !

14 *Wake of William Orr*

HERE our murdered brother lies—
Wake him not with women's cries ;
Mourn the way that manhood ought ;
Sit in silent trance of thought.

WILLIAM DRENNAN

Write his merits on your mind—
Morals pure and manners kind;
In his head, as on a hill,
Virtue placed her citadel.

Why cut off in palmy youth?
Truth he spoke, and acted truth—
Countrymen, 'Unite!' he cried,
And died—for what his Saviour died.

God of Peace, and God of Love,
Let it not thy vengeance move!
Let it not thy lightnings draw—
A Nation guillotin'd by law!

Hapless nation! rent and torn,
Thou wert early taught to mourn,
Warfare of six hundred years—
Epochs marked with blood and tears!

Hunted thro' thy native grounds,
Or flung reward to human hounds;
Each one pull'd and tore his share,
Heedless of thy deep despair.

Hapless Nation—hapless Land,
Heap of uncementing sand!
Crumbled by a foreign weight,
And, by worse, domestic hate.

God of Mercy! God of Peace!
Make the mad confusion cease;
O'er the mental chaos move,
Through it speak the light of love.

WILLIAM DRENNAN

Monstrous and unhappy sight,
Brothers' blood will not unite ;
Holy oil and holy water,
Mix, and fill the world with slaughter.

Who is she with aspect wild ?
The widow'd mother with her child—
Child new stirring in the womb !
Husband waiting for the tomb !

Angel of this sacred place,
Calm her soul and whisper peace,
Cord, or axe, or guillotin'
Make the sentence—not the sin.

Here we watch our brother's sleep ;
Watch with us, but do not weep ;
Watch with us thro' dead of night,
But expect the morning light.

Conquer fortune—persevere !—
Lo ! it breaks, the morning clear !
The cheerful cock awakes the skies,
The day is come—arise !—arise !

ANDREW CHERRY

15 *The Green Little Shamrock of Ireland*

1762–1812

THERE'S a dear little plant that grows in our isle,
'Twas St. Patrick himself sure that set it ;
And the sun on his labour with pleasure did smile,
And with dew from his eye often wet it.

It thrives through the bog, through the brake, and
the mireland ;
And he called it the dear little shamrock of Ireland—
The sweet little shamrock, the dear little sham-
rock,
The sweet little, green little, shamrock of Ireland !

This dear little plant still grows in our land,
Fresh and fair as the daughters of Erin,
Whose smiles can bewitch, whose eyes can command,
In each climate that they may appear in ;
And shine through the bog, through the brake, and
the mireland,
Just like their own dear little shamrock of Ireland.
The sweet little shamrock, the dear little sham-
rock,
The sweet little, green little, shamrock of Ireland !

This dear little plant that springs from our soil,
When its three little leaves are extended,
Denotes on one stalk we together should toil,
And ourselves by ourselves be befriended ;
And still through the bog, through the brake, and
the mireland,
From one root should branch, like the shamrock of
Ireland.
The sweet little shamrock, the dear little sham-
rock,
The sweet little, green little, shamrock of Ireland !

EDWARD LYSAGHT

16 *The Man who led the Van of Irish Volunteers*

1763–1810

THE gen'rous sons of Erin, in manly virtue bold,
With hearts and hands preparing our country to uphold,
Tho' cruel knaves and bigot slaves disturbed our isle some years,
Now hail the man, who led the van of Irish Volunteers.

Just thirty years are ending, since first his glorious aid,
Our sacred rights defending, struck shackles from our trade;
To serve us still, with might and skill, the vet'ran now appears,
That gallant man, who led the van of Irish Volunteers.

He sows no vile dissensions; good will to all he bears;
He knows no vain pretensions, no paltry fears or cares;
To Erin's and to Britain's sons his worth his name endears;
They love the man, who led the van of Irish Volunteers.

Opposed by hirelings sordid, he broke oppression's chain;
On statute-books recorded his patriot acts remain;
The equipoise his mind employs of Commons, King and Peers,
The upright man, who led the van of Irish Volunteers.

A British constitution—to Erin ever true—
In spite of state pollution, he gained in 'Eighty-two';
'He watch'd it in its cradle, and bedew'd its hearse
with tears,'[1]
This gallant man, who led the van of Irish Volunteers.

While other nations tremble, by proud oppressors
gall'd,
On hustings we'll assemble, by Erin's welfare call'd;
Our Grattan, there we'll meet him, and greet him
with three cheers;
The gallant man, who led the van of Irish Volunteers.

17 *Garnyvillo*[2]

HAVE you been at Garnyvillo?
Have you seen at Garnyvillo
Beauty's train trip o'er the plain
With lovely Kate of Garnyvillo?
Oh! she's pure as virgin snows,
Ere they light on woodland hill-O;
Sweet as dew-drop on wild rose,
Is lovely Kate of Garnyvillo!

Philomel, I've listened oft
To thy lay, nigh weeping willow—
Oh, the strain's more sweet, more soft,
That flows from Kate of Garnyvillo!
Have you been, etc.

[1] 'I watched by the cradle of Irish Independence, and I followed its hearse.'—GRATTAN.
[2] Usually modernised into Garnavilla.

As a noble ship I've seen
  Sailing o'er the swelling billow,
So I've marked the graceful mien
  Of lovely Kate of Garnyvillo.
      Have you been, etc.

If poets' prayers can banish cares,
  No cares should come to Garnyvillo ;
Joy's bright rays shall gild her days,
  And dove-like peace perch on her pillow :
    Charming maid of Garnyvillo !
    Lovely maid of Garnyvillo !
    Beauty, grace, and virtue wait
    On lovely Kate of Garnyvillo !

RICHARD ALFRED MILLIKEN

18 *The Groves of Blarney*

1767–1815

THE groves of Blarney
  They look so charming,
Down by the purling
  Of sweet, silent brooks,
Being banked with posies
That spontaneous grow there,
Planted in order
  By the sweet 'Rock Close.'
'Tis there the daisy
And the sweet carnation,

RICHARD ALFRED MILLIKEN

The blooming pink
  And the rose so fair.
The daffodowndilly,
Likewise the lily,
All flowers that scent
  The sweet, fragrant air.

'Tis Lady Jeffers
That own this station ;
Like Alexander,
  Or Queen Helen fair,
There's no commander
In all the nation,
For emulation,
  Can with her compare.
Such walls surround her,
That no nine-pounder
Could dare to plunder
  Her place of strength ;
But Oliver Cromwell
Her he did pommell,
And made a breach
  In her battlement.

There's gravel walks there
For speculation
And conversation
  In sweet solitude.
'Tis there the lover
May hear the dove, or
The gentle plover
  In the afternoon ;

And if a lady
Would be so engaging
As to walk alone in
  Those shady bowers,
'Tis there the courtier
He may transport her
Into some fort, or
  All under ground.

For 'tis there's a cave where
No daylight enters,
But cats and badgers
  Are for ever bred ;
Being mossed by nature,
That makes it sweeter
Than a coach-and-six or
  A feather bed.
'Tis there the lake is,
Well stored with perches,
And comely eels in
  The verdant mud ;
Besides the leeches,
And groves of beeches,
Standing in order
  For to guard the flood.

There's statues gracing
This noble place in—
All heathen gods
  And nymphs so fair ;
Bold Neptune, Plutarch,
And Nicodemus,
All standing naked
  In the open air !

RICHARD ALFRED MILLIKEN

So now to finish
This brave narration,
Which my poor genii
  Could not entwine;
But were I Homer,
Or Nebuchadnezzar,
'Tis in every feature
  I would make it shine.

'Father Prout' in his *Reliques* varies the original here given, and adds the following lines:—

There is a boat on
The lake to float on,
And lots of beauties
  Which I can't entwine;
But were I a preacher,
Or a classic teacher,
In every feature
  I'd make 'em shine!

There is a stone there,
That whoever kisses,
Oh! he never misses
  To grow eloquent;
'Tis he may clamber
To a lady's chamber,
Or become a member
  Of parliament;
A clever spouter
He'll soon turn out, or
An out-and-outer,
  'To be let alone.'
Don't hope to hinder him,
Or to bewilder him,
Sure he's a pilgrim
  From the Blarney Stone!

GEORGE NUGENT REYNOLDS

19 *Kathleen O'More*

1770–1802

MY love, still I think that I see her once more,
But, alas! she has left me her loss to deplore—
My own little Kathleen, my poor little Kathleen,
My Kathleen O'More!

Her hair glossy black, her eyes were dark blue,
Her colour still changing, her smiles ever new—
So pretty was Kathleen, my sweet little Kathleen,
My Kathleen O'More!

She milked the dun cow, that ne'er offered to stir;
Though wicked to all, it was gentle to her—
So kind was my Kathleen, my poor little Kathleen,
My Kathleen O'More!

She sat at the door one cold afternoon,
To hear the wind blow, and to gaze on the moon,—
So pensive was Kathleen, my poor little Kathleen,
My Kathleen O'More!

Cold was the night-breeze that sighed round her bower,
It chilled my poor Kathleen, she drooped from that hour,
And I lost my poor Kathleen, my own little Kathleen,
My Kathleen O'More!

The bird of all birds that I love the best
Is the robin that in the churchyard builds his nest;
For he seems to watch Kathleen, hops lightly o'er Kathleen,
My Kathleen O'More.

20 *Mary le More*

AS I stray'd o'er the common on Cork's rugged border,
While the dew-drops of morn the sweet primrose array'd,
I saw a poor maiden whose mental disorder,
Her quick-glancing eye and wild aspect betray'd.
On the sward she reclined, by the green fern surrounded,
At her side speckled daisies and wild flow'rs abounded;
To its utmost recesses her heart had been wounded;
Her sighs were unceasing—'twas Mary le More.

Her charms by the keen blasts of sorrow were faded,
Yet the soft tinge of beauty still play'd on her cheek;
Her tresses a wreath of pale primroses braided,
And strings of fresh daisies hung loose on her neck.
While with pity I gazed, she exclaim'd, 'O my Mother!
See the blood on that lash, 'tis the blood of my brother;
They have torn his poor flesh, and they now strip another—
'Tis Connor, the friend of poor Mary le More.

'Though his locks were as white as the foam of the ocean,
Those wretches shall find that my father is brave;
My father!' she cried, with the wildest emotion,
'Ah! no, my poor father now sleeps in the grave!
They have toll'd his death-bell, they've laid the turf o'er him;
His white locks were bloody! no aid could restore him;
He is gone! he is gone! and the good will deplore him,
When the blue waves of Erin hide Mary le More.'

A lark, from the gold blossom'd furze that grew near her,
Now rose, and with energy caroll'd his lay;
'Hush! hush!' she continued, 'the trumpet sounds clearer;
The horsemen approach! Erin's daughters away!
Ah! soldiers, 'twas foul, while the cabin was burning,
And o'er a pale father a wretch had been mourning—
Go, hide with the sea-mew, ye maids, and take warning,
Those ruffians have ruin'd poor Mary le More.

'Away, bring the ointment—O God! see those gashes!
Alas! my poor brother, come dry the big tear;
Anon we'll have vengeance for these dreadful lashes;
Already the screech-owl and raven appear.

By day the green grave, that lies under the willow,
With wild flow'rs I'll strew, and by night make my pillow,
Till the ooze and dark sea-weed, beneath the curl'd billow,
Shall furnish a death-bed for Mary le More.'

Thus raved the poor maniac, in tones more heart-rending
Than sanity's voice ever pour'd on my ear,
When, lo ! on the waste, and their march tow'rds her bending,
A troop of fierce cavalry chanced to appear ;
'O ye fiends !' she exclaim'd, and with wild horror started,
Then through the tall fern, loudly screaming, she darted !
With an overcharged bosom I slowly departed,
And sigh'd for the wrongs of poor Mary le More.

JAMES ORR

21 *The Irishman*

1770-1816

THE savage loves his native shore,
Though rude the soil and chill the air ;
Then well may Erin's sons adore
Their isle, which Nature formed so fair.
What flood reflects a shore so sweet
As Shannon great, or pastoral Bann ?
Or who a friend or foe can meet
So generous as an Irishman ?

His hand is rash, his heart is warm,
  But honesty is still his guide ;
None more repents a deed of harm,
  And none forgives with nobler pride ;
He may be duped, but won't be dared—
  More fit to practise than to plan ;
He dearly earns his poor reward,
  And spends it like an Irishman.

If strange or poor, for you he'll pay,
  And guide to where you safe may be ;
If you're his guest, while e'er you stay
  His cottage holds a jubilee.
His inmost soul he will unlock,
  And if he may your secrets scan,
Your confidence he scorns to mock,
  For faithful is an Irishman.

By honour bound in woe or weal,
  Whate'er she bids he dares to do ;
Try him with bribes—they won't prevail ;
  Prove him in fire—you'll find him true.
He seeks not safety, let his post
  Be where it ought, in danger's van ;
And if the field of fame be lost,
  It won't be by an Irishman.

Erin ! loved land ! from age to age
  Be thou more great, more famed, and free ;
May peace be thine, or, should'st thou wage
  Defensive war, cheap victory.
May plenty bloom in every field
  Which gentle breezes softly fan,
And cheerful smiles serenely gild
  The home of every Irishman !

THOMAS DERMODY

22 *When I Sat by my Fair*

1775-1802

WHEN I sat by my fair, and she tremblingly told
The soft wishes and doubts of her heart,
How quickly old Time then delightfully rolled,
For love lent the plume from his dart!
From the blush of her cheek, how my bosom caught flame,
And her eyes spoke a fondness her lips would not name.

But her cheek, that once rivalled the summer's full rose,
Now as April's sad primrose is pale;
In her eye, now, no bright sensibillity glows,
Though I breathe forth truth's rapturous tale;
And thy moments, old Time, that on downy feet fled,
Ah me! are now fettered and weighty as lead.

Yet surely, though much of her passion is past,
Some sparks of affection remain;
And the clouds, that her meek-beaming brow have o'ercast,
May be melted in pity's soft rain.
If not, my wrung breast to distraction I bare;
For distraction itself is less hard than despair.

THOMAS DERMODY

23 *My Burial Place*

AH me! and must I like the tenant lie
  Of this dark cell—all hushed the witching song?
And will not Feeling bend his streaming eye
  On my green sod, as slow he wends along,
And, smiting his rapt bosom, softly sigh,
  'His genius soared above the vulgar throng'?

Will he not fence my weedless turf around,
  Sacred from dull-eyed Folly's vagrant feet;
And there, soft swelling in aerial sound,
  Will he not list, at eve, to voices sweet;
Strew with the Spring's first flowers the little mound,
  And often muse within the lone retreat?

Yes, though I not affect the immortal lay,
  Nor bold effusions of the learned quill,
Nor often have I wound my tedious way
  Up the steep summit of the muse's hill;
Yet, sometimes have I poured the incondite lay,
  And sometimes have I felt the rapturous thrill.

Him, therefore, whom, even once, the sacred muse
  Has blest, shall be to feeling ever dear;
And, soft as sweet, sad April's gleamy dews,
  On my cold clay shall fall the genial tear;
While, pensive as the springing herb he views,
  He cries, 'Though mute, there is a poet here!'

WILLIAM BLACKER

24 *Oliver's Advice* (1)

1777-1855

THE night is gathering gloomily, the day is closing fast—
The tempest flaps his raven wings in loud and angry blast;
The thunder clouds are driving athwart the lurid sky—
But 'put your trust in God, my boys, and keep your powder dry.'

There was a day when loyalty was hailed with honour due,
Our banner the protection waved to all the good and true—
And gallant hearts beneath its folds were linked in honour's tie,
We put our trust in God, my boys, and kept our powder dry.

When Treason bared her bloody arm, and maddened round the land,
For King, and laws, and order fair, we drew the ready brand;
Our gathering spell was William's name—our word was, 'Do or die.'
And still we put our trust in God, and kept our powder dry.

But now, alas! a wondrous change has come the nation o'er,
And worth and gallant services remembered are no more;
And, crushed beneath oppression's weight, in chains of grief we lie—
But put your trust in God, my boys, and keep your powder dry.

Forth starts the spawn of Treason, the 'scaped of Ninety-eight,
To bask in courtly favour, and seize the helm of state—
E'en they whose hands are reeking yet with murder's crimson dye;
But put your trust in God, my boys, and keep your powder dry.

They come, whose deeds incarnadined the Slaney's silver wave—
They come, who to the foreign foe the hail of welcome gave;
He comes, the open rebel fierce—he comes, the Jesuit sly;
But put your trust in God, my boys, and keep your powder dry.

They come, whose counsels wrapped the land in foul rebellious flame,
Their hearts unchastened by remorse, their cheeks untinged by shame.
Be still, be still, indignant heart—be tearless, too, each eye,
And put your trust in God, my boys, and keep your powder dry.

WILLIAM BLACKER

The Power that led his chosen, by pillared cloud and flame,
Through parted sea and desert waste, that Power is still the same;
He fails not—He, the loyal hearts that firm on him rely—
So put your trust in God, my boys, and keep your powder dry.

The Power that nerved the stalwart arms of Gideon's chosen few,
The Power that led great William, Boyne's reddening torrent through—
In his protecting aid confide, and every foe defy—
Then put your trust in God, my boys, and keep your powder dry.

Already see the star of hope emits its orient blaze,
The cheering beacon of relief it glimmers thro' the haze.
It tells of better days to come, it tells of succour nigh—
Then put your trust in God, my boys, and keep your powder dry.

See, see along the hills of Down its rising glories spread,
But brightest beams its radiance from Donard's lofty head.
Clanbrassil's vales are kindling wide, and 'Roden' is the cry—
Then put your trust in God, my boys, and keep your powder dry.

Then cheer, ye hearts of loyalty, nor sink in dark
despair,
Our banner shall again unfold its glories to the air.
The storm that raves the wildest the soonest passes by;
Then put your trust in God, my boys, and keep your
powder dry.

For 'happy homes,' for 'altars free,' we grasp the
ready sword—
For freedom, truth, and for our God's unmutilated word.
These, these the war-cry of our march, our hope the
Lord on high;
Then put your trust in God, my boys, and keep your
powder dry.

THOMAS MOORE

25 *Oft, in the Stilly Night*

1779–1852

OFT, in the stilly night,
Ere Slumber's chain has bound me,
Fond Memory brings the light
Of other days around me;
The smiles, the tears,
Of boyhood's years,
The words of love then spoken;
The eyes that shone,
Now dimmed and gone,
The cheerful hearts now broken!
Thus, in the stilly night,
Ere Slumber's chain hath bound me,
Sad Memory brings the light
Of other days around me.

When I remember all
The friends, so linked together,
I've seen around me fall,
Like leaves in wintry weather ;
I feel like one,
Who treads alone
Some banquet-hall deserted,
Whose lights are fled,
Whose garlands dead,
And all but he departed !
Thus, in the stilly night,
Ere Slumber's chain has bound me,
Sad Memory brings the light
Of other days around me.

26 *After the Battle*

NIGHT closed around the conqueror's way,
And lightnings showed the distant hill,
Where those who lost that dreadful day,
Stood few and faint, but fearless still.
The soldier's hope, the patriot's zeal,
For ever dimmed, for ever crost—
Oh ! who shall say what heroes feel,
When all but life and honour's lost ?

The last sad hour of freedom's dream,
And valour's task, moved slowly by,
While mute they watched, till morning's beam
Should rise and give them light to die.
There's yet a world, where souls are free,
Where tyrant's taint nor nature's bliss ;—
If death that world's bright opening be,
Oh ! who would live a slave in this ?

27 *When He who Adores Thee*

WHEN he who adores thee has left but the name
Of his faults and his sorrows behind,
Oh ! say wilt thou weep, when they darken the fame
Of a life that for thee was resigned ?
Yes, weep, and however my foes may condemn,
Thy tears shall efface their decree ;
For Heaven can witness, though guilty to them,
I have been but too faithful to thee.

With thee were the dreams of my earliest love ;
Every thought of my reason was thine ;
In my last humble prayer to the Spirit above
Thy name shall be mingled with mine.
Oh ! blest are the lovers and friends who shall live
The days of thy glory to see ;
But the next dearest blessing that Heaven can give
Is the pride of thus dying for thee.

28 *Echo*

HOW sweet the answer Echo makes
To music at night,
When, roused by lute or horn, she wakes,
And far away, o'er lawns and lakes,
Goes answering light !

Yet Love hath echoes truer far,
And far more sweet,
Than e'er beneath the moonlight's star,
Of horn, or lute, or soft guitar,
The songs repeat.

'Tis when the sigh, in youth sincere,
And only then—
The sigh that's breathed for one to hear,
Is by that one, that only dear,
Breathed back again!

29 *At the Mid Hour of Night*

AT the mid hour of night, when stars are weeping, I fly
To the lone vale we loved, when life shone warm in thine eye;
And I think oft, if spirits can steal from the regions of air,
To revisit past scenes of delight, thou wilt come to me there,
And tell me our love is remembered, even in the sky.

Then I sing the wild song 'twas once such pleasure to hear!
When our voices commingling breathed, like one, on the ear;
And, as Echo far off through the vale my sad orison rolls,
I think, oh my love! 'tis thy voice from the Kingdom of Souls,
Faintly answering still the notes that once were so dear.

30 *The Song of Fionnuala* (2)

SILENT, O Moyle, be the roar of thy water,
Break not, ye breezes, your chain of repose,
While, murmuring mournfully, Lir's lonely daughter
Tells to the night-star her tale of woes.
When shall the swan, her death-note singing,
Sleep, with wings in darkness furled?
When will Heaven, its sweet bell ringing,
Call my spirit from this stormy world?

Sadly, O Moyle, to thy winter-wave weeping,
Fate bids me languish long ages away;
Yet still in her darkness doth Erin lie sleeping,
Still doth the pure light its dawning delay.
When will that day-star, mildly springing,
Warm our isle with peace and love?
When will Heaven, its sweet bell ringing,
Call my spirit to the fields above?

31 *As Slow our Ship*

AS slow our ship her foamy track
Against the wind was cleaving,
Her trembling pennant still looked back
To that dear isle 'twas leaving.
So loath we part from all we love,
From all the links that bind us;
So turn our hearts, as on we rove,
To those we've left behind us.

When, round the bowl, of vanished years
We talk, with joyous seeming,—
With smiles that might as well be tears,
So faint, so sad their beaming;
While memory brings us back again
Each early tie that twined us,
Oh, sweet's the cup that circles then
To those we've left behind us!

And when, in other climes, we meet
Some isle, or vale enchanting,
Where all looks flowery, wild and sweet,
And nought but love is wanting;
We think how great had been our bliss,
If Heaven had but assigned us
To live and die in scenes like this,
With some we've left behind us!

As travellers oft look back at eve,
When eastward darkly going,
To gaze upon that light they leave
Still faint behind them glowing,—
So, when the close of pleasure's day
To gloom hath near consigned us,
We turn to catch one fading ray
Of joy that's left behind us.

32 *My Birth-Day*

'MY birth-day'—what a different sound
That word had in my youthful ears!
And how, each time the day comes round,
Less and less white its mark appears!

THOMAS MOORE

When first our scanty years are told,
It seems like pastime to grow old ;
And, as Youth counts the shining links,
That Time around him binds so fast,
Pleased with the task, he little thinks
How hard that chain will press at last.
Vain was the man, and false as vain,
Who said—'were he ordained to run
His long career of life again,
He would do all that he had done.'

Ah, 'tis not thus the voice, that dwells
In sober birth-days, speaks to me ;
Far otherwise—of time it tells,
Lavished unwisely, carelessly ;
Of counsel mocked ; of talents, made
Haply for high and pure designs, .
But oft, like Israel's incense, laid
Upon unholy, earthly shrines ;
Of nursing many a wrong desire ;
Of wandering after Love too far,
And taking every meteor fire,
That crossed my pathway, for his star.
All this it tells, and, could I trace
Th' imperfect picture o'er again,
With power to add, retouch, efface
The lights and shades, the joy and pain,
How little of the past would stay !
How quickly all should melt away—
All—but that Freedom of the Mind,
Which hath been more than wealth to me ;

Those friendships, in my boyhood twined,
And kept till now unchangingly;
And that dear home, that saving-ark,
Where Love's true light at last I've found,
Cheering within, when all grows dark,
And comfortless, and stormy round!

33 *Dear Harp of my Country*

DEAR harp of my country! in darkness I found thee,
The cold chain of silence had hung o'er thee long,
When, proudly, my own island harp, I unbound thee,
And gave all thy chords to light, freedom, and song!
The warm lay of love, and the light note of gladness,
Have wakened thy fondest, thy liveliest thrill;
But so oft hast thou echoed the deep sigh of sadness,
That e'en in thy mirth it will steal from thee still.

Dear harp of my country! farewell to thy numbers,
This sweet wreath of song is the last we shall twine;
Go, sleep, with the sunshine of Fame on thy slumbers,
Till touched by some hand less unworthy than mine;
If the pulse of the patriot, soldier, or lover,
Have throbbed at our lay, 'tis thy glory alone;
I was but as the wind, passing heedlessly over,
And all the wild sweetness I waked was thy own.

34 *Oh! Breathe not his Name*

OH! breathe not his name, let it sleep in the shade
Where, cold and unhonoured, his relics are laid:
Sad, silent, and dark, be the tears that we shed,
As the night-dew that falls on the grass o'er his head.

But the night-dew that falls, though in silence it weeps,
Shall brighten with verdure the grave where he sleeps;
And the tear that we shed, though in secret it rolls,
Shall long keep his memory green in our souls.

35 *She is Far from the Land*

SHE is far from the land where her young hero sleeps,
And lovers are round her, sighing:
But coldly she turns from their gaze, and weeps,
For her heart in his grave is lying!

She sings the wild song of her dear native plains,
Every note which he loved awaking;—
Ah! little they think who delight in her strains,
How the heart of the Minstrel is breaking!

He had lived for his love, for his country he died,
They were all that to life had entwined him;
Nor soon shall the tears of his country be dried,
Nor long will his love stay behind him.

Oh ! make her a grave where the sunbeams rest.
  When they promise a glorious morrow ;
They'll shine o'er her sleep, like a smile from the
    West,
  From her own loved Island of Sorrow !

36 *Lines on the Death of Sheridan*

YES, grief will have way—but the fast falling tear
  Shall be mingled with deep execrations on those,
Who could bask in that Spirit's meridian career,
  And yet leave it thus lonely and dark at its close :—

Whose vanity flew round him, only while fed
  By the odour his fame in its summer-time gave ;—
Whose vanity now, with quick scent for the dead
  Like the Ghole of the East, comes to feed at his grave.

Oh ! it sickens the heart to see bosoms so hollow,
  And spirits so mean in the great and high-born ;
To think what a long line of titles may follow
  The relics of him who died—friendless and lorn !

How proud they can press to the funeral array
  Of one whom they shunned in his sickness and
    sorrow :—
How bailiffs may seize his last blanket, to-day,
  Whose pall shall be held up by nobles to-morrow !

And Thou, too, whose life, a sick epicure's dream,
  Incoherent and gross, even grosser had passed,
Were it not for that cordial and soul-giving beam,
  Which his friendship and wit o'er thy nothingness
    cast :—

No, not for the wealth of the land, that supplies thee
  With millions to heap upon Foppery's shrine ;—
No, not for the riches of all who despise thee,
  Tho' this would make Europe's whole opulence mine ;—

Would I suffer what—e'en in the heart that thou hast—
  All mean as it is—must have consciously burned,
When the pittance, which shame had wrung from thee at last,
  And which found all his wants at an end, was returned.

'Was *this* then the fate,'—future ages will say,
  When some names shall live but in History's curse ;
When Truth will be heard, and these Lords of a day
  Be forgotten as fools, or remembered as worse ;—

'Was this then the fate of that high-gifted man,
  The pride of the palace, the bower and the hall,
The orator,—dramatist,—minstrel,—who ran
  Through each mode of the lyre, and was master of all ;—

'Whose mind was an essence, compounded with art
  From the finest and best of all other men's powers ;—
Who ruled, like a wizard, the world of the heart,
  And could call up its sunshine, or bring down its showers ;—

'Whose humour, as gay as the fire-fly's light,
  Played round every subject, and shone as it played ;—
Whose wit, in the combat, as gentle as bright,
  Ne'er carried a heart-stain away on its blade ;—

'Whose eloquence—brightening whatever it tried,
 Whether reason or fancy, the gay or the grave,—
Was as rapid, as deep, and as brilliant a tide,
 As ever bore Freedom aloft on its wave!'

Yes—such was the man, and so wretched his fate;—
 And thus, sooner or later, shall all have to grieve,
Who waste their morn's dew in the beams of the Great,
 And expect 'twill return to refresh them at eve.

In the woods of the North there are insects that prey
 On the brain of the elk till his very last sigh;
O Genius! thy patrons, more cruel than they,
 First feed on thy brains, and then leave thee to die!

JAMES KENNEY

37 *The Green Leaves all turn Yellow*

1780–1849

A SAGE once to a maiden sung,
 While summer leaves were growing;
Experience dwelt upon his tongue,
 With love her heart was glowing:
'The summer bloom will fade away,
 And will no more be seen;
These flowers, that look so fresh and gay,
 Will not be ever green—
 For the green leaves all turn yellow.

JAMES KENNEY

'’Tis thus with the delights of love,
   The youthful heart beguiling;
Believe me, you will find them prove
   As transient—though as smiling:
Not long they flourish, ere they fade,
   As sadly I have seen;
Yes, like the summer flowers, fair maid,
   Oh! none are ever green—
      For the green leaves all turn yellow.'

LUKE AYLMER CONOLLY

38 *The Enchanted Island*

c. 1786–1833

TO Rathlin's Isle I chanced to sail
   When summer breezes softly blew,
And there I heard so sweet a tale
   That oft I wished it could be true.

They said, at eve, when rude winds sleep,
   And hushed is ev'ry turbid swell,
A mermaid rises from the deep
   And sweetly tunes her magic shell.

And while she plays, rock, dell, and cave,
   In dying falls the sound retain,
As if some choral spirits gave
   Their aid to swell her witching strain.

Then summoned by that dulcet note,
   Uprising to th' admiring view,
A fairy island seems to float
   With tints of many a gorgeous hue.

And glittering fanes, and lofty towers,
 All on this fairy isle are seen:
And waving trees, and shady bowers,
 With more than mortal verdure green.

And as it moves, the western sky
 Glows with a thousand varying rays;
And the calm sea, tinged with each dye,
 Seems like a golden flood of haze.

They also say, if earth or stone
 From verdant Erin's hallowed land
Were on this magic island thrown,
 For ever fixed it then would stand.

But when for this some little boat
 In silence ventures from the shore,
The mermaid sinks—hushed is the note—
 The fairy isle is seen no more.

SIR AUBREY DE VERE

39 *The Benumbed Butterfly*

1788–1846

BEAUTIFUL creature, how I envy thee!
 Pillowed on that soft bosom, gently heaving
In its transparent purity; more fair
Thus exquisitely shadowed by thy wings
Of crimson, purple-eyed, bedropt with gold.
The morning chill nigh killed thee:—happy creature!
Thou wilt revive again, like a glad soul
In paradise; and tremble in thy bliss,

And wave thy wings rejoicing. Ha! even now
The breath of love that ruffles o'er thy down,
Like summer breezes o'er a bed of flowers,
Hath stirred the life within thee, and awakened
The fragile spirit of thy tender frame.

But see—she smiles, she smiles! her sunny mouth
Dimples with hope and joy; her dewy eyes
Are full of pity. Oh how sweet to watch
The heaven-like changes of that angel face!
She smiles upon thee; and, as if new life
Came like an emanation from her eye,
Thou leap'st to life again.—Ah, silly one;
Say, wilt thou leave that haven of delight
And safety, where she cherished thee, like Love,
And nourished thee with pity and warm sighs?
Alas! like Love ingrateful! So, poor elf,
Inebriate with joy, thy giddy wing
Shall, for a time, thy form from flower to flower
Waft; but autumnal dews shall soon benumb
The little feeble heart within thee; soon
Like the harsh season of adversity,
Night winds shall find thee out, and thou shalt die—
No gentle breast to shelter thee again.

Oh! what a throng of similes I wove
For thee, while, cradled in that happy place,
Thou slept'st supine! Methought that thou wert like
A delicate flower cast on a bank of snow;—
Like Cupid nestling in his mother's arms;—
Like a fair barque from winds and waves escaped,
Close harboured in a warm and sheltered creek;—
Like a star beaming from the Milky Way;—

A monarch on his throne of ivory ;—
A jewelled brooch ;—a bright autumnal leaf
Rocked on a limpid wave ;—a humming-bird
Perched on the blossom of the orange tree :—
Or fairy sprite, ethereal Oberon,
Sleeping within a lily's stainless cup ;—
Or, dearer still, as famous poets feign,
A Psyche, in her emblematic dress
Of life, and joy, and immortality,
Harmlessly dreaming near her wedded love.
Nor these alone—but thou art fled ; and I,
Ingrate ! have chattered more than thou art worth.

40 *Glengarriff*

I

GAZING from each low bulwark of this bridge,
How wonderful the contrast ! Dark as night,
Here, amid cliffs and woods, with headlong might,
The black stream whirls, through ferns and drooping sedge,
'Neath twisted roots moss-brown, and weedy ledge,
Gushing. Aloft, from yonder birch-clad height
Leaps into air a cataract, snow-white ;
Falling to gulfs obscure. The mountain ridge,
Like a gray Warder, guardian of the scene,
Above the cloven gorge gloomily towers,
O'er the dim woods a gathering tempest lowers ;
Save where athwart the moist leaves' lucid green
A sunbeam, glancing through disparted showers,
Sparkles along the rill with diamond sheen !

41 *Glengarriff*

2

A SUN-BURST on the bay! Turn and behold!
The restless waves, resplendent in their glory,
Sweep glittering past yon purpled promontory,
Bright as Apollo's breastplate. Bathed in gold,
Yon bastioned islet gleams. Thin mists are rolled,
Translucent, through each glen. A mantle hoary
Veils those peaked hills, shapely as e'er in story,
Delphic, or Alpine, or Vesuvian old,
Minstrels have sung. From rock and headland proud
The wild wood spreads its arms around the bay:
The manifold mountain cones, now dark, now bright,
Now seen, now lost, alternate from rich light
To spectral shade; and each dissolving cloud
Reveals new mountains while it floats away.

42 *The Sea-Cliffs of Kilkee*

AWFULLY beautiful art thou, O sea!
Viewed from the vantage of these giant rocks,
That vast in air lift their primeval blocks,
Screening the sandy cove of lone Kilkee.
Cautious, with outstretched arm, and bended knee,
I scan the dread abyss, till the depth mocks
My straining eyeballs, and the eternal shocks
Of billows rolling from infinity
Disturb my brain! Hark! the shrill sea-bird's scream!

Cloud-like they sweep the long wave's sapphire
gleam,
Ere the poised Osprey stoop in wrath from high.
Here Man, alone, is nought; Nature supreme,
Where all is simply great that meets the eye—
The precipice, the ocean, and the sky.

43 *Kilmallock*

WHAT ruined shapes of feudal pomp are there,
In the cold moonlight fading silently?
The castle, with its stern, baronial air,
Still frowning, as accustomed to defy;
The Gothic street, where Desmond's chivalry
Dwelt in their pride; the cloistered house of prayer;
The gate-towers, mouldering where the stream
moans by,
Now, but the owl's lone haunt, and fox's lair.
Here once the pride of princely Desmond flushed;
His courtiers knelt, his mailèd squadrons rushed;
And saintly brethren poured the choral strain:
Here Beauty bowed her head, and smiled and
blushed:—
Ah! of these glories what doth now remain?
The charnel of yon desecrated fane!

44 *Castleconnell*

BROAD, but not deep, along his rock-chafed bed,
In many a sparkling eddy winds the flood,
Clasped by a margin of green underwood:
A castled crag, with ivy garlanded,

SIR AUBREY DE VERE

Sheer o'er the torrent frowns : above the mead
   De Burgho's towers, crumbling o'er many a rood,
   Stand gauntly out in airy solitude
Backed by yon furrowed mountain's tinted head.
Sounds of far people, mingling with the fall
   Of waters, and the busy hum of bees,
   And larks in air, and throstles in the trees,
Thrill the moist air with murmurs musical.
   While cottage smoke goes drifting on the breeze ;
And sunny clouds are floating over all.

CHARLOTTE ELIZABETH TONNA

45 *The Maiden City*

1790–1846

WHERE Foyle his swelling waters
   Rolls northward to the main,
Here, Queen of Erin's daughters,
   Fair Derry fixed her reign ;
A holy temple crowned her,
   And commerce graced her street,
A rampart wall was round her,
   The river at her feet ;
And here she sat alone, boys,
   And, looking from the hill,
Vowed the Maiden on her throne, boys,
   Would be a Maiden still.

From Antrim crossing over,
   In famous eighty-eight,
A plumed and belted lover
   Came to the Ferry Gate :

She summoned to defend her
  Our sires—a beardless race—
They shouted ' No Surrender ! '
  And slammed it in his face.
Then, in a quiet tone, boys,
  They told him 'twas their will
That the Maiden on her throne, boys,
  Should be a Maiden still.

Next, crushing all before him,
  A kingly wooer came
(The royal banner o'er him
  Blushed crimson deep for shame) ;
He showed the Pope's commission,
  Nor dreamed to be refused ;
She pitied his condition,
  But begged to stand excused.
In short, the fact is known, boys,
  She chased him from the hill,
For the Maiden on the throne, boys,
  Would be a Maiden still.

On our brave sires descending,
  'Twas then the tempest broke,
Their peaceful dwellings rending,
  'Mid blood, and flame, and smoke.
That hallowed grave-yard yonder
  Swells with the slaughtered dead—
O brothers ! pause and ponder—
  It was for us they bled ;
And while their gift we own, boys—
  The fane that tops our hill—
Oh ! the Maiden on her throne, boys,
  Shall be a Maiden still !

Nor wily tongue shall move us,
  Nor tyrant arm affright,
We'll look to One above us
  Who ne'er forsook the right;
Who will, may crouch and tender
  The birthright of the free,
But, brothers, 'No Surrender,'
  No compromise for me!
We want no barrier stone, boys,
  No gates to guard the hill,
Yet the Maiden on her throne, boys,
  Shall be a Maiden still.

46 *No Surrender*

BEHOLD the crimson banners float
  O'er yonder turrets hoary;
They tell of days of mighty note,
  And Derry's deathless glory;
When her brave sons undaunted stood,
  Embattled to defend her,
Indignant stemmed oppression's flood,
  And sung out, 'No Surrender!'

Old Derry's walls were firm and strong,
  Well fenced in every quarter,
Each frowning bastion grim along,
  With culverin and mortar;
But Derry had a surer guard
  Than all that art could lend her,
Her 'prentice boys the gate who barred,
  And sung out, 'No Surrender!'

On came the force in bigot ire,
  And fierce the assault was given ;
By shot and shell, 'mid streams of fire,
  Her fated roofs were riven :
But baffled was the tyrant's wrath,
  And vain his hopes to bend her,
For still 'mid famine, fire, and death,
  She sung out, 'No Surrender !'

Again, when treason maddened round,
  And rebel hordes were swarming,
Were Derry's sons the foremost found,
  For king and country arming :
Forth, forth they rushed at honour's call,
  From age to boyhood tender,
Again to man their virgin wall,
  And sung out, 'No Surrender !'

Long may the crimson banner wave,
  A meteor streaming airy,
Portentous of the free and brave
  Who man the walls of Derry :
And Derry's sons alike defy
  Pope, traitor, or pretender ;
And peal to heaven their 'prentice cry,
  Their patriot—'No Surrender !'

CHARLES WOLFE

47 *The Burial of Sir John Moore* 1791–1823

NOT a drum was heard, not a funeral note,
  As his corse to the rampart we hurried ;
Not a soldier discharged his farewell shot
  O'er the grave where our hero we buried.

CHARLES WOLFE

We buried him darkly at dead of night,
The sods with our bayonets turning,
By the struggling moonbeam's misty light,
And the lantern dimly burning.

No useless coffin enclosed his breast,
Not in sheet or in shroud we wound him ;
But he lay like a warrior taking his rest,
With his martial cloak around him.

Few and short were the prayers we said,
And we spoke not a word of sorrow ;
But we steadfastly gazed on the face that was dead,
And we bitterly thought of the morrow.

We thought as we hollow'd his narrow bed,
And smooth'd down his lonely pillow,
That the foe and the stranger would tread o'er his head
And we far away on the billow !

Lightly they'll talk of the spirit that's gone,
And o'er his cold ashes upbraid him,—
But little he'll reck, if they let him sleep on
In the grave where a Briton has laid him.

But half of our heavy task was done,
When the clock struck the hour for retiring ;
And we heard the distant and random gun
That the foe was sullenly firing.

Slowly and sadly we laid him down,
From the field of his fame fresh and gory ;
We carved not a line, and we raised not a stone—
But we left him alone in his glory !

48

Go! Forget Me

GO ! forget me, why should sorrow
O'er that brow a shadow fling ?
Go ! forget me—and to-morrow
Brightly smile, and sweetly sing.
Smile—though I shall not be near thee ;
Sing—though I shall never hear thee.
May thy soul with pleasure shine,
Lasting as the gloom of mine.

Like the sun, thy presence glowing
Clothes the meanest thing in light ;
And when thou, like him, art going,
Loveliest objects fade in night.
All things looked so bright about thee,
That they nothing seem without thee.
By that pure and lucid mind
Earthly things were too refined.

Go ! thou vision, wildly gleaming,
Softly on my soul that fell,
Go ! for me no longer beaming,
Hope and beauty, fare ye well !
Go ! and all that once delighted
Take—and leave me, all benighted,
Glory's burning gen'rous swell,
Fancy and the poet's shell.

CHARLES WOLFE

49 *If I had thought Thou couldst have Died*

IF I had thought thou couldst have died,
  I might not weep for thee ;
But I forgot, when by thy side,
  That thou couldst mortal be ;
It never through my mind had past
  The time would e'er be o'er,
And I on thee should look my last,
  And thou shouldst smile no more.

And still upon that face I look,
  And think 'twill smile again ;
And still the thought I will not brook
  That I must look in vain.
But when I speak, thou dost not say
  What thou ne'er left'st unsaid ;
And now I feel, as well I may,
  Sweet Mary ! thou art dead.

If thou wouldst stay e'en as thou art,
  All cold, and all serene,
I still might press thy silent heart,
  And where thy smiles have been !
While e'en thy chill, bleak corse I have,
  Thou seemest still mine own ;
But there I lay thee in thy grave–
  And I am now alone.

I do not think, where'er thou art,
  Thou hast forgotten me ;
And I, perhaps, may soothe this heart
  In thinking, too, of thee.

Yet there was round thee such a dawn
Of light, ne'er seen before,
As fancy never could have drawn,
And never can restore.

50 *Sonnet*

MY spirit's on the mountains, where the birds
In wild and sportive freedom wing the air,
Amidst the heath flowers and the browsing herds,
Where Nature's altar is, my spirit's there.
It is my joy to tread the pathless hills,
Though but in fancy—for my mind is free
And walks by sedgy ways and trickling rills,
While I'm forbid the use of liberty.
This is delusion—but it is so sweet
That I could live deluded. Let me be
Persuaded that my springing soul may meet
The eagle on the hills—and I am free.
Who'd not be flattered by a fate like this?
To fancy is to feel our happiness.

51 *On hearing 'The Last Rose of Summer'*

THAT strain again? It seems to tell
Of something like a joy departed;
I love its mourning accents well,
Like voice of one, ah! broken-hearted.

That note that pensive dies away,
And can each answering thrill awaken,
It sadly, wildly, seems to say,
Thy meek heart mourns its truth forsaken.

Or there was one who never more
  Shall meet thee with the looks of gladness,
When all of happier life was o'er,
  When first began thy night of sadness.

Sweet mourner, cease that melting strain,
  Too well it suits the grave's cold slumbers ;
Too well—the heart that loved in vain
  Breathes, lives, and weeps in those wild numbers.

THOMAS FURLONG

52

Róisín Dubh[1] (3)

From the Irish

1794–1827

OH ! my sweet little rose, cease to pine for the past,
For the friends that came eastward shall see thee at last ;
They bring blessings and favours the past never knew,
To pour forth in gladness on my Róisín Dubh.

Long, long, with my dearest, through strange scenes I've gone,
O'er mountains and broad valleys I still have toiled on ;
O'er the Erne I have sailed as the rough gales blew,
While the harp poured its music for my Róisín Dubh.

[1] Little Black Rose—a mystical name for Ireland.

Though wearied, oh! my fair one! do not slight my
song,
For my heart dearly loves thee, and hath loved thee
long;
In sadness and in sorrow I still shall be true,
And cling with wild fondness round my Róisín Dubh.

There's no flower that e'er bloomed can my rose excel,
There's no tongue that e'er moved half my love can
tell,
Had I strength, had I skill the wide world to subdue,
Oh! the queen of that wide world should be Róisín
Dubh.

Had I power, oh! my loved one, but to plead thy right,
I should speak out in boldness for my heart's delight;
I would tell to all around me how my fondness grew,
And bid them bless the beauty of my Róisín Dubh.

The mountains, high and misty, through the moors
must go,
The rivers shall run backward, and the lakes overflow,
And the wild waves of old ocean wear a crimson hue,
Ere the world sees the ruin of my Róisín Dubh.

53 *John O'Dwyer of the Glen* (4)

From the Irish

BLITHE the bright dawn found me,
Rest with strength had crown'd me,
Sweet the birds sang round me,
Sport was all their toil.

THOMAS FURLONG

The horn its clang was keeping,
Forth the fox was creeping,
Round each dame stood weeping,
O'er the prowler's spoil.

Hark ! the foe is calling,
Fast the woods are falling,
Scenes and sights appalling
Mark the wasted soil.

War and confiscation
Curse the fallen nation ;
Gloom and desolation
Shade the lost land o'er.

Chill the winds are blowing,
Death aloft is going,
Peace or hope seems growing
For our race no more.

Hark ! the foe is calling,
Fast the woods are falling,
Scenes and sights appalling
Throng the blood-stained shore.

Nobles, once high-hearted,
From their homes have parted,
Scattered, scared, and started
By a base-born band.

Spots that once were cheering,
Girls beloved, endearing,
Friends from whom I'm steering,
Take this parting tear.

THOMAS FURLONG

Hark! the foe is calling,
Fast the woods are falling,
Scenes and sights appalling
Plague and haunt me here.

WILLIAM CARLETON

54 *Sir Turlough; or, the Churchyard Bride* (5)

1794-1869

THE bride, she bound her golden hair—
Killeevy, O Killeevy!
And her step was light as the breezy air
When it bends the morning flowers so fair,
By the bonnie green woods of Killeevy.

And oh, but her eyes they danced so bright,
Killeevy, O Killeevy!
As she longed for the dawn of to-morrow's light,
Her bridal vows of love to plight,
By the bonnie green woods of Killeevy.

The bridegroom is come with youthful brow,
Killeevy, O Killeevy!
To receive from his Eva her virgin vow;
'Why tarries the bride of my bosom now?'
By the bonnie green woods of Killeevy.

A cry! a cry! 'twas her maidens spoke,
Killeevy, O Killeevy!
'Your bride is asleep—she has not awoke,
And the sleep she sleeps will never be broke,'
By the bonnie green woods of Killeevy.

Sir Turlough sank down with a heavy moan,
  Killeevy, O Killeevy!
And his cheek became like the marble stone—
'Oh, the pulse of my heart is for ever gone!'
  By the bonnie green woods of Killeevy.

The keen is loud, it comes again,
  Killeevy, O Killeevy!
And rises sad from the funeral train,
As in sorrow it winds along the plain,
  By the bonnie green woods of Killeevy.

And oh, but the plumes of white were fair,
  Killeevy, O Killeevy!
When they flutter'd all mournful in the air
As rose the hymn of the requiem prayer,
  By the bonnie green woods of Killeevy.

There is a voice that but one can hear,
  Killeevy, O Killeevy!
And it softly pours from behind the bier,
Its note of death on Sir Turlough's ear,
  By the bonnie green woods of Killeevy.

The keen is loud, but that voice is low,
  Killeevy, O Killeevy!
And it sings its song of sorrow slow,
And names young Turlough's name with woe,
  By the bonnie green woods of Killeevy.

Now the grave is closed, and the mass is said,
  Killeevy, O Killeevy!
And the bride she sleeps in her lonely bed,
The fairest corpse among the dead,
  By the bonnie green woods of Killeevy.

WILLIAM CARLETON

The wreaths of virgin-white are laid,
  Killeevy, O Killeevy !
By virgin hands o'er the spotless maid ;
And the flowers are strewn, but they soon will fade,
  By the bonnie green woods of Killeevy.

'Oh ! go not yet—not yet away,
  Killeevy, O Killeevy !
Let us feel that Life is near our clay,'
The long-departed seem to say,
  By the bonnie green woods of Killeevy.

But the tramp and voices of Life are gone,
  Killeevy, O Killeevy !
And beneath each cold forgotten stone
The mouldering dead sleep all alone,
  By the bonnie green woods of Killeevy !

But who is he who lingereth yet ?
  Killeevy, O Killeevy !
The fresh green sod with his tears is wet,
And his heart in that bridal grave is set,
  By the bonnie green woods of Killeevy.

Oh, who but Sir Turlough, the young and brave,
  Killeevy, O Killeevy !
Should bend him o'er that bridal grave,
And to his death-bound Eva rave,
  By the bonnie green woods of Killeevy.

'Weep not—weep not,' said a lady fair,
  Killeevy, O Killeevy !
'Should youth and valour thus despair,
And pour their vows to the empty air ?'
  By the bonnie green woods of Killeevy.

There's charmed music upon her tongue,
Killeevy, O Killeevy!
Such beauty—bright and warm and young—
Was never seen the maids among,
By the bonnie green woods of Killeevy.

A laughing light, a tender grace,
Killeevy, O Killeevy!
Sparkled in beauty around her face,
That grief from mortal heart might chase,
By the bonnie green woods of Killeevy.'

'The maid for whom thy salt tears fall,
Killeevy, O Killeevy!
Thy grief or love can ne'er recall;
She rests beneath that grassy pall,
By the bonnie green woods of Killeevy.

'My heart it strangely cleaves to thee,
Killeevy, O Killeevy!
And now that thy plighted love is free,
Give its unbroken pledge to me,
By the bonnie green woods of Killeevy.'

The charm is strong upon Turlough's eye,
Killeevy, O Killeevy!
His faithless tears are already dry,
And his yielding heart has ceased to sigh,
By the bonnie green woods of Killeevy.

'To thee,' the charmèd chief replied,
Killeevy, O Killeevy!
'I pledge that love o'er my buried bride!
Oh! come, and in Turlough's hall abide,
By the bonnie green woods of Killeevy.'

Again the funeral voice came o'er
  Killeevy, O Killeevy!
The passing breeze, as it wailed before,
And streams of mournful music bore,
  By the bonnie green woods of Killeevy.

'If I to thy youthful heart am dear,
  Killeevy, O Killeevy!
One month from hence thou wilt meet me here
Where lay thy bridal, Eva's bier,'
  By the bonnie green woods of Killeevy.

He pressed her lips as the words were spoken,
  Killeevy, O Killeevy!
And his banshee's wail—now far and broken—
Murmur'd 'Death,' as he gave the token,
  By the bonnie green woods of Killeevy.

'Adieu! adieu!' said this lady bright,
  Killeevy, O Killeevy.
And she slowly passed like a thing of light,
Or a morning cloud, from Sir Turlough's sight,
  By the bonnie green woods of Killeevy.

Now Sir Turlough has death in every vein,
  Killeevy, O Killeevy!
And there's fear and grief o'er his wide domain,
And gold for those who will calm his brain,
  By the bonnie green woods of Killeevy.

'Come, haste thee, leech, right swiftly ride,
  Killeevy, O Killeevy!
Sir Turlough the brave, Green Truagha's pride,
Has pledged his love to the churchyard bride,
  By the bonnie green woods of Killeevy.'

The leech groaned loud, 'Come, tell me this,
  Killeevy, O Killeevy !
By all thy hopes of weal and bliss,
Has Sir Turlough given the fatal kiss,
  By the bonnie green woods of Killeevy ?'

'The banshee's cry is loud and long,
  Killeevy, O Killeevy !
At eve she weeps her funeral song,
And it floats in the twilight breeze along,
  By the bonnie green woods of Killeevy.

'Then the fatal kiss is given ;—the last,
  Killeevy, O Killeevy !
Of Turlough's race and name is past,
His doom is seal'd, his die is cast,
  By the bonnie green woods of Killeevy.'

'Leech, say not that thy skill is vain,
  Killeevy, O Killeevy !
Oh, calm the power of his frenzied brain,
And half his lands thou shalt retain,
  By the bonnie green woods of Killeevy.'

The leech has fail'd, and the hoary priest,
  Killeevy, O Killeevy !
With pious shrift his soul released,
And the smoke is high of his funeral feast
  By the bonnie green woods of Killeevy.

The shanachies now are assembled all,
  Killeevy, O Killeevy !
And the songs of praise, in Sir Turlough's hall,
To the sorrowing harp's dark music fall,
  By the bonnie green woods of Killeevy.

And there is trophy, banner, and plume,
  Killeevy, O Killeevy!
And the pomp of death, with its darkest gloom,
O'ershadows the Irish chieftain's tomb,
  By the bonnie green woods of Killeevy.

The month is closed, and Green Truagha's pride,
  Killeevy, O Killeevy!
Is married to death—and, side by side,
He slumbers now with his churchyard bride,
  By the bonnie green woods of Killeevy.

55 *A Sigh for Knockmany*

TAKE, proud ambition, take thy fill
  Of pleasures won through toil or crime;
Go, learning, climb thy rugged hill,
  And give thy name to future time:
Philosophy, be keen to see
  Whate'er is just, or false, or vain,
Take each thy meed, but, oh! give me
  To range my mountain glens again.

Pure was the breeze that fanned my cheek,
  As o'er Knockmany's brow I went;
When every lonely dell could speak
  In airy music, vision sent;
False world, I hate thy cares and thee,
  I hate the treacherous haunts of men;
Give back my early heart to me,
  Give back to me my mountain glen.

WILLIAM CARLETON

How light my youthful visions shone,
When spann'd by Fancy's radiant form ;
But now her glittering bow is gone,
And leaves me but the cloud and storm.
With wasted form, and cheek all pale—
With heart long seared by grief and pain ;
Dunroe, I'll seek thy native gale,
I'll tread my mountain glens again.

Thy breeze once more may fan my blood,
Thy valleys all are lovely still ;
And I may stand, where oft I stood,
In lonely musings on thy hill.
But, ah ! the spell is gone ;—no art
In crowded town, or native plain,
Can teach a crush'd and breaking heart
To pipe the song of youth again.

JEREMIAH JOSEPH CALLANAN

56 *Dirge of O'Sullivan Bear* (6)

From the Irish

1795–1829

THE sun on Ivera [1]
No longer shines brightly ;
The voice of her music
No longer is sprightly ;
No more to her maidens
The light dance is dear,
Since the death of our darling
O'Sullivan Bear.

[1] The old name of Bearhaven ; it is still preserved in the name of the barony of Iveragh.

Scully ! thou false one,
  You basely betrayed him,
In his strong hour of need,
  When thy right hand should aid him ;
He fed thee—he clad thee—
  You had all could delight thee :
You left him—you sold him—
  May heaven requite thee !

Scully ! may all kinds
  Of evil attend thee !
On thy dark road of life
  May no kind one befriend thee !
May fevers long burn thee,
  And agues long freeze thee !
May the strong hand of God
  In his red anger seize thee !

Had he died calmly,
  I would not deplore him ;
Or if the wild strife
  Of the sea-war closed o'er him ;
But with ropes round his white limbs
  Through ocean to trail him,
Like a fish after slaughter—
  'Tis therefore I wail him.

Long may the curse
  Of his people pursue them ;
Scully, that sold him,
  And soldier that slew him !
One glimpse of heaven's light
  May they see never !
May the hearthstone of hell
  Be their best bed for ever !

In the hole which the vile hands
  Of soldiers had made thee,
Unhonour'd, unshrouded,
  And headless they laid thee ;
No sigh to regret thee,
  No eye to rain o'er thee,
No dirge to lament thee,
  No friend to deplore thee !

Dear head of my darling,
  How gory and pale,
These aged eyes see thee,
  High spiked on their gaol !
That cheek in the summer sun
  Ne'er shall grow warm ;
Nor that eye e'er catch light,
  But the flash of the storm.

A curse, blessed ocean,
  Is on thy green water,
From the haven of Cork,
  To Ivera of slaughter :
Since thy billows were dyed
  With the red wounds of fear
Of Muiertach Oge,[1]
  Our O'Sullivan Bear !

57 *Gougaune Barra* (7)

THERE is a green island in lone Gougaune Barra,
  Where Allua of songs rushes forth as an arrow ;
In deep-valley'd Desmond—a thousand wild fountains
Come down to that lake, from their home in the mountains.

1 Young Morty.

There grows the wild ash, and a time-stricken willow
Looks chidingly down on the mirth of the billow;
As, like some gay child, that sad monitor scorning,
It lightly laughs back to the laugh of the morning.

And its zone of dark hills—oh! to see them all
bright'ning,
When the tempest flings out its red banner of
lightning,
And the waters rush down, 'mid the thunder's deep
rattle,
Like clans from their hills at the voice of the battle;
And brightly the fire-crested billows are gleaming,
And wildly from Mullagh the eagles are screaming.
Oh! where is the dwelling in valley or highland,
So meet for a bard as this lone little island?

How oft when the summer sun rested on Clara,
And lit the dark heath on the hills of Ivera,
Have I sought thee, sweet spot, from my home by the
ocean,
And trod all thy wilds with a minstrel's devotion,
And thought of thy bards, when assembling together,
In the cleft of thy rocks, or the depth of thy heather;
They fled from the Saxon's dark bondage and slaughter,
And waked their last song by the rush of thy
water.

High sons of the lyre, oh! how proud was the feeling,
To think while alone through that solitude stealing,
Though loftier Minstrels green Erin can number,
I only awoke your wild harp from its slumber,

And mingled once more with the voice of those
fountains
The songs even Echo forgot on her mountains;
And glean'd each grey legend, that darkly was sleeping
Where the mist and the rain o'er their beauty were
creeping.

Least bard of the hills! were it mine to inherit
The fire of thy harp, and the wing of thy spirit,
With the wrongs which like thee to our country have
bound me,
Did your mantle of song fling its radiance around me,
Still, still in those wilds might young liberty rally,
And send her strong shout over mountain and valley,
The star of the west might yet rise in its glory,
And the land that was darkest be brightest in story.

I too shall be gone;—but my name shall be spoken
When Erin awakes, and her fetters are broken;
Some Minstrel will come, in the summer eve's gleaming,
When Freedom's young light on his spirit is beaming,
And bend o'er my grave with a tear of emotion,
Where calm Avon-Bwee seeks the kisses of ocean,
Or plant a wild wreath, from the banks of that river,
O'er the heart and the harp that are sleeping for ever.

58 *The Lament of O'Gnive* [1]

From the Irish

HOW dimm'd is the glory that circled the Gael,
And fall'n the high people of green Innisfail!
The sword of the Saxon is red with their gore,
And the mighty of nations is mighty no more.

[1] O'Gnive was bard to the O'Neill of Clandeboy about 1556.

JEREMIAH JOSEPH CALLANAN

Like a bark on the ocean long shatter'd and tost,
On the land of your fathers at length you are lost,
The hand of the spoiler is stretch'd on your plains,
And you're doomed from your cradles to bondage and
chains.

Oh where is the beauty that beam'd on thy brow?
Strong hand in the battle, how weak art thou now!
That heart is now broken that never would quail,
And thy high songs are turn'd into weeping and wail.

Bright shades of our sires! from your home in the skies
Oh blast not your sons with the scorn of your eyes!
Proud spirit of Gollamh, how red is thy cheek!
For thy freemen are slaves, and thy mighty are weak!

O'Neill of the Hostages, Con, whose high name
On a hundred red battles has floated to fame,
Let the long grass still sigh undisturbed o'er thy sleep,
Arise not to shame us, awake not to weep!

In thy broad wing of darkness infold us, oh night?
Withhold, oh bright sun, the reproach of thy light!
For freedom or valour no more canst thou see,
In the home of the Brave, in the isle of the Free.

Affliction's dark waters your spirits have bow'd,
And oppression hath wrapped all your land in its shroud,
Since first from the Brehons' pure justice you stray'd,
And bent to those laws the proud Saxon has made.

We know not our country, so strange is her face,
Her sons once her glory are now her disgrace;
Gone, gone is the beauty of fair Innisfail,
For the stranger now rules in the land of the Gael.

Where, where are the woods that oft rung to your
cheer,
Where you waked the wild chase of the wolf and the
deer?
Can those dark heights, with ramparts all frowning
and riven,
Be the hills where your forests waved brightly in
Heaven?

Oh bondsmen of Egypt, no Moses appears
To light your dark steps thro' this desert of tears;
Degraded and lost ones, no Hector is nigh,
To lead you to freedom, or teach you to die!

59 *The Outlaw of Loch Lene*

From the Irish

OH, many a day have I made good ale in the glen,
That came not of stream or malt—like the
brewing of men!
My bed was the ground; my roof, the greenwood
above,
And the wealth that I sought, one far kind glance
from my love.

Alas! on that night when the horses I drove from the
field,
That I was not near from terror my angel to shield.
She stretched forth her arms—her mantle she flung to
the wind,
And swam o'er Loch Lene her outlawed lover to find.

Oh would that a freezing, sleet-wing'd tempest did
sweep,
And I and my love were alone, far off on the deep!
I'd ask not a ship, or a bark, or pinnace, to save,—
With her hand round my waist I'd fear not the wind
or the wave.

'Tis down by the lake where the wild-tree fringes its
sides,
The maid of my heart, my fair one of Heaven resides;
I think as at eve she wanders its mazes along,
The birds go to sleep by the sweet, wild twist of her
song.

60 *O Say, my Brown Drimin*[1]

OH say, my brown Drimin, thou 'Silk of the Kine,'[2]
Where, where are thy strong ones, last hope of
thy line?
Too deep and too long is the slumber they take,
At the loud call of freedom why don't they awake?

My strong ones have fallen—from the bright eye of day
All darkly they sleep in their dwelling of clay;
The cold turf is o'er them—they hear not my cries,
And since Lewis no aid gives, I cannot arise.

Oh! where art thou, Lewis? our eyes are on thee—
Are thy lofty ships walking in strength o'er the sea?
In freedom's last strife, if you linger or quail,
No morn e'er shall break on the night of the Gael.

[1] Ireland is spoken of here under 'Drimin,' the favourite name of a cow.
[2] Another name for Ireland.

But should the King's son, now bereft of his right,
Come proud in his strength for his country to fight;
Like leaves on the trees, will new people arise,
And deep from their mountains shout back to my cries.

When the Prince, now an exile, shall come for his own,
The Isles of his father, his rights, and his throne,
My people in battle the Saxons will meet,
And kick them before, like old shoes from their feet.

O'er mountains and valleys they'll press on their rout,
The five ends of Erin shall ring to their shout;
My sons all united, shall bless the glad day
When the flint-hearted Saxon they've chased far away.

61 *The Convict of Clonmel*

From the Irish

HOW hard is my fortune,
And vain my repining!
The strong rope of fate
For this young neck is twining.
My strength is departed;
My cheek sunk and sallow;
While I languish in chains,
In the gaol of Clonmala.[1]

[1] Ir. *Cluain-meala* = Field of honey.

No boy in the village
  Was ever yet milder,
I'd play with a child,
  And my sport would be wilder.
I'd dance without tiring
  From morning till even,
And the goal-ball I'd strike
  To the lightning of Heaven.

At my bed-foot decaying,
  My hurlbat is lying,
Through the boys of the village
  My goal-ball is flying;
My horse 'mong the neighbours
  Neglected may fallow,—
While I pine in my chains,
  In the gaol of Clonmala.

Next Sunday the patron
  At home will be keeping,
And the young active hurlers
  The field will be sweeping.
With the dance of fair maidens
  The evening they'll hallow,
While this heart, once so gay,
  Shall be cold in Clonmala.

62 *On Cleada's Hill the Moon is Bright*

ON Cleada's[1] hill the moon is bright,
  Dark Avondu still rolls in light,
All changeless in that mountain's head,
That river still seeks ocean's bed:

[1] One of the mountain ranges between Millstreet and Killarney.

JEREMIAH JOSEPH CALLANAN

The calm blue waters of Loch Lene
Still kiss their own sweet isles of green,
But where's the heart as firm and true
As hill, or lake, or Avondu?[1]

It may not be, the firmest heart
From all it loves must often part,
A look, a word, will quench the flame
That time or fate could never tame;
And there are feelings proud and high
That through all changes cannot die,
That strive with love, and conquer too;
I knew them all by Avondu.

How cross and wayward still is fate
I've learned at last, but learned too late.
I never spoke of love, 'twere vain;
I knew it, still I dragg'd my chain.
I had not, never had a hope—
But who 'gainst passion's tide can cope?
Headlong it swept this bosom through,
And left it waste by Avondu.

Oh Avondu! I wish I were
As once upon that mountain bare,
Where thy young waters laugh and shine
On the wild breast of Meenganine;
I wish I were by Cleada's hill,
Or by Glenluachra's rushy rill.
But no!—I never more shall view
Those scenes I loved by Avondu.

Farewell, ye soft and purple streaks
Of evening on the beauteous Reeks;

[1] The Munster Blackwater.

JEREMIAH JOSEPH CALLANAN

Farewell, ye mists that loved to ride
On Cahir-bearna's stormy side ;
Farewell, November's moaning breeze,
Wild minstrel of the dying trees ;
Clara ! a fond farewell to you,
No more we meet by Avondu.

No more—but thou, O glorious hill !
Lift to the moon thy forehead still ;
Flow on, flow on, thou dark swift river,
Upon thy free wild course for ever.
Exult, young heart, in lifetime's spring,
And taste the joys pure love can bring ;
But, wanderer, go—they're not for you !
Farewell, farewell, sweet Avondu !

GEORGE DARLEY

1795–1846

63

Osme's Song

From 'Sylvia'

HITHER ! hither !
O come hither !
Lads and lasses come and see !
Trip it neatly,
Foot it featly,
O'er the grassy turf to me !

Here are bowers
Hung with flowers,
Richly curtain'd halls for you !
Meads for rovers,
Shades for lovers,
Violet beds, and pillows too !

GEORGE DARLEY

Purple heather
You may gather
Sandal-deep in seas of bloom !
Pale-faced lily,
Proud sweet-willy,
Gorgeous rose, and golden broom !

Odorous blossoms
For sweet bosoms,
Garlands green to bind the hair ;
Crowns and kirtles
Weft of myrtles,
Youth may choose, and Beauty wear !

Brightsome glasses
For bright faces
Shine in every rill that flows ;
Every minute
You look in it
Still more bright your beauty grows !

Banks for sleeping,
Nooks for peeping,
Glades for dancing, smooth and fine !
Fruits delicious
For who wishes,
Nectar, dew, and honey-wine !

Hither ! hither !
O come hither !
Lads and lasses come and see !
Trip it neatly,
Foot it featly,
O'er the grassy turf to me !

64 *The Crowning of Sylvia*

Peasants' Song

HERE'S a bank with rich cowslips, and cuckoo-
buds strewn,
To exalt your bright looks, gentle Queen of the
May;
Here's a cushion of moss for your delicate shoon,
And a woodbine to weave you a canopy gay!

Here's a garland of red maiden-roses for you,
Such a beautiful wreath is for Beauty alone!
Here's a golden king-cup, brimming over with dew,
To be kiss'd by a lip just as sweet as its own!

Here are bracelets of pearl from the fount in the dale,
That the Nymph of the wave on your wrists doth
bestow;
Here's a lily-wrought scarf, your sweet blushes to veil,
Or to lie on that bosom like snow upon snow!

Here's a myrtle enwreath'd with a jessamine band,
To express the fond twining of Beauty and Youth;
Take this emblem of love in thy exquisite hand,
And do thou sway the evergreen sceptre of Truth!

Then around you we'll dance, and around you we'll
sing!
To soft pipe, and sweet tabor we'll foot it away!
And the hills, and the vales, and the forests shall ring
While we hail you our lovely young Queen of the
May!

GEORGE DARLEY

65 *Runilda's Chant*

From 'Ethelstan'

O'ER the wild gannet's bath
Come the Norse coursers!
O'er the whale's heritance
Gloriously steering!
With beaked heads peering,
Deep-plunging, high-rearing,
Tossing their foam abroad,
Shaking white manes aloft,
Creamy-neck'd, pitchy ribb'd,
Steeds of the Ocean!

O'er the Sun's mirror green
Come the Norse coursers!
Trampling its glassy breadth
Into bright fragments!
Hollow-back'd, huge-bosom'd,
Fraught with mail'd riders,
Clanging with hauberks,
Shield, spear, and battleaxe.
Canvas-wing'd, cable-rein'd,
Steeds of the Ocean!

O'er the Wind's ploughing-field
Come the Norse coursers!
By a hundred each ridden,
To the bloody feast bidden,
They rush in their fierceness
And ravine all round them!

Their shoulders enriching
With fleecy-light plunder,
Fire-spreading, foe-spurning,
Steeds of the Ocean !

66 *Lay of the Forlorn*

FAREWELL to Sliev Morna,
The hills of the winds !
Where the hunters of Ullin
Pursue the brown hinds !
Farewell to Loch Ern where the wild eagles dwell !
Farewell to Shan-avon, Shan-avon, farewell !

Farewell to bright tresses,
Farewell to bright eyes,
To the snow-covered bosoms
That heave with their sighs !
Long, long for their heroes in vain may they swell,
Farewell to fair maidens, fair maidens, farewell !

Farewell to our castles,
Our oak-blazing halls,
Where the red fox is prowling
Alone in the walls !
Farewell to the joys of the harp and the shell,
Farewell to Ierné, Ierné, farewell.

GEORGE DARLEY

67 *The Sea-Ritual*

From 'Syren Songs'

PRAYER unsaid, and mass unsung,
Deadman's dirge must still be rung:
Dingle-dong, the dead-bells sound!
Mermen chant his dirge around!

Wash him bloodless, smooth him fair,
Stretch his limbs, and sleek his hair:
Dingle-dong, the dead-bells go!
Mermen swing them to and fro!

In the wormless sand shall he
Feast for no foul glutton be:
Dingle-dong, the dead-bells chime!
Mermen keep the tone and time!

We must with a tombstone brave
Shut the shark out from his grave:
Dingle-dong, the dead-bells toll!
Mermen dirgers ring his knoll!

Such a slab will we lay o'er him
All the dead shall rise before him!
Dingle-dong, the dead-bells boom!
Mermen lay him in his tomb!

68 *It is not Beauty I demand*

IT is not Beauty I demand,
  A crystal brow, the moon's despair,
Nor the snow's daughter, a white hand,
  Nor mermaid's yellow pride of hair.

Tell me not of your starry eyes,
  Your lips that seem on roses fed,
Your breast where Cupid trembling lies,
  Nor sleeps for kissing of his bed.

A bloomy pair of vermeil cheeks,
  Like Hebe's in her ruddiest hours,
A breath that softer music speaks
  Than summer winds a-wooing flowers.

These are but gauds ; nay what are lips ?
  Coral beneath the ocean stream,
Whose brink, when your adventurer sips
  Full oft he perishes on them.

And what are cheeks but ensigns oft
  That wave hot youths to fields of blood ?
Did Helen's breast though ne'er so soft,
  Do Greece or Ilium any good ?

Eyes can with baleful ardour burn,
  Poison can breath that erst perfumed,
There's many a white hand holds an urn
  With lovers' hearts to dust consumed.

For crystal brows—there's nought within,
  They are but empty cells for pride ;
He who the Syren's hair would win
  Is mostly strangled in the tide.

Give me instead, of Beauty's bust,
  A tender heart, a loyal mind,
Which with temptation I could trust,
  Yet never linked with error find.

One in whose gentle bosom I
  Could pour my secret heart of woes,
Like the care-burthened honey-fly
  That hides his murmur in the rose.

My earthly comforter ! whose love
  So indefeasible might be,
That when my spirit won above
  Hers could not stay for sympathy.

69 *The Fallen Star*

A STAR is gone ! a star is gone !
  There is a blank in Heaven,
One of the cherub choir has done
  His airy course this even.

He sat upon the orb of fire
  That hung for ages there,
And lent his music to the choir
  That haunts the nightly air.

But when his thousand years were past,
With a cherubic sigh
He vanish'd with his car at last,
For even cherubs die!

Hear how his angel-brothers mourn—
The minstrels of the spheres—
Each chiming sadly in his turn
And dropping splendid tears.

The Planetary Sisters all
Join in the fatal song,
And weep this hapless brother's fall
Who sang with them so long.

But deepest of the choral band
The Lunar Spirit sings,
And with a bass according hand
Sweeps all her sullen strings.

From the deep chambers of the dome
Where sleepless Uriel lies,
His rude harmonic thunders come
Mingled with mighty sighs.

The thousand car-borne cherubim,
The wandering Eleven,
All join to chant the dirge of him
Who fell just now from Heaven.

70

The Call of the Morning

VALE of the waterfalls !
  Glen of the streams !
Wake from your slumbering !
  Wake from your dreams !

Wild sings the mountain-lark,
  Bird of the air !
Calling the valley-birds
  Up to him there !

Sweet ring the mountain-bells
  High o'er the dale,
Waking the little bells
  Down in the vale.

Fresh breathes the morning-wind,
  Bright looks the day,—
Up to the heather hills,
  Lilian, away !

71

The Wild Bee's Tale

WHEN the sun steps from the billow
  On the steep and stairless sky,
'Up !' I say, and quit my pillow,
  'Bed, for many an hour, good-bye !'

Swiftly to the East I turn me,
  Where the world's great lustre beams,
Warm to bathe, but not to burn me,
  In its radiant fount of streams.

Then unto the glittering valley,
  Where Aurora strews her pearls,
With my favourite flowers to dally,
  Jewelled all, like princely girls !

There I hum amid the bushes,
  Eating honey, as it grows,
Off the cheek of maiden blushes,
  And the red lip of the rose.

In the ear of every flower
  Buzzing many a secret thing,
Every bright bell of the bower
  Thinks it is for her I sing.

But the valley and the river,
  That go with me as I go,
Know me for a grand deceiver,
  All my pretty pranks they know.

How I lulled a rose with humming
  Gentle ditties in her ear,
Then into her bosom coming,
  Rifled all the treasure there.

How I kissed a pair of sisters
  Hanging from one parent tree,
Whilst each bud-mouth, as I kissed hers,
  Called me her own little bee !

Now my flower-gentle sighing,
  To so wild a lover true,
Tells me she is just a-dying,
  So I must go kiss her too.

GEORGE DARLEY

Down the honeysuckle bending,
  As I light upon her crest,
And her silken tucker rending,
  Creep I bold into her breast.

There entranced, but scarcely sleeping,
  For one odorous while I lie,
But for all her woe and weeping
  In a moment out I fly.

Golden-chain, with all her tresses,
  Cannot bind me for an hour ;
Soon I break her amorous jesses,
  And desert the drooping flower.

They may talk of happy Heaven,
  Of another world of bliss ;
Were I choice and freedom given
  I would ask no world but this.

Have they lawns so wide and sunny ?
  Have they such sweet valleys there ?
Are their fields so full of honey ?
  What care I for fields of air ?

Give me Earth's rich sun and flowers,
  Give me Earth's green fields and groves,
Let him fly to Eden's bowers,
  He who such cold bowers loves.

O'er the broom and furze and heather,
  That betuft the mountain side,
In the sweet sunshiny weather
  Let me here for ever glide.

Let me o'er the woodland wander
  On my wild bassooning wing,
Let me, as the streams meander,
  Murmur to their murmuring.

I can dream of nothing sweeter
  Under or above the moon ;
Tell me anything that's better
  And I'll change my song as soon.

But if Heaven must be, I prythee,
  God of woodlands, grant my prayer,
Let me bring my woodland with me,
  Or find such another there !

72 *Serenade of a Loyal Martyr*

SWEET in her green cell the Flower of Beauty slumbers,
  Lulled by the faint breezes sighing through her hair ;
Sleeps she, and hears not the melancholy numbers
  Breathed to my sad lute amid the lonely air ?

Down from the high cliffs the rivulet is teeming,
  To wind round the willow banks that lure him from above :
Oh that in tears from my rocky prison streaming,
  I too could glide to the bower of my love !

Ah! where the woodbines with sleepy arms have
wound her,
Opes she her eyelids at the dream of my lay,
Listening like the dove, while the fountains echo
round her,
To her lost mate's call in the forests far away?

Come, then, my Bird!—for the peace thou ever
bearest,
Still heaven's messenger of comfort to me,
Come!—this fond bosom, my faithfullest, my fairest!
Bleeds with its death-wound, but deeper yet for thee.

SAMUEL LOVER

73 *Widow Machree*

1797–1868

WIDOW Machree, it's no wonder you frown,
Och hone! Widow Machree;
Faith, it ruins your looks, that same dirty black gown,
Och hone! Widow Machree.
How altered your air,
With that close cap you wear—
'Tis destroying your hair,
Which should be flowing free;
Be no longer a churl
Of its black silken curl,
Och hone! Widow Machree.

Widow Machree, now the summer is come,
Och hone! Widow Machree;
When everything smiles, should a beauty look glum?
Och hone! Widow Machree.

See the birds go in pairs,
And the rabbits and hares,—
Why, even the bears
    Now in couples agree;
And the mute little fish,
Though they can't spake, they wish,
    Och hone! Widow Machree.

Widow Machree, and when winter comes in,
    Och hone! Widow Machree;
To be poking the fire all alone is a sin,
    Och hone! Widow Machree.
  Sure the shovel and tongs
  To each other belongs,
  And the kittle sings songs
    Full of family glee;
  Yet alone with your cup
  Like a hermit you sup.
      Och hone! Widow Machree.

And how do you know, with the comforts I've towld,
    Och hone! Widow Machree.
But you're keeping some poor fellow out in the cowld!
    Och hone! Widow Machree.
  With such sins on your head,
  Sure your peace would be fled,
  Could you sleep in your bed,
    Without thinking to see
  Some ghost or some sprite,
  That would wake you each night,
    Crying, 'Och hone! Widow Machree'?

Then take my advice, darling Widow Machree,
          Och hone! Widow Machree;
And with my advice, faith I wish you'd take me,
          Och hone! Widow Machree.
     You'd have me to desire
     Then to stir up the fire,
     And sure Hope is no liar
          In whispering to me
     That the ghosts would depart
     When you'd me near your heart,
          Och hone! Widow Machree.

74 *Rory O'More*

YOUNG Rory O'More courted Kathleen bán,
     He was bold as a hawk,—and she soft as the dawn;
He wished in his heart pretty Kathleen to please,
And he thought the best way to do that was to tease;
'Now Rory, be aisy,' sweet Kathleen would cry—
Reproof on her lip, but a smile in her eye;
'With your tricks, I don't know, in troth, what I'm
     about;
Faith, you've teased me till I've put on my cloak
     inside out';
'Och, jewel,' says Rory, 'that same is the way
You've thrated my heart for this many a day,
And 'tis plased that I am, and why not, to be sure?
For 'tis all for good luck,' says bold Rory O'More.

'Indeed, then,' says Kathleen, 'don't think of the like,
For I half gave a promise to soothering Mike;
The ground that I walk on, he loves, I'll be bound.'
'Faith,' says Rory, 'I'd rather love you than the
     ground.'

'Now, Rory, I'll cry, if you don't let me go;
Sure I dhrame every night that I'm hating you so.'
'Och,' says Rory, 'that same I'm delighted to hear,
For dhrames always go by contraries, my dear;
So, jewel, keep dhramin' that same till you die,
And bright mornin' will give dirty night the black lie;
And 'tis plased that I am, and why not, to be sure?
Since 'tis all for good luck,' says bold Rory O'More.

'Arrah, Kathleen, my darlint, you've teased me enough,
And I've thrashed for your sake Dinny Grimes and James Duff,
And I've made myself, drinkin' your health, quite a baste,
So I think, after that, *I may talk to the priest.*'
Then Rory, the rogue, stole his arm round her neck,
So soft and so white, without freckle or speck,
And he looked in her eyes that were beaming with light,
And he kissed her sweet lips—don't you think he was right?
'Now, Rory, leave off, sir; you'll hug me no more;
That's eight times to-day that you've kissed me before.'
'Then here goes another,' says he, 'to make sure,
For there's luck in odd numbers,' says Rory O'More.

75 *The Low-Backed Car*

WHEN first I saw sweet Peggy,
'Twas on a market day,
A low-backed car she drove, and sat
Upon a truss of hay;

But when that hay was blooming grass,
  And decked with flowers of Spring,
No flow'r was there that could compare
  With the blooming girl I sing.
As she sat in the low-backed car—
The man at the turnpike bar
  Never asked for the toll,
  But just rubbed his ould poll
And looked after the low-backed car.

In battle's wild commotion,
  The proud and mighty Mars,
With hostile scythes, demands his tithes
  Of death—in warlike cars ;
While Peggy, peaceful goddess,
  Has darts in her bright eye,
That knock men down, in the market town,
  As right and left they fly—
While she sits in her low-backed car,
Than battle more dangerous far—
  For the doctor's art
  Cannot cure the heart
That is hit from that low-backed car.

Sweet Peggy, round her car, sir,
  Has strings of ducks and geese,
But the scores of hearts she slaughters
  By far outnumber these ;
While she among her poultry sits,
  Just like a turtle-dove,
Well worth the cage, I do engage,
  Of the blooming god of love !

While she sits in her low-backed car
The lovers come near and far,
 And envy the chicken
 That Peggy is pickin'
As she sits in the low-backed car.

Oh, I'd rather own that car, sir,
 With Peggy by my side,
Than a coach-and-four and goold galore,
 And a lady for my bride;
For the lady would sit forninst me,
 On a cushion made with taste,
While Peggy would sit beside me
 With my arm around her waist—
While we drove in the low-backed car,
To be married by Father Maher,
 Oh, my heart would beat high
 At her glance and her sigh—
Though it beat in a low-backed car.

76 *The Whistlin' Thief*

WHEN Pat came over the hill,
 His colleen fair to see,
His whistle low, but shrill,
 The signal was to be.

(*Pat whistles.*)

'Mary,' the mother said,
 'Someone is whistling sure;'
Says Mary, ''Tis only the wind
 Is whistling through the door.'

(*Pat whistles a bit of a popular air.*)

'I've lived a long time, Mary,
  In this wide world, my dear,
But a door to whistle like that
  I never yet did hear.'

'But, mother, you know the fiddle
  Hangs close beside the chink,
And the wind upon the strings
  Is playing the tune I think.'
(*The pig grunts.*)
'Mary, I hear the pig,
  Unaisy in his mind.'
'But, mother, you know, they say
  The pigs can see the wind.'

'That's true enough in the day,
  But I think you may remark
That pigs no more nor we,
  Can see anything in the dark.'
(*The dog barks.*)
'The dog is barking now,
  The fiddle can't play the tune.'
'But, mother, the dogs will bark
  Whenever they see the moon.'

'But how could he see the moon,
  When, you know, the dog is blind?
Blind dogs won't bark at the moon,
  Nor fiddles be played by the wind.

'I'm not such a fool as you think,
  I know very well it is Pat:
Shut your mouth, you whistlin' thief,
  And go along home out o' that!

'And you be off to your bed,
 Don't play upon me your jeers ;
For though I have lost my eyes,
 I haven't lost my ears !'

77 *The Angel's Whisper*

A BABY was sleeping,
 Its mother was weeping,
For her husband was far on the wild-raging sea,
 And the tempest was swelling
 Round the fisherman's dwelling—
And she cried, 'Dermot, darling, oh ! come back to me.'

Her beads while she numbered,
 The baby still slumbered,
And smiled in her face, as she bended her knee ;
 'Oh ! blessed be that warning,
 My child, thy sleep adorning,
For I know that the angels are whispering with thee.

'And while they are keeping
 Bright watch o'er thy sleeping,
Oh ! pray to them softly, my baby, with me—
 And say thou would'st rather
 They'd watch o'er thy father,
For I know that the angels are whispering with thee.'

The dawn of the morning
Saw Dermot returning,
And the wife wept with joy her babe's father to see,
And closely caressing
Her child, with a blessing,
Said, 'I knew that the angels were whispering with thee.'

78 *The Fairy Boy*

A MOTHER came when stars were paling,
Wailing round a lonely spring;
Thus she cried while tears were falling,
Calling on the Fairy King:
'Why with spells my child caressing,
Courting him with fairy joy—
Why destroy a mother's blessing,
Wherefore steal my baby boy?

'O'er the mountain, through the wild wood,
Where his childhood loved to play;
Where the flowers are freshly springing,
There I wander, day by day.
There I wander, growing fonder
Of the child that made my joy;
On the echoes wildly calling,
To restore my fairy boy.

'But in vain my plaintive calling,
Tears are falling all in vain;
He now sports with fairy pleasure,
He's the treasure of their train!

Fare thee well, my child, for ever,
In this world I've lost my joy,
But in the next we ne'er shall sever,
There I'll find my angel boy!'

JOHN BANIM

79

Soggarth Aroon[1]

1798-1842

AM I the slave they say,
Soggarth aroon?
Since you did show the way,
Soggarth aroon!
Their slave no more to be,
While they would work with me
Old Ireland's slavery,
Soggarth aroon!

Why not her poorest man,
Soggarth aroon!
Try and do all he can,
Soggarth aroon!
Her commands to fulfil
Of his own heart and will,
Side by side with you still,
Soggarth aroon?

Loyal and brave to you,
Soggarth aroon!
Yet be not slave to you,
Soggarth aroon!

[1] Priest, dear.

Nor, out of fear to you—
Stand up so near to you—
Och! out of fear to you,
Soggarth aroon!

Who, in the winter's night,
Soggarth aroon!
When the cold blast did bite,
Soggarth aroon!
Came to my cabin-door,
And, on my earthen-floor,
Knelt by me, sick and poor,
Soggarth aroon?

Who, on the marriage day,
Soggarth aroon!
Made the poor cabin gay,
Soggarth aroon?—
And did both laugh and sing,
Making our hearts to ring,
At the poor christening,
Soggarth aroon?

Who, as friend only met,
Soggarth aroon!
Never did flout me yet,
Soggarth aroon?
And when my heart was dim,
Gave, while his eye did brim,
What I should give to him,
Soggarth aroon?

Och! you, and only you,
Soggarth aroon!
And for this I was true to you,
Soggarth aroon!
In love they'll never shake,
When for ould Ireland's sake,
We a true part did take,
Soggarth aroon!

80 *Ailleen*

'TIS not for love of gold I go,
'Tis not for love of fame;
Tho' fortune should her smile bestow
And I may win a name,
Ailleen,
And I may win a name.

And yet it is for gold I go,
And yet it is for fame,
That they may deck another brow,
And bless another name,
Ailleen,
And bless another name.

For this, but this, I go—for this
I lose thy love awhile;
And all the soft and quiet bliss
Of thy young, faithful smile,
Ailleen,
Of thy young, faithful smile.

And I go to brave a world I hate,
  And woo it o'er and o'er,
And tempt a wave, and try a fate
  Upon a stranger shore,
            Ailleen,
  Upon a stranger shore.

O! when the bays are all my own,
  I know a heart will care!
O! when the gold is wooed and won,
  I know a brow shall wear,
            Ailleen,
  I know a brow shall wear!

And when with both returned again,
  My native land to see,
I know a smile will meet me there,
  And a hand will welcome me,
            Ailleen,
  And a hand will welcome me!

81 *The Irish Mother in the Penal Days*

NOW welcome, welcome, baby-boy, unto a mother's fears,
The pleasure of her sufferings, the rainbow of her tears,
The object of your father's hope, in all the hopes to do,
A future man of his own land, to live him o'er anew!

How fondly on thy little brow a mother's eye would
trace,
And in thy little limbs, and in each feature of thy face,
His beauty, worth, and manliness, and everything
that's his,
Except, my boy, the answering mark of where the
fetter is!

Oh! many a weary hundred years his sires that fetter
wore,
And he has worn it since the day that him his mother
bore;
And now, my son, it waits on you, the moment you
are born,
The old hereditary badge of suffering and scorn!

Alas, my boy so beautiful!—alas, my love so brave!
And must your gallant Irish limbs still drag it to the
grave?
And you, my son, yet have a son, freedom'd a slave
to be,
Whose mother still must weep o'er him the tears I
weep o'er thee!

GERALD GRIFFIN

82 *Eileen Aroon* [1]

1803–1840

WHEN, like the early rose,
Eileen aroon!
Beauty in childhood blows,
Eileen aroon!

[1] Eileen, my treasure. See No. 269.

GERALD GRIFFIN

When, like a diadem,
Buds blush around the stem,
Which is the fairest gem?
Eileen aroon!

Is it the laughing eye,
Eileen aroon!
Is it the timid sigh,
Eileen aroon!
Is it the tender tone,
Soft as the stringed harp's moan?
Oh! it is Truth alone,
Eileen aroon!

When, like the rising day,
Eileen aroon!
Love sends his early ray,
Eileen aroon!
What makes his dawning glow
Changeless through joy or woe?
Only the constant know—
Eileen aroon!

I know a valley fair,
Eileen aroon!
I knew a cottage there,
Eileen aroon!
Far in that valley's shade
I knew a gentle maid,
Flower of a hazel glade,
Eileen aroon!

Who in the song so sweet?
Eileen aroon!
Who in the dance so fleet?
Eileen aroon!
Dear were her charms to me,
Dearer her laughter free,
Dearest her constancy,
Eileen aroon!

Were she no longer true,
Eileen aroon!
What should her lover do?
Eileen aroon!
Fly with his broken chain
Far o'er the sounding main,
Never to love again,
Eileen aroon!

Youth must with time decay,
Eileen aroon!
Beauty must fade away,
Eileen aroon!
Castles are sacked in war,
Chieftains are scattered far,
Truth is a fixéd star,
Eileen aroon!

83 *Hy-Brasail—The Isle of the Blest* (8)

ON the ocean that hollows the rocks where ye dwell,
A shadowy land has appeared, as they tell;
Men thought it a region of sunshine and rest,
And they called it Hy-Brasail, the isle of the blest.

GERALD GRIFFIN

From year unto year on the ocean's blue rim,
The beautiful spectre showed lovely and dim;
The golden clouds curtained the deep where it lay,
And it looked like an Eden, away, far away!

A peasant who heard of the wonderful tale,
In the breeze of the Orient loosened his sail;
From Ara, the holy, he turned to the west,
For though Ara was holy, Hy-Brasail was blest.
He heard not the voices that called from the shore—
He heard not the rising wind's menacing roar;
Home, kindred, and safety he left on that day,
And he sped to Hy-Brasail, away, far away!

Morn rose on the deep, and that shadowy isle,
O'er the faint rim of distance, reflected its smile;
Noon burned on the wave, and that shadowy shore
Seemed lovelily distant, and faint as before;
Lone evening came down on the wanderer's track,
And to Ara again he looked timidly back;
Oh, far on the verge of the ocean it lay,
Yet the isle of the blest was away, far away!

Rash dreamer, return! O, ye winds of the main,
Bear him back to his own peaceful Ara again.
Rash fool! for a vision of fanciful bliss,
To barter thy calm life of labour and peace.
The warning of reason was spoken in vain;
He never revisited Ara again!
Night fell on the deep, amidst tempest and spray,
And he died on the waters, away, far away!

84

Gille Machree

GILLE machree,[1]
Sit down by me,
We now are joined and ne'er shall sever;
This hearth's our own,
Our hearts are one,
And peace is ours for ever!

When I was poor
Your father's door
Was closed against your constant lover;
With care and pain
I tried in vain
My fortunes to recover.
I said, 'To other lands I'd roam,
Where fate may smile on me, love;'
I said, 'Farewell, my own old home!'
And I said, 'Farewell to thee, love!'
Sing, Gille machree, etc.

I might have said,
My mountain maid,
Come live with me, your own true lover—
I know a spot,
A silent cot,
Your friends can ne'er discover,
Where gently flows the waveless tide
By one small garden only;
Where the heron waves his wings so wide,
And the linnet sings so lonely!
Sing, Gille machree, etc.

[1] Brightener of my heart.

I might have said,
My mountain maid,
A father's right was never given
True hearts to curse
With tyrant force
That have been blest in heaven.
But then I said, 'In after years,
When thoughts of home shall find her,
My love may mourn with secret tears
Her friends thus left behind her.'
Sing, Gille machree, etc.

Oh no, I said,
My own dear maid,
For me, though all forlorn for ever,
That heart of thine
Shall ne'er repine
O'er slighted duty—never !
From home and thee though wandering far,
A dreary fate be mine, love—
I'd rather live in endless war,
Than buy my peace with thine, love.
Sing, Gille machree, etc.

Far, far away,
By night and day,
I toiled to win a golden treasure ;
And golden gains
Repaid my pains
In fair and shining measure.
I sought again my native land,
Thy father welcomed me, love ;
I poured my gold into his hand,
And my guerdon found in thee, love.

Sing, Gille machree,
Sit down by me,
We now are joined, and ne'er shall sever ;
This hearth's our own,
Our hearts are one,
And peace is ours for ever !

85

Orange and Green

THE night was falling dreary,
In merry Bandon town,
When, in his cottage weary,
An Orangeman lay down.
The summer sun in splendour
Had set upon the vale,
And shouts of 'No surrender !'
Arose upon the gale.

Beside the waters, laving
The feet of aged trees,
The Orange banners waving,
Flew boldly in the breeze—
In mighty chorus meeting,
A hundred voices join,
And fife and drum were beating
The 'Battle of the Boyne.'

Ha ! tow'rd his cottage hieing,
What form is speeding now,
From yonder thicket flying,
With blood upon his brow ?

'Hide—hide me, worthy stranger,
  Though Green my colour be,
And, in the day of danger,
  May heaven remember thee!

'In yonder vale contending
  Alone against that crew,
My life and limbs defending,
  An Orangeman I slew;
Hark! hear that fearful warning,
  There's death in every tone—
O, save my life till morning,
  And heav'n prolong your own!'

The Orange heart was melted
  In pity to the Green;
He heard the tale, and felt it
  His very soul within,
'Dread not that angry warning
  Though death be in its tone—
I'll save your life till morning,
  Or I will lose my own.'

Now, round his lowly dwelling,
  The angry torrent press'd,
A hundred voices swelling,
  The Orangeman addressed—
'Arise, arise, and follow
  The chase along the plain!
In yonder stony hollow
  Your only son is slain!'

With rising shouts they gather
  Upon the track amain,
And leave the childless father
  Aghast with sudden pain.
He seeks the righted stranger
  In covert where he lay—
'Arise!' he said, 'all danger
  Is gone and passed away.

'I had a son—one only,
  One lovéd as my life,
Thy hand has left me lonely,
  In that accursed strife.
I pledged my word to save thee
  Until the storm should cease,
I keep the pledge I gave thee—
  Arise, and go in peace!'

The stranger soon departed
  From that unhappy vale:
The father, broken-hearted,
  Lay brooding o'er that tale.
Full twenty summers after,
  To silver turned his beard,
And yet the sound of laughter
  From him was never heard.

The night was falling dreary
  In merry Wexford town,
When, in his cabin, weary,
  A peasant laid him down.

And many a song was singing
  Along the summer vale,
And Wexford town was ringing
  With shouts of 'Granua Uile!'

Beside the waters, laving
  The feet of aged trees,
The green flag, gaily waving,
  Was spread against the breeze—
In mighty chorus meeting,
  Loud voices filled the town,
And fife and drum were beating,
  'Down, Orangemen, lie down!'

Hark! 'mid the stirring clangour
  That woke the echoes there,
Loud voices, high in anger,
  Rise on the evening air.
Like billows of the ocean,
  He sees them hurry on—
And, 'mid the wild commotion,
  An Orangeman alone.

'My hair,' he said, 'is hoary,
  And feeble is my hand,
And I could tell a story
  Would shame your cruel band.
Full twenty years and over
  Have changed my heart and brow,
And I am grown a lover
  Of peace and concord now.

'It was not thus I greeted
  Your brother of the Green ;
When fainting and defeated
  I freely took him in.
I pledged my word to save him,
  From vengeance rushing on,
I kept the pledge I gave him,
  Though he had kill'd my son.'

That aged peasant heard him,
  And knew him as he stood,
Remembrance kindly stirr'd him,
  And tender gratitude.
With gushing tears of pleasure,
  He pierced the listening train,
'I'm here to pay the measure
  Of kindness back again.'

Upon his bosom falling,
  That old man's tears came down ;
Deep memory recalling
  That cot and fatal town.
'The hand that would offend thee,
  My being first shall end ;
I'm living to defend thee,
  My saviour and my friend !'

He said, and slowly turning,
  Address'd the wondering crowd,
With fervent spirit burning,
  He told the tale aloud.

Now pressed the warm beholders,
  Their aged foe to greet;
They raised him on their shoulders
  And chaired him through the street.

As he had saved that stranger
  From peril scowling dim,
So in his day of danger
  Did heav'n remember him.
By joyous crowds attended,
  The worthy pair were seen,
And their flags that day were blended
  Of Orange and of Green.

86 *The Bridal of Malahide* (8*a*)

THE joy-bells are ringing
  In gay Malahide,
The fresh wind is singing
  Along the sea-side;
The maids are assembling
  With garlands of flowers,
And the harpstrings are trembling
  In all the glad bowers.

Swell, swell the gay measure!
  Roll trumpet and drum!
'Mid greetings of pleasure
  In splendour they come!
The chancel is ready,
  The portal stands wide
For the lord and the lady,
  The bridegroom and bride.

What years, ere the latter
  Of earthly delight,
The future shall scatter
  O'er them in its flight !
What blissful caresses
  Shall fortune bestow,
Ere those dark-flowing tresses
  Fall white as the snow !

Before the high altar
  Young Maud stands array'd,
With accents that falter
  Her promise is made—
From father and mother
  For ever to part,
For him and no other
  To treasure her heart.

The words are repeated,
  The bridal is done,
The rite is completed—
  The two, they are one ;
The vow, it is spoken
  All pure from the heart,
That must not be broken
  Till life shall depart.

Hark ! 'mid the gay clangour
  That compass'd their car,
Loud accents in anger
  Come mingling afar !

GERALD GRIFFIN

The foe's on the border,
  His weapons resound
Where the lines in disorder
  Unguarded are found.

As awakes the good shepherd
  The watchful and bold,
When the ounce or the leopard
  Is seen in the fold,
So rises already
  The chief in his mail,
While the new-married lady
  Looks fainting and pale.

'Son, husband, and brother,
  Arise to the strife,
For the sister and mother,
  For children and wife!
O'er hill and o'er hollow,
  O'er mountain and plain,
Up, true men, and follow!
  Let dastards remain!'

Farrah! to the battle!
  They form into line—
The shields, how they rattle!
  The spears, how they shine!
Soon, soon, shall the foeman
  His treachery rue—
On, burgher and yeoman,
  To die or to do!

GERALD GRIFFIN

The eve is declining
  In lone Malahide,
The maidens are twining
  Gay wreaths for the bride!
She marks them unheeding—
  Her heart is afar,
Where the clansmen are bleeding
  For her in the war.

Hark! loud from the mountain
  'Tis Victory's cry!
O'er woodland and fountain
  It rings to the sky!
The foe has retreated!
  He flies to the shore;
The spoiler's defeated—
  The combat is o'er!

With foreheads unruffled
  The conquerors come—
But why have they muffled
  The lance and the drum?
What form do they carry
  Aloft on his shield?
And where does he tarry,
  The lord of the field?

Ye saw him at morning,
  How gallant and gay!
In bridal adorning,
  The star of the day:

GERALD GRIFFIN

Now weep for the lover—
  His triumph is sped,
His hope it is over!
  The chieftain is dead!

But oh, for the maiden
  Who mourns for that chief,
With heart overladen
  And rending with grief!
She sinks on the meadow
  In one morning-tide,
A wife and a widow,
  A maid and a bride!

Ye maidens attending,
  Forbear to condole!
Your comfort is rending
  The depths of her soul.
True—true, 'twas a story
  For ages of pride;
He died in his glory—
  But oh, he has died!

The war-cloak she raises
  All mournfully now,
And steadfastly gazes
  Upon the cold brow.
That glance may for ever
  Unalter'd remain,
But the bridegroom will never
  Return it again.

GERALD GRIFFIN

The dead-bells are tolling
  In sad Malahide,
The death-wail is rolling
  Along the sea-side;
The crowds, heavy-hearted,
  Withdraw from the green,
For the sun has departed
  That brighten'd the scene!

Even yet in that valley,
  Though years have roll'd by,
When through the wild sally
  The sea-breezes sigh,
The peasant, with sorrow,
  Beholds in the shade
The tomb where the morrow
  Saw Hussey convey'd.

How scant was the warning,
  How briefly reveal'd,
Before on that morning
  Death's chalice was fill'd!
The hero who drunk it
  There moulders in gloom,
And the form of Maud Plunket
  Weeps over his tomb.

The stranger who wanders
  Along the lone vale
Still sighs while he ponders
  On that heavy tale:

'Thus passes each pleasure
That earth can supply—
Thus joy has its measure—
We live but to die!'

87 *Lines to a Seagull*

WHITE bird of the tempest! O beautiful thing!
With the bosom of snow and the motionless wing,
Now sweeping the billow, now floating on high,
Now bathing thy plumes in the light of the sky,
Now poising o'er ocean thy delicate form,
Now breasting the surge with thy bosom so warm,
Now darting aloft with a heavenly scorn,
Now shooting along like a ray of the morn,
Now lost in the folds of the cloud-curtained dome,
Now floating abroad like a flake of the foam,
Now silently poised o'er the war of the main,
Like the spirit of Charity brooding o'er pain,
Now gliding with pinion all silently furled,
Like an angel descending to comfort the world!
Thou seem'st to my spirit, as upward I gaze,
And see thee, now clothed in mellowest rays,
Now lost in the storm-driven vapours that fly
Like hosts that are routed across the broad sky,
Like a pure spirit true to its virtue and faith,
'Mid the tempests of Nature, and passion, and death!

Rise, beautiful emblem of purity, rise!
On the sweet winds of Heaven to thine own brilliant skies;
Still higher—still higher—till lost to our sight,
Thou hidest thy wings in a mantle of light;

And I think, how a pure spirit gazing on thee,
Must long for the moment—the joyous and free—
When the soul disembodied from nature shall spring
Unfettered at once to her Maker and King;
When the bright day of service and suffering past,
Shapes fairer than thine shall shine round her at last,
While, the standard of battle triumphantly furled,
She smiles like a victor, serene on the world!

88 *Céad Míle Fáilte,*[1] *Elim!*

Song from 'The Invasion'

CÉAD Míle Fáilte! child of the Ithian!
Céad Míle Fáilte, Elim!
Aisneach, thy temple in ruins is lying,
In Druim na Druid the dark blast is sighing,
Lonely we shelter in grief and in danger,
Yet have we welcome and cheer for the stranger.
Céad Míle Fáilte! child of the Ithian!
Céad Míle Fáilte, Elim!

Woe for the weapons that guarded our slumbers,
Temreach, they said, was too small for our numbers;
Little is left for our sons to inherit,
Yet what we have, thou art welcome to share it.
Céad Míle Fáilte! child of the Ithian!
Céad Míle Fáilte, Elim!

[1] A hundred thousand welcomes.

Corman, thy teachers have died broken-hearted ;
Voice of the trilithon, thou art departed !
All have forsaken our mountains so dreary,
All but the spirit that welcomes the weary.
Céad Míle Fáilte ! child of the Ithian !
Céad Míle Fáilte, Elim !

Vainly the Draithe, alone in the mountain,
Look to the torn cloud or eddying fountain ;
The spell of the Christian has vanquished their power,
Yet is he welcome to rest in our bower.
Céad Míle Fáilte ! child of the Ithian !
Céad Míle Fáilte, Elim !

Wake for the Christian your welcoming numbers !
Strew the dry rushes to pillow his slumbers ;
Long let him cherish, with deep recollection,
The eve of our feast, and the Druid's affection.
Céad Míle Fáilte ! child of the Ithian !
Céad Míle Fáilte, Elim !

JAMES CLARENCE MANGAN

89 *A Lament for the Tyronian and Tyrconnellian Princes Buried at Rome* (9)

From the Irish

1803–1849

O, WOMAN of the Piercing Wail,
Who mournest o'er yon mound of clay
With sigh and groan,
Would God thou wert among the Gael !
Thou would'st not then from day to day
Weep thus alone.

'Twere long before, around a grave
In green Tirconnell, one could find
This loneliness;
Near where Beann-Boirche's banners wave
Such grief as thine could ne'er have pined
Compassionless.

Beside the wave, in Donegal,
In Antrim's glens, or fair Dromore,
Or Killilee,
Or where the sunny waters fall,
At Assaroe, near Erna's shore,
This could not be.
On Derry's plains—in rich Drumclieff—
Throughout Armagh the Great, renowned
In olden years,
No one could pass but woman's grief
Would rain upon the burial-ground
Fresh floods of tears!

O, no!—from Shannon, Boyne, and Suir,
From high Dunluce's castle-walls,
From Lissadill,
Would flock alike both rich and poor,
One wail would rise from Cruachan's halls
To Tara's hill;
And some would come from Barrow-side,
And many a maid would leave her home,
On Leitrim's plains,
And by melodious Banna's tide,
And by the Mourne and Erne, to come
And swell thy strains!

O, horses' hoofs would trample down
The Mount whereon the martyr-saint (10)
Was crucified !
From glen and hill, from plain and town,
One loud lament, one thrilling plaint,
Would echo wide.
There would not soon be found, I ween,
One foot of ground among those bands
For museful thought,
So many shriekers of the keen [1]
Would cry aloud and clap their hands,
All woe-distraught ?

Two princes of the line of Conn
Sleep in their cells of clay beside
O'Donnell Roe ;
Three royal youths, alas ! are gone,
Who lived for Erin's weal, but died
For Erin's woe !
Ah ! could the men of Ireland read
The names these noteless burial-stones
Display to view,
Their wounded hearts afresh would bleed,
Their tears gush forth again, their groans
Resound anew !

The youths whose relics moulder here
Were sprung from Hugh, high Prince and Lord
Of Aileach's lands !
Thy noble brothers, justly dear,
Thy nephew, long to be deplored
By Ulster's bands.

[1] Ir. *Caoine*. The funeral wail.

Theirs were not souls wherein dull Time
  Could domicile Decay or house
    Decrepitude!
They passed from Earth ere Manhood's prime,
  Ere years had power to dim their brows
    Or chill their blood.

And who can marvel o'er thy grief,
  Or who can blame thy flowing tears,
    That knows their source?
O'Donnell, Dunnasava's chief,
  Cut off amid his vernal years,
    Lies here a corse.
Beside his brother Cathbar, whom
  Tirconnell of the Helmets mourns
    In deep despair—
For valour, truth, and comely bloom,
  For all that greatens and adorns
    A peerless pair.

O, had these twain, and he, the third,
  The Lord of Mourne, O'Niall's son,
    Their mate in death—
A prince in look, in deed, and word—
  Had these three heroes yielded on
    The field their breath,—
O, had they fallen on Criffan's plain,
  There would not be a town or clan
    From shore to sea,
But would with shrieks bewail the slain,
  Or chant aloud the exulting rann [1]
    Of Jubilee!

[1] Song.

When high the shout of battle rose,
  On fields where Freedom's torch still burned
    Through Erin's gloom,
If one, if barely one of those
  Were slain, all Ulster would have mourned
    The hero's doom!
If at Athboy, where hosts of brave
  Ulidian horsemen sank beneath
    The shock of spears,
Young Hugh O'Neill had found a grave,
  Long must the North have wept his death
    With heart-wrung tears!

If on the day of Ballach-myre
  The Lord of Mourne had met thus young,
    A warrior's fate,
In vain would such as thou desire
  To mourn, alone, the champion sprung
    From Niall the Great!
No marvel this—for all the dead,
  Heaped on the field, pile over pile,
    At Mullach-brack,
Were scarce an eric[1] for his head,
  If death had stayed his footsteps while
    On victory's track!

If on the Day of Hostages
  The fruit had from the parent bough
    Been rudely torn
In sight of Munster's bands—Mac-Nee's—
  Such blow the blood of Conn, I trow,
    Could ill have borne.

[1] A fine or compensation.

If on the day of Ballach-boy
  Some arm had laid, by foul surprise,
    The chieftain low,
Even our victorious shout of joy
  Would soon give place to rueful cries
    And groans of woe!

If on the day the Saxon host
  Were forced to fly—a day so great
    For Ashanee [1]—
The Chief had been untimely lost,
  Our conquering troops should moderate
    Their mirthful glee.
There would not lack on Lifford's day,
  From Galway, from the glens of Boyle,
    From Limerick's towers,
A marshalled file, a long array
  Of mourners to bedew the soil
    With tears in showers!

If on the day a sterner fate
  Compelled his flight from Athenree,
    His blood had flowed,
What numbers all disconsolate,
  Would come unasked, and share with thee
    Affliction's load!
If Derry's crimson field had seen
  His life-blood offered up, though 'twere
    On Victory's shrine,
A thousand cries would swell the keen,
  A thousand voices of despair
    Would echo thine!

[1] Ballyshannon.

O, had the fierce Dalcassian swarm
  That bloody night on Fergus' banks
    But slain our Chief,
When rose his camp in wild alarm—
  How would the triumph of his ranks
    Be dashed with grief!
How would the troops of Murbach mourn
  If on the Curlew Mountains' day
    Which England rued,
Some Saxon hand had left them lorn,
  By shedding there, amid the fray,
    Their prince's blood!

Red would have been our warriors' eyes
  Had Roderick found on Sligo's field
    A gory grave,
No Northern Chief would soon arise
  So sage to guide, so strong to shield,
    So swift to save.
Long would Leith-Cuinn have wept if Hugh
  Had met the death he oft had dealt
    Among the foe;
But, had our Roderick fallen too,
  All Erin must, alas! have felt
    The deadly blow!

What do I say? Ah, woe is me!
  Already we bewail in vain
    Their fatal fall!
And Erin, once the Great and Free,
  Now vainly mourns her breakless chain,
    And iron thrall!

Then, daughter of O'Donnell! dry
Thine overflowing eyes, and turn
Thy heart aside;
For Adam's race is born to die,
And sternly the sepulchral urn
Mocks human pride!

Look not, nor sigh, for earthly throne,
Nor place thy trust in arm of clay—
But on thy knees
Uplift thy soul to God alone,
For all things go their destined way
As He decrees.
Embrace the faithful Crucifix,
And seek the path of pain and prayer
Thy Saviour trod!
Nor let thy spirit intermix
With earthly hope and worldly care
Its groans to God!

And Thou, O mighty Lord! whose ways
Are far above our feeble minds
To understand,
Sustain us in these doleful days,
And render light the chain that binds
Our fallen land!
Look down upon our dreary state,
And through the ages that may still
Roll sadly on,
Watch Thou o'er hapless Erin's fate,
And shield at least from darker ill
The blood of Conn!

90 *The Fair Hills of Eiré, O!*

From the Irish

TAKE a blessing from my heart to the land of my birth,
And the fair Hills of Eiré, O!
And to all that yet survive of Eibhear's tribe on earth,
On the fair Hills of Eiré, O!
In that land so delightful the wild thrush's lay
Seems to pour a lament forth for Eiré's decay—
Alas! alas! why pine I a thousand miles away
From the fair Hills of Eiré, O!

The soil is rich and soft—the air is mild and bland,
Of the fair Hills of Eiré, O!
Her barest rock is greener to me than this rude land—
O, the fair Hills of Eiré, O!
Her woods are tall and straight, grove rising over grove;
Trees flourish in her glens below, and on her heights above;
Oh, in heart and in soul, I shall ever, ever love
The fair Hills of Eiré, O!

A noble tribe, moreover, are the now hapless Gael,
On the fair Hills of Eiré, O!
A tribe in battle's hour unused to shrink or fail
On the fair Hills of Eiré, O!
For this is my lament in bitterness outpoured,
To see them slain or scattered by the Saxon sword:
Oh, woe of woes, to see a foreign spoiler horde
On the fair Hills of Eiré, O!

Broad and tall rise the Cruachs[1] in the golden morning's glow,
On the fair Hills of Eiré, O!
O'er her smooth grass for ever sweet cream and honey flow
On the fair Hills of Eiré, O!
Oh, I long, I am pining again to behold
The land that belongs to the brave Gael of old;
Far dearer to my heart than a gift of gems or gold
Are the fair Hills of Eiré, O!

The dew-drops lie bright 'mid the grass and yellow corn
On the fair Hills of Eiré, O!
The sweet-scented apples blush redly in the morn
On the fair Hills of Eiré, O!
The water-cress and sorrel fill the vales below;
The streamlets are hush'd, till the evening breezes blow,
While the waves of the Suir, noble river! ever flow
Near the fair Hills of Eiré, O!

A fruitful clime is Eiré's, through valley, meadow, plain,
And the fair land of Eiré, O!
The very 'Bread of Life' is in the yellow grain
On the fair Hills of Eiré, O!
Far dearer unto me than the tones music yields,
Is the lowing of the kine and the calves in her fields,
And the sunlight that shone long ago on the shields
Of the Gaels, on the fair Hills of Eiré, O!

[1] Hills in co. Waterford.

91 *Dark Rosaleen* (II)

From the Irish

O MY Dark Rosaleen,
  Do not sigh, do not weep!
The priests are on the ocean green,
  They march along the deep.
There's wine from the royal Pope,
  Upon the ocean green;
And Spanish ale shall give you hope,
  My Dark Rosaleen!
  My own Rosaleen!
Shall glad your heart, shall give you hope,
Shall give you health, and help, and hope,
  My Dark Rosaleen!

Over hills and through dales
  Have I roamed for your sake;
All yesterday I sailed with sails
  On river and on lake.
The Erne, at its highest flood,
  I dashed across unseen,
For there was lightning in my blood,
  My Dark Rosaleen!
  My own Rosaleen!
O! there was lightning in my blood,
Red lightning lightened through my blood,
  My Dark Rosaleen!

All day long, in unrest,
  To and fro do I move,
The very soul within my breast
  Is wasted for you, love!

The heart in my bosom faints
  To think of you, my Queen,
My life of life, my saint of saints,
  My Dark Rosaleen!
  My own Rosaleen!
To hear your sweet and sad complaints,
My life, my love, my saint of saints,
  My Dark Rosaleen!

Woe and pain, pain and woe,
  Are my lot, night and noon,
To see your bright face clouded so,
  Like to the mournful moon.
But yet will I rear your throne
  Again in golden sheen;
'Tis you shall reign, shall reign alone,
  My Dark Rosaleen!
  My own Rosaleen!
'Tis you shall have the golden throne,
'Tis you shall reign, and reign alone,
  My Dark Rosaleen!

Over dews, over sands,
  Will I fly for your weal:
Your holy, delicate white hands
  Shall girdle me with steel.
At home in your emerald bowers,
  From morning's dawn till e'en,
You'll pray for me, my flower of flowers,
  My Dark Rosaleen!
  My fond Rosaleen!
You'll think of me through daylight's hours,
My virgin flower, my flower of flowers,
  My Dark Rosaleen?

I could scale the blue air,
  I could plough the high hills,
O, I could kneel all night in prayer,
  To heal your many ills!
And one beamy smile from you
  Would float like light between
My toils and me, my own, my true,
  My Dark Rosaleen!
  My fond Rosaleen!
Would give me life and soul anew,
A second life, a soul anew,
  My Dark Rosaleen!

O! the Erne shall run red
  With redundance of blood,
The earth shall rock beneath our tread,
  And flames warp hill and wood,
And gun-peal and slogan cry,
  Wake many a glen serene,
Ere you shall fade, ere you shall die,
  My Dark Rosaleen!
  My own Rosaleen!
The Judgement Hour must first be nigh,
Ere you can fade, ere you can die,
  My Dark Rosaleen!

92 *Kathaleen Ny-Houlahan*[1]

A Jacobite Relic from the Irish

LONG they pine in weary woe, the nobles of our land,
Long they wander to and fro, proscribed, alas! and banned;

[1] One of the many emblematic names for Ireland.

Feastless, houseless, altarless, they bear the exile's brand;
But their hope is in the coming-to of Kathaleen Ny-Houlahan!

Think her not a ghastly hag, too hideous to be seen;
Call her not unseemly names, our matchless Kathaleen;
Young she is, and fair she is, and would be crowned queen,
Were the king's son at home here with Kathaleen Ny-Houlahan?

Sweet and mild would look her face, oh none so sweet and mild,
Could she crush the foes by whom her beauty is reviled;
Woollen plaids would grace herself, and robes of silk her child,
If the king's son were living here with Kathaleen Ny-Houlahan!

Sore disgrace it is to see the Arbitress of thrones,
Vassal to a Saxoneen of cold and sapless bones!
Bitter anguish wrings our souls—with heavy sighs and groans
We wait the Young Deliverer of Kathaleen Ny-Houlahan.

Let us pray to Him who holds life's issues in His hands—
Him who formed the mighty globe, with all its thousand lands;

Girdling them with seas and mountains, rivers deep,
and strands,
To cast a look of pity upon Kathaleen Ny-
Houlahan!

He who over sands and waves led Israel along—
He who fed, with heavenly bread, that chosen tribe
and throng—
He who stood by Moses, when his foes were fierce
and strong—
May He show forth His might in saving
Kathaleen Ny-Houlahan!

93

Kincora (12)

From the Irish

O, WHERE, Kincora! is Brian the Great?
And where is the beauty that once was thine?
O, where are the princes and nobles that sate
At the feast in thy halls, and drank the red wine?
Where, O, Kincora?

O, where, Kincora! are thy valorous lords?
O, whither, thou Hospitable! are they gone?
O, where are the Dalcassians of the golden swords?
And where are the warriors Brian led on?
Where, O, Kincora?

And where is Morogh, the descendant of kings;
The defeater of a hundred—the daringly brave—
Who set but slight store by jewels and rings;
Who swam down the torrent and laughed at its wave?
Where, O, Kincora?

And where is Donogh, King Brian's son ?
  And where is Conaing, the beautiful chief ?
And Kian and Corc ? Alas ! they are gone ;
  They have left me this night alone with my grief !
          Left me, Kincora !

And where are the chiefs with whom Brian went forth,
  The never-vanquished sons of Erin the brave,
The great King of Onaght, renowned for his worth,
  And the hosts of Baskinn from the western wave ?
          Where, O, Kincora ?

O, where is Duvlann of the Swift-footed Steeds ?
  And where is Kian, who was son of Molloy ?
And where is King Lonergan, the fame of whose deeds
  In the red battle-field no time can destroy ?
          Where, O, Kincora ?

And where is that youth of majestic height,
  The faith-keeping Prince of the Scots ? Even he,
As wide as his fame was, as great as was his might,
  Was tributary, O Kincora, to thee !
          Thee, O, Kincora !

They are gone, those heroes of royal birth,
  Who plundered no churches, and broke no trust ;
'Tis weary for me to be living on earth
  When they, O Kincora, be low in the dust !
          Low, O, Kincora !

O, never again will Princes appear,
To rival the Dalcassians of the Cleaving Swords;
I can never dream of meeting afar or anear,
In the east or the west such heroes and lords!
Never, Kincora!

O, dear are the images my memory calls up
Of Brian Boru!—how he never would miss
To give me at the banquet the first bright cup!
Ah! why did he heap on me honour like this?
Why, O, Kincora?

I am MacLiag, and my home is on the Lake:
Thither often, to that palace whose beauty is fled,
Came Brian, to ask me, and I went for his sake,
O, my grief! that I should live, and Brian be dead!
Dead, O, Kincora!

94 *O'Hussey's Ode to The Maguire*

From the Irish

WHERE is my Chief, my Master, this bleak night, movrone!
Oh, cold, cold, miserably cold is this bleak night for Hugh;
Its showery, arrowy, speary sleet pierceth one through and through,
Pierceth one to the very bone!

Rolls real thunder? Or was that red, livid light
Only a meteor? I scarce know; but through the midnight dim
The pitiless ice-wind streams. Except the hate that persecutes him
Nothing hath crueller venomy might.

An awful, a tremendous night is this, meseems!
  The flood-gates of the rivers of heaven, I think, have been burst wide—
  Down from the overcharged clouds, like unto headlong ocean's tide,
Descends grey rain in roaring streams.

Though he were even a wolf ranging the round green woods,
  Though he were even a pleasant salmon in the unchainable sea,
  Though he were a wild mountain eagle, he could scarce bear, he,
This sharp, sore sleet, these howling floods.

Oh, mournful is my soul this night for Hugh Maguire!
  Darkly, as in a dream he strays! Before him and behind
  Triumphs the tyrannous anger of the wounding wind,
The wounding wind, that burns as fire!

It is my bitter grief—it cuts me to the heart—
  That in the country of Clan Darry this should be his fate!
  Oh, woe is me, where is he? Wandering, houseless, desolate,
Alone, without or guide or chart!

Medreams I see just now his face, the strawberry-bright,
  Uplifted to the blackened heavens, while the tempestuous winds
  Blow fiercely over and round him, and the smiting sleet-shower blinds
The hero of Galang to-night!

Large, large affliction unto me and mine it is,
That one of his majestic bearing, his fair, stately form,
Should thus be tortured and o'erborne—that this unsparing storm
Should wreak its wrath on head like his!

That his great hand, so oft the avenger of the oppressed,
Should this chill churlish night, perchance, be paralysed by frost—
While through some icicle-hung thicket—as one lorn and lost—
He walks and wanders without rest.

The tempest-driven torrent deluges the mead;
It overflows the low banks of the rivulets and ponds—
The lawns and pasture-grounds lie locked in icy bonds,
So that the cattle cannot feed.

The pale bright margins of the streams are seen by none;
Rushes and sweeps along the untamable flood on every side—
It penetrates and fills the cottagers' dwellings far and wide—
Water and land are blent in one.

Through some dark wood, 'mid bones of monsters, Hugh now strays,
As he confronts the storm with anguished heart, but manly brow—
Oh, what a sword-wound to that tender heart of his were now
A backward glance of peaceful days!

But other thoughts are his—thoughts that can still
inspire
With joy and onward-bounding hope the bosom of
Mac-Nee—
Thoughts of his warriors charging like bright billows
of the sea,
Borne on the wind's wings, flashing fire !

And though frost glaze to-night the clear dew of
his eyes,
And white ice-gauntlets glove his noble fine fair
fingers o'er,
A warm dress is to him that lightning-garb he ever
wore,
The lightning of the soul, not skies.

Avran

Hugh marched forth to the fight—I grieved to see
him so depart ;
And lo ! to-night he wanders frozen, rain-drenched,
sad, betrayed—
But the memory of the lime-white mansions his
right hand hath laid
In ashes, warms the hero's heart !

95 *The Woman of Three Cows*

From the Irish

O, WOMAN of Three Cows, agrah ![1] don't let
your tongue thus rattle !
O, don't be saucy, don't be stiff, because you may
have cattle.

[1] My love.

I have seen—and, here's my hand to you, I only say what's true—
A many a one with twice your stock not half so proud as you.

Good luck to you, don't scorn the poor, and don't be their despiser;
For worldly wealth soon melts away, and cheats the very miser;
And death soon strips the proudest wreath from haughty human brows—
Then don't be stiff, and don't be proud, good Woman of Three Cows.

See where Momonia's heroes lie, proud Owen More's descendants,
'Tis they that won the glorious name, and had the grand attendants!
If they were forced to bow to Fate, as every mortal bows,
Can you be proud, can you be stiff, my Woman of Three Cows?

The brave sons of the Lord of Clare, they left the land to mourning;
Movrone![1] for they were banished, with no hope of their returning—
Who knows in what abodes of want those youths were driven to house?
Yet you can give yourself these airs, O Woman of Three Cows.

[1] My Grief.

O, think of Donnell of the Ships, the Chief whom
nothing daunted—
See how he fell in distant Spain, unchronicled, un-
chanted!
He sleeps, the great O'Sullivan, where thunder
cannot rouse—
Then, ask yourself, should you be proud, good
Woman of Three Cows?

O'Ruark, Maguire, those souls of fire, whose names
are shrined in story—
Think how their high achievements once made
Erin's greatest glory:
Yet now their bones lie mouldering under weeds and
cypress boughs—
And so, for all your pride, will yours, O Woman
of Three Cows.

The O'Carrolls also, famed when fame was only
for the boldest,
Rest in forgotten sepulchres with Erin's best and
oldest;
Yet who so great as they of yore in battle or carouse?
Just think of that, and hide your head, good Woman
of Three Cows.

Your neighbour's poor, and you it seems are big with
vain ideas,
Because, inagh![1] you've got three cows—one more,
I see, than she has;
That tongue of yours wags more at times than charity
allows,
But, if you are strong, be merciful—great Woman
of Three Cows.

[1] Forsooth.

Avran

Now, there you go! You still, of course, keep up your scornful bearing,
And I'm too poor to hinder you; but, by the cloak I'm wearing,
If I had but four cows myself, even though you were my spouse,
I'd thwack you well to cure your pride, my Woman of Three Cows.

96 *The Karamanian Exile*

I SEE thee ever in my dreams,
Karaman!
Thy hundred hills, thy thousand streams,
Karaman! O Karaman!
As when thy gold-bright morning gleams,
As when the deepening sunset seams
With lines of light thy hills and streams,
Karaman!
So thou loomest on my dreams,
Karaman! O Karaman!

The hot bright plains, the sun, the skies,
Karaman!
Seem death-black marble to mine eyes,
Karaman! O Karaman!
I turn from Summer's blooms and dyes;
Yet in my dreams thou dost arise
In welcome glory to my eyes,
Karaman!

JAMES CLARENCE MANGAN

In thee my life of life yet lies,
Karaman!
Thou still art holy in mine eyes,
Karaman! O Karaman!

Ere my fighting years were come,
Karaman!
Troops were few in Erzerome,
Karaman! O Karaman!
Their fiercest came from Erzerome,
They came from Ukhbar's palace dome,
They dragged me forth from thee, my home,
Karaman!
Thee, my own, my mountain home,
Karaman!
In life and death, my spirit's home,
Karaman! O Karaman!

Oh, none of all my sisters ten,
Karaman!
Loved like me my fellow-men,
Karaman!
I was mild as milk till then,
I was soft as silk till then;
Now my breast is as a den,
Karaman!
Foul with blood and bones of men,
Karaman!
With blood and bones of slaughtered men,
Karaman! O Karaman!

My boyhood's feelings newly born,
Karaman!
Withered like young flowers uptorn,
Karaman! O Karaman!

And in their stead sprang weed and thorn ;
What once I loved now moves my scorn ;
My burning eyes are dried to horn,
Karaman !
I hate the blessed light of morn,
Karaman !
It maddens me, the face of morn,
Karaman ! O Karaman !

The Spahi wears a tyrant's chains,
Karaman !
But bondage worse than this remains,
Karaman ! O Karaman !
His heart is black with million stains :
Thereon, as on Kaf's blasted plains,
Shall never more fall dews and rains,
Karaman !
Save poison-dews and bloody rains,
Karaman !
Hell's poison-dews and bloody rains,
Karaman ! O Karaman !

But life at worst must end ere long,
Karaman !
Azreel avengeth every wrong,
Karaman ! O Karaman !
Of late my thoughts rove more among
Thy fields ; o'ershadowing fancies throng
My mind, and texts of bodeful song,
Karaman !
Azreel is terrible and strong,
Karaman !
His lightning sword smites all ere long,
Karaman ! O Karaman !

There's care to-night in Ukhbar's halls,
Karaman !
There's hope, too, for his trodden thralls,
Karaman ! O Karaman !
What lights flash red along your walls ?
Hark ! hark !—the muster-trumpet calls !—
I see the sheen of spears and shawls,
Karaman !
The foe ! the foe !—they scale the walls,
Karaman !
To-night Murad or Ukhbar falls,
Karaman ! O Karaman !

97 *Siberia*

IN Siberia's wastes
The Ice-wind's breath
Woundeth like the toothéd steel.
Lost Siberia doth reveal
Only blight and death.

Blight and death alone.
No Summer sun shines.
Night is interblent with Day
In Siberia's wastes alway
The blood blackens, the heart pines.

In Siberia's wastes
No tears are shed,
For they freeze within the brain.
Nought is felt but dullest pain.
Pain acute, yet dead.

JAMES CLARENCE MANGAN

Pain as in a dream,
When years go by
Funeral-paced, yet fugitive,
When man lives and doth not live,
Doth not live—nor die.

In Siberia's wastes
Are sands and rocks.
Nothing blooms of green or soft,
But the snow-peaks rise aloft
And the gaunt ice-blocks.

And the exile there
Is one with those ;
They are part and he is part,
For the sands are in his heart,
And the killing snows.

Therefore, in those wastes
None curse the Czar.
Each man's tongue is cloven by
The North Blast, who heweth nigh
With sharp scimitar.

And such doom each drees,
Till, hunger-gnawn,
And cold-slain, he at length sinks there,
Yet scarce more a corpse than ere
His last breath was drawn.

JAMES CLARENCE MANGAN

98 *Gone in the Wind*

SOLOMON! where is thy throne? It is gone in the wind.
Babylon! where is thy might? It is gone in the wind.
Like the swift shadows of Noon, like the dreams of the Blind,
Vanish the glories and pomps of the earth in the wind.

Man! canst thou build upon aught in the pride of thy mind?
Wisdom will teach thee that nothing can tarry behind;
Though there be thousand bright actions embalmed and enshrined,
Myriads and millions of brighter are snow in the wind.

Solomon! where is thy throne? It is gone in the wind.
Babylon! where is thy might? It is gone in the wind.
All that the genius of man hath achieved or designed
Waits but its hour to be dealt with as dust by the wind.

Say, what is Pleasure? A phantom, a mask undefined.
Science? An almond, whereof we can pierce but thc rind.
Honour and Affluence? Firmans that Fortune hath signed,
Only to glitter and pass on the wings of the wind.

Solomon! where is thy throne? It is gone in the
wind.
Babylon! where is thy might? It is gone in the
wind.
Who is the Fortunate? He who in anguish hath
pined!
He shall rejoice when his relics are dust in the wind.

Mortal! be careful with what thy best hopes are
entwined;
Woe to the miners for Truth—where the Lampless
have mined!
Woe to the seekers on earth for—what none ever
find!
They and their trust shall be scattered like leaves
on the wind.

Solomon! where is thy throne? It is gone in the
wind.
Babylon! where is thy might? It is gone in the
wind.
Happy in death are they only whose hearts have
consigned
All Earth's affections and longings and cares to the
wind.

Pity, thou, reader! the madness of poor humankind,
Raving of knowledge—and Satan so busy to blind!
Raving of glory,—like me,—for the garlands I bind
(Garlands of Song) are but gathered, and strewn in
the wind.

Solomon! where is thy throne! It is gone in the
wind.
Babylon! where is thy might? It is gone in the
wind.
I, Abdul-Namez, must rest; for my fire hath declined,
And I hear voices from Hades like bells on the wind.

99 *The Nameless One*

ROLL forth, my song, like the rushing river
That sweeps along to the mighty sea;
God will inspire me while I deliver
My soul to thee!

Tell thou the world, when my bones lie whitening
Amid the last homes of youth and eld,
That there once was one whose veins ran lightning
No eye beheld.

Tell how his boyhood was one drear night-hour,
How shone for him, through his griefs and gloom,
No star of all heaven sends to light our
Path to the tomb.

Roll on, my song, and to after-ages
Tell how, disdaining all earth can give,
He would have taught men from wisdom's pages
The way to live.

And tell how trampled, derided, hated,
And worn by weakness, disease and wrong,
He fled for shelter to God, who mated
His soul with song—

With song which alway, sublime or vapid,
  Flowed like a rill in the morning beam,
Perchance not deep, but intense and rapid—
    A mountain stream.

Tell how the Nameless, condemned for years long
  To herd with demons from hell beneath,
Saw things that made him, with groans and tears, long
    For even death.

Go on to tell how, with genius wasted,
  Betrayed in friendship, befooled in love,
With spirit shipwrecked, and young hopes blasted,
    He still, still strove.

Till, spent with toil, dreeing death for others,
  And some whose hands should have wrought for him
(If children live not for sires and mothers),
    His mind grew dim.

And he fell far through that pit abysmal,
  The gulf and grave of Maginn and Burns,
And pawned his soul for the Devil's dismal
    Stock of returns.

But yet redeemed it in days of darkness,
  And shapes and signs of the final wrath
When death, in hideous and ghastly starkness,
    Stood in his path.

And tell how now, amid wreck and sorrow,
  And want, and sickness, and houseless nights,
He bides in calmness the silent morrow
    That no ray lights.

And lives he still, then ? Yes ! Old and hoary
  At thirty-nine, from despair and woe,
He lives, enduring what future story
          Will never know.

Him grant a grave to, ye pitying noble,
  Deep in your bosoms ! There let him dwell !
He, too, had tears for all souls in trouble,
          Here and in hell.

100 *The One Mystery*

'TIS idle ! we exhaust and squander
  The glittering mine of thought in vain.
All-baffled reason cannot wander
          Beyond her chain.
The flood of life runs dark—dark clouds
  Make lampless night around its shore :
The dead, where are they ! In their shrouds—
          Man knows no more.

Evoke the ancient and the past,
  Will one illumining star arise ?
Or must the film, from first to last
          O'erspread thine eyes ?
When life, love, glory, beauty, wither,
  Will wisdom's page, or science chart,
Map out for thee the region whither
          Their shades depart ?

Supposest thou the wondrous powers,
  To high imagination given,
Pale types of what shall yet be ours,
          When earth is heaven ?

JAMES CLARENCE MANGAN

When this decaying shell is cold,
  Oh! sayest thou the soul shall climb
What magic mount she trod of old,
      Ere childhood's time?

And shall the sacred pulse that thrilled,
  Thrill once again to glory's name?
And shall the conquering love that filled
      All earth with flame,
Reborn, revived, renewed, immortal,
  Resume his reign in prouder might,
A sun beyond the ebon portal
      Of death and night?

No more, no more—with aching brow,
  And restless heart, and burning brain,
We ask the When, the Where, the How,
      And ask in vain.
And all philosophy, all faith,
  All earthly—all celestial lore,
Have but one voice, which only saith
      Endure—adore!

FRANCIS SYLVESTER MAHONEY

('FATHER PROUT')

101 *The Bells of Shandon*

1804–1866

WITH deep affection and recollection
  I often think of the Shandon bells,
Whose sounds so wild would, in days of childhood,
  Fling round my cradle their magic spells—

On this I ponder, where'er I wander,
And thus grow fonder, sweet Cork, of thee;
With thy bells of Shandon,
That sound so grand on
The pleasant waters of the river Lee.

I have heard bells chiming full many a clime in,
Tolling sublime in cathedral shrine;
While at a glib rate brass tongues would vibrate,
But all their music spoke nought to thine;
For memory dwelling on each proud swelling
Of thy belfry knelling its bold notes free,
Made the bells of Shandon
Sound far more grand on
The pleasant waters of the river Lee.

I have heard bells tolling 'old Adrian's mole' in,
Their thunder rolling from the Vatican,
With cymbals glorious, swinging uproarious
In the gorgeous turrets of Notre Dame;
But thy sounds were sweeter than the dome of Peter
Flings o'er the Tiber, pealing solemnly.
Oh! the bells of Shandon
Sound far more grand on
The pleasant waters of the river Lee.

There's a bell in Moscow, while on tower and Kiosko,
In St. Sophia the Turkman gets,
And loud in air, calls men to prayer,
From the tapering summit of tall minarets.
Such empty phantom I freely grant them,
But there's an anthem more dear to me,
It's the bells of Shandon,
That sound so grand on
The pleasant waters of the river Lee.

EDWARD WALSH

1805-1850

102 *Mairgréad ni Chealleadh* (13)

AT the dance in the village
  Thy white foot was fleetest;
Thy voice 'mid the concert
  Of maidens was sweetest;
The swell of thy white breast
  Made rich lovers follow;
And thy raven hair bound them,
  Young Mairgréad ni Chealleadh.

Thy neck was, lost maid,
  Than the ceanabhan [1] whiter,
And the glow of thy cheek
  Than the monadan [2] brighter;
But death's chain hath bound thee,
  Thine eye's glazed and hollow,
That shone like a sunburst,
  Young Mairgréad ni Chealleadh.

No more shall mine ear drink
  Thy melody swelling;
Nor thy beamy eye brighten
  The outlaw's dark dwelling;
Or thy soft heaving bosom
  My destiny hallow,
When thine arms twine around me,
  Young Mairgréad ni Chealleadh.

[1] The bog-cotton plant.
[2] A red-berry plant found on wild marshy mountains.

The moss couch I brought thee
To-day from the mountain,
Has drank the last drop
Of thy young heart's red fountain—
For this good skian beside me
Struck deep and rung hollow
In thy bosom of treason,
Young Mairgréad ni Chealleadh.

With strings of rich pearls
Thy white neck was laden,
And thy fingers with spoils
Of the Sassanach maiden :
Such rich silks enrob'd not
The proud dames of Mallow—
Such pure gold they wore not
As Mairgréad ni Chealleadh.

Alas ! that my loved one
Her outlaw would injure—
Alas ! that he e'er proved
Her treason's avenger !
That this right hand should make thee
A bed cold and hollow,
When in death's sleep it laid thee,
Young Mairgréad ni Chealleadh.

And while to this lone cave
My deep grief I'm venting,
The Saxon's keen bandog
My footsteps is scenting ;
But true men await me
Afar in Duhallow.
Farewell, cave of slaughter,
And Mairgréad ni Chealleadh.

EDWARD WALSH

103 *Mo Craoibhin Cno*[1]

MY heart is far from Liffey's tide
And Dublin town;
It strays beyond the southern side
Of Cnoc-Maol-Donn,[2]
Where Capa-chuinn[3] hath woodlands green,
Where Amhan-mór's[4] waters flow,
Where dwells unsung, unsought, unseen,
Mo craoibhin cno,
Low clustering in her leafy screen,
Mo craoibhin cno!

The high-bred dames of Dublin town
Are rich and fair,
With wavy plume and silken gown,
And stately air;
Can plumes compare thy dark brown hair?
Can silks thy neck of snow?
Or measur'd pace thine artless grace,
Mo craoibhin cno,
When harebells scarcely show thy trace,
Mo craoibhin cno?

I've heard the songs by Liffey's wave
That maidens sung—
They sung their land the Saxon's slave,
In Saxon tongue—

[1] Mo Creevin Cno, My cluster of nuts, figuratively signifying —My nut-brown maid.

[2] Knockmealdown, the range of hills between Tipperary and Waterford.

[3] Cappoquin.

[4] Avon-more (Great river), the Blackwater.

Oh! bring me here that Gaelic dear
Which cursed the Saxon foe,
When thou didst charm my raptured ear,
Mo craoibhin cno!
And none but God's good angels near
Mo craoibhin cno!

I've wandered by the rolling Lee!
And Lene's green bowers—
I've seen the Shannon's wide-spread sea,
And Limerick's towers—
And Liffey's tide, where halls of pride
Frown o'er the flood below;
My wild heart strays to Amhan-mór's side,
Mo craoibhin cno!
With love and thee for aye to bide,
Mo craoibhin cno!

104 *A Munster Keen* (14)

ON Monday morning, the flowers were gaily springing,
The skylark's hymn in middle air was singing,
When, grief of griefs, my wedded husband left me,
And since that hour of hope and health bereft me.
Ulla gulla, gulla g'one! etc.

Above the board, where thou art low reclining,
Have parish priests and horsemen high been dining,
And wine and usquebaugh, while they were able,
They quaffed with thee—the soul of all the table.
Ulla gulla, gulla g'one! etc.

Why didst thou die? Could wedded wife adore thee
With purer love than that my bosom bore thee?
Thy children's cheeks were peaches ripe and mellow,
And threads of gold their tresses long and yellow.
Ulla gulla, gulla g'one! etc.

In vain for me are pregnant heifers lowing;
In vain for me are yellow harvests growing;
Or thy nine gifts of love in beauty blooming—
Tears blind my eyes, and grief's my heart consuming!
Ulla gulla, gulla g'one! etc.

Pity her plaints whose wailing voice is broken,
Whose finger holds our early wedding token,
The torrents of whose tears have drain'd their fountain,
Whose piled-up grief on grief is past recounting.
Ulla gulla, gulla g'one! etc.

I still might hope, did I not thus behold thee,
That high Knockferin's airy peak might hold thee,
Or Crohan's fairy halls, or Corrin's towers,
Or Lene's bright caves, or Cleana's magic bowers.
Ulla gulla, gulla g'one! etc.

But oh! my black despair! when thou wert dying
O'er thee no tear was wept, no heart was sighing—
No breath of prayer did waft thy soul to glory;
But lonely thou didst lie, and maim'd and gory!
Ulla gulla, gulla g'one! etc.

Oh! may your dove-like soul on whitest pinions
Pursue her upward flight to God's dominions,

Where saints' and martyrs' hands shall gifts provide
thee—
And oh! my grief that I am not beside thee!
Ulla gulla, gulla g'one! etc.

105 *O'Donovan's Daughter*

ONE midsummer's eve, when the Bel-fires were
lighted,
And the bagpiper's tone call'd the maidens delighted,
I join'd a gay group by the Araglin's water,
And danced till the dawn with O'Donovan's
Daughter.

Have you seen the ripe monadan glisten in Kerry,
Have you mark'd on the Galteys the black whortle-
berry,
Or ceanabhan wave by the wells of Blackwater?
They're the cheek, eye, and neck of O'Donovan's
Daughter.

Have you seen a gay kidling on Claragh's round
mountain,
The swan's arching glory on Sheeling's blue foun-
tain,
Heard a weird woman chant what the fairy choir
taught her?
They've the step, grace, and tone of O'Donovan's
Daughter!

EDWARD WALSH

Have you marked in its flight the black wing of the
raven,
The rosebuds that breathe in the summer breeze
waven,
The pearls that lie hid under Lene's magic water?
They're the teeth, lip, and hair of O'Donovan's
Daughter!

Ere the Bel-fire was dimmed or the dancers departed,
I taught her a song of some maid broken-hearted:
And that group, and that dance, and that love-song
I taught her
Haunt my slumbers at night with O'Donovan's
Daughter.

God grant, 'tis no fay from Cnoc-Firinn [1] that woos
me,
God grant, 'tis not Cliodhna [2] the queen that pursues
me,
That my soul lost and lone has no witchery wrought
her,
While I dream of dark groves and O'Donovan's
Daughter.

If, spell-bound, I pine with an airy disorder,
Saint Gobnate has sway over Musgry's [3] wide border;
She'll scare from my couch, when with prayer I've
besought her.
That bright airy sprite like O'Donovan's Daughter.

[1] A fairy-hill in co. Limerick.
[2] Or Cleena, the fairy queen of South Munster.
[3] Muskerry—the name of two baronies in co. Cork.

EDWARD WALSH

106 *Song of the Penal Days*

1720

YE dark-haired youths and elders hoary,
  List to the wandering harper's song.
My cláirseach weeps my true love's story,
  In my true love's native tongue:
She's bound and bleeding 'neath the oppressor,
  Few her friends and fierce her foe,
And brave hearts cold who would redress her—
  Ma chreevin evin alga, O![1]

My love had riches once and beauty,
  Till want and sorrow paled her cheek,
And stalwart hearts for honour's duty—
  They're crouching now, like cravens sleek.
O Heaven! that e'er this day of rigour
  Saw sons of heroes abject, low—
And blood and tears thy face disfigure,
  Ma chreevin evin alga, O!

I see young virgins step the mountain
  As graceful as the bounding fawn,
With cheeks like heath-flower by the fountain,
  And breasts like downy ceanabhan.
Shall bondsmen share those beauties ample?
  Shall their pure bosoms' current flow
To nurse new slaves for them that trample?
  Ma chreevin evin alga, O!

[1] My fair noble maid.

Around my cláirseach's speaking measures
  Men, like their fathers tall, arise ;
Their heart the same deep hatred treasures—
  I read it in their kindling eyes !
The same proud brow to frown at danger—
  The same long coulin's graceful flow—
The same dear tongue to curse the stranger—
  Ma chreevin evin alga, O !

I'd sing ye more, but age is stealing
  Along my pulse and tuneful fires ;
Far bolder woke my chord appealing,
  For craven Sheamus, to your sires.
Arouse to vengeance, men of bravery,
  For broken oaths—for altars low—
For bonds that bind in bitter slavery—
  Ma chreevin evin alga, O !

107 *Brighidin bán mo Stór* (15)

I AM a wandering minstrel man,
  And Love my only theme,
I've strayed beside the pleasant Bann,
  And eke the Shannon's stream ;
I've piped and played to wife and maid
  By Barrow, Suir, and Nore,
But never met a maiden yet
  Like Brighidin bán mo stór.

My girl hath ringlets rich and rare,
  By Nature's fingers wove—
Loch-Carra's swan is not so fair
  As is her breast of love ;

And when she moves, in Sunday sheen,
  Beyond our cottage door,
I'd scorn the high-born Saxon queen
  For Brighidin bán mo stór.

It is not that thy smile is sweet,
  And soft thy voice of song—
It is not that thou fliest to meet
  My comings lone and long!
But that doth rest beneath thy breast
  A heart of purest core,
Whose pulse is known to me alone,
  Brighidin bán mo stór.

108 *From the Cold Sod that's o'er You*

From the Irish

FROM the cold sod that's o'er you
  I never shall sever;
Were my hands twined in yours, Love,
  I'd hold them for ever.
My fondest, my fairest,
  We may now sleep together!
I've the cold earth's damp odour,
  And I'm worn from the weather.

This heart filled with fondness
  Is wounded and weary;
A dark gulf beneath it
  Yawns jet-black and dreary.

EDWARD WALSH

When death comes, a victor,
  In mercy to greet me,
On the wings of the whirlwind
  In the wild wastes you'll meet me.

When the folk of my household
  Suppose I am sleeping,
On your cold grave till morning
  The lone watch I'm keeping.
My grief to the night wind
  For the mild maid to render,
Who was my betrothed
  Since infancy tender.

Remember the lone night
  I last spent with you, Love,
Beneath the dark sloe-tree
  When the icy wind blew, Love.
High praise to thy Saviour
  No sin-stain had found you,
That your virginal glory
  Shines brightly around you.

The priests and the friars
  Are ceaselessly chiding,
That I love a young maiden
  In life not abiding.
O! I'd shelter and shield you
  If wild storms were swelling!
And O, my wrecked hope,
  That the cold earth's your dwelling!

MICHAEL DOHENY

109 *A Cushla gal mo Chree*[1]

1805-1863

THE long, long wished-for hour has come,
  Yet come astór, in vain ;
And left thee but the wailing hum
  Of sorrow and of pain ;
My light of life, my only love !
  Thy portion, sure, must be
Man's scorn below, God's wrath above—
  A cuisle geal mo chroidhe !

I've given for thee my early prime,
  And manhood's teeming years ;
I've blessed thee in my merriest time,
  And shed with thee my tears ;
And, mother, though thou cast away
  The child who'd die for thee,
My fondest wishes still should pray
  For cuisle geal mo chroidhe !

For thee I've tracked the mountain's sides,
  And slept within the brake,
More lonely than the swan that glides
  On Lua's fairy lake.
The rich have spurned me from their door,
  Because I'd make thee free ;
Yet still I love thee more and more,
  A cuisle geal mo chroidhe !

[1] Bright vein of my heart.

I've run the outlaw's wild career,
And borne his load of ill;
His rocky couch—his dreamy fear—
With fixed, sustaining will;
And should his last dark chance befall,
Even that shall welcome be;
In death I'd love thee best of all,
A cuisle geal mo chroidhe!

'Twas told of thee the world around,
'Twas hoped for thee by all,
That with one gallant sunward bound
Thou'dst burst long ages' thrall;
Thy faith was tried, alas! and those
Who perilled all for thee
Were cursed and branded as thy foes,
A cuisle geal mo chroidhe!

What fate is thine, unhappy Isle,
When even the trusted few
Would pay thee back with hate and guile,
When most they should be true!
'Twas not my strength or spirit quailed,
Or those who'd die for thee—
Who loved thee truly have not failed,
A cuisle gael mo chroidhe!

110

The Shan Van Vocht[1]

1176

THE sainted isle of old,
Says the Shan Van Vocht,
The sainted isle of old,
Says the Shan Van Vocht.

[1] The poor old woman—a name typifying Ireland.

MICHAEL DOHENY

The parent and the mould
Of the beautiful and bold,
Has her blithesome heart waxed cold?
Says the Shan Van Vocht.

The Saxon and the Dane,
Says the Shan Van Vocht,
The Saxon and the Dane
Says the Shan Van Vocht,
The Saxon and the Dane
Our immortal hills profane;
Oh! confusion seize the twain,
Says the Shan Van Vocht.

What are the chiefs to do?
Says the Shan Van Vocht,
What are the chiefs to do?
Says the Shan Van Vocht.
What should the chieftains do
But to treat the hireling crew
To a touch of Brian Boru,
Says the Shan Van Vocht.

They came across the wave,
Says the Shan Van Vocht,
They came across the wave,
Says the Shan Van Vocht,
They came across the wave
But to plunder and enslave,
And should find a robber's grave,
Says the Shan Van Vocht.

MICHAEL DOHENY

Then be the trusty brand,
        Says the Shan Van Vocht,
Then be the trusty brand,
        Says the Shan Van Vocht,
Then be the trusty brand,
Firmly clutched in every hand,
And we'll scourge them from the land,
        Says the Shan Van Vocht.

There's courage yet and truth,
        Says the Shan Van Vocht,
There's courage yet and truth,
        Says the Shan Van Vocht;
There's a God above us all,
And, whatever may befall,
No invader shall enthrall,
        Says the Shan Van Vocht.

ELLEN FITZSIMON

111 *The Woods of Kylinoe* (16)

Song of the Irish Emigrant in North America

1805-1883

MY heart is heavy in my breast—my eyes are full of tears,
My memory is wandering back to long departed years—
To those bright days long, long ago,
When nought I dream'd of sordid care, of worldly woe—
But roved, a gay, light-hearted boy, the woods of Kylinoe.

There, in the spring-time of my life, and spring-time
of the year,
I've watched the snowdrop start from earth, the first
young buds appear;
The sparkling stream o'er pebbles flow,
The modest violet, and the golden primrose blow,
Within thy deep and mossy dells, beloved Kylinoe!

'Twas there I wooed my Mary Dhuv, and won her
for my bride,
Who bore me three fair daughters, and four sons, my
age's pride;
Though cruel fortune was our foe,
And steep'd us to the lips in bitter want and woe,
Yet cling our hearts to those sad days we pass'd near
Kylinoe.

At length, by misery bowed to earth, we left our
native strand,
And crossed the wide Atlantic to this free and happy
land;
Though toils we had to undergo,
Yet soon content and happy peace 'twas ours to
know,
And plenty, such as never blessed our hearth near
Kylinoe!

And Heaven a blessing has bestow'd more precious far
than wealth,
He spared us to each other, full of years, yet strong
in health;
Across the threshold when we go,
We see our children's children round us grow,
Like sapling oaks within thy woods, far distant
Kylinoe.

Yet sadness clouds our hearts to think that when we
are no more,
Our bones must find a resting-place far, far from
Erin's shore!
For us—no funeral sad and slow—
Within the ancient abbey's burial ground shall go—
No, we must slumber far from home, far, far from
Kylinoe!

Yet, oh! if spirits e'er can leave the appointed place
of rest,
Once more will I revisit thee, dear Isle that I love
best;
O'er thy green vales will hover slow,
And many a tearful parting blessing will bestow
On all—but most of all on thee, my native Kylinoe.

CHARLES LEVER

112 *Widow Malone*

1806–1872

DID you hear of the Widow Malone,
Ohone!
Who lived in the town of Athlone?
Ohone!
Oh, she melted the hearts
Of the swains in them parts,
So lovely the Widow Malone,
Ohone!
So lovely the Widow Malone.

Of lovers she had a full score,
Or more,
And fortunes they all had galore,
In store;
From the minister down
To the clerk of the Crown,
All were courting the Widow Malone,
Ohone!
All were courting the Widow Malone.

But so modest was Mistress Malone,
'Twas known,
That no one could see her alone,
Ohone!
Let them ogle and sigh,
They could ne'er catch her eye,
So bashful the Widow Malone,
Ohone!
So bashful the Widow Malone.

Till one Mister O'Brien, from Clare,—
How quare!
It's little for blushing they care
Down there,
Put his arm round her waist—
Gave ten kisses at laste—
'Oh,' says he, 'you're my Molly Malone,
My own!'
'Oh,' says he, 'you're my Molly Malone.'

And the widow they all thought so shy,
My eye!
Ne'er thought of a simper or sigh,
For why?

But 'Lucius,' says she,
'Since you've now made so free,
You may marry your Mary Malone,
Ohone!
You may marry your Mary Malone.'

There's a moral contained in my song,
Not wrong,
And one comfort, it's not very long,
But strong,—
If for widows you die,
Learn to kiss, not to sigh,
For they're all like sweet Mistress Malone.
Ohone!
Oh, they're all like sweet Mistress Malone.

113 *Larry M'Hale*

OH! Larry M'Hale he had little to fear,
And never could want when the crops didn't fail;
He'd a house and demesne and eight hundred a year,
And the heart for to spend it, had Larry M'Hale!

The soul of a party—the life of a feast,
And an illigant song he could sing, I'll be bail;
He would ride with the rector, and drink with the priest,
Oh! the broth of a boy was old Larry M'Hale.

It's little he cared for the judge or recorder,
His house was as big and as strong as a jail;
With a cruel four-pounder, he kept all in great order,
He'd murder the country, would Larry M'Hale.

He'd a blunderbuss too ; of horse pistols a pair ;
  But his favourite weapon was always a flail ;
I wish you could see how he'd empty a fair,
  For he handled it nately, did Larry M'Hale.

His ancestors were kings before Moses was born ;
  His mother descended from great Grana Uaile ;
He laughed all the Blakes and the Frenches to scorn ;
  They were mushrooms compared to old Larry
    M'Hale.

He sat down every day to a beautiful dinner,
  With cousins and uncles enough for a tail ;
And, though loaded with debt, oh ! the devil a thinner
  Could law or the sheriff make Larry M'Hale.

With a larder supplied, and a cellar well stored,
  None lived half so well from Fair-Head to Kinsale,
And he piously said, 'I've a plentiful board,
  And the Lord he is good to old Larry M'Hale.'

So fill up your glass, and a high bumper give him,
  It's little we'd care for the tithes or repale ;
For ould Erin would be a fine country to live in,
  If we only had plenty, like Larry M'Hale.

114 *The Man for Galway*

TO drink a toast,
  A proctor roast,
    Or bailiff, as the case is ;
To kiss your wife,
Or take your life
    At ten or fifteen paces ;

To keep game cocks, to hunt the fox,
  To drink in punch the Solway,
With debts galore, but fun far more;
  Oh! that's 'the man for Galway.'
                    With debts, etc.

    The King of Oude
    Is mighty proud,
      And so were onest the Caysars;
    But ould Giles Eyre
    Would make them stare,
      Av he had them with the Blazers.
To the devil I fling ould Runjeet Sing,
  He's only a prince in a small way,
And knows nothing at all of a six-foot wall;
  Oh! he'd never 'do for Galway.'
                    With debts, etc.

    Ye think the Blakes
    Are no 'great shakes';
      They're all his blood relations;
    And the Bodkins sneeze
    At the grim Chinese,
      For they come from the Phenaycians.
So fill to the brim, and here's to him
  Who'd drink in punch the Solway;
With debts galore, but fun far more;
  Oh! that's 'the man for Galway.'
                    With debts, etc.

LADY DUFFERIN

115 *Lament of the Irish Emigrant*

1807-1867

I'M sittin' on the stile, Mary,
  Where we sat side by side
On a bright May mornin', long ago,
  When first you were my bride:
The corn was springin' fresh and green,
  And the lark sang loud and high—
And the red was on your lip, Mary,
  And the love-light in your eye.

The place is little changed, Mary,
  The day is bright as then,
The lark's loud song is in my ear,
  And the corn is green again;
But I miss the soft clasp of your hand,
  And your breath, warm on my cheek,
And I still keep list'nin' for the words
  You never more will speak.

'Tis but a step down yonder lane,
  And the little church stands near—
The church where we were wed, Mary,
  I see the spire from here.
But the graveyard lies between, Mary,
  And my step might break your rest—
For I've laid you, darling! down to sleep,
  With your baby on your breast.

LADY DUFFERIN

I'm very lonely now, Mary,
  For the poor make no new friends ;
But, oh ! they love the better still,
  The few our Father sends !
And you were all I had, Mary,
  My blessin' and my pride !
There's nothin' left to care for now,
  Since my poor Mary died.

Yours was the good, brave heart, Mary,
  That still kept hoping on,
When the trust in God had left my soul,
  And my arm's young strength was gone ;
There was comfort ever on your lip,
  And the kind look on your brow—
I bless you, Mary, for that same,
  Though you cannot hear me now.

I thank you for the patient smile
  When your heart was fit to break,
When the hunger pain was gnawin' there,
  And you hid it for my sake ;
I bless you for the pleasant word,
  When your heart was sad and sore—
Oh ! I'm thankful you are gone, Mary,
  Where grief can't reach you more !

I'm biddin' you a long farewell,
  My Mary—kind and true !
But I'll not forget you, darling,
  In the land I'm goin' to :

They say there's bread and work for all,
  And the sun shines always there—
But I'll not forget old Ireland,
  Were it fifty times as fair !

And often in those grand old woods
  I'll sit and shut my eyes,
And my heart will travel back again
  To the place where Mary lies ;
And I'll think I see the little stile
  Where we sat side by side,
And the springin' corn, and the bright May morn,
  When first you were my bride.

116 *Terence's Farewell*

SO, my Kathleen, you're going to leave me
  All alone by myself in this place,
But I'm sure you will never deceive me—
  Oh no, if there's truth in that face.
Though England's a beautiful city,
  Full of illigant boys—oh, what then ?
You would not forget your poor Terence ;
  You'll come back to ould Ireland again.

Och ! those English, deceivers by nature,
  Though maybe you'd think them sincere,
They'll say you're a sweet charming creature,
  But don't you believe them, my dear.
No, Kathleen, agrah ! [1] don't be minding
  The flattering speeches they'll make ;
Just tell them a poor boy in Ireland
  Is breaking his heart for your sake.

[1] My love.

It's folly to keep you from going,
Though, faith, it's a mighty hard case—
For, Kathleen, you know, there's no knowing
When next I shall see your sweet face.
And when you come back to me, Kathleen,
None the better will I be off then—
You'll be spaking such beautiful English,
Sure, I won't know my Kathleen again.

Eh, now, where's the need of this hurry?
Don't flutter me so in this way,—
I've forgot, 'twixt the grief and the flurry,
Every word I was maning to say;
Now just wait a minute, I bid ye,—
Can I talk if you bother me so?
Oh, Kathleen, my blessing go wid ye,
Ev'ry inch of the way that you go!

JOHN KEEGAN

117 *Caoch*[1] *the Piper*

1809–1849

ONE winter's day, long, long ago,
When I was a little fellow,
A piper wandered to our door,
Grey-headed, blind, and yellow:
And, oh! how glad was my young heart,
Though earth and sky looked dreary,
To see the stranger and his dog—
Poor 'Pinch' and Caoch O'Leary.

[1] Blind.

And when he stowed away his 'bag,'
  Cross-barred with green and yellow,
I thought and said, 'In Ireland's ground
  There's not so fine a fellow.'
And Fineen Burke, and Shaun Magee,
  And Eily, Kate, and Mary,
Rushed in, with panting haste, to see
  And welcome Caoch O'Leary.

O! God be with those happy times!
  O! God be with my childhood!
When I, bare-headed, roamed all day—
  Bird-nesting in the wild-wood.
I'll not forget those sunny hours,
  However years may vary;
I'll not forget my early friends,
  Nor honest Caoch O'Leary.

Poor Caoch, and 'Pinch,' slept well that night,
  And in the morning early
He called me up to hear him play
  'The wind that shakes the barley';
And then he stroked my flaxen hair,
  And cried, 'God mark my deary!'
And how I wept when he said, 'Farewell,
  And think of Caoch O'Leary!'

And seasons came and went, and still
  Old Caoch was not forgotten,
Although we thought him dead and gone,
  And in the cold grave rotten;
And often, when I walked and talked
  With Eily, Kate, and Mary,
We thought of childhood's rosy hours,
  And prayed for Caoch O'Leary.

Well—twenty summers had gone past,
  And June's red sun was sinking,
When I, a man, sat by my door,
  Of twenty sad things thinking.
A little dog came up the way,
  His gait was slow and weary,
And at his tail a lame man limped—
  'Twas 'Pinch' and Caoch O'Leary!

Old Caoch, but, oh! how woe-begone!
  His form is bowed and bending,
His fleshless hands are stiff and wan,
  Ay—Time is even blending
The colours on his threadbare 'bag'—
  And 'Pinch' is twice as hairy
And 'thin-spare' as when first I saw
  Himself and Caoch O'Leary.

'God's blessing here!' the wanderer cried,
  'Far, far be hell's black viper;
Does anybody hereabouts
  Remember Caoch the Piper?'
With swelling heart I grasped his hand;
  The old man murmured, 'Deary,
Are you the silky-headed child
  That loved poor Caoch O'Leary?'

'Yes, yes,' I said—the wanderer wept
  As if his heart was breaking—
'And where, a vic machree,'[1] he sobbed,
  'Is all the merrymaking

[1] Son of my heart.

I found here twenty years ago?'
  'My tale,' I sighed, 'might weary;
Enough to say—there's none but me
  To welcome Caoch O'Leary.'

'Vo, vo, vo!' the old man cried,
  And wrung his hands in sorrow,
'Pray let me in, astór machree,[1]
  And I'll go home to-morrow.
My "peace is made"; I'll calmly leave
  This world so cold and dreary;
And you shall keep my pipes and dog,
  And pray for Caoch O'Leary.'

With 'Pinch' I watched his bed that night;
  Next day his wish was granted:
He died; and Father James was brought,
  And the Requiem Mass was chanted.
The neighbours came; we dug his grave
  Near Eily, Kate, and Mary,
And there he sleeps his last sweet sleep.
  God rest you! Caoch O'Leary.

118 *The Irish Reaper's Harvest Hymn*

ALL hail! Holy Mary, our hope and our joy!
  Smile down, blessed Queen! on the poor Irish boy
Who wanders away from his dear beloved home;
O Mary! be with me wherever I roam.
    Be with me, O Mary!
    Forsake me not, Mary!

[1] Treasure of my heart.

JOHN KEEGAN

From the home of my fathers in anguish I go,
To toil for the dark-livered, cold-hearted foe,
Who mocks me, and hates me, and calls me a slave,
An alien, a savage—all names but a knave.
    But, blessed be Mary!
    My sweet, holy Mary!
The bodagh[1] he never dare call me a knave.

From my mother's mud sheeling an outcast I fly,
With a cloud on my heart and a tear in my eye;
Oh! I burn as I think that if Some One would say,
'Revenge on your tyrants!'—but, Mary! I pray
    From my soul's depth, O Mary!
    And hear me, sweet Mary!
For union and peace to old Ireland I pray.

The land that I fly from is fertile and fair,
And more than I ask or I wish for is there,
But I must not taste the good things that I see—
'There's nothing but rags and green rushes for me.'
    O mild Virgin Mary!
    O sweet Mother Mary!
Who keeps my rough hand from red murder but thee?

But sure in the end our dear freedom we'll gain,
And wipe from the green flag each Sassanach stain,
And oh! Holy Mary, your blessing we crave!
Give hearts to the timid, and hands to the brave;
    And then, Mother Mary!
    Our own blessed Mary!
Light Liberty's flame in the hut of the slave!

[1] A clown, a churl.

JOHN KEEGAN

119 *The 'Dark Girl' by the 'Holy Well'* (17)

'MOTHER! is that the passing bell?
  Or yet the midnight chime?
Or rush of angels' golden wings?
  Or is it near the time—
The time when God, they say, comes down
  This weary world upon,
With Holy Mary at His right,
  And at His left St. John?

'I'm dumb! my heart forgets to throb;
  My blood forgets to run;
But vain my sighs—in vain I sob—
  God's will must still be done.
I hear but tone of warning bell,
  For holy priest or nun;
On earth, God's face I'll never see!
  Nor Mary, nor St. John!

'Mother, my hopes are gone again;
  My heart is black as ever.
Mother! I say, look forth once more,
  And see can you discover
God's glory in the crimson clouds—
  See, does He ride upon
That perfumed breeze—or do you see
  The Virgin, or St. John?

'Ah, no! ah, no! Well, God of Peace,
  Grant me Thy blessing still;
O, make me patient with my doom,
  And happy at Thy will;

And guide my footsteps so on earth,
  That, when I'm dead and gone,
My eyes may catch Thy shining light
  With Mary, and St. John!

'Yet, mother, could I see thy smile,
  Before we part below—
Or watch the silver moon or stars
  Where Slaney's ripples flow;
Oh, could I see the sweet sun shine
  My native hills upon,
I'd never love my God the less,
  Nor Mary, nor St. John!

'But, no! ah, no! it cannot be;
  Yet, mother, do not mourn—
Come, kneel again, and pray to God,
  In peace, let us return;
The Dark Girl's doom must aye be mine—
  But Heaven will light me on,
Until I find my way to God,
  And Mary, and St. John!'

120 *Bouchalleen Bawn* (18)

OH, pray have you heard of my Bouchalleen bawn?[1]
Can you tell me at all of my Bouchalleen bawn;
Have you come by the 'rath,' on the hill of Knock-awn:
Or what can you tell of my Bouchalleen bawn?

[1] Ir. *Bhuachailín bán* (pron. *vouchaleen bawn*) = Fair-haired little boy.

JOHN KEEGAN

The pulse of my heart was my Bouchalleen bawn;
The light of my eyes was my Bouchalleen bawn.
From Dinan's red wave to the tower of Kilvawn,
You'd not meet the like of my Bouchalleen bawn!

The first time I saw my own Bouchalleen bawn,
'Twas a Midsummer eve on the fair-green of bawn.
He danced at the 'Baal-fire,' as light as a fawn,
And away went my heart with my Bouchalleen bawn.

I loved him as dear as I love my own life;
And he vowed on his knees he would make me his wife.
I looked in his eyes, flashing bright as the dawn,
And drank love from the lips of my Bouchalleen bawn.

But, Christ save the hearers! his angel forsook him—
My curse on the queen of the fairies—she took him—
Last All-hallow's eve as he came by Knockawn,
She saw—loved, and 'struck' my poor Bouchalleen bawn.

Like the primrose when April her last sigh has breathed,
My Bouchalleen drooped and his young beauty faded;
He died—and his white limbs were stretched in Kilvawn,
And I wept by the grave of my Bouchalleen bawn.

JOHN KEEGAN

I said to myself, sure it cannot be harm,
To go to the wise man, and ask for a charm ;
'Twill cost but a crown, and my heart's blood I'd pawn,
To purchase from bondage my Bouchalleen bawn.

I went to the priest, and he spoke about heaven ;
And said that my failings would not be forgiven,
If ever I'd cross the grey fairy-man's bawn ;
Or try his weird spells for my Bouchalleen bawn.

I'll take his advice, though God knows my heart's breaking ;
I start in my sleep, and I weep when I'm waking.
Oh, I long for the blush of eternity's dawn,
When again I shall meet my own Bouchalleen bawn !

JOHN DE JEAN FRAZER

121 *The Holy Wells*

1809-1852

THE holy wells—the living wells—the cool, the fresh, the pure—
A thousand ages rolled away, and still those founts endure,
As full and sparkling as they flowed ere slave or tyrant trod
The Emerald garden, set apart for Irishmen by God.

And while their stainless chastity and lasting life have
birth
Amid the oozy cells and caves of gross material earth,
The Scripture of creation holds no fairer type than
they—
That an immortal spirit can be linked with human
clay.

How sweet of old the bubbling gush—no less to
antlered race,
Than to the hunter and the hound that smote them
in the chase!
In forest depths the water-fount beguiled the Druid's
love,
From that adored high fount of fire which sparkled
far above;
Inspired apostles took it for a centre to the ring,
When sprinkling round baptismal life—salvation—
from the spring;
And in the sylvan solitude, or lonely mountain cave,
Beside it passed the hermit's life, as stainless as its
wave.

The cottage hearth, the convent's wall, the battle-
mented tower,
Grew up around the crystal springs, as well as flag
and flower;
The brooklime and the water-cress were evidence of
health,
Abiding in those basins, free to poverty and wealth;
The city sent pale sufferers there the faded brow to
dip,
And woo the water to depose some bloom upon the
lip;

The wounded warrior dragged him towards the unforgotten tide,
And deemed the draught a heavenlier gift than triumph to his side.

The stag, the hunter, and the hound, the Druid and the saint,
And anchorite are gone, and even the lineaments grown faint,
Of those old ruins into which, for monuments, had sunk
The glorious homes that held, like shrines, the monarch and the monk.
So far into the heights of God the mind of man has ranged,
It learned a lore to change the earth—its very self it changed
To some more bright intelligence; yet still the springs endure,
The same fresh fountains, but become more precious to the poor!

For knowledge has abused its powers, an empire to erect
For tyrants, on the rights the poor had given them to protect;
Till now the simple elements of nature are their all,
That from the cabin is not filched, and lavished in the hall—
And while night, noon, or morning meal no other plenty brings,
No beverage than the water-draught from old, spontaneous springs:

They, sure, may deem them holy wells, that yield from day to day,
One blessing that no tyrant hand can taint or take away.

122 *Song for July* 12, 1843

COME—pledge again thy heart and hand—
One grasp that ne'er shall sever;
Our watchword be—'Our native land'—
Our motto—'Love for ever.'
And let the Orange lily be
Thy badge, my patriot brother—
The everlasting Green for me;
And we for one another.

Behold how green the gallant stem
On which the flower is blowing;
How in one heavenly breeze and beam
Both flower and stem are glowing.
The same good soil, sustaining both,
Makes both united flourish
But cannot give the Orange growth,
And cease the Green to nourish.

Yea, more—the hand that plucks the flow'r
Will vainly strive to cherish;
The stem blooms on—but in that hour
The flower begins to perish.
Regard them, then, of equal worth
While lasts their genial weather;
The time's at hand when into earth
The two shall sink together.

Ev'n thus be, in our country's cause,
Our party feelings blended;
Till lasting peace, from equal laws,
On both shall have descended.
Till then the Orange lily be
Thy badge, my patriot brother—
The everlasting Green for me;
And—we for one another.

123 *A Lament for Thomas Davis*

IS he gone from our struggle—the pure of the purest—
The staff that upheld our green banner the surest—
Is he gone from our struggle away?
Oh, Heaven! that the man who gave soul to our strife—
The heart with the lightnings of liberty rife,
Should be suddenly stricken to clay;
But yesterday lending a people new life,
Cold—mute—in the coffin to-day!
Woe, woe—
Strong myriads stunned by the one fatal blow—
The loved is departed—the lofty laid low!

Though his form was to me as a far-dwelling stranger,
Did I need a defender from falsehood or danger,
I would call on his voice—or his arm!
Romance and reality blended, in sooth,
The firmest of manhood, and freshest of youth,
In honour's most beautiful form;

JOHN DE JEAN FRAZER

Not even to save the whole cargo of truth,
Would he cast out a part in the storm!
Gloom, gloom—
The firmness and freshness are nipped in the bloom!
Broad and dark is the shadow that falls from his tomb!

Go—mix with the crowds where his praises are spoken,
Go—watch the wet eyes that hang over each token
His genius hath given of its birth:
Would millions in one common grief be combined,
If some spell-work embracing the heart and the mind
Of man in its magical girth,
Were not left, like a scroll from his spirit, behind,
To circle and gird up the earth?
Grief, grief—
The minstrel-magician, the patriot chief,
To praise him is some—oh! how little—relief.

The water runs clear from the high, rocky fountain,
And rapid the river that bursts from the mountain:
So rapid and clear was the stream
Of his song—for the bard was exalted above
The gross of the world, both by lore and by love,
When country and kind were his theme,—
Oh! his soul was a seraph that ceaselessly strove
To soar to its own native beam.
Dear, dear—
Are the prunings of pinion that dropped from him here;
His own is the torch-light that flames round his bier.

JOHN DE JEAN FRAZER

From a spirit intensely to liberty cleaving—
From a heart that grew yet more enlarged by its
heaving,
He fired into energy all,
Whose nature looks up to the loftiest mind,
Since, like loftiest bough, it first catches the wind,
And is last into stillness to fall ;
He banded the glowing—he guided the blind,
Who grappled and tugged with their thrall—
Grave, grave—
Onward may still be the sweep of the brave ;
But the bright crest of foam—it is gone from the
wave.

To cowards and despots a hatred undying,
For freedom a passion intense and relying,
A pride in the resolute hand ;
A hope that could see not a danger to shun,
When bonds should be broken, and liberty won—
A faith in the book and the brand,
The song and the standard—had made him the sun
Of a fair, but a shadowy land—
Blight, blight—
How sad are the banner and book in our sight,
Ah ! the brow of the country grew grey in a
night !

The gallant, good heart, that was fitted to clamber
The rockiest path, is now cold in the chamber
Of death, as the basest can be—
No minstrel again to his greatness shall grow,
Though many shall spring from the one lying low,
Like twigs from the felled forest tree ;

But still, at his bidding, the fettered shall throw
Their chains on the earth, and be free!
Clay, clay—
Thou sooner shalt steal the broad sun from the day,
Than the luminous spirit of Davis away!

124 *Brosna's Banks*

YES, yes, I idled many an hour—
Oh! would that I could idle now,
In wooing back the wither'd flower
Of health into my wasted brow!
But from my life's o'ershadowing close,
My unimpassioned spirit ranks
Among its happiest moments those
I idled on the Brosna's Banks.

For there upon my boyhood broke
The dreamy voice of nature first;
And every word the vision spoke
How deeply has my spirit nursed?
A woman's love, a lyre, or pen,
A rescued land, a nation's thanks,
A friendship with the world, and then
A grave upon the Brosna's Banks.

For these I sued, and sought, and strove,
But now my youthful days are gone,
In vain, in vain—for woman's love
Is still a blessing to be won;
And still my country's cheek is wet,
And still unbroken fetter clanks,
And I may not forsake her yet
To die upon the Brosna's Banks.

Yet idle as those visions seem,
  They were a strange and faithful guide,
When Heaven itself had scarce a gleam
  To light my darken'd life beside;
And if from grosser guilt escaped
  I feel no dying dread, the thanks
Are due unto the Power that shaped
  My visions on the Brosna's Banks.

And love, I feel, will come at last,
  Albeit too late to comfort me;
And fetters from the land be cast,
  Though I may not survive to see.
If then the gifted, good, and brave,
  Admit me to their glorious ranks,
My memory may, tho' not my grave,
  Be green upon the Brosna's Banks.

JOHN FRANCIS WALLER

125 *Kitty Neil*

1810–1894

'AH, sweet Kitty Neil, rise up from that wheel—
  Your neat little foot will be weary from spinning;
Come trip down with me to the sycamore tree,
Half the parish is there and the dance is beginning.
The sun is gone down, but the full harvest moon
Shines sweetly and cool in the dew-whitened valley;
While all the air rings with the soft loving things,
Each little bird sings in the green shaded alley.'

With a blush and a smile, Kitty rose up the while,
Her eye in the glass, as she bound her hair, glancing;
'Tis hard to refuse when a young lover sues—
So she couldn't but choose to go off to the dancing.
And now on the green, the glad groups are seen—
Each gay-hearted lad with the lass of his choosing,
And Pat, without fail, leads out sweet Kitty Neil—
Somehow when he asked, she ne'er thought of refusing.

Now Felix Magee puts his pipes to his knee,
And with flourish so free sets each couple in motion;
With a cheer and a bound the lads patter the ground—
The maids move around just like swans on the ocean.
Cheeks bright as the rose—feet light as the doe's,
Now coyly retiring, now boldly advancing—
Search the world all around, from the sky to the ground,
No such sight can be found as an Irish lass dancing!

Sweet Kate! who could view your bright eyes of deep blue
Beaming humidly through their dark lashes as mildly,
Your fair-turned arm, heaving breast, rounded form,
Nor feel his heart warm, and his pulses throb wildly?
Young Pat feels his heart, as he gazes, depart,
Subdued by the smart of such painful yet sweet love;
The sight leaves his eye, as he cries with a sigh,
'Dance light, for my heart it lies under your feet, love.'

JOHN FRANCIS WALLER

126 *The Spinning Wheel*

MELLOW the moonlight to shine is beginning,
Close by the window young Eileen is spinning;
Bent over the fire her blind grandmother, sitting,
Is crooning, and moaning, and drowsily knitting:—
'Eileen, achora, I hear some one tapping.'
''Tis the ivy, dear mother, against the glass flapping.'
'Eily, I surely hear somebody sighing.'
''Tis the sound, mother dear, of the summer wind dying.'
Merrily, cheerily, noiselessly whirring,
Swings the wheel, spins the wheel, while the foot's stirring;
Sprightly, and brightly, and airily ringing
Thrills the sweet voice of the young maiden singing.

'What's that noise that I hear at the window, I wonder?'
''Tis the little birds chirping the holly-bush under.'
'What makes you be shoving and moving your stool on,
And singing, all wrong, that old song of "The Coolun"?'
There's a form at the casement—the form of her true-love—
And he whispers, with face bent, 'I'm waiting for you, love;
Get up on the stool, through the lattice step lightly,
We'll rove in the grove while the moon's shining brightly.'
Merrily, cheerily, noiselessly whirring, etc.

The maid shakes her head, on her lips lays her fingers,
Steals up from her seat—longs to go, and yet lingers;
A frightened glance turns to her drowsy grand-
mother,
Puts one foot on the stool, spins the wheel with the
other,
Lazily, easily, swings now the wheel round,
Slowly and lowly is heard now the reel's sound;
Noiseless and light to the lattice above her
The maid steps—then leaps to the arms of her lover.
Slower—and slower—and slower the wheel swings;
Lower—and lower—and lower the reel rings;
Ere the reel and the wheel stopped their ringing
and moving,
Through the grove the young lovers by moonlight
are roving.

127 *Quien Sabe?*

From 'Peter Brown'

THE breeze of the evening that cools the hot air,
That kisses the orange and shakes out thy hair,
Is its freshness less welcome, less sweet its perfume
That you know not the region from which it is
come?
Whence the wind blows, where the wind goes,
Hither and thither and whither—who knows?
Who knows?
Hither and thither—but whither—who knows?

The river for ever glides singing along,
The rose on the bank bends a-down to its song;

And the flower, as it listens, unconsciously dips,
Till the rising wave glistens and kisses its lips.
But why the wave rises and kisses the rose,
And why the rose stoops for those kisses—who knows?
Who knows?
And away flows the river—but whither—who knows?

Let me be the breeze, love, that wanders along,
The river that ever rejoices in song;
Be thou to my fancy the orange in bloom,
The rose by the river that gives its perfume.
Would the fruit be so golden, so fragrant the rose,
If no breeze and no wave were to kiss them? Who knows?
Who knows?
If no breeze and no wave were to kiss them? Who knows?

128 *A Waking Dream*

From 'Isabel Clare'

DREAMING in the twilight,
When the shades creep o'er the hill—
Watching, when the sun is gone,
How the grey, cold night comes on—
Awake, yet dreaming still.

Then I dream of dead ones,
Of my life the joy and light,
And I see them round me rise,
And I feel their cold, calm eyes
Gaze on me through the night.

JOHN FRANCIS WALLER

Dreaming by the firelight,
When the wintry night is chill—
Watching fire-sparks upward fly,
While the embers sink and die—
Awake, yet dreaming still.

Then I dream of fair souls
From dead ashes issuing bright,
And I see my dead arise,
Soaring heavenward through the skies,
In the death-dark night.

Dreaming in the sunlight,
When the summer noon is still—
Watching in the deep blue sky
Clouds of white, gold-cinctured lie—
Awake, yet dreaming still.

Then I dream of heaven,
Far beyond those tranquil skies,
And I see, 'mid angels bright,
My dead, in robes of gold and white,
Alive before my eyes.

SAMUEL FERGUSON

129 *The Burial of King Cormac* (19)

1810–1886

'CROM Cruach and his sub-gods twelve,'
Said Cormac, 'are but carven treene;
The axe that made them, halt or helve,
Had worthier of our worship been.

'But he who made the tree to grow,
  And hid in earth the iron-stone,
And made the man with mind to know,
  The axe's use, is God alone.'

Anon to priests of Crom was brought—
  Where, girded in their service dread,
They minister'd on red Moy Slaught—
  Word of the words King Cormac said.

They loosed their curse against the king;
  They cursed him in his flesh and bones;
And daily in their mystic ring
  They turned the maledictive stones, (20)

Till, where at meat the monarch sate,
  Amid the revel and the wine,
He choked upon the food he ate,
  At Sletty, southward of the Boyne.

High vaunted then the priestly throng,
  And far and wide they noised abroad
With trump and loud liturgic song
  The praise of their avenging God.

But ere the voice was wholly spent
  That priest and prince should still obey,
To awed attendants o'er him bent
  Great Cormac gather'd breath to say,—

'Spread not the beds of Brugh for me (21)
  When restless death-bed's use is done:
But bury me at Rossnaree
  And face me to the rising sun.

'For all the kings who lie in Brugh
  Put trust in gods of wood and stone;
And 'twas at Ross that first I knew
  One, Unseen, who is God alone.

'His glory lightens from the east;
  His message soon shall reach our shore;
And idol-god and cursing priest
  Shall plague us from Moy Slaught no more.'

Dead Cormac on his bier they laid:—
  'He reign'd a king for forty years,
And shame it were,' his captains said,
  'He lay not with his royal peers.

'His grandsire, Hundred-battle, sleeps
  Serene in Brugh: and, all around,
Dead kings in stone sepulchral keeps
  Protect the sacred burial ground.

'What though a dying man should rave
  Of changes o'er the eastern sea?
In Brugh of Boyne shall be his grave,
  And not in noteless Rossnaree.'

There northward forth they bore the bier,
  And down from Sletty side they drew,
With horsemen and with charioteer,
  To cross the fords of Boyne to Brugh.

There came a breath of finer air
  That touched the Boyne with ruffling wings,
It stirr'd him in his sedgy lair
  And in his mossy moorland springs.

And as the burial train came down
  With dirge and savage dolorous shows,
Across their pathway, broad and brown
  The deep, full-hearted river rose ;

From bank to bank through all his fords,
  'Neath blackening squalls he swell'd and boil'd ;
And thrice the wondering gentile lords
  Essay'd to cross, and thrice recoil'd.

Then forth stepp'd grey-hair'd warriors four :
  They said, 'Through angrier floods than these
On link'd shields once our king we bore
  From Dread-Spear and the hosts of Deece.

'And long as loyal will holds good,
  And limbs respond with helpful thews,
Nor flood, nor fiend within the flood,
  Shall bar him of his burial dues.'

With slanted necks they stoop'd to lift ;
  They heaved him up to neck and chin ;
And, pair and pair, with footsteps swift,
  Lock'd arm and shoulder, bore him in.

'Twas brave to see them leave the shore ;
  To mark the deep'ning surges rise,
And fall subdued in foam before
  The tension of their striding thighs.

'Twas brave, when now a spear-cast out,
  Breast-high the battling surges ran ;
For weight was great, and limbs were stout,
  And loyal man put trust in man.

But ere they reached the middle deep,
  Nor steadying weight of clay they bore,
Nor strain of sinewy limbs could keep
  Their feet beneath the swerving four.

And now they slide, and now they swim,
  And now, amid the blackening squall,
Grey locks afloat, with clutchings grim,
  They plunge around the floating pall.

While, as the youth with practised spear
  Through justling crowds bears off the ring,
Boyne from their shoulders caught the bier
  And proudly bore away the king.

At morning, on tne grassy marge
  Of Rossnaree, the corpse was found,
And shepherds at their early charge
  Entomb'd it in the peaceful ground.

A tranquil spot : a hopeful sound
  Comes from the ever youthful stream,
And still on daisied mead and mound
  The dawn delays with tenderer beam.

Round Cormac Spring renews her buds :
  In march perpetual by his side,
Down come the earth-fresh April floods,
  And up the sea-fresh salmon glide ;

And life and time rejoicing run
  From age to age their wonted way ;
But still he waits the risen Sun,
  For still 'tis only dawning Day.

130 *Aideen's Grave* (22)

THEY heaved the stone; they heap'd the cairn.
Said Ossian, 'In a queenly grave
We leave her, 'mong her fields of fern,
Between the cliff and wave.

'The cliff behind stands clear and bare,
And bare, above, the heathery steep
Scales the clear heaven's expanse, to where
The Danaan Druids sleep. (23)

'And all the sands that, left and right,
The grassy isthmus-ridge confine,
In yellow bars lie bare and bright
Among the sparkling brine.

'A clear pure air pervades the scene,
In loneliness and awe secure;
Meet spot to sepulchre a Queen
Who in her life was pure.

'Here, far from camp and chase removed,
Apart in Nature's quiet room;
The music that alive she loved
Shall cheer her in the tomb.

'The humming of the noontide bees,
The lark's loud carol all day long,
And, borne on evening's salted breeze.
The clanking sea-bird's song

'Shall round her airy chamber float,
  And with the whispering winds and streams
Attune to Nature's tenderest note
  The tenor of her dreams.

'And oft, at tranquil eve's decline,
  When full tides lip the Old Green Plain,[1]
The lowing of Moynalty's kine
  Shall round her breathe again,

'In sweet remembrance of the days
  When, duteous, in the lowly vale,
Unconscious of my Oscar's gaze,
  She fill'd the fragrant pail,

'And, duteous, from the running brook
  Drew water for the bath; nor deem'd
A king did on her labour look,
  And she a fairy seem'd.

'But when the wintry frosts begin,
  And in their long-drawn, lofty flight,
The wild geese with their airy din
  Distend the ear of night,

'And when the fierce De Danaan ghosts
  At midnight from their peak come down
When all around the enchanted coasts
  Despairing strangers drown;

'When, mingling with the wreckful wail,
  From low Clontarf's wave-trampled floor
Comes booming up the burthen'd gale,
  The angry Sand-Bull's roar; (24)

[1] The plain of Moynalty, part of Dublin and Meath.

'Or, angrier than the sea, the shout
  Of Erin's hosts in wrath combined,
When Terror heads Oppression's rout,
  And Freedom cheers behind :

'Then o'er our lady's placid dream,
  Where safe from storms she sleeps, may steal
Such joy as will not misbeseem
  A Queen of men to feel :

'Such thrill of free, defiant pride
  As wrapt her in her battle car
At Gavra, when by Oscar's side
  She rode the ridge of war,

'Exulting, down the shouting troops,
  And through the thick confronting kings,
With hands on all their javelin loops
  And shafts on all their strings ;

'E'er closed the inseparable crowds,
  No more to part for me, and show,
As bursts the sun through scattering clouds,
  My Oscar issuing so.

'No more, dispelling battle's gloom,
  Shall son for me from fight return ;
The great green rath's ten-acred tomb
  Lies heavy on his urn.

'A cup of bodkin-pencill'd clay
  Holds Oscar ; mighty heart and limb
One handful now of ashes grey :
  And she has died for him.

'And here, hard by her natal bower
  On lone Ben Edar's side, we strive
With lifted rock and sign of power
  To keep her name alive.

'That while, from circling year to year,
  Her Ogham-letter'd stone is seen,
The Gael shall say, "Our Fenians here
  Entomb'd their loved Aideen."

'The Ogham from her pillar-stone
  In tract of time will wear away ;
Her name at last be only known
  In Ossian's echo'd lay.

'The long-forgotten lay I sing
  May only ages hence revive
(As eagle with a wounded wing
  To soar again might strive),

'Imperfect, in an alien speech,
  When, wandering here, some child of chance
Through pangs of keen delight shall reach
  The gift of utterance,—

'To speak the air, the sky to speak,
  The freshness of the hill to tell,
Who, roaming bare Ben Edar's peak
  And Aideen's briary dell,

'And gazing on the Cromlech vast,
  And on the mountain and the sea,
Shall catch communion with the past
  And mix himself with me.

'Child of the Future's doubtful night,
  Whate'er your speech, whoe'er your sires,
Sing while you may with frank delight
  The song your hour inspires.

'Sing while you may, nor grieve to know
  The song you sing shall also die;
Atharna's lay has perish'd so, (25)
  Though once it thrill'd this sky

Above us, from his rocky chair,
  There, where Ben Edar's landward crest
O'er eastern Bregia bends, to where
  Dun Almon crowns the west;

'And all that felt the fretted air
  Throughout the song-distemper'd clime,
Did droop, till suppliant Leinster's prayer
  Appeased the vengeful rhyme.

'Ah me, or e'er the hour arrive
  Shall bid my long-forgotten tones,
Unknown One, on your lips revive,
  Here, by these moss-grown stones,

'What change shall o'er the scene have cross'd;
  What conquering lords anew have come;
What lore-arm'd, mightier Druid host
  From Gaul or distant Rome!

'What arts of death, what ways of life,
  What creeds unknown to bard or seer,
Shall round your careless steps be rife,
  Who pause and ponder here;

'And haply, where yon curlew calls
  Athwart the marsh, 'mid groves and bowers
See rise some mighty chieftain's halls
  With unimagined towers :

'And baying hounds, and coursers bright,
  And burnish'd cars of dazzling sheen,
With courtly train of dame and knight,
  Where now the fern is green.

'Or, by yon prostrate altar-stone
  May kneel, perchance, and, free from blame,
Hear holy men with rites unknown
  New names of God proclaim.

'Let change as may the Name of Awe,
  Let right surcease and altar fall,
The same One God remains, a law
  For ever and for all.

'Let change as may the face of earth,
  Let alter all the social frame,
For mortal men the ways of birth
  And death are still the same.

'And still, as life and time wear on,
  The children of the waning days
(Though strength be from their shoulders gone
  To lift the loads we raise),

'Shall weep to do the burial rites
  Of lost ones loved ; and fondly found,
In shadow of the gathering nights,
  The monumental mound.

'Farewell! the strength of men is worn;
The night approaches dark and chill:
Sleep, till perchance an endless morn
Descend the glittering hill.'

Of Oscar and Aideen bereft,
So Ossian sang. The Fenians sped
Three mighty shouts to heaven; and left
Ben Edar to the dead.

131 *Deirdra's Lament for the Sons of Usnach* (26)

From the Irish

THE lions of the hill are gone,
And I am left alone—alone—
Dig the grave both wide and deep,
For I am sick, and fain would sleep!

The falcons of the wood are flown,
And I am left alone—alone—
Dig the grave both deep and wide,
And let us slumber side by side.

The dragons of the rock are sleeping,
Sleep that wakes not for our weeping:
Dig the grave and make it ready;
Lay me on my true-love's body.

Lay their spears and bucklers bright
By the warriors' side aright;
Many a day the three before me
On their linkéd bucklers bore me.

SAMUEL FERGUSON

Lay upon the low grave floor,
'Neath each head, the blue claymore ;
Many a time the noble three
Redden'd these blue blades for me.

Lay the collars, as is meet,
Of their greyhounds at their feet ;
Many a time for me have they
Brought the tall red deer to bay.

In the falcon's jesses throw,
Hook and arrow, line and bow ;
Never again by stream or plain
Shall the gentle woodsmen go.

Sweet companions ye were ever—
Harsh to me, your sister, never ;
Woods and wilds and misty valleys
Were, with you, as good's a palace.

Oh ! to hear my true love singing,
Sweet as sound of trumpets ringing ;
Like the sway of ocean swelling
Roll'd his deep voice round our dwelling.

Oh ! to hear the echoes pealing
Round our green and fairy sheeling,
When the three, with soaring chorus,
Pass'd the silent skylark o'er us.

Echo now, sleep, morn and even—
Lark alone enchant the heaven !—
Ardan's lips are scant of breath,
Naisi's tongue is cold in death.

Stag, exult on glen and mountain—
Salmon, leap from loch to fountain—
Heron, in the free air warm ye—
Usnach's sons no more will harm ye!

Erin's stay no more you are,
Rulers of the ridge of war;
Nevermore 'twill be your fate
To keep the beam of battle straight!

Woe is me! by fraud and wrong,
Traitors false and tyrants strong,
Fell clan Usnach, bought and sold,
For Barach's feast and Conor's gold!

Woe to Eman, roof and wall!
Woe to Red Branch, hearth and hall!—
Tenfold woe and black dishonour
To the foul and false clan Conor!

Dig the grave both wide and deep,
Sick I am and fain would sleep!
Dig the grave and make it ready,
Lay me on my true-love's body!

132 *The Downfall of the Gael*

From the Irish

MY heart is in woe,
And my soul deep in trouble,—
For the mighty are low,
And abased are the noble:

SAMUEL FERGUSON

The Sons of the Gael
  Are in exile and mourning,
Worn, weary, and pale,
  As spent pilgrims returning ;

Or men who, in flight
  From the field of disaster,
Beseech the black night
  On their flight to fall faster ;

Or seamen aghast
  When their planks gape asunder,
And the waves fierce and fast
  Tumble through in hoarse thunder ;

Or men whom we see
  That have got their death-omen—
Such wretches are we
  In the chains of our foemen !

Our courage is fear,
  Our nobility vileness,
Our hope is despair,
  And our comeliness foulness.

There is mist on our heads,
  And a cloud chill and hoary
Of black sorrow, sheds
  An eclipse on our glory.

From Boyne to the Linn
  Has the mandate been given,
That the children of Finn
  From their country be driven.

That the sons of the King—
  Oh, the treason and malice!
Shall no more ride the ring
  In their own native valleys;

No more shall repair
  Where the hill foxes tarry,
Nor forth to the air
  Fling the hawk at her quarry:

For the plain shall be broke
  By the share of the stranger,
And the stone-mason's stroke
  Tell the woods of their danger;

The green hills and shore
  Be with white keeps disfigured,
And the Moat of Rathmore
  Be the Saxon churl's haggard!

The land of the lakes
  Shall no more know the prospect
Of valleys and brakes—
  So transform'd is her aspect!

The Gael cannot tell,
  In the uprooted wild-wood
And red ridgy dell,
  The old nurse of his childhood:

The nurse of his youth
  Is in doubt as she views him,
If the wan wretch, in truth,
  Be the child of her bosom.

We starve by the board,
  And we thirst amid wassail—
For the guest is the lord,
  And the host is the vassal!

Through the woods let us roam,
  Through the wastes wild and barren;
We are strangers at home!
  We are exiles in Erin!

And Erin's a bark
  O'er the wide waters driven!
And the tempest howls dark,
  And her side planks are riven!

And in billows of night
  Swell the Saxon before her,—
Unite, oh, unite!
  Or the billows burst o'er her!

133 *Lament over the Ruins of the Abbey of Timoleague*

From the Irish

LONE and weary as I wander'd
  By thc bleak shore of the sea,
Meditating and reflecting
  On the world's hard destiny;

Forth the moon and stars 'gan glimmer,
  In the quiet tide beneath,—
For on slumbering spray and blossom
  Breathed not out of heaven a breath.

On I went in sad dejection,
  Careless where my footsteps bore,
Till a ruin'd church before me
  Open'd wide its ancient door,—

Till I stood before the portals,
  Where of old were wont to be,
For the blind, the halt, and leper,
  Alms and hospitality.

Still the ancient seat was standing,
  Built against the buttress grey,
Where the clergy used to welcome
  Weary travellers on their way.

There I sat me down in sadness,
  'Neath my cheek I placed my hand,
Till the tears fell hot and briny
  Down upon the grassy land.

There, I said in woeful sorrow,
  Weeping bitterly the while,
Was a time when joy and gladness
  Reign'd within this ruin'd pile ;—

Was a time when bells were tinkling,
  Clergy preaching peace abroad,
Psalms a-singing, music ringing
  Praises to the mighty God.

Empty aisle, deserted chancel,
  Tower tottering to your fall,
Many a storm since then has beaten
  On the grey head of your wall !

SAMUEL FERGUSON

Many a bitter storm and tempest
  Has your roof-tree turn'd away,
Since you first were form'd a temple
  To the Lord of night and day.

Holy house of ivied gables,
  That were once the country's pride,
Houseless now in weary wandering
  Roam your inmates far and wide.

Lone you are to-day, and dismal,—
  Joyful psalms no more are heard
Where, within your choir, her vesper
  Screeches the cat-headed bird.

Ivy from your eaves is growing,
  Nettles round your green hearth-stone,
Foxes howl, where, in your corners,
  Dropping waters make their moan.

Where the lark to early matins
  Used your clergy forth to call,
There, alas! no tongue is stirring,
  Save the daw's upon the wall.

Refectory cold and empty,
  Dormitory bleak and bare,
Where are now your pious uses,
  Simple bed and frugal fare?

Gone your abbot, rule and order,
  Broken down your altar stones;
Nought see I beneath your shelter,
  Save a heap of clayey bones.

Oh ! the hardship, oh ! the hatred,
Tyranny, and cruel war.
Persecution and oppression,
That have left you as you are !

I myself once also prosper'd ;—
Mine is, too, an alter'd plight ;
Trouble, care, and age have left me
Good for nought but grief to-night.

Gone, my motion and my vigour,—
Gone, the use of eye and ear ;
At my feet lie friends and children,
Powerless and corrupting here :

Woe is written on my visage,
In a nut my heart would lie—
Death's deliverance were welcome—
Father, let the old man die.

134 *Cean dubh Deelish* [1]

From the Irish

PUT your head, darling, darling, darling,
Your darling black head my heart above ;
Oh, mouth of honey, with the thyme for fragrance,
Who, with heart in breast, could deny you love ?
Oh, many and many a young girl for me is pining,
Letting her locks of gold to the cold wind free,
For me, the foremost of our gay young fellows ;
But I'd leave a hundred, pure love, for thee !

[1] Dear black head.

Then put your head, darling, darling, darling,
  Your darling black head my heart above ;
Oh, mouth of honey, with the thyme for fragrance,
  Who, with heart in breast, could deny you love ?

135 *The Fairy Thorn*

An Ulster Ballad

'GET up, our Anna dear, from the weary spinning-wheel ;
  For your father's on the hill, and your mother is asleep ;
Come up above the crags, and we'll dance a Highland reel
  Around the Fairy Thorn on the steep.'

At Anna Grace's door 'twas thus the maidens cried,
  Three merry maidens fair in kirtles of the green ;
And Anna laid the rock and the weary wheel aside,
  The fairest of the four, I ween.

They're glancing through the glimmer of the quiet eve,
  Away in milky wavings of neck and ankle bare ;
The heavy-sliding stream in its sleepy song they leave,
  And the crags in the ghostly air.

And linking hand-in-hand, and singing as they go,
  The maids along the hill-side have ta'en their fearless way,
Till they come to where the rowan trees in lonely beauty grow
  Beside the Fairy Hawthorn grey.

SAMUEL FERGUSON

The Hawthorn stands between the ashes tall and slim,
  Like matron with her twin grand-daughters at her knee;
The rowan berries cluster o'er her low head grey and dim
  In ruddy kisses sweet to see.

The merry maidens four have ranged them in a row,
  Between each lovely couple a stately rowan stem,
And away in mazes wavy, like skimming birds they go,
  Oh, never carolled bird like them!

But solemn is the silence of the silvery haze
  That drinks away their voices in echoless repose,
And dreamily the evening has stilled the haunted braes,
  And dreamier the gloaming grows.

And sinking one by one, like lark-notes from the sky,
  When the falcon's shadow saileth across the open shaw,
Are hushed the maidens' voices, as cowering down they lie
  In the flutter of their sudden awe.

For, from the air above and the grassy ground beneath,
  And from the mountain-ashes and the old Whitethorn between,
A power of faint enchantment doth through their beings breathe,
  And they sink down together on the green.

They sink together silent, and stealing side to side,
  They fling their lovely arms o'er their drooping necks so fair,
Then vainly strive again their naked arms to hide,
  For their shrinking necks again are bare.

Thus clasped and prostrate all, with their heads together bowed,
  Soft o'er their bosoms beating—the only human sound—
They hear the silky footsteps of the silent fairy crowd,
  Like a river in the air gliding round.

Nor scream can any raise, nor prayer can any say,
  But wild, wild the terror of the speechless three—
For they feel fair Anna Grace drawn silently away,
  By whom they dare not look to see.

They feel their tresses twine with her parting locks of gold,
  And the curls elastic falling, as her head withdraws;
They feel her sliding arms from their trancèd arms unfold,
  But they dare not look to see the cause;

For heavy on their senses the faint enchantment lies
  Through all that night of anguish and perilous amaze;
And neither fear nor wonder can ope their quivering eyes,
  Or their limbs from the cold ground raise;

Till out of Night the Earth has rolled her dewy side,
With every haunted mountain and streamy vale below;
When, as the mist dissolves in the yellow morning tide,
The maidens' trance dissolveth so.

Then fly the ghastly three as swiftly as they may,
And tell their tale of sorrow to anxious friends in vain—
They pined away and died within the year and day,
And ne'er was Anna Grace seen again.

136 *The Fair Hills of Ireland*

From the Irish

A PLENTEOUS place is Ireland for hospitable cheer,
Uileacán dubh O![1]
Where the wholesome fruit is bursting from the yellow barley ear;
Uileacán dubh O!
There is honey in the trees where her misty vales expand,
And her forest paths in summer are by falling waters fanned;
There is dew at high noontide there, and springs i' the yellow sand,
On the fair hills of holy Ireland.

[1] O sad lamentation.

Curled he is and ringleted, and plaited to the knee,
Uileacán dubh O!
Each captain who comes sailing across the Irish sea;
Uileacán dubh O!
And I will make my journey, if life and health but stand,
Unto that pleasant country, that fresh and fragrant strand,
And leave your boasted braveries, your wealth and high command,
For the fair hills of holy Ireland.

Large and profitable are the stacks upon the ground,
Uileacán dubh O!
The butter and the cream do wondrously abound,
Uileacán dubh O!
The cresses on the water and the sorrels are at hand,
And the cuckoo's calling daily his note of music bland,
And the bold thrush sings so bravely his song i' the forests grand,
On the fair hills of holy Ireland.

137 *The Pretty Girl of Loch Dan*

THE shades of eve had crossed the glen
That frowns o'er infant Avonmore,
When, nigh Loch Dan, two weary men,
We stopped before a cottage door.

'God save all here!' my comrade cries,
And rattles on the raised latch-pin;
'God save you kindly!' quick replies
A clear sweet voice, and asks us in.

We enter; from the wheel she starts,
 A rosy girl with soft black eyes;
Her fluttering court'sy takes our hearts,
 Her blushing grace and pleased surprise.

Poor Mary, she was quite alone—
 For, all the way to Glenmalure,
Her mother had that morning gone,
 And left the house in charge with her.

But neither household cares, nor yet
 The shame that startled virgins feel,
Could make the generous girl forget
 Her wonted hospitable zeal.

She brought us, in a beechen bowl,
 Sweet milk that smacked of mountain thyme,
Oat cake, and such a yellow roll
 Of butter—it gilds all my rhyme!

And, while we ate the grateful food
 (With weary limbs on bench reclined),
Considerate and discreet, she stood
 Apart, and listened to the wind.

Kind wishes both our souls engaged,
 From breast to breast spontaneous ran
The mutual thought—we stood and pledged,
 The modest rose above Loch Dan.

'The milk we drink is not more pure,
 Sweet Mary—bless those budding charms!—
Than your own generous heart, I'm sure,
 Nor whiter than the breast it warms!'

She turned and gazed, unused to hear
  Such language in that homely glen;
But, Mary, you have nought to fear,
  Though smiled on by two stranger men.

Not for a crown would I alarm
  Your virgin pride by word or sign,
Nor need a painful blush disarm
  My friend of thoughts as pure as mine.

Her simple heart could not but feel
  The words we spoke were free from guile,
She stooped, she blushed—she fixed her wheel—
  'Tis all in vain—she can't but smile!

Just like sweet April's dawn appears
  Her modest face—I see it yet—
And though I lived a hundred years,
  Methinks I never could forget

The pleasure that, despite her heart,
  Fills all her downcast eyes with light—
The lips reluctantly apart,
  The white teeth struggling into sight,

The dimples eddying o'er her cheek,—
  The rosy cheek that won't be still!
Oh! who could blame what flatterers speak,
  Did smiles like this reward their skill?

For such another smile, I vow,
  Though loudly beats the midnight rain,
I'd take the mountain-side e'en now,
  And walk to Luggelaw again!

SAMUEL FERGUSON

138 *Boatman's Hymn*

From the Irish

BARK that bears me through foam and squall,
You in the storm are my castle-wall :
Though the sea should redden from bottom to top,
From tiller to mast she takes no drop ;
On the tide-top, the tide-top,
Wherry aroon, my land and store !
On the tide-top, the tide-top,
She is the boat can sail go-leor.[1]

She dresses herself and goes gliding on,
Like a dame in her robes of the Indian lawn ;
For God has blessed her, gunnel and wale—
And oh ! if you saw her stretch out to the gale,
On the tide-top, the tide-top, etc.

Whillan,[2] ahoy ! old heart of stone,
Stooping so black o'er the beach alone,
Answer me well—on the bursting brine
Saw you ever a bark like mine ?
On the tide-top, the tide-top, etc.

Says Whillan, 'Since first I was made of stone,
I have looked o'er the beach alone—
But till to-day, on the bursting brine
Saw I never a bark like thine !'
On the tide-top, the tide-top, etc.

[1] Abundantly well.

[2] A rock on the shore near Blacksod Harbour.

'God of the air!' the seamen shout,
When they see us tossing the brine about:
'Give us the shelter of strand or rock,
Or through and through us she goes with a shock!'
On the tide-top, the tide-top,
Wherry aroon, my land and store!
On the tide-top, the tide-top,
She is the boat can sail go-leor.

139 *The Forester's Complaint*

THROUGH our wild wood-walks here,
Sunbright and shady,
Free as the forest deer
Roams a lone lady:
Far from her castle keep,
Down in the valley,
Roams she, by dingle deep,
Green holm, and alley,
With her sweet presence bright
Gladd'ning my dwelling—
Oh, fair her face of light,
Past the tongue's telling!
Woe was me
E'er to see
Beauty so shining;
Ever since, hourly,
Have I been pining!

In our blithe sports' debates
Down by the river,

I, of my merry mates,
  Foremost was ever ;
Skilfullest with my flute
  Leading the maidens,
Heark'ning by moonlight mute
  To its sweet cadence ;
Sprightliest in the dance
  Tripping together—
Such a one was I once
  Ere she came hither !
          Woe was me
          E'er to see
  Beauty so shining ;
    Ever since, hourly,
  Have I been pining !

Loud now my comrades laugh
  As I pass by them ;
Broadsword and quarter-staff,
  No more I ply them :
Coy now the maidens frown,
  Wanting their dances ;
How can their faces brown
  Win one, who fancies
Even an angel's face
  Dark to be seen would
Be, by the Lily-grace
  Gladd'ning the greenwood ?
          Woe was me
          E'er to see
  Beauty so shining ;
    Ever since, hourly,
  Have I been pining !

Wolf, by my broken bow
  Idle is lying,
While through the woods I go,
  All the day, sighing,
Tracing her footsteps small
  Through the moss'd cover,
Hiding then, breathless all,
  At the sight of her,
Lest my rude gazing should
  From her haunt scare her—
Oh, what a solitude
  Wanting her, there were!
        Woe was me
        E'er to see
  Beauty so shining;
    Ever since, hourly,
  Have I been pining!

140 *Pastheen Finn* (27)

From the Irish

OH, my fair Pastheen is my heart's delight,
  Her gay heart laughs in her blue eye bright;
Like the apple blossom her bosom white,
And her neck like the swan's on a March morn bright!
  Then, Oro, come with me! come with me! come with me!
  Oro, come with me! brown girl, sweet!
  And oh! I would go through snow and sleet,
  If you would come with me, brown girl, sweet!

SAMUEL FERGUSON

Love of my heart, my fair Pastheen!
Her cheeks are as red as the rose's sheen,
But my lips have tasted no more, I ween,
Than the glass I drank to the health of my queen!
    Then, Oro, come with me! come with me! come with me!
    Oro, come with me! brown girl, sweet!
    And oh! I would go through snow and sleet,
    If you would come with me, brown girl, sweet!

Were I in the town, where's mirth and glee,
Or 'twixt two barrels of barley bree,
With my fair Pastheen upon my knee,
'Tis I would drink to her pleasantly!
    Then, Oro, come with me! come with me! come with me!
    Oro, come with me! brown girl, sweet!
    And oh! I would go through snow and sleet,
    If you would come with me, brown girl, sweet!

Nine nights I lay in longing and pain,
Betwixt two bushes, beneath the rain,
Thinking to see you, love, once again;
But whistle and call were all in vain!
    Then, Oro, come with me! come with me! come with me!
    Oro, come with me! brown girl, sweet!
    And oh! I would go through snow and sleet,
    If you would come with me, brown girl, sweet!

I'll leave my people, both friend and foe;
From all the girls in the world I'll go;

But from you, sweetheart, oh, never ! oh, no !
Till I lie in the coffin, stretched cold and low !
Then, Oro, come with me ! come with me ! come with me !
Oro, come with me ! brown girl, sweet !
And oh ! I would go through snow and sleet,
If you would come with me, brown girl, sweet !

GEORGE FOX

141 *The County of Mayo* (28)

From the Irish

— 1880

ON the deck of Patrick Lynch's boat I sat in woeful plight,
Through my sighing all the weary day, and weeping all the night,
Were it not that full of sorrow from my people forth I go,
By the blessed sun ! 'tis royally I'd sing thy praise, Mayo !

When I dwelt at home in plenty, and my gold did much abound,
In the company of fair young maids the Spanish ale went round—
'Tis a bitter change from those gay days that now I'm forced to go,
And must leave my bones in Santa Cruz, far from my own Mayo.

They are altered girls in Irrul now; 'tis proud
they're grown and high,
With their hair-bags and their top-knots—for I pass
their buckles by;
But it's little now I heed their airs, for God will
have it so,
That I must depart for foreign lands, and leave my
sweet Mayo.

'Tis my grief that Patrick Loughlin is not Earl of
Irrul still,
And that Brian Duff no longer rules as Lord upon
the hill:
And that Colonel Hugh MacGrady should be lying
dead and low,
And I sailing, sailing swiftly from the county of
Mayo.

FRANCIS DAVIS

142 *Kathleen bán Adair*

1810–1885

THE battle blood of Antrim had not dried on
freedom's shroud,
And the rosy ray of morning was but struggling thro'
the cloud;
When, with lightning foot and deathly cheek, and
wildly waving hair,
O'er grass and dew, scarce breathing, flew young
Kathleen bán Adair.

Behind, her native Antrim in a reeking ruin lies;
Before her, like a silvery path, Kell's sleeping waters
rise;
And many a pointed shrub has pierc'd those feet so
white and bare,
But, oh! thy heart is deeper rent, young Kathleen
bán Adair.

And Kathleen's heart but one week since was like a
harvest morn;
When hope and joy are kneeling round the sheaf of
yellow corn;
But where's the bloom then made her cheek so ripe,
so richly fair?
Thy stricken heart hath fed on it, young Kathleen
bán Adair.

And now she gains a thicket, where the sloe and hazel
rise;
But why those shrieking whispers, like a rush of
worded sighs?
Ah, low and lonely bleeding lies a wounded patriot
there,
And every pang of his is thine, young Kathleen
bán Adair.

'I see them, oh! I see them, in their fearful red
array;
The yeomen, love! the yeomen come—ah! heavens
away, away!
I know, I know they mean to track my lion to his
lair;
Ah! save thy life—ah! save it for thy Kathleen
bán Adair!'

'May Heaven shield thee, Kathleen!—when my
soul has gone to rest;
May comfort rear her temple in thy pure and faithful
breast;
But to fly them, oh! to fly them, like a bleeding,
hunted hare;
No! not to purchase Heaven, with my Kathleen
bán Adair.

'I loved, I love thee, Kathleen, in my bosom's
warmest core—
And Erin, injured Erin, oh! I loved thee even more;
And death I feared him little when I drove him thro'
their square,
Nor now, though eating at my heart, my Kathleen
bán Adair.'

With feeble hand his blade he grasp'd yet dark with
spoilers' blood;
And then, as though with dying bound, once more
erect he stood;
But scarcely had he kiss'd that cheek, so pale, so
purely fair,
When flash'd their bayonets round him and his
Kathleen bán Adair!

Then up arose his trembling, yet his dreaded hero's
hand,
And up arose, in struggling sounds, his cheer for
mother land:
A thrust—a rush—their foremost falls; but ah! good
God! see there,
Thy lover's quivering at thy feet, young Kathleen
bán Adair!

But heavens! men, what recked he then your
heartless taunts and blows,
When from his lacerated heart ten dripping bayonets
rose?
And maiden, thou with frantic hands, what boots
it kneeling there?
The winds heed not thy yellow locks, young Kathleen
bán Adair.

Oh! what were tears, or shrieks, or swoons, but
shadows of the rest,
When torn was frantic Kathleen from the slaughtered
hero's breast?
And hardly had his last-heaved sigh grown cold upon
the air,
When oh! of all but life they robb'd young Kathleen
bán Adair!

But whither now shall Kathleen fly?—already is
she gone;
Thy water, Kells, is tempting fair, and thither speeds
she on;
A moment on its blooming banks she kneels in
hurried prayer—
Now in its wave she finds a grave, poor Kathleen bán
Adair!

143 *My Betrothed*

OH! come, my betrothed, to thine anxious bride,
Too long have they kept thee from my side;
Sure I sought thee by meadow and mountain, astór,
And I watch'd and I wept till my heart was sore,

While the false to the false did say,—
We will lead her away by the mound and the rath,
And we'll nourish her heart in its worse than death,
Till her tears shall have traced a pearly path,
For the work of a future day.

Ah! little they knew what their guile could do—
It has won me a host of the stern and true,
Who have sworn by the eye of the yellow sun,
That my home is their hearts till thy hand be won;
And they've gathered my tears and sighs;
And they've woven them into a cloudy frown,
That shall gird my brow like an ebony crown,
Till these feet, in my wrath, shall have trampled down
All, all that betwixt us rise.

Then come, my betrothed, to thine anxious bride!
Thou art dear to my breast as my heart's red tide;
And a wonder it is you can tarry so long,
And your soul so proud, and your arm so strong,
And your limb without a chain;
And your feet in their flight like the midnight wind,
When he laughs at the flash that he leaves behind;
And your heart so warm, and your look so kind—
Oh! come to my arms again!

Oh, my dearest has eyes like the noontide sun;
So bright that my own dare scarce look on;
And the clouds of a thousand years gone by,
Brought back, and again on the crowded sky,
Heaped haughtily pile o'er pile,
Then all in a boundless blaze outspread,
Rent, shaken, and tossed o'er their flaming bed,
Till each heart by the light of the heavens was read,
Were as nought to his softest smile!

And to hear my love in his wild mirth sing
To the flap of the battle-god's fiery wing!
How his chorus shrieks through the iron tones
Of crashing towers and creaking thrones,
  And the crumbling of bastions strong!
Yet, sweet to my ear as the sigh that slips
From the nervous dance of a maiden's lips,
When the eye first wanes in its love eclipse,
  Is his soul-creating song!

Then come, my betrothed, to thine anxious bride!
Thou has tarried too long, but I may not chide;
For the prop and the hope of my home thou art,
Ay, the vein that suckles my growing heart:
  Oh, I'd frown on the world for thee!
And it is not a dull, cold, soulless clod,
With a lip in the dust at a tyrant nod,
Unworthy one glance of the Patriot's God,
  That you ever shall find in me!

144 *Nanny*

OH, for an hour when the day is breaking,
  Down by the shore when the tide is making,
Fair as a white cloud, thou, love, near me,
None but the waves and thyself to hear me!
Oh, to my breast how these arms would press thee;
Wildly my heart in its joy would bless thee;
Oh, how the soul thou hast won would woo thee,
Girl of the snow-neck! closer to me.

Oh, for an hour as the day advances,
Out where the breeze on the broom-bush dances
Watching the lark, with the sun-ray o'er us,
Winging the notes of his heaven-taught chorus !
Oh, to be there, and my love before me,
Soft as a moonbeam smiling o'er me ;
Thou would'st but love, and I would woo thee,
Girl of the dark eye ! closer to me.

Oh, for an hour where the sun first found us,
Out in the eve with its red sheets round us,
Brushing the dew from the gale's soft winglets,
Pearly and sweet, with their long dark ringlets !
Oh, to be there on the sward beside thee,
Telling my tale, though I know you'd chide me ;
Sweet were thy voice, though it should undo me—
Girl of the dark locks ! closer to me.

Oh, for an hour by night or by day, love,
Just as the heavens and thou might say, love,
Far from the stare of the cold-eyed many,
Bound in the breath of my dove-souled Nanny !
Oh, for the pure chains that have bound me,
Warm from thy red lips circling round me !
Oh, in my soul, as the light above me,
Queen of the pure hearts ! do I love thee.

145 *Our Own Land*

IS this a time to cut and carve
Each other's souls for trifles,
When at our hearts the foe's reserve
Prepare to point their rifles ?

Up! up! ye true—
Prepare to do!
But hear it, high and low, man:
By Erin's faith,
One angry breath,
And Erin writes you foeman!
Our own land, our dear land,
The green land that bore us;
Let's firmer grasp her bleeding hand,
And faction sweep before us.

Her page of every bloody trace,
Before ye'd dream to close it,
To cleanse ye vowed in Heaven's face,
And mark ye, Heaven knows it:
And sure this day
Her green's as gay
As when your vows were plighted:
And now as then,
Ye know it, men,
She's full as banned and blighted.
Our own land, our green land,
The dear land that bore us;
Oh, who would drop her bleeding hand,
And aught of hope before us.

Oh, no! we've none, be Heaven praised,
To bite his lip and falter,
Till freedom's sacrifice has blazed
On every cottage altar;
And here we swear
By sea and air,

FRANCIS DAVIS

Though earth and hell oppose it,
However won,
It must be done,
And that's the way to close it !
Our own land, our dear land,
The green land that bore us ;
We'll firmer grasp her bleeding hand,
And sweep her foes before us !

ARTHUR GERALD GEOGHEGAN

146 *The Mountain Fern*

1810–1889

OH, the Fern ! the Fern !—the Irish hill Fern !—
That girds our blue lakes from Lough Ine to Lough Erne,
That waves on our crags like the plume of a king,
And bends, like a nun, over clear well and spring !
The fairy's tall palm tree ! the heath-bird's fresh nest,
And the couch the red deer deems the sweetest and best,
With the free winds to fan it, and dew-drops to gem,—
Oh, what can ye match with this beautiful stem ?

From the shrine of Saint Finbar, by lone Avonbuie,
To the halls of Dunluce, with its towers by the sea,
From the hill of Knockthu to the rath of Moyvore,
Like a chaplet it circles our green island o'er—
In the bawn of the chief, by the anchorite's cell,
On the hill-top, or greenwood, by streamlet or well,
With a spell on each leaf, which no mortal can learn,—
Oh, there never was plant like the Irish hill Fern !

ARTHUR GERALD GEOGHEGAN

Oh, the Fern! the Fern!—the Irish hill Fern!—
That shelters the weary, or wild roe, or kern.
Through the glens of Kilcoe rose a shout on the
gale,
As the Saxons rushed forth, in their wrath, from the
Pale,
With bandog and blood-hound, all savage to see,
To hunt through Clunealla the wild Rapparee!
Hark! a cry from yon dell on the startled ear rings,
And forth from the wood the young fugitive springs.

Through the copse, o'er the bog, and, oh saints be his
guide!
His fleet step now falters—there's blood on his side!
Yet onward he strains, climbs the cliff, fords the
stream,
And sinks on the hill-top 'mid bracken leaves green,
And thick o'er his brow are their fresh clusters piled,
And they cover his form, as a mother her child;
And the Saxon is baffled!—they never discern
Where it shelters and saves him—the Irish hill
Fern!

Oh, the Fern! the Fern!—the Irish hill Fern!—
That pours a wild keen o'er the hero's grey cairn;
Go, hear it at midnight, when stars are all out,
And the wind o'er the hill-side is moaning about,
With a rustle and stir, and a low wailing tone
That thrills through the heart with its whispering
lone;
And ponder its meaning, when haply you stray
Where the halls of the stranger in ruin decay.

With night-owls for warders, the goshawk for guest,
And their dais of honour by cattle-hoofs prest,
With its fosse choked with rushes, and spider-webs
flung
Over walls where the marchmen their red weapons
hung,
With a curse on their name, and a sigh for the hour
That tarries so long—look! what waves on the tower?
With an omen and sign, and an augury stern,
'Tis the Green Flag of Time!—'tis the Irish hill Fern!

147 *After Aughrim*

DO you remember, long ago,
Kathaleen?
When your lover whispered low,
'Shall I stay or shall I go,
Kathaleen?'
And you answered proudly, 'Go!
And join King James and strike a blow
For the Green!'

Movrone, your hair is white as snow,
Kathaleen;
Your heart is sad and full of woe.
Do you repent you made him go,
Kathaleen?
And quick you answer proudly, 'No!
For better die with Sarsfield so
Than live a slave without a blow
For the Green!'

SIR STEPHEN E. DE VERE

148

The Land Betrayed

1881–3

1812–1904

NEAR to the grave's mysterious brink,
  Weary, weary, sighing for rest,
I pause awhile, ere yet I sink
  Once more into my mother's breast.

In youth I sought a sterner rest,—
  To labour, labouring not in vain,
To help the friendless and distrest,
  Asking no guerdon save the gain

Of conscience clear, and gratitude,
  And calm content. Long years went by;
I saw but evil spring from good
  And dear-bought sacrifices lie

The sport of fools, the scoff of knaves,
  Dead ere they blossomed, barren, blighted,
By greedy dupes, and willing slaves,
  Wasted, unhonoured, unrequited.

My country, in thy jocund youth
  Nursling of faith, of love, and song,
Thou wert not made for shame or ruth,
  For trampled right, triumphant wrong.

Thy hope was high, thy heart was true,
  The fire of freedom lit thine eye;
Thy homes were pure as morning dew;
  Reverence was thine, and charity.

But glozing tongues turned love to hate,
And honour died, and faith decayed ;—
Land self-abased, self-immolate,
By thy best virtues worst betrayed !

Thy sun is set in gloom and storm :
Piled waters of a barren deep,
And the pale tempest's spectral form
Above his tomb their night-watch keep.

Farewell ! if, bursting prison caves,
That Orb once more shall flame in air,
Trampling with light the conquered waves,
And scattering from his wind-tossed hair

A myriad diamond chains,—bow down
Thy humbled head to Him, the King,
Who chastens, yet vouchsafes a crown
To Penitence and Suffering.

THOMAS OSBORNE DAVIS

149 *Lament for the Death of Eoghan Ruadh O'Neill* (29)

COMMONLY CALLED OWEN ROE O'NEILL

Time—10th November 1649. *Scene*—Ormond's camp, co. Waterford. *Speakers*—A veteran of Owen O'Neill's clan, and one of the horsemen just arrived with an account of his death.

1814–1845

'DID they dare, did they dare, to slay Owen Roe O'Neill ?'
'Yes, they slew with poison him they feared to meet with steel.'

'May God wither up their hearts! May their blood cease to flow!
May they walk in living death, who poisoned Owen Roe!

'Though it break my heart to hear, say again the bitter words.'
'From Derry, against Cromwell, he marched to measure swords;
But the weapon of the Saxon met him on his way,
And he died at Cloc Uactair, upon Saint Leonard's Day.'

'Wail, wail ye for the Mighty One! Wail, wail ye for the Dead!
Quench the hearth, and hold the breath—with ashes strew the head!
How tenderly we loved him! How deeply we deplore!
Holy Saviour! but to think we shall never see him more!

'Sagest in the council was he, kindest in the hall:
Sure we never won a battle—'twas Owen won them all.
Had he lived, had he lived, our dear country had been free;
But he's dead, but he's dead, and 'tis slaves we'll ever be.

'O'Farrell and Clanrickarde, Preston and Red Hugh,
Audley and MacMahon, ye are valiant, wise, and true;
But what—what are ye all to our darling who is gone?
The rudder of our ship was he — our castle's corner-stone!

'Wail, wail him through the island! Weep, weep for our pride!
Would that on the battle-field our gallant chief had died!
Weep the Victor of Beinn Burb—weep him, young men and old!
Weep for him, ye women—your Beautiful lies cold!

'We thought you would not die—we were sure you would not go,
And leave us in our utmost need to Cromwell's cruel blow—
Sheep without a shepherd, when the snow shuts out the sky—
Oh! why did you leave us, Owen? why did you die?

'Soft as woman's was your voice, O'Neill! bright was your eye!
Oh! why did you leave us, Owen? why did you die?
Your troubles are all over—you're at rest with God on high;
But we're slaves, and we're orphans, Owen!—why did you die?'

THOMAS OSBORNE DAVIS

150

My Land

SHE is a rich and rare land ;
  Oh ! she's a fresh and fair land,
She is a dear and rare land—
  This native land of mine.

No men than hers are braver—
Her women's hearts ne'er waver ;
I'd freely die to save her,
  And think my lot divine.

She's not a dull or cold land ;
No ! she's a warm and bold land ;
Oh ! she's a true and old land—
  This native land of mine.

Could beauty ever guard her,
And virtue still reward her,
No foe would cross her border—
  No friend within it pine.

Oh ! she's a fresh and fair land,
Oh ! she's a true and rare land !
Yes, she's a rare and fair land—
  This native land of mine.

THOMAS OSBORNE DAVIS

151 *The Sack of Baltimore* (30)

THE summer sun is falling soft on Carbery's hundred isles—
The summer's sun is gleaming still through Gabriel's rough defiles—
Old Inisherkin's crumbled fane looks like a moulting bird;
And in a calm and sleepy swell the ocean tide is heard:
The hookers lie upon the beach; the children cease their play;
The gossips leave the little inn; the households kneel to pray—
And full of love, and peace, and rest—its daily labour o'er—
Upon that cosy creek there lay the town of Baltimore.

A deeper rest, a starry trance, has come with midnight there;
No sound, except that throbbing wave, in earth, or sea, or air,
The massive capes and ruined towers seem conscious of the calm;
The fibrous sod and stunted trees are breathing heavy balm.
So still the night, these two long barques, round Dunashad that glide
Must trust their oars—methinks not few—against the ebbing tide—
Oh! some sweet mission of true love must urge them to the shore—
They bring some lover to his bride who sighs in Baltimore!

All, all asleep within each roof along that rocky
street,
And these must be the lovers' friends, with gently
gliding feet—
A stifled gasp! a dreamy noise! 'the roof is in a
flame!'
From out their beds, and to their doors, rush maid,
and sire, and dame—
And meet, upon the threshold stone, the gleaming
sabre's fall,
And o'er each black and bearded face the white or
crimson shawl—
The yell of 'Allah!' breaks above the prayer, and
shriek, and roar—
O, blessed God! the Algerine is lord of Baltimore!

Then flung the youth his naked hand against the
shearing sword;
Then sprung the mother on the brand with which
her son was gor'd;
Then sunk the grandsire on the floor, his grand-babes
clutching wild;
Then fled the maiden moaning faint, and nestled with
the child:
But see yon pirate strangled lies, and crushed with
splashing heel,
While o'er him in an Irish hand there sweeps his
Syrian steel—
Though virtue sink, and courage fail, and misers yield
their store,
There's one hearth well avenged in the sack of Balti-
more!

Midsummer morn, in woodland nigh, the birds begin
to sing—
They see not now the milking maids, deserted is the
spring!
Midsummer day—this gallant rides from distant Bandon's town—
These hookers crossed from stormy Skull, that skiff
from Affadown;
They only found the smoking walls, with neighbours'
blood besprent,
And on the strewed and trampled beach awhile they
wildly went—
Then dash'd to sea, and passed Cape Clear, and saw
five leagues before
The pirate-galley vanishing that ravaged Baltimore.

Oh! some must tug the galley's oar, and some must
tend the steed—
This boy will bear a Scheik's chibouk, and that a
Bey's jerreed.
Oh! some are for the arsenals, by beauteous Dardanelles;
And some are in the caravan to Mecca's sandy
dells.
The maid that Bandon gallant sought is chosen for
the Dey,
She's safe—she's dead—she stabb'd him in the midst
of his Serai;
And when, to die a death of fire, that noble maid they
bore,
She only smiled—O'Driscoll's child—she thought of
Baltimore.

'Tis two long years since sunk the town beneath that bloody band,
And all around its trampled hearths a larger concourse stand,
Where high upon a gallows-tree, a yelling wretch is seen—
'Tis Hackett of Dungarvan—he who steered the Algerine!
He fell amid a sullen shout, with scarce a passing prayer,
For he had slain the kith and kin of many a hundred there.
Some muttered of MacMorrogh, who had brought the Norman o'er—
Some cursed him with Iscariot, that day in Baltimore.

152 *Native Swords*

A Volunteer Song—July 1, 1792

WE'VE bent too long to braggart wrong,
While force our prayers derided;
We've fought too long ourselves among,
By knaves and priests divided;
United now, no more we'll bow;
Foul faction, we discard it;
And now, thank God! our native sod
Has Native Swords to guard it.

Like rivers which, o'er valleys rich,
Bring ruin in their water,
On native land a native hand
Flung foreign fraud and slaughter.

From Dermod's crime to Tudor's time
Our clans were our perdition ;
Religion's name, since then, became
Our pretext for division.

But, worse than all ! with Limerick's fall
Our valour seemed to perish ;
Or, o'er the main, in France and Spain,
For bootless vengeance flourish.
The peasant here grew pale for fear
He'd suffer for our glory,
While France sang joy for Fontenoy,
And Europe hymned our story.

But now no clan nor factious plan
The east and west can sunder—
Why Ulster e'er should Munster fear
Can only wake our wonder.
Religion's crost when Union's lost,
And 'royal gifts' retard it ;
And now, thank God ! our native sod
Has Native Swords to guard it.

153 *Nationality*

A NATION'S voice, a nation's voice—
It is a solemn thing !
It bids the bondage-sick rejoice—
'Tis stronger than a king.
'Tis like the light of many stars,
The sound of many waves ;

Which brightly look through prison-bars
  And sweetly sound in caves.
Yet is it noblest, godliest known,
When righteous triumph swells its tone.

A nation's flag, a nation's flag—
  If wickedly unrolled,
May foes in adverse battle drag
  Its every fold from fold.
But in the cause of Liberty,
  Guard it 'gainst Earth and Hell;
Guard it till Death or Victory—
  Look you, you guard it well!
No saint or king has tomb so proud
As he whose flag becomes his shroud.

A nation's right, a nation's right—
  God gave it, and gave, too,
A nation's sword, a nation's might,
  Danger to guard it through.
'Tis freedom from a foreign yoke,
  'Tis just and equal laws,
Which deal unto the humblest folk
  As in a noble's cause.
On nations fixed in right and truth
God would bestow eternal youth.

May Ireland's voice be ever heard
  Amid the world's applause!
And never be her flag-staff stirred
  But in an honest cause!
May freedom be her very breath,
  Be justice ever dear;

And never an ennobled death
  May son of Ireland fear!
So the Lord God will ever smile,
With guardian grace, upon our isle.

154 *Maire bán Astór*[1]

IN a valley far away,
  With my Maire bán astór,
Short would be the summer day,
  Ever loving more and more;
Winter days would all grow long,
  With the light her heart would pour,
With her kisses and her song,
  And her loving mait go leór.[2]
      Fond is Maire bán astór,
      Fair is Maire bán astór,
      Sweet as ripple on the shore,
      Sings my Maire bán astór.

Oh! her sire is very proud,
  And her mother cold as stone;
But her brother bravely vow'd
  She should be my bride alone;
For he knew I loved her well,
  And he knew she loved me too,
So he sought their pride to quell,
  But 'twas all in vain to sue.
      True is Maire bán astór,
      Tried is Maire bán astór,
      Had I wings I'd never soar
      From my Maire bán astór

[1] Fair Mary, my treasure. [2] In much plenty.

There are lands where manly toil
  Surely reaps the crop it sows,
Glorious woods and teeming soil,
  Where the broad Missouri flows ;
Through the trees the smoke shall rise,
  From our hearth with mait go leór,
There shall shine the happy eyes
    Of my Maire bán astór,
        Mild is Maire bán astór,
        Mine is Maire bán astór,
        Saints will watch about the door
        Of my Mairc bán astór.

155 *My Grave*

SHALL they bury me in the deep,
  Where wind-forgetting waters sleep ?
Shall they dig a grave for me
Under the green-wood tree ?
Or on the wild heath,
Where the wilder breath
Of the storm doth blow ?
Oh, no ! oh, no !

Shall they bury me in the palace tombs,
Or under the shade of cathedral domes ?
Sweet 'twere to lie on Italy's shore ;
Yet not there—nor in Greece, though I love it more.
In the wolf or the vulture my grave shall I find ?
Shall my ashes career on the world-seeing wind ?
Shall they fling my corpse in the battle mound,
Where coffinless thousands lie under the ground—
Just as they fall they are buried so ?
Oh, no ! oh, no !

THOMAS OSBORNE DAVIS

No! on an Irish green-hill side,
On an opening lawn, but not too wide!
For I love the drip of the wetted trees;
I love not the gales, but a gentle breeze
To freshen the turf; put no tombstone there,
But green sods, decked with daisies fair;
Nor sods too deep, but so that the dew
The matted grass-roots may trickle through.
Be my epitaph writ on my country's mind:
'He served his country, and loved his kind.'
Oh! 'twere merry unto the grave to go,
If one were sure to be buried so.

AUBREY DE VERE

156 *The Ballad of the Bier that Conquered; or, O'Donnell's Answer* (31)

A.D. 1257.

1814–1902

LAND which the Norman would make his own!
(Thus sang the bard 'mid a host o'erthrown,
While their white cheeks some on the clench'd hand propp'd,
And from some the life-blood unheeded dropp'd)
There are men in thee that refuse to die,
Though they scorn to live, while a foe stands nigh!

AUBREY DE VERE

O'Donnell lay sick with a grievous wound :
  The leech had left him ; the priest had come ;
The clan sat weeping upon the ground,
  Their banners furl'd, and their minstrels dumb.

Then spake O'Donnell, the King : ' Although
My hour draws nigh, and my dolours grow ;
And although my sins I have now confess'd,
And desire in the land, my charge, to rest,
Yet leave this realm, nor will I nor can,
While a stranger treads on her, child or man.

' I will languish no longer a sick King here :
My bed is grievous ; build up my Bier.
The white robe a King wears over me throw ;
Bear me forth to the field where he camps—your foe,
With the yellow torches and dirges low.
The heralds have brought his challenge and fled ;
The answer they bore not I bear instead.
My people shall fight, my pain in sight,
And I shall sleep well when their wrong stands right.'

Then the clan rose up from the ground, and gave ear,
And they fell'd great oak-trees and built a Bier ;
Its plumes from the eagle's wing were shed,
And the wine-black samite above it spread
Inwov'n with sad emblems and texts divine,
And the braided bud of Tyrconnell's pine,
And all that is meet for the great and brave
When past are the measured years God gave,
And a voice cries ' Come ' from the waiting grave.

When the Bier was ready they laid him thereon ;
And the army forth bare him with wail and moan :
With wail by the sea-lakes and rock-abysses ;
With moan through the vapour-trail'd wildernesses ;
And men sore wounded themselves drew nigh
And said, 'We will go with our King and die ;'
And women wept as the pomp pass'd by.
The yellow torches far off were seen ;
No war-note peal'd through the gorges green ;
But the black pines echo'd the mourners' keen.

What, said the Invader, that pomp in sight ?
'They sue for the pity they shall not win.'
But the sick King sat on his bier upright,
And said, 'So well ! I shall sleep to-night :—
Rest here my couch, and my peace begin.'

Then the war-cry sounded—'Lamb-dearg Aboo !'[1]
And the whole clan rush'd to the battle plain :
They were thrice driven back, but they closed anew
That an end might come to their King's great pain.
'Twas a nation, not army, that onward rush'd,
'Twas a nation's blood from their wounds that gush'd :
Bare-bosom'd they fought, and with joy were slain ;
Till evening their blood fell fast like rain ;
But a shout swell'd up o'er the setting sun,
And O'Donnell died, for the field was won.

So they buried their King upon Aileach's shore ;
And in peace he slept ;—O'Donnell More.

[1] Red-hand for ever.

AUBREY DE VERE

157 *Dirge of Rory O'More* (32)

A.D. 1642

UP the sea-saddened valley at evening's decline,
A heifer walks lowing—'the Silk of the Kine;'[1]
From the deep to the mountains she roams, and again
From the mountain's green urn to the purple-rimmed main.

What seek'st thou, sad mother? Thine own is not thine!
He dropped from the headland; he sank in the brine!
'Twas a dream! but in dreams at thy foot did he follow
Through the meadow-sweet on by the marish and mallow!

Was he thine? Have they slain him? Thou seek'st him, not knowing
Thyself, too, art theirs, thy sweet breath and sad lowing!
Thy gold horn is theirs; thy dark eye and thy silk!
And that which torments thee, thy milk is their milk!

'Twas no dream, Mother Land! 'Tis no dream, Innisfail!
Hope dreams, but grief dreams not—the grief of the Gael!
From Leix and Ikerrin to Donegal's shore
Rolls the dirge of thy last and thy bravest—O'More!

[1] One of the mystical names of Ireland.

158 *The New Race*

O YE who have vanquished the land and retain it,
How little ye know what ye miss of delight!
There are worlds in her heart—could ye seek it or gain it—
That would clothe a true noble with glory and might.

What is she, this Isle which ye trample and ravage,
Which ye plough with oppression, and reap with the sword,
But a harp, never strung, in the hall of a savage,
Or a fair wife embraced by a husband abhorred?

The chiefs of the Gael were the people embodied;
Thy chiefs were the blossoms, the people the root!
Their conquerors, the Normans, high-souled and high-blooded,
Grew Irish at last from the scalp to the foot.

And ye!—ye are hirelings and satraps, not nobles!
Your slaves, they detest you; your masters, they scorn!
The river lives on—but the sun-painted bubbles
Pass quick, to the rapids insensibly borne.

159 *The Dirge of Desmond* (33)

RUSH, dark dirge, o'er hills of Erin! Woe for Desmond's name and race!
Loving conqueror whom the conquered caught so soon to her embrace:

AUBREY DE VERE

There's a veil on Erin's forehead : cold at last is
Desmond's hand :—
Halls that roofed her outlawed prelates blacken like a
blackening brand.

Strongbow's sons forsook their strong one, served so
long with loving awe ;
Roche the Norman, Norman Barry, and the Baron
of Lixnaw :
Gaelic lords—that once were princes—holp not—
Thomond or Clancar :
Ormond, ill-crowned Tudor's kinsman, ranged her
hosts, and led her war.

One by one his brothers perished : fate down drew
them to their grave :
Smerwick's cliffs beheld his Spaniards wrestling with
the yeasty wave.
Swiftly sweep the eagles westward, gathering where
the carcase lies :
There's a blacker crowd behind them : vultures next
will rend their prize.

'Twas not War that wrought the ruin ! Sister por-
tents, yoked for hire,
Side by side dragged on the harrow—Famine's plague,
and plague of Fire :
Slain the herds, and burned the harvests, vale and
plain with corpses strown,
'Mid the waste they spread their feast ; within the
charnel reigned—alone.

In the death-hunt she was nigh him ; she that scorned
to leave his side :
By her lord she stood and spake not, neck-deep in
the freezing tide :
Round them waved the osiers ; o'er them drooped
the willows, rank on rank :
Troopers spurred ; and bayed the bloodhounds, up
and down the bleeding bank.

From the East sea to the West sea rings the death-keen
long and sore :
Erin's curse be his that led them, found the hovel,
burst the door !
O'er the embers dead an old man silent bent with
head to knee :
Slowly rose he : backward fell they :—'Seek ye Desmond ? I am he !'

London Bridge ! thy central archway props that grey
head year by year :
But to God that head is holy ; and to Erin it is dear :
When that bridge is dust, that river in the last fire-
judgement dried,
The man shall live who fought for God ; the man
who for his country died.

160 *Roisin Dubh ;*[1] *or, The Bleeding Heart*

O WHO art thou with that queenly brow
And uncrown'd head ?
And why is the vest that binds thy breast,
O'er the heart, blood-red ?

[1] Little Black Rose—Ireland.

Like a rose-bud in June was that spot at noon,
    A rose-bud weak ;
But it deepens and grows like a July rose :
    Death-pale thy cheek !

'The babes I fed at my foot lay dead ;
    I saw them die ;
In Ramah a blast went wailing past ;
    It was Rachel's cry.
But I stand sublime on the shores of Time,
    And I pour mine ode,
As Miriam sang to the cymbals' clang,
    On the wind to God.

'Once more at my feasts my bards and priests
    Shall sit and eat :
And the Shepherd whose sheep are on every steep
    Shall bless my meat !
Oh, sweet, men say, is the song by day,
    And the feast by night ;
But on poisons I thrive, and in death survive
    Through ghostly night.'

161 *The March to Kinsale*

DECEMBER, A.D. 1601

O'ER many a river bridged with ice,
    Through many a vale with snow-drifts dumb,
Past quaking fen and precipice
  The Princes of the North are come !

Lo, these are they that, year by year,
  Roll'd back the tide of England's war ;—
Rejoice, Kinsale ! thy help is near !
  That wondrous winter march is o'er.
    And thus they sang, 'To-morrow morn
      Our eyes shall rest upon the foe :
    Roll on, swift night, in silence borne,
      And blow, thou breeze of sunrise, blow !'

Blithe as a boy on march'd the host
  With droning pipe and clear-voiced harp ;
At last above that southern coast
  Rang out their war-steed's whinny sharp :
And up the sea-salt slopes they wound,
  And airs once more of ocean quaff'd ;
Those frosty woods, the blue wave's bound,
  As though May touched them waved and laugh'd.
    And thus they sang, 'To-morrow morn
      Our eyes shall rest upon our foe :
    Roll on, swift night, in silence borne,
      And blow, thou breeze of sunrise, blow !'

Beside their watchfires couch'd all night
  Some slept, some danced, at cards some play'd,
While, chanting on a central height
  Of moonlit crag, the priesthood pray'd :
And some to sweetheart, some to wife
  Sent message kind ; while others told
Triumphant tales of recent fight,
  Or legends of their sires of old.
    And thus they sang, 'To-morrow morn
      Our eyes at last shall see the foe :
    Roll on, swift night, in silence borne,
      And blow, thou breeze of sunrise, blow !'

162 *Dunluce Castle, County of Antrim*

O! of the fallen most fallen, yet of the proud
Proudest; sole-seated on thy tower-girt rock;
Breasting for ever circling ocean's shock;
With blind sea-caves for ever dinned and loud;
Now sunset-gilt; now wrapt in vapoury shroud;
Till distant ships—so well thy bastions mock
Primeval nature's style in joint and block—
Misdeem her ramparts, round thee bent and bowed,
For thine, and on her walls, men say, have hurled
The red artillery stored designed for thee:
Thy wars are done! Henceforth perpetually
Thou restest, like some judged, impassive world
Whose sons, their probatory period past,
Have left that planet void amid the vast.

163 *Horn Head, County of Donegal*

SISTER of Earth, her sister eldest-born,
Huge world of waters, how unlike are ye!
Thy thoughts are not as her thoughts: unto thee
Her pastoral fancies are as things to scorn:
Thy heart is still with that old hoary morn
When on the formless deep, the procreant sea,
God moved alone: of that Infinity,
Thy portion then, thou art not wholly shorn.
Scant love hast thou for dells where every leaf
Boasts its own life, and every brook its song;
Thy massive floods down stream from reef to reef
With one wide pressure; thy worn cliffs along
The one insatiate Hunger moans and raves,
Hollowing its sunless crypts and sanguine caves.

164 *Plorans Ploravit*

SHE sits alone on the cold grave-stone
And only the dead are nigh her ;
In the tongue of the Gael she makes her wail :
The night wind rushes by her.

'Few, oh few are the leal and true,
And fewer shall be, and fewer ;
The land is a corse ; no life, no force :
O wind with sere leaves strew her !

'Men ask what scope is left for hope
To one who has known her story :—
I trust her dead ! The graves are red ;
But their souls are with God in glory.'

165 *Song*

SEEK not the tree of silkiest bark
And balmiest bud,
To carve her name, while yet 'tis dark,
Upon the wood.
The world is full of noble tasks,
And wreaths hard-won :
Each work demands strong hearts, strong hands,
Till day is done.

Sing not that violet-veinéd skin ;
That cheek's pale roses ;—
The lily of that form wherein
Her soul reposes !

Forth to the fight, true man, true knight!
The clash of arms
Shall more prevail than whispered tale
To win her charms.

The warrior for the True, the Right,
Fights in Love's name.
The love that lures thee from that fight
Lures thee to shame.
That love which lifts the heart, yet leaves
The spirit free;
That love, or none, is fit for one
Man-shaped like thee.

166 *The Dignity of Sorrow*

I HAVE not seen you since the Shadow fell
From Heaven against your door.
I know not if you bear your sorrow well:
I only know your hearth is cold; your floor
Will hear that soft and gliding tread no more.

I know our ancient friendship now is over.
I can love still, and so will not complain:
I have not loved in vain;
Taught long that art of sadness to discover
Which draws stern solace from the wells of Pain.
You love the Dead alone;—or you have lost
The power and life of Love in Time's untimely
frost.

AUBREY DE VERE

You have stood up in the great monarch's court—
  The court of Death : in spirit you have seen
    His lonely shades serene
Where all the mighty men of old resort.
  The eyes of Proserpine
Heavy and black have rested upon thine.

Her vintage, wine from laurel-berries prest,
  You raised—and laid you then the dark urn down,
  Scared by that Queen's inevitable frown,
Just as the marble touched your panting breast?
  O! in the mirror of that poison cold
  What Shadow or what Shape did you behold?

And she is dead : and you have long been dying ;
  And are recovered, and live on!—O, friend,
    Say, what shall be the end
Of leaf-lamenting boughs and wintry sighing?
  When will the woods that moan
    Resume their green array?
  When will the dull, sad clouds be overblown,
    And a calm sunset close our stormy day?

My thoughts pursue you still. I call them back.
  Once more they seek you, like the birds that rise
Up from their reeds, and in a winding track
  Circle the field in which their forage lies ;—
Or like some poor and downcast pensioner,
  Depressed and timid though his head be grey,
    That moves with curving steps to greet his lord,
      Whom he hath watched all day—
    Yet lets him pass away without a word ;
And gazes on his footsteps from afar.

167 *Song*

Scene in a Madhouse

SHE sings her wild dirges, and smiles 'mid the strain;
  Then turns to remember her sorrow.
Men gaze on that smile till their tears fall like rain,
  And she from their weeping doth borrow.
She forgets her own story: and none, she complains,
  Of the cause for her grief will remind her:
She fancies but one of her kindred remains—
  She is certain he never can find her.
Whence caught you, sweet mourner, the swell of that
    song?
  'From the arch of yon wind-laden billow.'
Whence learned you, sweet lady, your sadness?—
    'From Wrong.'
  Your meekness who taught you?—'The Willow.'

She boasts that her tresses have never grown grey;
  Yet murmurs—'How long I am dying!
My sorrows but make me more lovely, men say;
  But I soon in my grave shall be lying!
My grave will embrace me all round and all round,
  More warmly than thou, my false lover:—
No rival will steal to my couch without sound;
  No sister will come to discover!'
Whence caught you, sweet mourner, the swell of that
    song?
  'From the arch of the wind-laden billow.'
Whence learned you, sweet lady, your sadness?—
    'From Wrong.'
  Your meekness who taught you?—'The Willow.'

She courts the cold wind when the tempests blow
 hard,
 And at first she exults in their raving.
She clasps with her fingers the lattice close-barred—
 Like the billows her bosom is waving :—
But ere long with strange pity her spirit is crossed,
 And she sighs for poor mariners drowning :
And—'thus in my passion of old I was tossed'—
 And—'thus stood my grey father frowning!'
Whence caught you, sweet mourner, the swell of that
 song?
 'From the arch of the wind-laden billow.'
Whence learned you, sweet lady, your sadness?—
 'From Wrong.'
 Your meekness who taught you?—'The Willow.'

On the wall the rough water chafes ever its
 breast;
 'Mid the willows my bark was awaiting;
Passing by, on her cold hand a sad kiss I prest,
 And slowly moved on to the grating.
'For my lips, not my fingers, your bounty I
 crave!'
 She cried with a laugh and light shiver:
'You drift o'er the ocean, and I to the grave;
 Henceforward we meet not for ever!'
Where found you, sweet mourner, the swell of that
 song?
 'In the arch of yon wind-laden billow.'
Whence caught you, sweet lady, your sadness?—
 'From Wrong.'
 Your meekness who taught you?—'The Willow.'

JAMES McKOWEN

168 *Bonnie Twinkling Starnies*

1814-1889

BONNIE twinklin' starnies!
  Sae gentle and sae bright—
Ye woo me and ye win me
  With your soft and silver light.
Now peepin' o'er the mountain—
  Now glintin' in the streams—
Now kissin' the red heather bell
  All with your winsome beams:
    Bonnie twinklin' starnies!
      Sae gentle and sae bright—
    Ye woo me and ye win me
      With your soft and silver light.

Bonnie twinklin' starnies!
  When gloamin' sheds its tinge,
And strings the crystal dew-drop
  Around the gowan's fringe—
How often do I linger,
  With keen and anxious eye,
To watch your bonnie faces
  Come glintin' frae the sky.
    Starnies! twinklin' starnies!
      Sae gentle and sae bright—
    Ye woo me and ye win me
      With your soft and silver light.

Bonnie twinklin' starnies!
  Bright guardians of the skies—
How can we dream of wickedness
  Beneath your sleepless eyes?

Cold and pulseless is the heart
  And deeply fraught with guile,
Who does na feel the 'lowe o' love,'
  When ye look down and smile.
    Bonnie twinklin' starnies!
      Sae gentle and sae bright—
    Ye woo me and ye win me
      With your soft and silver light.

169 *Oh! if I were yon Gossamer*

OH! if I were yon gossamer,
    That's trembling o'er the green,
I know the sunny tresses where
  I'd hide and be unseen.
Or if I were the fitful wind,
  That wanders east and west,
I know a gentle bosom where
  I'd nestle me to rest.

Oh! were I yon marsh Mary-buds
  With nests of ripening gold,
I know a hand of slender make
  That should my treasures hold.
Or if I were the velvet bee,
  Of which I've heard you speak,
'Tis on your lip, fair Alice bán,
  My honey I would seek.

JOSEPH SHERIDAN LE FANU

170 *From 'The Legend of the Glaive'*

1814-1873

THROUGH the woods of Morrua and over its root-knotted flooring,
The hero speeds onward, alone, on his terrible message;
When faint and far-off, like the gathering gallop of battle,
The hoofs of the hurricane louder and louder come leaping,
There's a gasp and a silence around him, a swooning of nature,
And the forest trees moan, and complain with a presage of evil.
And nearer, like great organ's wailing, high-piping through thunder,
Subsiding, then lifted again to a thousand-tongued tumult,
And crashing, and deafening and yelling in clangorous uproar.
Soaring onward, down-riding, and rending the wreck of its conquest,
The tempest swoops on: all the branches before it bend, singing
Like cordage in shipwreck; before it sear leaves fly like vapour;
Before it bow down like wide armies, plumed heads of the forest,
In frenzy dark-rolling, up-tossing their scathed arms like Mænads.

Dizzy lightnings split this way and that in the blind
void above him ;
For a moment long passages reeling and wild with the
tempest,
In the blue map and dazzle of lightning, throb vivid
and vanish ;
And white glare the wrinkles and knots of the oak-
trees beside him,
While close overhead clap the quick mocking palms of
the Storm-Fiend.

171 *Hymn*

From 'Beatrice'

HUSH ! oh ye billows,
Hush ! oh thou wind,
Watch o'er us, angels,
Mary, be kind !

Fishermen followed
The steps of the Lord ;
Oft in their fishing boats
Preached He the Word.

Pray for us, Pietro,
Pray for us, John,
Pray for us, Giacomo,
Zebedee's son.

If it be stormy,
Fear not the sea ;
Jesus upon it
Is walking by thee.

Billows, be gentle,
  Soft blow the wind,
Watch o'er us, angels,
  Mary, be kind !

Soft be the billows,
  Gentle the wind,
Angels watch over thee,
  Mary, be kind !

172 *From the Same*

NOW by a stranger hand the lamp is placed,
  And little Beatrice no longer lights
The star he steered by on the moonless nights ;
And when, like spirits lost, the sea-bird shrieks,
And when close-reefed across the roaring waste,
O'er breakers thundering in the shrilly winds,
His starless boat his wild home darkly seeks,
His eye at last the soulless beacon finds,
Thrills to his heart the ray of other years
Starred dimly in the dark by gathering tears.

In summer evenings, when the isles grow dim,
And seas float silvery round the darkened shore,
Never again awakes the distant hymn,
The laughing, sweet-voiced welcome in the door,
The loving prattle and the glad surprise,
When down the rocky stair the true steps flies
To meet him at the gunwale by the shore.
That laughing, loving welcome as of yore,
That dancing step will wake again no more.

The cold sea breaks along the pebbles there,
The door is dark—the stair is but a stair—
And through the struggling roses, weeds wave high,
And summer breezes wildering rock and sigh.

173 *Abhain au Bhuideil*

Address of a Drunkard to a Bottle of Whiskey

FROM what dripping cell, through what fairy glen,
Where 'mid old rocks and ruins the fox makes his den;
Over what lonesome mountain,
Acushla machree!
Where gauger never has trod,
Sweet as the flowery sod,
Wild as the breath
Of the breeze on the heath,
And sparkling all o'er like the moon-lighted fountain,
Are you come to me—
Sorrowful me?

Dancing—inspiring—
My wild blood firin';
Oh! terrible glory—
Oh! beautiful siren—
Come, tell the old story—
Come light up my fancy, and open my heart.
Oh, beautiful ruin—
My life—my undoin'—
Soft and fierce as a pantheress,
Dream of my longing, and wreck of my soul,
I never knew love till I loved you, enchantress!

JOSEPH SHERIDAN LE FANU

At first, when I knew you, 'twas only flirtation,
The touch of a lip and the flash of an eye;
But 'tis different now—'tis desperation!
I worship before you,
I curse and adore you,
And without you I'd die.

Wirrasthrue!
I wish 'twas again
The happy time when
I cared little about you,
Could do well without you,
But would just laugh and view you;
'Tis little I knew you!

Oh! terrible darling,
How have you sought me,
Enchanted, and caught me?
See, now, where you've brought me—
To sleep by the road-side, and dress out in rags.
Think how you found me;
Dreams come around me—
The dew of my childhood, and life's morning beam;
Now I sleep by the road-side, a wretch all in rags.
My heart that sang merrily when I was young,
Swells up like a billow and bursts in despair;
And the wreck of my hopes on sweet memory flung,
And cries on the air,
Are all that is left of the dream.

Wirrasthrue!
My father and mother,
The priest, and my brother—
Not a one has a good word for you.

But I can't part you, darling, their preaching's all vain ;
You'll burn in my heart till these thin pulses stop ;
And the wild cup of life in your fragrance I'll drain
To the last brilliant drop.
Then oblivion will cover
The shame that is over,
The brain that was mad, and the heart that was sore ;
Then, beautiful witch,
I'll be found—in a ditch,
With your kiss on my cold lips, and never rise more.

(MRS.) MARY DOWNING

174 *The Grave of MacCaura* (34)

1815–1881

AND this is thy grave, MacCaura,[1]
Here by the pathway lone ;
Where the thorn blossoms are bending
Over thy mouldered stone.
Alas ! for the sons of glory ;
Oh ! thou of the darkened brow,
And the eagle plume, and the belted clans,
Is it here thou art sleeping now ?

Oh ! wild is the spot, MacCaura,
In which they have laid thee low—
The field where thy people triumphed
Over a slaughtered foe ;
And loud was the banshee's wailing,
And deep was the clansmen's sorrow,
When with bloody hands and burning tears
They buried thee here, MacCaura.

[1] The old name of MacCarthy.

And now thy dwelling is lonely—
  King of the rushing horde ;
And now thy battles are over—
  Chief of the shining sword.
And the rolling thunder echoes
  O'er torrent and mountain free,
But alas ! and alas ! MacCaura,
  It will not awaken thee.

Farewell to thy grave, MacCaura,
  Where the slanting sunbeams shine,
And the briar and waving fern
  Over thy slumbers twine ;
Thou whose gathering summons
  Could waken the sleeping glen ;
MacCaura ! alas for thee and thine,
  'Twill never be heard again !

175 *The Banshee's Wail*

THY life was like the mountain stream,
  That in the rocky dell has birth,
Now rushing, while its waters gleam,
Exulting in the sun's warm beam ;
And, when its wild waves brightest seem,
  Dark sinking in its native earth.

Who, now, shall bid the clansmen speed
  The signal and the gathering-cry ?
Who, now, shall rein the stalwart steed ?
Who, now, shall urge the glorious deed ?
Who, now, the warrior clans shall lead
  When the battle-shout is nigh ?

(MRS.) MARY DOWNING

Though many a noble one lies dead—
    Though groaning heaps around thee lie—
Though many a gallant chief, who led
His clans, o'er night, has bravely bled;
Though many a daring soul has fled—
    Yet, oh! what were they all to thee?

The day-beam breaks on the green hill-side,
    And gleams o'er hill and river;
And the Saxon banner is floating wide,
With the blood of the hapless heroes dyed;
But MacCaura's boast, and MacCaura's pride,
    Is faded and lost for ever.

CHARLES GAVAN DUFFY

176 *Fag an Bealagh* (35)

1816–1903

'HOPE no more for fatherland,
    All its ranks are thinned or broken;'
Long a base and coward band
  Recreant words like these have spoken:
  But we preach a land awoken;
Fatherland is true and tried
  As your fears are false and hollow;
Slaves and dastards, stand aside—
  Knaves and traitors, 'Fag an Bealagh!'

Know, ye suffering brethren ours,
  Might is strong, but Right is stronger;
Saxon wiles or Saxon pow'rs
  Can enslave our land no longer
  Than your own dissensions wrong her;

Be ye one in might and mind—
  Quit the mire where cravens wallow—
And your foes shall flee like wind
  From your fearless 'Fag an Bealagh!'

Thus the mighty multitude
  Speak in accents hoarse with sorrow:
'We are fallen, but unsubdued;
  Show us whence we hope may borrow,
  And we'll fight your fight to-morrow.
Be but cautious, true, and brave,
  Where you lead us we will follow;
Hill and valley, rock and wave,
  Soon shall hear our "Fag an Bealagh!"'

Fling our banner to the wind,
  Studded o'er with names of glory;
Worth, and wit, and might, and mind,
  Poet young, and patriot hoary,
  Long shall make it shine in story.
Close your ranks—the moment's come—
  Now, ye men of Ireland! follow;
Friends of Freedom, charge them home—
  Foes of Freedom, 'Fag an Bealagh!'

177 *A Lay Sermon*

BROTHER, do you love your brother?
  Brother, are you all you seem?
Do you live for more than living?
  Has your life a law and scheme?
Are you prompt to bear its duties,
  As a brave man may beseem?

CHARLES GAVAN DUFFY

Brother, shun the mist exhaling
  From the fen of pride and doubt ;
Neither seek the house of bondage,
  Walling straitened souls about—
Bats ! who, from their narrow spy-hole,
  Cannot see a world without.

Anchor in no stagnant shallow ;
  Trust the wide and wondrous sea,
Where the tides are fresh for ever,
  And the mighty currents free :
There, perchance, O young Columbus !
  Your New World of truth may be.

Favour will not make deserving—
  Can the sunshine brighten clay ?—
Slowly must it grow to blossom,
  Fed by labour and delay ;
And the fairest bud of promise
  Bears the taint of quick decay.

You must strive for better guerdons—
  Strive to be the thing you'd seem ;
Be the thing that God hath made you,
  Channel for no borrowed stream ;
He hath lent you mind and conscience—
  See you travel in their beam !

See you scale life's misty highlands
  By this light of living truth !
And, with bosom braced for labour,
  Breast them in your manly youth ;
So, when age and care have found you,
  Shall your downward path be smooth.

CHARLES GAVAN DUFFY

Fear not, on that rugged highway,
  Life may want its lawful zest ;
Sunny glens are in the mountain,
  Where the weary feet may rest,
Cooled in streams that gush for ever
  From a loving mother's breast.

'Simple heart and simple pleasures,'
  So they write life's golden rule.
Honour won by supple baseness,
  State that crowns a cankered fool,
Gleam as gleam the gold and purple
  On a hot and rancid pool.

Wear no show of wit or science,
  But the gems you've won and weighed ;
Thefts, like ivy on a ruin,
  Make the rifts they seem to shade :
Are you not a thief and beggar
  In the rarest spoils arrayed ?

Shadows deck a sunny landscape,
  Making brighter all the bright ;
So, my brother ! care and danger
  On a loving nature light,
Bringing all its latent beauties
  Out upon the common sight.

Love the things that God created,
  Make your brother's need your care ;
Scorn and hate repel God's blessings,
  But where love's is, they are there ;
As the moonbeams light the waters,
  Leaving rock and sand-bank bare.

Thus, my brother, grow and flourish,
Fearing none and loving all ;
For the true man needs no patron—
He shall climb, and never crawl ;
Two things fashion their own channel—
The strong man and the waterfall.

178 *Inis-Eoghain* (36)

GOD bless the grey mountains of Dun-na-n-gall ! [1]
God bless royal Aileach ! the pride of them all ;
For she sits, evermore, like a queen on her throne,
And smiles on the valleys of green Inis-Eoghain.
And fair are the valleys of green Inis-Eoghain,
And hardy the fishers that call them their own—
A race that nor traitor nor coward has known
Enjoys the fair valleys of green Inis-Eoghain.

Oh ! simple and bold are the bosoms they bear,
Like the hills that with silence and nature they share ;
For our God, who hath planted their home near his own,
Breath'd His Spirit abroad upon fair Inis-Eoghain.
Then praise to our Father for wild Inis-Eoghain,
Where fiercely for ever the surges are thrown ;
Nor weather nor fortune a tempest hath blown
Could shake the strong bosoms of brave Inis-Eoghain.

[1] Donegal.

See the beautiful Cul-daim [1] careering along,
A type of their manhood so stately and strong—
On the weary for ever its tide is bestown,
So they share with the stranger in fair Inis-Eoghain.
God guard the kind homesteads of fair Inis-Eoghain,
Which manhood and virtue have chosen for their own;
Not long shall the nation in slavery groan
That rears the tall peasants of fair Inis-Eoghain.

Like the oak of St. Bride, which nor devil nor Dane,
Nor Saxon nor Dutchman, could rend from her fane,
They have clung by the creed and the cause of their own,
Through the midnight of danger, in true Inis-Eoghain.
Then shout for the glories of old Inis-Eoghain,
The stronghold that foeman has never o'erthrown—
The soul and the spirit, the blood and the bone
That guard the green valleys of true Inis-Eoghain.

Nor purer of old was the tongue of the Gael
When the charging 'aboo' made the foreigner quail,
Than it gladdens the stranger in welcome's soft tone
In the home-loving cabins of kind Inis-Eoghain.
Oh! flourish, ye homesteads of kind Inis-Eoghain,
Where seeds of a people's redemption are sown;
Right soon shall the fruit of that sowing have grown,
To bless the kind homesteads of Green Inis-Eoghain.

When they tell us the tale of a spell-stricken band,
All entranced, with their bridles and broadswords in hand,
Who await but the word to give Erin her own,
They can read you that riddle in proud Inis-Eoghain!

[1] The Culdaff, a river in the Inishowen peninsula.

Hurrah for the spæmen [1] of proud Inis-Eoghain !
Long live the wild seers of stout Inis-Eoghain ;
May Mary, our mother, be deaf to their moan
Who love not the promise of proud Inis-Eoghain !

179 *The Irish Rapparees* (37)

A Peasant Ballad of 1691

RIGH Shemus [2] he has gone to France, and left his crown behind ;
Ill luck be theirs, both day and night, put running in his mind !
Lord Lucan followed after, with his Slashers brave and true,
And now the doleful keen is raised—'What will poor Ireland do ? (38)
What must poor Ireland do ?
Our luck,' they say, 'has gone to France—what can poor Ireland do ?'

Oh ! never fear for Ireland, for she has soldiers still ;
For Rory's boys are in the wood, and Remy's on the hill ;
And never had poor Ireland more loyal hearts than these—
May God be kind and good to them, the faithful Rapparees !
The fearless Rapparees !
The jewel were you, Rory, with your Irish Rapparees !

[1] Persons gifted with second sight.
[2] King James II.

Oh, black's your heart, Clan Oliver, and colder than the clay!
Oh, high's your head, Clan Sassenach, since Sarsfield's gone away!
It's little love you bear to us, for sake of long ago;
But hold your hand, for Ireland still can strike a deadly blow—
Can strike a mortal blow—
Och, dar-a-Críost![1] 'tis she that still could strike a deadly blow!

The Master's bawn, the Master's seat, a surly bodagh[2] fills;
The Master's son, an outlawed man, is riding on the hills.
But God be praised that round him throng, as thick as summer bees,
The swords that guarded Limerick wall—his loyal Rapparees!
His loving Rapparees!
Who dare say 'no' to Rory Oge, with all his Rapparees?

Black Billy Grimes of Latnamard, he racked us long and sore—
God rest the faithful hearts he broke!—we'll never see them more!
But I'll go bail he'll break no more, while Truagh has gallows-trees;
For why?—he met, one lonely night, the fearless Rapparees!
The angry Rapparees!
They never sin no more, my boys, who cross the Rapparees!

[1] Word of Christ. [2] A churl.

Now, Sassenach and Cromweller, take heed of what
I say—
Keep down your black and angry looks, that scorn us
night and day:
For there's a just and wrathful Judge, that every
action sees,
And He'll make strong, to right our wrong, the
faithful Rapparees!
The fearless Rapparees!
The men that rode at Sarsfield's side, the roving
Rapparees!

FRANCES BROWN

180 *Songs of our Land*

1816–1879

SONGS of our land, ye are with us for ever:
The power and the splendour of thrones pass
away;
But yours is the might of some far flowing river,
Through summer's bright roses, or autumn's decay.
Ye treasure each voice of the swift-passing ages,
And truth, which time writeth on leaves or on
sand;
Ye bring us the bright thoughts of poets and sages,
And keep them among us, old songs of our land.

The bards may go down to the place of their
slumbers;
The lyre of the charmer be hushed in the grave;
But far in the future the power of their numbers
Shall kindle the hearts of our faithful and brave.

It will waken an echo in souls deep and lonely,
Like voices of reeds by the summer breeze fanned;
It will call up a spirit of freedom, when only
Her breathings are heard in the songs of our land.

For they keep a record of those, the true-hearted,
Who fell with the cause they had vowed to maintain;
They show us bright shadows of glory departed,
Of the love that grew cold, and the hope that was vain.
The page may be lost and the pen long forsaken,
And weeds may grow wild o'er the brave heart and hand;
But ye are still left when all else hath been taken,
Like streams in the desert, sweet songs of our land.

Songs of our land! ye have followed the stranger
With power over ocean and desert afar,
Ye have gone with our wand'rers through distance and danger,
And gladdened their path like a home-guiding star;
With the breath of our mountains in summers long vanished,
And visions that passed like a wave from our strand;
With hope for their country and joy from her banished,
Ye come to us ever, sweet songs of our land.

The spring-time may come with the song of her glory,
To bid the green heart of the forest rejoice ;
But the pine of the mountain, though blasted and hoary,
And rock in the desert can send forth a voice.
It is thus in their triumphs for deep desolations,
While ocean waves roll, or the mountains shall stand,
Still hearts that are bravest and best of the nations,
Shall glory and live in the songs of our land.

181 *The Streams*

YOUR murmurs bring the pleasant breath
Of many a sylvan scene ;
They tell of sweet and sunny vales,
And woodlands wildly green ;
Ye cheer the lonely heart of age,—
Ye fill the exile's dreams
With hope and home and memory,—
Ye unforgotten streams.

Too soon the blessèd springs of love
To bitter fountains turn,
And deserts drink the stream that flows
From hope's exhaustless urn ;
And faint, upon the waves of life,
May fall the summer beams ;
But they linger long and bright with you,
Ye sweet unchanging streams.

FRANCES BROWN

The bards—the ancient bards—who sang
  When thought and song were new,—
O mighty waters! did they learn
  Their minstrelsy from you?
For still, methinks, your voices blend
  With all their glorious themes,
That flow for ever fresh and free
  As the eternal streams.

Well might the sainted seer of old,
  Who trod the tearless shore,
Like many waters deem the voice
  The angel hosts adore!
For still, where deep the rivers roll,
  Or far the torrent gleams,
Our spirits hear the voice of God
  Amid the rush of streams!

MICHAEL JOSEPH BARRY

182 *The Sword*

1817–1889

WHAT rights the brave?
    The sword!
What frees the slave?
    The sword!
What cleaves in twain
The despot's chain,
And makes his gyves and dungeons vain?
    The sword!

Chorus

Then cease thy proud task never
While rests a link to sever !
Guard of the free,
We'll cherish thee,
And keep thee bright for ever !

What checks the knave ?
The sword !
What smites to save ?
The sword !
What wreaks the wrong
Unpunished long,
At last, upon the guilty strong ?
The sword ?

Chorus

Then cease thy proud task never, etc.

What shelters right ?
The sword !
What makes it might ?
The sword !
What strikes the crown
Of tyrants down,
And answers with its flash their frown ?
The sword !

Chorus

Then cease thy proud task never, etc.

Still be thou true,
Good sword!
We'll die or do,
Good sword!
Leap forth to light
If tyrants smite,
And trust our arms to wield thee right,
Good sword!

Chorus

Yes! cease thy proud task never
While rests a link to sever!
Guard of the free,
We'll cherish thee,
And keep thee bright for ever!

183 *Hymn of Freedom*

GOD of Peace! before thee,
Peaceful, here we kneel,
Humbly to implore thee
For a nation's weal.
Calm her sons' dissensions,
Bid their discord cease,
End their mad contentions—
Hear us, God of Peace!

God of Love! low bending,
To thy throne we turn;
Let thy rays, descending,
Through our island burn.

Let no strife divide us,
  But, from Heaven above,
Look on us and guide us—
  Hear us, God of Love!

God of Battles! aid us;
  Let no despot's might
Trample or degrade us,
  Seeking this our right!
Arm us for the danger;
  Keep all craven fear
To our breasts a stranger—
  God of Battles! hear.

God of Right! preserve us
  Just—as we are strong;
Let no passion swerve us
  To one act of wrong;
Let no thought unholy
  Come our cause to blight;
Thus we pray thee, lowly—
  Hear us, God of Right!

God of Vengeance! smite us
  With thy shaft sublime,
If one bond unite us
  Forged in fraud or crime!
But if, humbly kneeling,
  We implore thine ear,
For our rights appealing—
  God of Nations! hear.

MICHAEL JOSEPH BARRY

184 *The Wild Geese* (39)

THE Wild Geese—the Wild Geese—'tis long since
they flew
O'er the billowy ocean's bright bosom of blue;
For the foot of the false-hearted stranger had curst
The shores on whose fond breast they'd settled at first;
And they sought them a home afar off o'er the sea,
Where their pinions, at least, might be chainless and
free.

The Wild Geese—the Wild Geese—sad, sad was the
wail
That followed their flight on the easterly gale;
But the eyes that had wept o'er their vanishing track
Ne'er brightened to welcome the wanderers back;
The home of their youth was the land of the slave,
And they died on that shore far away o'er the wave.

The Wild Geese—the Wild Geese—their coming
once more,
Was the long-cherished hope of that desolate shore,
For the loved ones behind knew it would yet be free,
If they flew on their white pinions back o'er the sea;
But vainly the hope of these lonely ones burned,
The Wild geese—the Wild geese—they never returned.

The Wild Geese—the Wild Geese—hark! heard ye
that cry?
And marked ye that white flock o'erspreading the sky?
Can ye read not the omen? Joy, joy to the slave,
And gladness and strength to the hearts of the brave;
For Wild Geese are coming at length o'er the sea,
And Eirinn, green Eirinn, once more shall be free!

DENIS FLORENCE McCARTHY

185 *The Clan of MacCaura* (40)

1817–1882

OH! bright are the names of the chieftains and sages,
That shine like the stars through the darkness of ages,
Whose deeds are inscribed on the pages of story,
There for ever to live in the sunshine of glory—
Heroes of history, phantoms of fable,
Charlemagne's champions, and Arthur's Round Table;
Oh! but they all a new lustre could borrow
From the glory that hangs round the name of MacCaura!

Proud should thy heart beat, descendant of Heber,
Lofty thy head as the shrines of the Guebre,
Like them are the halls of thy forefathers shattered,
Like theirs is the wealth of thy palaces scattered.
Their fire is extinguished—your flag long unfurled—
But how proud were ye both in the dawn of the world!
And should both fade away, oh! what heart would not sorrow
O'er the towers of the Guebre—the name of MacCaura!

What a moment of glory to cherish and dream on,
When far o'er the sea came the ships of Heremon,
With Heber, and Ir,[1] and the Spanish patricians,
To free Inisfail from the spells of magicians.

[1] Heremon and Ir were sons of Milesius.

Oh ! reason had these for their quaking and pallor,
For what magic can equal the strong sword of
valour ?
Better than spells are the axe and the arrow,
When wielded or flung by the hand of MacCaura !

From that hour a MacCaura had reigned in his pride
O'er Desmond's green valleys and rivers so wide,
From thy waters, Lismore, to the torrents and rills
That are leaping for ever down Brandon's brown
hills ;
The billows of Bantry, the meadows of Bear,
The wilds of Evaugh, and the groves of Glancare,
From the Shannon's soft shores to the banks of the
Barrow—
All owned the proud sway of the princely MacCaura !

In the house of Miodchuart, by princes surrounded, (41)
How noble his step when the trumpet was sounded,
And his clansmen bore proudly his broad shield before
him,
And hung it on high in that bright palace o'er him !
On the left of the monarch the chieftain was seated,
And happy was he whom his proud glances greeted,
'Mid monarchs and chiefs at the great Feis of Tara—
Oh ! none was to rival the princely MacCaura !

To the halls of the Red Branch, when conquest was
o'er, (42)
The champions their rich spoils of victory bore,
And the sword of the Briton, the shield of the Dane,
Flashed bright as the sun on the walls of Eamhain ;

There Dathy and Niall bore trophies of war,
From the peaks of the Alps and the waves of the
Loire; (43)
But no knight ever bore from the hills of Iveragh
The breastplate or axe of a conquered MacCaura!

In chasing the red deer what step was the fleetest,
In singing the love-song what voice was the sweetest,
What breast was the foremost in courting the
danger—
What door was the widest to shelter the stranger?
In friendship the truest, in battle the bravest—
In revel the gayest, in council the gravest—
A hunter to-day and a victor to-morrow?
Oh! who but a chief of the princely MacCaura!

But, oh! proud MacCaura, what anguish to touch on
The one fatal stain of thy princely escutcheon—
In thy story's bright garden the one spot of bleak-
ness—
Through ages of valour the one hour of weakness!
Thou, the heir of a thousand chiefs, sceptred and
royal—
Thou, to kneel to the Norman and swear to be loyal!
Oh! a long night of horror, and outrage, and sorrow,
Have we wept for thy treason, base Diarmid Mac-
Caura!

Soon, soon, didst thou pay for that error in woe—(44)
Thy life to the Butler—thy crown to the foe—
Thy castles dismantled, and strewn on the sod,
And the homes of the weak, and the abbeys of
God!

No more in thy halls is the wayfarer fed,
Nor the rich mead sent round, nor the soft heather
spread,
Nor the clairseach's sweet notes, now in mirth, now in
sorrow,—
All, all have gone by, but the name of MacCaura!

MacCaura, the pride of thy house is gone by,
But its name cannot fade, and its fame cannot die,
Though the Arigideen, with its silver waves, shine (45)
Around no green forests or castles of thine,—
Though the shrines that you founded no incense doth
hallow,
Nor hymns float in peace down the echoing Allo—
One treasure thou keepest — one hope for the
morrow,—
True hearts yet beat of the clan of MacCaura!

186 *The Dead Tribune*

THE awful shadow of a great man's death
Falls on this land, so sad and dark before,—
Dark with the famine and the fever breath,
And mad dissensions gnawing at its core.
Oh! let us hush foul discord's maniac roar,
And make a mournful truce, however brief,
Like hostile armies when the day is o'er!
And thus devote the night-time of our grief
To tears and prayers for him, the great departed
Chief.

DENIS FLORENCE McCARTHY

In 'Genoa the Superb' O'Connell dies—
  That city of Columbus by the sea,
Beneath the canopy of azure skies,
  As high and cloudless as his fame must be.
Is it mere chance or higher destiny
  That brings these names together? One, the bold
Wanderer in ways that none had trod but he—
  The other, too, exploring paths untold;
One a new world would seek, and one would save the old!

With childlike incredulity we cry,
  It cannot be that great career has run,
It cannot be but in the eastern sky
  Again will blaze that mighty world-watch'd sun!
Ah! fond deceit, the east is black and dun,
  Death's black, impervious cloud is on the skies;
Toll the deep bell, and fire the evening gun,
  Let honest sorrow moisten manly eyes:
A glorious sun has set that never more shall rise!

Brothers, who struggle yet in Freedom's van,
  Where'er your forces o'er the world are spread,
The last great Champion of the Rights of Man—
  The last great Tribune of the World is dead!
Join in our grief, and let our tears be shed
  Without reserve or coldness on his bier;
Look on his life as on a map outspread—
  His fight for Freedom—Freedom far and near—
And if a speck should rise, oh! hide it with a tear!

To speak his praises little need have we—
  To tell the wonders wrought within these waves:
Enough, so well he taught us to be free,
  That even to him we could not kneel as slaves.
Oh! let our tears be fast-destroying graves,
  Where doubt and difference may for ever lie,
Buried and hid as in sepulchral caves;
  And let Love's fond and reverential eye
Alone behold the Star new risen in the sky!

But can it be, that well-known form is stark?
  Can it be true, that burning heart is chill?
Oh! can it be that twinkling eye is dark?
  And that great thunder voice is hush'd and still?
Never again upon the famous hill
  Will he preside as Monarch of the Land,
With myriad myriads subject to his will;
  Never again shall raise that powerful hand,
To rouse, to warm, to check, to kindle, and command!

The twinkling eye, so full of changeful light,
  Is dimmed and darkened in a dread eclipse;
The withering scowl—the smile so sunny bright,
  Alike have faded from his voiceless lips.
The words of power, the mirthful, merry quips,
  The mighty onslaught, and the quick reply,
The biting taunts that cut like stinging whips,
  The homely truth, the lessons grave and high,
All—all are with the past, but cannot, shall not die!

DENIS FLORENCE McCARTHY

187 *A Lament*

THE dream is over,
  The vision has flown,
Dead leaves are lying
Where roses have blown ;
Wither'd and strown
Are the hopes I cherished,—
All hath perished
But grief alone.

My heart was a garden
Where fresh leaves grew ;
Flowers there were many,
And weeds a few ;
Cold winds blew,
And the frosts came thither,
For flowers will wither,
And weeds renew !

Youth's bright palace
Is overthrown,
With its diamond sceptre
And golden throne ;
As a time-worn stone
Its turrets are humbled,—
All hath crumbled
But grief alone !

Whither, oh ! whither
Have fled away
The dreams and hopes
Of my early day ?

DENIS FLORENCE McCARTHY

Ruined and grey
Are the towers I builded ;
And the beams that gilded—
Ah ! where are they ?

Once this world
Was fresh and bright,
With its golden noon
And its starry night ;
Glad and light,
By mountain and river,
Have I bless'd the Giver
With hushed delight.

These were the days
Of story and song,
When Hope had a meaning
And Faith was strong.
'Life will be long,
And lit with love's gleamings :'
Such were my dreamings,
But, ah ! how wrong.

Youth's illusions,
One by one,
Have passed like clouds
That the sun looked on.
While morning shone,
How purple their fringes !
How ashy their tinges
When that was gone !

DENIS FLORENCE McCARTHY

Darkness that cometh
Ere morn has fled—
Boughs that wither
Ere fruits are shed—
Death bells instead
Of a bridal's pealings—
Such are my feelings,
Since Hope is dead!

Sad is the knowledge
That cometh with years—
Bitter the tree
That is watered with tears;
Truth appears,
With his wise predictions,
Then vanish the fictions
Of boyhood's years.

As fire-flies fade
When the nights are damp—
As meteors are quenched
In a stagnant swamp—
Thus Charlemagne's camp,
Where the Paladins rally,
And the Diamond Valley,
And the Wonderful Lamp,

And all the wonders
Of Ganges and Nile,
And Haroun's rambles,
And Crusoe's isle,
And Princes who smile
On the Genii's daughters
'Neath the Orient's waters
Full many a mile,

And all that the pen
Of Fancy can write,
Must vanish
In manhood's misty light—
Squire and knight,
And damosel's glances,
Sunny romances
So pure and bright !

These have vanished,
And what remains ?
Life's budding garlands
Have turned to chains—
Its beams and rains
Feed but docks and thistles,
And sorrow whistles
O'er desert plains !

The dove will fly
From a ruined nest—
Love will not dwell
In a troubled breast—
The heart has no zest
To sweeten life's dolour—
If Love, the Consoler,
Be not its guest !

The dream is over,
The vision has flown ;
Dead leaves are lying
Where roses have blown ;
Wither'd and strown
Are the hopes I cherished,—
All hath perished
But grief alone !

DENIS FLORENCE McCARTHY

188 *Over the Sea*

SAD eyes! why are ye steadfastly gazing
Over the sea?
Is it the flock of the Ocean-shepherd grazing
Like lambs on the lea?—
Is it the dawn on the orient billows blazing
Allureth ye?

Sad heart! why art thou tremblingly beating—
What troubleth thee?
There where the waves from the fathomless water come greeting,
Wild with their glee!
Or rush from the rocks, like a routed battalion retreating,
Over the sea?

Sad feet! why are ye constantly straying
Down by the sea?
There where the winds in the sandy harbour are playing
Child-like and free;
What is the charm, whose potent enchantment obeying,
There chaineth ye?

Oh! sweet is the dawn, and bright are the colours it glows in!
Yet not to me!
To the beauty of God's bright creation my bosom is frozen!
Nought can I see!

Since she has departed—the dear one, the loved one,
the chosen,
Over the sea !

Pleasant it was when the billows did struggle and
wrestle,
Pleasant to see !
Pleasant to climb the tall cliffs where the sea-birds
nestle,
When near to thee !
Nought can I now behold but the track of thy vessel
Over the sea !

Long as a Lapland winter, which no pleasant sunlight
cheereth,
The summer shall be :
Vainly shall autumn be gay, in the rich robes it
weareth,
Vainly for me !
No joy can I feel till the prow of thy vessel appeareth
Over the sea !

Sweeter than summer, which tenderly, motherly
bringeth
Flowers to the bee !
Sweeter than autumn, which bounteously, lovingly
flingeth
Fruits on the tree !
Shall be winter, when homeward returning, thy swift
vessel wingeth
Over the sea !

DENNY LANE

189 *Kate of Araglen*

1818–1896

WHEN first I saw thee, Kate,
That summer evening late,
Down at the orchard gate
Of Araglen,
I felt I'd ne'er before
Seen one so fair, astór ;
I feared I'd never more
See thee again.
I stopped and gazed at thee—
My footfall, luckily,
Reached not thy ear, though we
Stood there so near ;
While from thy lips a strain,
Soft as the summer rain,
Sad as a lover's pain,
Fell on my ear.

I've heard the lark in June,
The harp's wild, plaintive tune,
The thrush, that aye too soon
Gives o'er his strain—
I've heard in hushed delight
The mellow horn at night,
Waking the echoes light
Of wild Loch Lein ;
But neither echoing horn,
Nor thrush upon the thorn,
Nor lark at early morn
Hymning in air,

DENNY LANE

Nor harper's lay divine,
E'er witched this heart of mine,
Like that sweet voice of thine,
That evening there.

And when some rustling, dear,
Fell on thy listening ear,
You thought your brother near,
And named his name,
I could not answer, though,
As luck would have it so,
His name and mine, you know,
Were both the same;
Hearing no answering sound,
You glanced in doubt around
With timid look, and found
It was not he;
Turning away your head,
And blushing rosy red,
Like a wild fawn you fled,
Far, far, from me.

The swan upon the lake,
The wild rose in the brake,
The golden clouds that make
The west their throne,
The wild ash by the stream,
The full moon's silver beam,
The evening star's soft gleam,
Shining alone;
The lily robed in white—
All, all are fair and bright;
But ne'er on earth was sight
So bright, so fair,

As that one glance of thee,
That I caught then, machree,
It stole my heart from me
That evening there.

And now you're mine alone,
That heart is all my own—
That heart that ne'er hath known
A flame before.
That form of mould divine,
That snowy hand of thine,
Those locks of gold, are mine
For evermore.
Was lover ever seen,
As blest as thine, Kathleen?
Hath lover ever been
More fond, more true?
Thine is my ev'ry vow!
For ever dear, as now!
Queen of my heart be thou,
Mo cailin ruadh![1]

190 *Lament of the Irish Maiden*

ON Carrigdhoun the heath is brown,
The clouds are dark o'er Ardnalee,
And many a stream comes rushing down
To swell the angry Ownabwee;
The moaning blast is sweeping fast
Through many a leafless tree,
And I'm alone, for he is gone,
My hawk has flown, ochone machree!

[1] My golden-haired girl.

DENNY LANE

The heath was green on Carrigdhoun,
  Bright shone the sun on Ardnalee,
The dark green trees bent trembling down
  To kiss the slumbering Ownabwee ;
That happy day, 'twas but last May,
  'Tis like a dream to me,
When Donnell swore, ay, o'er and o'er,
  We'd part no more, astór machree !

Soft April show'rs and bright May flowers
  Will bring the summer back again,
But will they bring me back the hours
  I spent with my brave Donnell then ?
'Tis but a chance, for he's gone to France,
  To wear the fleur-de-lis ;
But I'll follow you, my Donnell Dhu,[1]
  For still I'm true to you, machree !

CECIL FRANCES ALEXANDER

191 *Ruth*

1823–1895

IN the land of Bethlehem Judah
  Let us linger, let us wander :
Ephrath's sorrow, Rachel's pillar,
Lieth in the valley yonder ;
And the yellow barley harvest
Floods it with a golden glory.
Let us back into the old time,
Dreaming of her tender story,

[1] Black Daniel.

Of her true heart's strong devotion,
From beyond the Dead Sea water,
From the heathen land of Moab—
Mahlon's wife, and Mara's daughter.

On the terebinth and fig-tree
Suns of olden time are shining,
And the dark leaf of the olive
Scarcely shows its silver lining ;
For still noon is on the thicket,
Where the blue-neck'd pigeons listen
To their own reproachful music ;
And the red pomegranates glisten.
As a queen a golden circlet,
As a maid might wear a blossom,
So the valley wears the cornfields
Heaving on her fertile bosom :
And the round grey hills stand o'er them,
All their terraced vineyards swelling,
Like the green waves of a forest,
Up to David's royal dwelling.

Lo ! the princely-hearted Boaz
Moves among his reapers slowly,
And the widow'd child of Moab
Bends behind the gleaners lowly ;
Gathering, gleaning as she goeth
Down the slopes, and up the hollows,
While the love of old Naomi,
Like a guardian angel, follows ;
And he speaketh words of kindness,
Words of kindness calm and stately,
Till he breaks the springs of gladness
That lay cold and frozen lately ;

And the love-flowers that had faded
Deep within her bosom lonely,
Slowly open as he questions,
Soon for him to blossom only,—
When that spring shall fill with music,
Like an overflowing river,
All his homestead, and those flowers
Bloom beside his hearth for ever.
Mother of a line of princes,
Wrought into that race's story,
Whom the Godhead, breaking earthward,
Mark'd with an unearthly glory.

Still he walks among the reapers :
The long day is nearly over,
And the lonely mountain partridge
Seeks afar his scanty cover ;
And the flocks of wild blue pigeons,
That had glean'd behind the gleaner,
Find their shelter in the thicket :
And the cloudless sky grows sheener
With a sudden flush of crimson,
Steeping in a fiery lustre
Every sheaf-top in the valley,
On the hill-side every cluster.

Slowly, slowly fade, fair picture,
Yellow lights and purple shadows,
On the valley, on the mountain,
And sweet Ruth among the meadows.
Yet delay, true heart, and teach us,
Pausing in thy matron beauty,
Care of elders, love of kindred,
All unselfish thought and duty.

Linger, Boaz, noble minded!
Teach us, haughty and unsparing,
Tender care for lowlier station,
Kindly speech, and courteous bearing,
Still each softest, loveliest colour,
Shrine the form beloved and loving,
Heroine of our hearts' first poem,
Through our childhoods' dreamland moving;
When the great old Bible open'd,
And a pleasant pastoral measure,
As our mothers read the story,
Fill'd our infant hearts with pleasure.

192 *The Irish Mother's Lament*

HALF the long night, my children, I lie waking
Till the dawn rustles in the old thorn-tree,
Then dream of you, while the red morn is breaking
Beyond that broad salt sea;

In this poor room, where many a time the measure
Of your low, regular breathing in mine ear,
Brought to my listening heart a keener pleasure
Than any music clear;

Here, where, your soft heads in my bosom laying,
Ye nestled, with your hearts to my heart press'd;
And I have felt your little fingers playing,
All night, around my breast;

On the brown hill-side, where so oft together,
Roaming forth idly, when our work was done,
We heard the moor-fowl in the purple heather,
Crowing at set of sun;

CECIL FRANCES ALEXANDER

I am alone—still on my threshold lieth
The shadow of the thorn ye play'd beneath,
Still to her mate, at eve, the brown bird crieth,
Out of the lonely heath :

But in my desolate house no sound of laughter,
And by my dreary hearth no daughter's face ;
I watch the black smoke curling round the rafter,
I see each empty place.

How could ye leave me ? Did ye think a mother
Was natured like a bird in summer's prime,
Who leaves her young brood, hopeful of another
In the next glad spring time ?

They tell me your new home is rich and sunny,
More than this dwelling on the mountain cold,
Fair as the land that flowed with milk and honey,
In the great Book of old.

They tell me flowers most beautiful are blowing
Out on your waysides, on your common trees,
But will ye find the mother's love there growing,
Ye gave for things like these ?

And some have told me souls are never parted,
Faith leads us all unto the same bright Heaven,
Nor meet it is, that woman, Christian-hearted,
To such wild grief be given ;

Ah ! But I know in that bright land is wanting,
On Sunday morn, the sweet church-calling bell,
The pastoral word, the gather'd voices chanting
Hymns that ye loved so well.

The cares of this great world, its toils, its beauty,
  Will dim your eyes, and grow about your heart,
And shut out heavenly hope and Christian duty,
    And every better part.

The prayers we pray'd together at God's altar,
  The creed ye lisp'd into my ear at night,
The verses that I taught your lips to falter
    Will be forgotten quite.

Ah me! could I but think those lips were making,
  In some far church, the vows they used to pour,
I could lie down without this wild heart-aching
    Lest we should meet no more.

Sad mother! for the visible presence pining
  Of eyes that smile, and lips that fondly move,
Things that, like dewy nights and bright sun's shining,
    Nurse the sweet flowers of love.

But, sadder far, when the wild waves that sever,
  Sing to her ear in one foreboding strain:—
'We part you now, but must ye part for ever?'
    Echoing the heart's dull pain.

193 *The Place of Remembrance*

WHERE wouldst thou think of her? Where the young flowers
  Spring through the turf where so often she lay,
Wearily watching the long summer hours,
  Last of her lifetime, fleet slowly away?

There by the garden-wall, cover'd with roses,
  Where, in the shelter, she linger'd so late,
Under the tree where the shadow reposes,
  Over the spot where at noontime she sate?

Down the green walk where you drew her so slowly,
  Patient and sweet in her helpless decay,
In her own chamber, the haunted and holy,
  There wouldst thou dream of thy darling to-day?

Where wouldst thou think of her, darkling and
    dreary?
  In the lone room where her spirit took flight,
Passing away, as a child that is weary
  Turns to its cradle, nor wishes good-night?

Where, like a wild dream, thy heart still remembers
  The lingering smile on the motionless clay—
A flame that lives on in the light of its embers—
  There wouldst thou dream of thy darling to-day?

Not in the greenwood glade—hearts need not borrow
  Helps from dead nature to teach them to weep,
Not in that lonely room;—why should thy sorrow
  Brood o'er her, silent and shrouded in sleep?

Go to the altar, where, morning and even,
  The low voice has mingled, the bright head bow'd
    down,
Pouring her heart out in commune with Heaven,
  Taking His cross up who gave her the crown.

Everywhere, everywhere holdeth communion,
  Loving and cheering, her spirit with thine,
But in a holier, happier union,
  Meet you with praises to-night at the shrine.

Then in the vale, when the waters are swelling,
  Go where the desolate bird finds a nest,
Go to His holy and beautiful dwelling,
  The Courts of the Lord, where she dwelt and was
    blest.

Where the Church mingles her happy departed,
  Victors gone home with the strugglers who stay,
Bringing forth balm for the desolate-hearted,—
  There shouldst thou dream of thy darling to-day!

194 *Dreams*

BEYOND, beyond the mountain line,
  The grey-stone and the boulder,
Beyond the growth of dark green pine,
  That crowns its western shoulder,
There lies that fairy-land of mine,
  Unseen of a beholder.

Its fruits are all like rubies rare;
  Its streams are clear as glasses;
There golden castles hang in air,
  And purple grapes in masses,
And noble knights and ladies fair
  Come riding down the passes.

CECIL FRANCES ALEXANDER

Ah me! they say if I could stand
  Upon those mountain ledges,
I should but see on either hand
  Plain fields and dusty hedges;
And yet I know my fairy-land
  Lies somewhere o'er their edges.

RALPH VARIAN

195 *Mo Bouchailín Bán*[1]

c. 1820–1889

MO Bouchailín bán
  Is up with the dawn,
And over the mountain, through forest and lawn;
  By green bank and slip,
  Where golden flowers dip,
The dew of the morning is still on his lip.

And down by the castle, right over the hill,
Mo Bouchailín works, the brown lands to till;
But still at the dawn we meet at the slip,
Where white lilies float and golden flowers dip.

  Through field as he goes,
  He pulls the wild rose,
And blossoms of blue from the green rushy bawn;
  But over the rose
  His damask cheek glows,
And the blue eye is bright of my Bouchailín bán.

[1] *Mo Bhuachailín* (pron. *vouchaleen*) *Bán* = Fair-haired little boy.

RALPH VARIAN

He talks not like men who think woman can't know
When Liberty rises or Freedom is low ;
And often our thoughts for old Ireland are high,
Like the sun on the mountain when painting the sky.
My Bouchailín bán
Is clear as the dawn,
No shadow of falsehood to cloud his blue eye ;
The plans of untruth
'Tis he can confute,
And tyranny shrinks when he stands to defy.

And sometimes his blue eyes will dream in the dawn ;
And fitful and wild is mo Bouchailín bán ;
But as infancy kind, he is dear to my mind,
And the shield of my life is mo Bouchailín bán !
Mo Bouchailín bán.
The dew on the lip of mo Bouchailín bán
Is gossamer gold, strung with beads of the dawn ;
What hard heart shall dare to brush them away ?
No hard heart but mine, at the dawning of day !
Mo Bouchailín bán.

LADY WILDE (46)

196 *The Exodus*

1820?–1896

'A MILLION a decade !' Calmly and cold
The units are read by our statesmen sage ;
Little they think of a Nation old,
Fading away from history's page ;
Outcast weeds by a desolate sea—
Fallen leaves of humanity.

LADY WILDE

'A million a decade!'—of human wrecks,
  Corpses lying in fever sheds—
Corpses huddled on foundering decks,
  And shroudless dead on their rocky beds;
    Nerve and muscle, and heart and brain,
    Lost to Ireland—lost in vain.

'A million a decade!' Count ten by ten,
  Column and line of the record fair;
Each unit stands for ten thousand men,
  Staring with blank, dead eye-balls there;
    Strewn like blasted trees on the sod,
    Men that were made in the image of God.

'A million a decade!'—and nothing done;
  The Cæsars had less to conquer a world;
And the war for the Right not yet begun,
  The banner of Freedom not yet unfurled:
    The soil is fed by the weed that dies;
    If forest leaves fall, yet they fertilise.

But ye—dead, dead, not climbing the height,
  Not clearing a path for the future to tread;
Not opening the golden portals of light,
  Ere the gate was choked by your piled-up dead:
    Martyrs ye, yet never a name
    Shines on the golden roll of Fame.

Had ye rent one gyve of the festering chain,
  Strangling the life of the Nation's soul;
Poured your life-blood by river and plain,
  Yet touched with your dead hand Freedom's goal;
    Left of heroes one footprint more
    On our soil, tho' stamped in your gore—

LADY WILDE

We could triumph while mourning the brave,
  Dead for all that was holy and just,
And write, through our tears, on the grave,
  As we flung down the dust to dust—
    'They died for their country, but led
    Her up from the sleep of the dead.'

'A million a decade!' What does it mean?
  A Nation dying of inner decay—
A churchyard silence where life has been—
  The base of the pyramid crumbling away:
    A drift of men gone over the sea,
    A drift of the dead where men should be.

Was it for this ye plighted your word,
  Crowned and crownless rulers of men?
Have ye kept faith with your crucified Lord,
  And fed His sheep till He comes again?
    Or fled like hireling shepherds away,
    Leaving the fold the gaunt wolf's prey?

Have ye given of your purple to cover,
  Have ye given of your gold to cheer,
Have ye given of your love, as a lover
  Might cherish the bride he held dear,
    Broken and Sacrament-bread to feed
    Souls and bodies in uttermost need?

Ye stand at the Judgement-bar to-day—
  The Angels are counting the dead-roll, too;
Have ye trod in the pure and perfect way,
  And ruled for God as the crowned should do?
    Count our dead—before Angels and men,
    Ye're judged and doomed by the statist's pen.

197 *The Famine Year*

WEARY men, what reap ye?—Golden corn for the stranger.
What sow ye?—Human corses that wait for the avenger.
Fainting forms, hunger-stricken, what see ye in the offing?—
Stately ships to bear our food away, amid the stranger's scoffing.
There's a proud array of soldiers—what do they round your door?
They guard our master's granaries from the thin hands of the poor.
Pale mothers, wherefore weeping? Would to God that we were dead—
Our children swoon before us, and we cannot give them bread.

Little children, tears are strange upon your infant faces,
God meant you but to smile within your mother's soft embraces.
Oh, we know not what is smiling, and we know not what is dying;
But we're hungry, very hungry, and we cannot stop our crying.
And some of us grow cold and white—we know not what it means;
But, as they lie beside us we tremble in our dreams.
There's a gaunt crowd on the highway—are you come to pray to man,
With hollow eyes that cannot weep, and for words your faces wan?

No; the blood is dead within our veins—we care not now for life;
Let us die hid in the ditches, far from children and from wife!
We cannot stay and listen to their raving famished cries—
Bread! Bread! Bread! and none to still their agonies.
We left our infants playing with their dead mother's hand:
We left our maidens maddened by the fever's scorching brand:
Better, maiden, thou wert strangled in thy own dark-twisted tresses—
Better, infant, thou wert smothered in thy mother's first caresses.

We are fainting in our misery, but God will hear our groan;
Yet, if fellowmen desert us, will He hearken from His throne?
Accursed are we in our own land, yet toil we still and toil;
But the stranger reaps our harvest—the alien owns our soil.
O Christ! how have we sinned, that on our native plains
We perish homeless, naked, starved, with branded brow like Cain's?
Dying, dying wearily, with a torture sure and slow—
Dying as a dog would die, by the wayside as we go.

One by one they're falling round us, their pale faces
to the sky ;
We've no strength left to dig them graves—there let
them lie.
The wild bird, if he's stricken, is mourned by the
others,
But we—we die in Christian land,—we die amid our
brothers,
In a land which God has given us, like a wild beast in
his cave,
Without a tear, a prayer, a shroud, a coffin, or a
grave.
Ha ! but think ye the contortions on each livid face
ye see,
Will not be read on Judgement-day by eyes of
Deity ?

We are wretches, famished, scorned, human tools to
build your pride,
But God will yet take vengeance for the souls for
whom Christ died.
Now in your hour of pleasure—bask ye in the world's
caress ;
But our whitening bones against ye will rise as
witnesses,
From the cabins and the ditches in their charred,
uncoffined masses,
For the Angel of the Trumpet will know them as he
passes.
A ghastly spectral army, before the great God we'll
stand,
And arraign ye as our murderers, the spoilers of our
land !

198 *The Dawn*

WHAT of the night, O Watcher on the Tower?
Is the Day dawning through the golden bars?
Comes it through the midnight, over clouds that lower,
Trailing robes of crimson 'mid the fading stars?

'Through the rent clouds I see a splendour gleaming,
Rolling down the darkness to the far Heaven's rim,
While through the mist the glorious Dawn up-streaming
Rises like the music of a grand choral hymn.'

From the deep valleys where the whirlwind passes,
Hear you the tramp of the coming hosts of men,
Strong in their manhood, mighty in their masses,
Swift as rushing torrents down a mountain glen?

'Far as eye can reach, where purple mists are lifted,
Thousands upon thousands are gathering in might,
Powerful as tempests when giant sails are rifted,
Beautiful as ocean in the sun's silver light.'

See you their Banner in the free air proudly
Waving, as an oriflamme a king might bear,
Has it no legend—dare we utter loudly
All that a people may have written there?

'I see their Banner in the red dawn flashing—
Haughty is the legend, plain to all men's sight,
Traced in their heart's blood, which the breeze up-catching,
Flings out in flame-words—Liberty and Right!

'Onward they come, still gathering in power,
Serried ranks of men o'er the crimson-clouded lawn;
Banners glisten brightly in the golden shower,
Pouring through the portals of the golden Dawn.

'Each bears a symbol, glorious in its meaning,
Holy as the music of the crown'd Bard's psalm:
Faith gazing upward, on her Anchor leaning,
Peace with the Olive, and Mercy with the Palm.'

Long have we waited, O Watcher, for the vision,
Splendid in promise we now can see it rise,
Scattering the darkness, while with hero-mission
Brave hands uplift Hope's banner to the skies!

Not with vain clamour, but the soul's strength revealing
In the golden silence of all great true deeds,
Banded in strength for human rights appealing,
Banded in love for our poor human needs.

Bitter was the past; let it rest, a new æon
Preaches a new Gospel to man not in vain,
Earth through all her kingdoms echoes back the pæan
Chanted once by Angels on the star-lit plain.

Brotherhood of Nations, disdaining ancient quarrel,
Brotherhood of Peoples, flushed with a nobler rage,
Palm branch and Olive let us mingle with the Laurel
In the radiant future of the coming age!

MICHAEL TORMEY

199 *The Ancient Race*

1820–1893

WHAT shall become of the ancient race,
The noble Celtic island race?
Like cloud on cloud o'er the azure sky,
When winter storms are loud and high,
Their dark ships shadow the ocean's face—
What shall become of the Celtic race?

What shall befall the ancient race—
The poor, unfriended, faithful race?
Where ploughman's song made the hamlet ring,
The hawk and the owlet flap their wing;
The village homes, oh, who can trace—
God of our persecuted race!

What shall befall the ancient race?
Is treason's stigma on their face?
Be they cowards or traitors? Go—
Ask the shade of England's foe;
See the gems her crown that grace;
They tell a tale of the ancient race.

They tell a tale of the ancient race—
Of matchless deeds in danger's face;
They speak of Britain's glory fed
With blood of Celts, right bravely shed;
Of India's spoil and Frank's disgrace—
Such tale they tell of the ancient race.

MICHAEL TORMEY

What shall befall the ancient race?
Shall all forsake their dear birth-place,
Without one struggle strong to keep
The old soil where their fathers sleep?
The dearest land on earth's wide space—
Why leave it so, oh, ancient race?

What shall befall the ancient race?
Light up one hope for the ancient race;
O, priest of God—Soggarth aroon!
Lead but the way, we'll go full soon;
Is there a danger we will not face,
To keep old homes for the Irish race?

They shall not go, the ancient race—
They must not go, the ancient race!
Come, gallant Celts, and take your stand—
And form a league to save the land;
The land of faith, the land of grace,
The land of Erin's ancient race!

They must not go, the ancient race!
They shall not go, the ancient race!
The cry swells loud from shore to shore,
From emerald vale to mountain hoar,
From altar high to market-place—
'They shall not go, the ancient race!'

WILLIAM PEMBROKE MULCHINOCK

200 *Fill High To-Night*

1820?–1864

FILL high to-night in your halls of light,
The toast on our lips shall be—
'The sinewy hand, the glittering brand,
Our homes and our altars free.'

Though the coward pale, like the girl, may wail
And sleep in his chains for years,
The sound of our mirth shall pass over earth
With balm for a nation's tears.

A curse for the cold, a cup for the bold,
A smile for the girls we love;
And for him who'd bleed in his country's need
A home in the skies above.

We have asked the page of a former age,
For hope secure and bright,
And the spell it gave to the stricken slave
Was in one strong word—'Unite.'

Though the wind howl free o'er a simple tree
Till it bends beneath its frown—
For many a day it will howl away
Ere a forest be stricken down.

By the martyred dead who for freedom bled,
By all that man deems divine,
Our patriot band for a sainted land
Like brothers shall all combine.

Then fill to-night in our halls of light,
The toast on our lips must be—
'The sinewy hand, the glittering brand,
Our homes and our altars free.'

JOHN O'HAGAN (47)

201 *Eiré a Rúin*

1822–1890

LONG thy fair cheek was pale,
Eiré a rúin—
Too well it spake thy tale,
Eiré a rúin—
Fondly nursed hopes betrayed,
Gallant sons lowly laid,
All anguish there portrayed,
Eiré a rúin.

Long my dear clairseach's string,
Eiré a rúin,
Sang but as captives sing,
Eiré a rúin.
'Twas sorrow's broken sigh
Blent with mirth's reckless cry,
Saddest of minstrelsy!
Eiré a rúin.

Still was it thine to cope,
Eiré a rúin—
Still against hope to hope,
Eiré a rúin,

JOHN O'HAGAN

Ever through blackest woe
Fronting that tyrant foe,
Whom thou shalt yet lay low,
Eiré a rúin.

Though he should sue thee now,
Eiré a rúin,
Heed not his traitor vow,
Eiré a rúin ;
When didst thou e'er believe,
When his false words receive,
But sorely thou didst grieve,
Eiré a rúin ?

Millions of hearts are thine,
Eiré a rúin ;
Millions as one combine,
Eiré a rúin ;
Closer in peril knit,
Patient, though passion-lit—
For such is triumph writ,
Eiré a rúin.

Then let thy clairseach pour,
Eiré a rúin,
Wailings of grief no more,
Eiré a rúin ;
But strains like flash of steel,
Kindling that fire of zeal
Which melts their chains who feel,
Eiré a rúin.

JOHN O'HAGAN

202 *Ourselves Alone* (48)

THE work that should to-day be wrought,
  Defer not till to-morrow ;
The help that should within be sought,
  Scorn from without to borrow.
Old maxims these—yet stout and true—
  They speak in trumpet tone,
To do at once what is to do,
  And trust Ourselves Alone.

Too long our Irish hearts we schooled
  In patient hope to bide,
By dreams of English justice fooled
  And English tongues that lied.
That hour of weak delusion's past—
  The empty dream has flown :
Our hope and strength, we find at last,
  Is in Ourselves Alone.

Aye ! bitter hate, or cold neglect,
  Or lukewarm love, at best,
Is all we've found, or can expect,
  We Aliens of the West.
No friend, beyond our own green shore,
  Can Erin truly own ;
Yet stronger is her trust, therefore,
  In her brave sons Alone.

Remember, when our lot was worse—
  Sunk, trampled to the dust—
'Twas long our weakness and our curse
  In stranger aid to trust.

And if, at length, we proudly trod
  On bigot laws o'erthrown,
Who won that struggle? Under God,
  Ourselves—Ourselves Alone.

Oh! let its memory be enshrined
  In Ireland's heart for ever!
It proves a banded people's mind
  Must win in just endeavour;
It shows how wicked to despair,
  How weak to idly groan—
If ills at others' hands ye bear,
  The cure is in Your Own.

The foolish word 'impossible'
  At once, for aye, disdain;
No power can bar a people's will,
  A people's right to gain.
Be bold, united, firmly set,
  Nor flinch in word or tone—
We'll be a glorious nation yet,
  Redeemed—Erect—Alone!

203 *An Ancient Tale*

HE came across the meadow-pass,
  That summer eve of eves—
The sunlight streamed along the grass
  And glanced amid the leaves;
And from the shrubbery below,
  And from the garden trees,

JOHN O'HAGAN

He heard the thrushes' music flow
  And humming of the bees ;
The garden gate was swung apart—
  The space was brief between ;
But there, for throbbing of his heart,
  He paused perforce to lean.

He leaned upon the garden gate ;
  He looked, and scarce he breathed ;
Within the little porch she sate,
  With woodbine overwreathed ;
Her eyes upon her work were bent,
  Unconscious who was nigh ;
But oft the needle slowly went,
  And oft did idle lie ;
And ever to her lips arose
  Sweet fragments sweetly sung,
But ever, ere the notes could close,
  She hushed them on her tongue.

'O ! beauty of my heart,' he said,
  'O ! darling, darling mine,
Was ever light of evening shed
  On loveliness like thine ?
Why should I ever leave this spot,
  But gaze until I die ?'
A moment from that bursting thought
  She felt his footstep nigh.
One sudden, lifted glance—but one,
  A tremor and a start,
So gently was their greeting done
  That who would guess their heart ?

JOHN O'HAGAN

Long, long the sun had sunken down,
  And all his golden trail
Had died away to lines of brown,
  In duskier hues that fail.
The grasshopper was chirping shrill—
  No other living sound
Accompanied the tiny rill
  That gurgled under ground—
No other living sound, unless
  Some spirit bent to hear
Low words of human tenderness
  And mingling whispers near.

The stars, like pallid gems at first,
  Deep in the liquid sky,
Now forth upon the darkness burst,
  Sole kings and lights on high ;
For splendour, myriadfold, supreme,
  No rival moonlight strove ;
Nor lovelier e'er was Hesper's beam,
  Nor more majestic Jove.
But what if hearts there beat that night
  That recked not of the skies,
Or only felt their imaged light
  In one another's eyes ;

And if two worlds of hidden thought
  And fostered passion met,
Which, passing human language, sought
  And found an utterance yet,
And if they trembled as the flowers
  That droop across the stream,
The while the silent starry hours
  Wait o'er them like a dream ;

JOHN O'HAGAN

And if, when came the parting time,
  They faltered still and clung ;
What is it all ?—an ancient rhyme
  Ten thousand times besung—
That part of Paradise which man
  Without the portal knows—
Which hath been since the world began,
  And shall be till its close.

RICHARD DALTON WILLIAMS

204 *The Munster War-Song* (49)

A.D. 1190

1822–1862

CAN the depths of the ocean afford you not graves,
  That you come thus to perish afar o'er the waves—
To redden and swell the wild torrents that flow
Through the valley of vengeance, the dark Eatharlach ?[1]

The clangour of conflict o'erburthens the breeze,
From the stormy Sliabh Bloom to the stately Galtees ;
Your caverns and torrents are purple with gore,
Sliabh na m-Ban,[2] Gleann Colaich, and sublime Galtee Mór !

The sunburst that slumbered, embalmed in our tears,
Tipperary ! shall wave o'er thy tall mountaineers !
And the dark hill shall bristle with sabre and spear,
While one tyrant remains to forge manacles here.

[1] Aharlow Glen, county Tipperary. [2] Slievenaman.

RICHARD DALTON WILLIAMS

The riderless war-steed careers o'er the plain
With a shaft in his flank and a blood-dripping
mane,
His gallant breast labours, and glare his wild eyes!
He plunges in torture—falls—shivers—and dies.

Let the trumpets ring triumph! the tyrant is
slain!
He reels o'er his charger deep-pierced through the
brain;
And his myriads are flying like leaves on the
gale—
But who shall escape from our hills with the tale?

For the arrows of vengeance are show'ring like
rain,
And choke the strong rivers with islands of slain,
Till thy waves, 'lordly Sionainn,'[1] all crimsonly
flow,
Like the billows of hell, with the blood of the foe.

Ay! the foemen are flying, but vainly they fly—
Revenge with the fleetness of lightning can vie;
And the septs of the mountains spring up from each
rock,
And rush down the ravines like wolves on the flock.

And who shall pass over the stormy Sliabh Bloom,
To tell the pale Saxon of tyranny's doom,
When, like tigers from ambush, our fierce moun-
taineers
Leap along from the crags with their death-dealing
spears?

[1] Shannon.

They came with high boasting to bind us as slaves,
But the glen and the torrent have yawned on their
graves?
From the gloomy Ard Fionnain to wild Teampoll
Mór—[1]
From the Suir to the Sionainn—is red with their gore.

By the soul of Heremon! our warriors may smile,
To remember the march of the foe through our isle;
Their banners and harness were costly and gay,
And proudly they flashed in the summer sun's ray;

The hilts of their falchions were crusted with gold,
And the gems of their helmets were bright to behold;
By Saint Bride of Cildare! but they moved in fair show—
To gorge the young eagles of dark Eatharlach!

205 *A Breeze through the Forest*

THE sounding forest towers
Through the tinted blossom showers—
Green heavens raining flowers,
Like my heart in the days that are gone.

O, thousand-pillared shrine
Of an Architect divine!
What chancel meet as thine
For praise to the days that are gone?

But oh! what forest hath
Such unforgotten path,
As the haunted fairy rath
Where we met in the days that are gone?

[1] Ardfinan and Templemore.

For an Irish Venus there,
Twining shamrocks in her hair,
Smiled a glory through the air
  Pure as dawn in the days that are gone.

Oh! the soul within her eyes,
And our mingled tears and sighs—
Hush! in Irish clay she lies;
  Hang a pall o'er the days that are gone.

Now a wailing phantom there
Wrings the death-dew from her hair,
Gazing westwards in despair
  Through the mist, where the black ships have
    gone.

Thou shalt not long alone
O'er our joy's abandoned throne
To the midnight breezes moan
  O'er the hopes of the days that are gone.

My life is ebbing fast,
On the fiery southern blast
I spring to thee at last,
  First love of the days that are gone.

Prophetic shadows loom
O'er my spirit from the tomb—
In glory, or in gloom,
  Thou art mine, by the days that are gone.

There too the white-thorn blows
O'er the mother's dust, whose woes
One heart—one only—knows;
  Child of tears, it is well thou art gone.

RICHARD DALTON WILLIAMS

As I bore thee home to die,
The lark filled all the sky ;
'Twas thine angel's call on high—
Let us pray for the souls that are gone.

I miss the cloister bells
Through the ruin-hallowed dells,
The round towers and holy wells,
That were part of the days that are gone.

And the friends—alas ! how few—
In the hours of anguish true,
Whose inmost hearts I knew,
In the fire of the days that are gone.

And the dreams that once I dreamed
Of a nation's soul redeemed
From the hell in which she seemed
A saint in the days that are gone.

Still the tomb, the rath, the shrine,
And love's memories divine,
O rich in tears ! are thine,
Widowed queen of the days that are gone.

Sad isle of chains and graves,
Though thy sons are slaves of slaves,
I bless thee o'er the waves,
For the sake of the days that are gone.

Thus memory like a breeze
Through the strong and silent trees,
Bows my manhood, strewing these
Withered leaves of the days that are gone.

RICHARD DALTON WILLIAMS

206 *The Dying Girl*

FROM a Munster vale they brought her,
  From the pure and balmy air ;
An Ormond peasant's daughter,
  With blue eyes and golden hair.
They brought her to the city,
  And she faded slowly there—
Consumption has no pity
  For blue eyes and golden hair.

When I saw her first reclining
  Her lips were mov'd in prayer,
And the setting sun was shining
  On her loosen'd golden hair.
When our kindly glances met her,
  Deadly brilliant was her eye ;
And she said that she was better,
  While we knew that she must die.

She speaks of Munster valleys,
  The pattern, dance, and fair,
And her thin hand feebly dallies
  With her scattered golden hair.
When silently we listen'd
  To her breath with quiet care,
Her eyes with wonder glisten'd,
  And she asked us, 'What was there ?'

The poor thing smiled to ask it,
  And her pretty mouth laid bare,
Like gems within a casket,
  A string of pearlets rare.

We said that we were trying
  By the gushing of her blood
And the time she took in sighing
  To know if she were good.

Well, she smil'd and chatted gaily,
  Though we saw in mute despair
The hectic brighter daily,
  And the death-dew on her hair.
And oft her wasted fingers
  Beating time upon the bed :
O'er some old tune she lingers,
  And she bows her golden head.

At length the harp is broken ;
  And the spirit in its strings,
As the last decree is spoken,
  To its source exulting springs.
Descending swiftly from the skies
  Her guardian angel came,
He struck God's lightning from her eyes,
  And bore Him back the flame.

Before the sun had risen
  Through the lark-loved morning air,
Her young soul left its prison,
  Undefiled by sin or care.
I stood beside the couch in tears
  Where pale and calm she slept,
And though I've gaz'd on death for years,
  I blush not that I wept.

I check'd with effort pity's sighs
And left the matron there,
To close the curtains of her eyes
And bind her golden hair.

207 *St. Kevin and Kathleen*

COME, Kathleen, pure and soft as dew,
The lake is heaving at our feet,
The stars ascend the eternal blue,
Primeval granite makes our seat.
Beneath eternal skies above,
'Mid everlasting hills around,
I speak of love—immortal love !—
Such as in Eden first was found.
Let each look through the other's soul,
Until each thought within that lies,
Like spar o'er which these clear waves roll,
Unveil its lustre to our eyes.

I bless thee, Kathleen, o'er and o'er,
For all the joy thy smiles have brought me,
And mysteries of loving lore
Thy very presence oft hath taught me.
For beauty innocent as thine—
Such lovely soul in lovely form—
Still makes diviner aught divine,
And calms the spirit's wildest storm.
Whene'er I muse—how oft !—on thee,
Half-seen, each high and holy feeling
Of love and immortality
Take shape, like angels round me wheeling.

To thee I owe the purest flowers
  Of song that o'er my pathway burst,
And holy thought, at midnight hours,
  From thine unconscious beauty nurst.
There is no stain on flowers like these,
  That from my heart to thine are springing;
And thoughts of thee are like the breeze,
  When bells for midnight mass are ringing.
Without thy knowledge from thee beams
  Some gentle and refining light,
That fills my heart with childhood's dreams,
  And I grow purer in thy sight.

Thou art no queen—no hero I—
  But thou'rt the fairest Christian maid
To whom the worship of a sigh,
  By Christian bard was ever paid.
And this I am—Sire—God above,
  Who made my soul of that rich flame,
All adoration, song, and love,
  That from thine own great Spirit came!
Than mine no purer, warmer zeal
  For justice and sublime desire
Of freedom, truth, and human weal
  Glows in the seraph ranks of fire.

I've bower'd thee in a lonely shrine—
  My bosom's convent-garden, sweet—
Where song and pray'r their signs combine,
  Where love and adoration meet.
I've rob'd thee like Ban-Tierna olden
  Of Eirè, in a vesture green;
And clasped thee with a girdle golden
  O'er all my dream-world saint and queen.

RICHARD DALTON WILLIAMS

I've starr'd thy hands with Irish gems,
  And sought to wreathe thy rich brown hair,
The oakwood's dewy diadems,
  And won the sacred shamrocks there.

Oh, would that thou could'st read my heart,
  Or that my lips might be unseal'd,
And by love's lamp, in every part,
  My spirit's inmost crypt reveal'd!
Within, like maid in minstrel tale,
  One lovely vision sleeping lies;
Beside her Hope, with forehead pale,
  And timid Joy, with downcast eyes.
'Tis Love, in long enchantment bound,
  I know not how, in torpor there;
The spells obey but one sweet sound—
  When Kathleen sings, they melt in air.

See! over yonder mountains, crack'd
  And sunder'd by volcanic fire,
Sings Glendalough's white cataract—
  Fit chord of such a granite lyre.
And then the cloud-born waterfall
  Summons aloud, from rock and wood,
The child-like springs, and leads them all,
  With laughter to this gloomy flood.
And thus thy love my heart shall lave—
  When sorrow's rocks, faith-cloven, sever,
Giving a glimpse of God—and save
  Life's current pure and fresh for ever!

DION BOUCICAULT

208 *The Wearing of the Green* (50)

1822–1890

O PADDY dear, and did you hear the news that's going round?
The shamrock is forbid by law to grow on Irish ground;
St. Patrick's Day no more we'll keep, his colours can't be seen,
For there's a bloody law again the wearing of the Green.
I met with Napper Tandy, and he took me by the hand,
And he said, 'How's poor old Ireland, and how does she stand?'
She's the most distressful country that ever yet was seen,
They are hanging men and women for the wearing of the Green.

Then since the colour we must wear is England's cruel Red,
Sure Ireland's sons will ne'er forget the blood that they have shed.
You may take the shamrock from your hat and cast it on the sod,
But 'twill take root and flourish there, though under foot 'tis trod.
When law can stop the blades of grass from growing as they grow,
And when the leaves in summer-time their verdure dare not show,

Then I will change the colour that I wear in my
caubeen,
But till that day, please God, I'll stick to wearing of
the Green.

But if at last our colour should be torn from Ireland's
heart,
Her sons with shame and sorrow from the dear old
isle will part;
I've heard a whisper of a country that lies beyond the
sea,
Where rich and poor stand equal in the light of
freedom's day.
O Erin, must we leave you, driven by a tyrant's hand?
Must we ask a mother's blessing from a strange and
distant land?
Where the cruel cross of England shall nevermore be
seen,
And where, please God, we'll live and die still wearing
of the Green.

209 *A Peasant Woman's Song* (51)

1864

I'M very happy where I am,
Far across the say,
I'm very happy far from home,
In North Amerikay.

It's lonely in the night, when Pat
Is sleeping by my side,
I lie awake, and no one knows
The big tears that I've cried;

For a little voice still calls me back
  To my far, far counthrie,
And nobody can hear it spake,
  Oh! nobody but me.

There is a little spot of ground
  Behind the chapel wall,
It's nothing but a tiny mound,
  Without a stone at all;

It rises like my heart just now,
  It makes a dawny[1] hill;
It's from below the voice comes out,
  I cannot keep it still.

Oh! little Voice; ye call me back
  To my far, far counthrie,
And nobody can hear ye spake,
  Oh! nobody but me.

JOHN KELLS INGRAM

210 *The Memory of the Dead* (52)

1823–1907

WHO fears to speak of Ninety-Eight?
  Who blushes at the name?
When cowards mock the patriot's fate,
  Who hangs his head for shame?
He's all a knave, or half a slave,
  Who slights his country thus;
But a true man, like you, man,
  Will fill your glass with us.

[1] Little.

JOHN KELLS INGRAM

We drink the memory of the brave,
  The faithful and the few :
Some lie far off beyond the wave,
  Some sleep in Ireland, too ;
All, all are gone ; but still lives on
  The fame of those who died ;
All true men, like you, men,
  Remember them with pride.

Some on the shores of distant lands
  Their weary hearts have laid,
And by the stranger's heedless hands
  Their lonely graves were made ;
But, though their clay be far away
  Beyond the Atlantic foam,
In true men, like you, men,
  Their spirit's still at home.

The dust of some is Irish earth,
  Among their own they rest,
And the same land that gave them birth
  Has caught them to her breast ;
And we will pray that from their clay
  Full many a race may start
Of true men, like you, men,
  To act as brave a part.

They rose in dark and evil days
  To right their native land ;
They kindled here a living blaze
  That nothing shall withstand.

Alas! that Might can vanquish Right—
They fell and passed away;
But true men, like you, men,
Are plenty here to-day.

Then here's their memory—may it be
For us a guiding light,
To cheer our strife for liberty,
And teach us to unite—
Through good and ill, be Ireland's still,
Though sad as theirs your fate,
And true men be you, men,
Like those of Ninety-Eight.

211 *A Fragment*

From the Norse

I

'NOBLE warrior! droop not thus;
Tower of strength thou hast in us.
Yonder stand our anvils ten,
Round them, see, are stalwart men—
Bare broad shoulder, sinewy limb,
Black-brow'd feature sooty-grim;
Eye like glare of smouldering fire,
Lighted with a dull desire.
These shall sweat; their hammers swinging,
They will keep the anvils ringing,
Forging thee such trusty mail,
Nought against it will prevail.'

II

'God-like artist, spare thy pain :
Strength and skill alike are vain.
When upon the destin'd day
Balder meets me in the fray,
Were my breast-plate triple steel,
If his shaft but once it feel,—
Such that weapon's magic power—
Like a guilty thing 'twill cower,
And, smit through with fear and wonder,
Shrink, and cleave, and fall asunder.
Well I know this weird is mine—
I am human, he divine.'

212 *National Presage*

UNHAPPY Erin, what a lot was thine !
Half-conquer'd by a greedy robber band ;
Ill govern'd with now lax, now ruthless hand ;
Misled by zealots, wresting laws divine
To sanction every dark or mad design ;
Lured by false lights of pseudo-patriot league
Through crooked paths of faction and intrigue ;
And drugg'd with selfish flattery's poison'd wine.
Yet, reading all thy mournful history,
Thy children, with a mystic faith sublime,
Turn to the future, confident that Fate,
Become at last thy friend, reserves for thee,
To be thy portion in the coming time,
They know not what—but surely something great.

213 *The Social Future*

AS, with enforc'd yet unreluctant pace
We downward move along life's westward slope,
Slow fades the once bright gleam of personal hope,
And larger looms the future of the race;
Our wistful eyes the goodly prospect trace,
Seen through a haze of forecast; there outspread
Lie the fair fields our children's feet shall tread
When we have passed to our abiding place.
Oh! sons and daughters of the coming age,
Give worthy meed of gratitude and praise
To those true souls who, in less happy days,
Have lived for others—most of all for you,—
Have stored the wealth which is your heritage,
And plann'd the work it will be yours to do.

214 *Winged Thoughts*

LITTLE they know us, ev'n who know us best.
Oft, when the social circle, frank and gay,
Sports with the topics of the passing day,
I seem, at friendly challenge, with keen zest
To catch and echo back the flying jest;
Yet will my inmost thought be far away—
Like bird that lights, and lights, but does not stay—
Beside my lost ones in their long low rest.
One sleeps in Erin, near the home she bless'd,
Where grateful hearts still worship her; and one,
Who pass'd, his active manhood scarce begun,
And all his poet-soul yet unexpress'd,
Lies under tamarisk boughs, where Afric's sun
Looks down on hallow'd ground at Beaufortwest.

JOHN KELLS INGRAM

215 *To A. J.*[1]

A Monody

BRIGHT spirit! wheresoe'er thou art,
Take this sad tribute of my heart;
Or if within the realms of space
Thou ownest now no dwelling-place,
Yet let me hum my descant o'er,
Though ear of thine it reach no more.

Not often mov'd thy thoughts away
From active duties of the day,
Yet was thy faith, I doubt not, sure
That after death our lives endure,
And, safe on some far distant shore,
They dwell whom here we meet no more.

Such golden dream I do not share;
My promis'd land is here, not there;
Here, where the brethren of my race
Love, work, and weep their little space,
And, with green hillocks cover'd o'er,
Lie those who bless our homes no more.

That earlier vision fades away,
As twilight kindles into day.
Another prospect greets our view—
Of Earth array'd in vesture new.
Nor need we grieve that now no more
We shape the future as of yore.

[1] Mrs. Jellicoe, foundress of Alexandra College, Dublin, 1866.

JOHN KELLS INGRAM

For truth is truth, and love is love,
Though never register'd above ;
And Duty looks her mute appeal,
As we its mastering force can feel,
Though it may be we live no more
When this our earthly life is o'er.

We need no verdict from the skies
To tell us thou wert good and wise.
Though angel trump ne'er break thy rest,
Thy heart was pure, thy work was blest ;
Nor is thy sacred service o'er,
Though here thy face is seen no more.

Thy quickening power is with us still,
Thy memory spurs the laggard will ;
Thy call to labour while we may,
And reap the harvest of the day,
Inspires our souls not less, but more,
Because thy well-wrought task is o'er.

And oft the wish will haunt my breast
To earn like thee my final rest.
Might I, at parting, leave behind
Some worthy gift to human kind,—
Perchance a not unvalued store,
When I on earth am seen no more !

O well for those who chant a song
That through the ages echoes long,
Or rear some pile of thought sublime,
Strong to withstand the shocks of time ;
And so, when this first life is o'er,
Still live in others evermore.

Not such my lot—I have but power
To breathe the feeling of the hour—
Half said, half sung—in simple strain,
Like this, whose sorrowful refrain
Some kindly souls may murmur o'er,
When my poor voice is heard no more.

Yet do I fret not, nor repine,
Because no loftier gifts are mine;
Lamenting rather that my past
With stains of sin is overcast,
Which, if anew I traced it o'er,
I trust, should soil the page no more.

Be still, sad heart, nor thus complain,
Nor spend thy waning strength in vain.
Thou canst not by repentant tears
Efface the record of the years.
Be true, be loving now, the more
That love and life will soon be o'er.

MARTIN MACDERMOTT

1823-

216 *Girl of the Red Mouth*

GIRL of the red mouth,
Love me! Love me!
Girl of the red mouth,
Love me!

MARTIN MACDERMOTT

'Tis by its curve, I know,
Love fashioneth his bow,
And bends it—ah, even so !
  Oh, girl of the red mouth, love me !

Girl of the blue eye,
  Love me ! Love me !
Girl of the dew eye,
    Love me !
Worlds hang for lamps on high ;
And thought's world lives in thy
Lustrous and tender eye—
  Oh, girl of the blue eye, love me !

Girl of the swan's neck,
  Love me ! Love me !
Girl of the swan's neck,
    Love me !
As a marble Greek doth grow
To his steed's back of snow,
Thy white neck sits thy shoulder so,—
  Oh, girl of the swan's neck, love me !

Girl of the low voice,
  Love me ! Love me !
Girl of the sweet voice,
    Love me !
Like the echo of a bell,—
Like the bubbling of a well—
Sweeter ! Love within doth dwell,—
  Oh, girl of the low voice, love me !

MARTIN MACDERMOTT

217 *The Coolun* (53)

THE scene is beside where the Avonmore[1] flows—
'Tis the spring of the year, and the day's near its close;
And an old woman sits with a boy on her knee—
She smiles like the evening, but he like the lea!
Her hair is as white as the flax ere it's spun—
His brown as yon tree that is hiding the sun!
Beside the bright river—
The calm, glossy river,
That's sliding and gliding all peacefully on.

'Come, granny,' the boy says, 'you'll sing me, I know,
The beautiful Coolun, so sweet and so low;
For I love its soft tones more than blackbird or thrush,
Though often the tears in a shower will gush
From my eyes when I hear it. Dear granny, say why,
When my heart's full of pleasure, I sob and I cry
To hear the sweet Coolun—
The beautiful Coolun—
An angel first sang it above in the sky?'

And she sings and he listens; but many years pass,
And the old woman sleeps 'neath the chapel-yard grass;
And a couple are seated upon the same stone,
Where the boy sat and listened so oft to the crone—

[1] The Munster Blackwater.

'Tis the boy—'tis the man, and he says while he
    sighs,
To the girl at his side with the love-streaming eyes,
        'Oh! sing me, sweet Oonagh,
        My beautiful Oonagh,
  Oh! sing me the Coolun,' he says and he sighs.

'That air, mo stór, brings back the days of my youth,
That flowed like a river there, sunny and smooth!
And it brings back the old woman, kindly and dear—
If her spirit, dear Oonagh, is hovering near,
'Twill glad her to hear the old melody rise
Warm, warm, on the wings of our love and our sighs—
        Oh! sing me the Coolun,
        The beautiful Coolun!'
  Is't the dew or a tear-drop is moistening his eyes?

There's a change on the scene, far more grand, far
    less fair—
By the broad rolling Hudson are seated the pair;
And the dark hemlock-fir waves its branches above,
As they sigh for their land, as they murmur their love;
Hush!—the heart hath been touched, and its musical
    strings
Vibrate into song—'tis the Coolun she sings—
        The home-sighing Coolun,
        The love-breathing Coolun—
  The well of all memory's deep-flowing springs.

They think of the bright stream they sat down beside,
When he was a bridegroom and she was his bride;
The pulses of youth seem to throb in the strain—
Old faces, long vanished, look kindly again—

Kind voices float round them, and grand hills are
near,
Their feet have not touched, ah, this many a year—
And, as ceases the Coolun,
The home-loving Coolun,
Not the air, but their native land faints on the ear.

Long in silence they weep, with hand clasped in
hand—
Then to God send up prayers for the far-off old
land;
And while grateful to Him for the blessings He's
sent—
They know 'tis His hand that withholdeth content—
For the exile and Christian must evermore sigh
For the home upon earth and the home in the
sky—
So they sing the sweet Coolun,
The sorrowful Coolun,
That murmurs of both homes—they sing and they
sigh.

Heaven bless thee, old bard, in whose bosom were
nurst
Emotions that into such melody burst!
Be thy grave ever green!—may the softest of
showers
And brightest of beams nurse its grass and its flowers—
Oft, oft, be it moist with the tear-drop of love,
And may angels watch round thee, for ever above!
Old bard of the Coolun,
The beautiful Coolun,
That's sobbing, like Eirè, with sorrow and love.

THOMAS CAULFIELD IRWIN

218 *The Vine Song*

From 'The Minstrel's Appointment'

1823–1892

THE grape is the only fruit of the skies:
  'Tis suckled with dew in the springtime bright;
Then, lapped in leaves, awhile it lies,
  To learn their songs in the evening light.
Crimson sunsets lend it a hue—
  Airs of summer, being and breath;
Under the heaven's palace of blue
  None that drink of it dream of death.
    In each grape there dwells a sprite,
    Born of fancy, pleasure, and light;
    Every bubble that sparks the bowl
    Holds in its dome a starry soul.
        Then would you think
        Like a spirit, drink—
    Drink, drink of the joyous wine,
        Up to the brain,
        Again and again,
    Those wits of the stars shall mount and shine.

    Lovers, shed your happiest smiles
      Under the vine where'er you go.
    The tendrils shoot like passion's wiles,
      The blushes under their shadows glow.
    Friends, who around the bright hearth sing,
      Pray by the vine where'er you roam,
    That friendship, like his arms, may cling
      For ever around the walls of home.

Poets, looking through fancy's glass
  Round the world for beauty and light,
Wheresoever the day you pass,
  Under some old vine rest at night.
Every bough shall guard their guest,
  And bend to his lip their rosiest wine ;
And every leaf that lulls to rest
  Shall fill your spirits with dreams divine.

Oh ! when this heart has ceased to blow,
  Oh ! when its love has failed to burn,
Scatter it still in its wit-bright glow
  Into some cup's funereal urn :
Songs and smiles that charmed and shone
  Over its bright brim many a night,
Murmuring yet of pleasures gone,
  Shall charm its rest with echo and light.

219 *The Troubadour's Pilgrimage*

EASTWARD, moonlit peaks are glancing
  O'er the dusk with silvery eyes ;
Westward, tracts of Summer forest
  Deepen down the crimson skies :
Pilgrims pass the bridge whose crescent
  Darkens o'er the gleaming frith,
And the noon heat camps its vapour
  O'er the bronzèd moorland's width—
    Toll, bell of sunset, toll
      Over listening land and river ;
    Sing, Memory, to my soul,
      Of spirits lost, but loved for ever !

THOMAS CAULFIELD IRWIN

Toward the norland distance yonder
  Listening, praying, forth I go ;
Starry stream and solemn mountain
  Lure me, shining in their snow ;
There, within a silent valley,
  Full of the cold planets' light,
Lies the grave to which my fancy,
  Dreaming, wanders through the night—
    Toll, bell of sunset, toll
      Over silent land and river ;
    Sing, Memory, to my soul,
      Of spirits lost, but loved for ever.

Onward, where awhile the Summer
  Slumbers round in twilight blooms—
Waters showering from the summits,
  Forest full of topaz glooms ;
Moon and sea beneath me rising,
  O'er me star and cottage nest—
Sadness in the eastern evening,
  Music in the golden west—
    Toll, bell of sunset, toll
      Down the gorgeous glooming river ;
    Sing, Memory, to my soul,
      Of spirits lost, but loved for ever.

Wheresoe'er the world I've wandered,
  Realm of life, or place of tombs ;
Through the Mediterranean splendours,
  Through the dumb Egyptian glooms ;
Radiant spirits round me hover,
  Watch my rest, or with me stray,

While our hearts, in mournful anthems
  Mingling, close the lonely day—
    Toll, bell of evening, toll
      O'er the starry trembling river ;
    Sing, Memory, to my soul,
      Of spirits lost, but loved for ever.

Oft I hear their charmed voices
  Lingering round some mountain height ;
Utterance rich as planet music
  Swooning through the magic night.
Oft great brows of meteor beauty,
  O'er the star-dim seas appear ;
Oft in noonlit towns a silence
  Falling, tells me they are near—
    Toll, bell of darkness, toll
      Fate like, down the ghostly river ;
    Sing, Memory, to my soul,
      Of spirits lost, but loved for ever.

Upward, where the moulder'd castle
  Guards the quick, unquiet fords,
All its moated depths of waters,
  Glossed with beams, like blades of swords :
Now the lowland's dark expansure
  Widens from the mountain crest ;
And a low star lights the valley,
  Where my pilgrim heart would rest—
    Toll, bell of silence, toll
      Down the silver rippled river ;
    Sing, Memory, to my soul,
      Of spirits lost, but loved for ever.

By this well, that bubbles sprayless,
  Shall I rest upon my way:
Earth is broadening in shadow—
  Heaven in brightness, while I pray.
'Blessed spirits, rise above me,
  When the death-dark round me flows,
Like a crescent o'er the sunset,
  Beaconing where the glory goes.'
    Toll, bell of Heaven, toll
      Down the sapphire radiant river.
    God, waft my trembling soul
      Where rest the spirits loved for ever.

220 *The Faerie's Child*

AMID the nut grove, still and brown,
  The Faerie's Child is walking.
List, list, as the leaves come down,
  To the sprites around her talking.
    Along the windy, waving grass
    Their evening whispers breathe and pass:
    From yon aged bending bough
    Their leafy language floats below;
And now o'erhead in the air 'tis streaming.
  Oh! who can tell what things she hears—
  What secrets of the faery spheres,
  That fill her eyes with silent tears!
Sweet wandering fancy-charmed child,
With cheek so pale, and eyes so wild.
Oh! what shall come of this lonely dreaming!

Down by the sun-dry harvest road,
  Through quiet evening's hours,

She paces with her scented load
  Of late-year moss and flowers.
    Blooms from the wood of every hue,
    Moon pale, purple, jet, and blue ;
    Woven in bunches, and lightly press'd
    Upon her simple, snowy breast,
    And through the brown locks wildly tressed
  Nodding in crownlets o'er her.
    And, lo ! as the cloud on ocean's brim
    With moonlight has enriched its rim,
    A quaint wild shape, with kindly eyes,
    And a smile like a star of the distant skies,
  Goes tripping along the path before her.

Now by her pillow, small and white,
  'Mid faded leaflets lying,
An eager star, like a taper light,
  O'er the curtain's edge is spying.
    The scent of the broom-buds fills the room;
    The window is full of the bare blue gloom,
    And by the low hearth ashily sinking,
    Half asleep is the faery winking.
    Out in the air there comes a sound
    Of music eddying round and round
    The ivied chimneys—swooning near
    The glassy pane, and streaming clear
    As moonlight into the little ear,
  Like a shell in brown weed gleaming ;
    And, just as the first bird, mounted high
    On the sycamore's tinkling canopy,
    Sings to the first red streak of day,
    Her soul with the faeries speeds away,
    O'er field, and stream, and hamlet grey,
  Where the weary folk are dreaming.

WILLIAM ALLINGHAM

221 *The Winding Banks of Erne; or, The Emigrant's Adieu to his Birthplace*

1824–1889

ADIEU to Belashanny,[1] where I was bred and born;
Go where I may I'll think of you, as sure as night and morn:
The kindly spot, the friendly town, where every one is known,
And not a face in all the place but partly seems my own;
There's not a house or window, there's not a field or hill,
But east or west, in foreign lands, I'll recollect them still;
I leave my warm heart with you, though my back I'm forced to turn—
Adieu to Belashanny, and the winding banks of Erne!

No more on pleasant evenings we'll saunter down the Mall,
When the trout is rising to the fly, the salmon to the fall.
The boat comes straining on her net, and heavily she creeps,
Cast off, cast off—she feels the oars, and to her berth she sweeps;

[1] Ballyshannon, at the mouth of the Erne, co. Donegal.

Now fore and aft keep hauling, and gathering up the
 clew,
Till a silver wave of salmon rolls in among the
 crew.
Then they may sit, with pipes a-lit, and many a joke
 and 'yarn':—
Adieu to Belashanny, and the winding banks of
 Erne!

The music of the waterfall, the mirror of the tide,
When all the green-hill'd harbour is full from side to
 side,
From Portnasun to Bulliebawns, and round the Abbey
 Bay,
From rocky Inis Saimer to Coolnargit sandhills
 grey;
While far upon the southern line, to guard it like a
 wall,
The Leitrim mountains clothed in blue gaze calmly
 over all,
And watch the ship sail up or down, the red flag at
 her stern—
Adieu to these, adieu to all the winding banks of
 Erne!

Farewell to you, Kildoney lads, and them that pull an
 oar,
A lugsail set, or haul a net, from the point to Mullagh-
 more;
From Killybegs to bold Slieve-League, that ocean-
 mountain steep,
Six hundred yards in air aloft, six hundred in the
 deep;

WILLIAM ALLINGHAM

From Dooran to the Fairy Bridge, and round by
    Tullen strand,
Level and long, and white with waves, where gull
    and curlew stand ;
Head out to sea, when on your lee the breakers you
    discern—
Adieu to all the billowy coast and winding banks of
    Erne !

Farewell, Coolmore, Bundoran ! and your summer
    crowds that run
From inland homes to see with joy th' Atlantic-setting
    sun ;
To breathe the buoyant salted air, and sport among
    the waves ;
To gather shells on sandy beach, and tempt the gloomy
    caves ;
To watch the flowing, ebbing tide, the boats, the
    crabs, the fish ;
Young men and maids to meet and smile, and form
    a tender wish ;
The sick and old in search of health, for all things
    have their turn—
And I must quit my native shore and the winding
    banks of Erne !

Farewell to every white cascade from the Harbour to
    Belleek,
And every pool where fins may rest, and ivy-shaded
    creek ;
The sloping fields, the lofty rocks, where ash and holly
    grow,
The one split yew-tree gazing on the curving flood
    below ;

WILLIAM ALLINGHAM

The Lough, that winds through islands under Turaw mountain green ;
And Castle Caldwell's stretching woods, with tranquil bays between ;
And Breesie Hill, and many a pond among the heath and fern—
For I must say adieu—adieu to the winding banks of Erne !

The thrush will call through Camlin groves the live-long summer day ;
The waters run by mossy cliff, and banks with wild flowers gay ;
The girls will bring their work and sing beneath a twisted thorn,
Or stray with sweethearts down the path among the growing corn ;
Along the riverside they go, where I have often been,—
O, never shall I see again the days that I have seen !
A thousand chances are to one I never may return—
Adieu to Belashanny, and the winding banks of Erne !

Adieu to evening dances, when merry neighbours meet,
And the fiddle says to boys and girls, 'Get up and shake your feet !'
To shanachas [1] and wise old talk of Erin's days gone by—
Who trench'd the rath on such a hill, and where the bones may lie

[1] History, genealogy, folk-lore.

Of saint, or king, or warrior chief; with tales of fairy
power,
And tender ditties sweetly sung to pass the twilight
hour.
The mournful song of exile is now for me to
learn—
Adieu, my dear companions on the winding banks of
Erne!

Now measure from the Commons down to each end
of the Purt,
Round the Abbey, Moy, and Knather,—I wish no
one any hurt;
The Main Street, Back Street, College Lane, the
Mall, and Portnasun,
If any foes of mine are there, I pardon every one.
I hope that man and womankind will do the same by
me;
For my heart is sore and heavy at voyaging the
sea.
My loving friends I'll bear in mind, and often fondly
turn
To think of Belashanny, and the winding banks of
Erne.

If ever I'm a money'd man, I mean, please God, to
cast
My golden anchor in the place where youthful years
were past;
Though heads that now are black and brown must
meanwhile gather grey,
New faces rise by every hearth, and old ones drop
away—

Yet dearer still that Irish hill than all the world beside;
It's home, sweet home, where'er I roam, through lands and waters wide.
And if the Lord allows me, I surely will return
To my native Belashanny, and the winding banks of Erne.

222 *Lovely Mary Donnelly*

OH, lovely Mary Donnelly, my joy, my only best!
If fifty girls were round you, I'd hardly see the rest;
Be what it may the time o' day, the place be where it will,
Sweet looks o' Mary Donnelly, they bloom before me still.

Her eyes like mountain water that's flowing on a rock,
How clear they are, how dark they are! they give me many a shock.
Red rowans warm in sunshine and wetted with a shower,
Could ne'er express the charming lip that has me in its power.

Her nose is straight and handsome, her eyebrows lifted up,
Her chin is very neat and pert, and smooth like a china cup,

Her hair's the brag of Ireland, so weighty and so fine;
It's rolling down upon her neck, and gather'd in a twine.

The dance o' last Whit-Monday night exceeded all before,
No pretty girl for miles about was missing from the floor;
But Mary kept the belt of love, and O but she was gay!
She danced a jig, she sung a song, that took my heart away.

When she stood up for dancing, her steps were so complete,
The music nearly killed itself to listen to her feet;
The fiddler moan'd his blindness, he heard her so much praised,
But bless'd his luck to not be deaf when once her voice she raised.

And evermore I'm whistling or lilting what you sung,
Your smile is always in my heart, your name beside my tongue;
But you've as many sweethearts as you'd count on both your hands,
And for myself there's not a thumb or little finger stands.

Oh, you're the flower o' womankind in country or in town;
The higher I exalt you, the lower I'm cast down.

If some great lord should come this way, and see your beauty bright,
And you to be his lady, I'd own it was but right.

O might we live together in a lofty palace hall,
Where joyful music rises, and where scarlet curtains fall!
O might we live together in a cottage mean and small,
With sods o' grass the only roof, and mud the only wall!

O lovely Mary Donnelly, your beauty's my distress,
It's far too beauteous to be mine, but I'll never wish it less.
The proudest place would fit your face, and I am poor and low;
But blessings be about you, dear, wherever you may go!

223 *The Fairies*

UP the airy mountain,
Down the rushy glen,
We daren't go a-hunting
For fear of little men;
Wee folk, good folk,
Trooping all together;
Green jacket, red cap,
And white owl's feather!

WILLIAM ALLINGHAM

Down along the rocky shore
  Some make their home,
They live on crispy pancakes
  Of yellow tide foam ;
Some in the reeds
  Of the black mountain lake,
With frogs for their watch-dogs,
  All night awake.

High on the hill-top
  The old King sits ;
He is now so old and grey
  He's nigh lost his wits.
With a bridge of white mist
  Columbkill he crosses,
On his stately journeys
  From Slieveleague to Rosses ;
Or going up with music
  On cold starry nights,
To sup with the queen
  Of the gay Northern Lights.

They stole little Bridget
  For seven years long ;
When she came down again
  Her friends were all gone.
They took her lightly back,
  Between the night and morrow,
They thought that she was fast asleep,
  But she was dead with sorrow.
They have kept her ever since
  Deep within the lake,
On a bed of flag-leaves,
  Watching till she wake.

By the craggy hill-side,
 Through the mosses bare,
They have planted thorn-trees
 For pleasure here and there.
Is any man so daring
 As dig them up in spite,
He shall find their sharpest thorns
 In his bed at night.

Up the airy mountain,
 Down the rushy glen,
We daren't go a-hunting
 For fear of little men ;
Wee folk, good folk,
 Trooping all together ;
Green jacket, red cap,
 And white owl's feather !

224 *Unknown Belov'd One*

O UNKNOWN Belov'd One ! to the perfect season
 Branches in the lawn make drooping bow'rs ;
Vase and plot burn scarlet, gold, and azure ;
Honeysuckles wind the tall grey turret,
 And pale passion-flow'rs.
Come thou, come thou to my lonely thought,
 O Unknown Belov'd One.

Now, at evening twilight, dusky dew down-wavers,
 Soft stars crown the grove-encircled hill ;

Breathe the new-mown meadows, broad and misty;
Through the heavy grass the rail is talking;
All beside is still.
Trace with me the wandering avenue,
Thou Unknown Belov'd One.

In the mystic realm, and in the time of visions,
I thy lover have no need to woo;
There I hold thy hand in mine, thou dearest,
And thy soul in mine, and feel its throbbing,
Tender, deep, and true:
Then my tears are love, and thine are love,
Thou Unknown Belov'd One!

Is thy voice a wavelet on the listening darkness?
Are thine eyes unfolding from their veil?
Wilt thou come before the signs of winter—
Days that shred the bough with trembling fingers,
Nights that weep and wail?
Art thou Love indeed, or art thou Death,
O Unknown Belov'd One?

225 *Æolian Harp*

WHAT saith the river to the rushes grey,
Rushes sadly bending,
River slowly wending?
Who can tell the whisper'd things they say?
Youth, and prime, and life, and time,
For ever, ever fled away!

WILLIAM ALLINGHAM

Drop your wither'd garlands in the stream,
Low autumnal branches,
Round the skiff that launches
Wavering downward through the lands of dream.
Ever, ever fled away!
This the burden, this the theme.

What saith the river to the rushes grey,
Rushes sadly bending,
River slowly wending?
It is near the closing of the day.
Near the night. Life and light
For ever, ever fled away!

Draw him tideward down; but not in haste.
Mouldering daylight lingers;
Night with her cold fingers
Sprinkles moonbeams on the dim sea-waste.
Ever, ever fled away!
Vainly cherish'd! vainly chased!

What saith the river to the rushes grey,
Rushes sadly bending,
River slowly wending?
Where in darkest glooms his bed we lay,
Up the cave moans the wave,
For ever, ever, ever fled away!

WILLIAM ALEXANDER

226 *Robert Burns*

1824–

ALL Scottish legends did his fancy fashion,
All airs that richly flow,
Laughing with frolic, tremulous with passion,
Broken with love-lorn woe ;

Ballads whose beauties years have long been stealing
And left few links of gold,
Under his quaint and subtle touch of healing
Grew fairer, not less old.

Grey Cluden, and the vestal's choral cadence,
His spell awoke therewith ;
Till boatmen hung their oars to hear the maidens
Upon the banks of Nith.

His, too, the strains of battle nobly coming
From Bruce, or Wallace wight,
Such as the Highlander shall oft be humming
Before some famous fight.

Nor only these—for him the hawthorn hoary
Was with new wreaths enwrought,
The 'crimson-tippèd daisy' wore fresh glory,
Born of poetic thought.

From the 'wee cow'ring beastie' he could borrow
A moral strain sublime,
A noble tenderness of human sorrow,
In wondrous wealth of rhyme.

Oh, but the mountain breeze must have been pleasant
Upon the sunburnt brow
Of that poetic and triumphant peasant
Driving his laurell'd plough !

227 *A Fine Day on Lough Swilly*

SOFT slept the beautiful autumn
In the heart, on the face of the Lough—
Its heart, whose pulses were hush'd
Till you knew the life of the tide
But by a wash on the shore.
A whisper like whispering leaves
In green abysses of forest—
Its face, whose violet melted,
Melted in roseate gold—
Roses and violets dying
Into a tender mystery
Of soft impalpable haze.

Calm lay the woodlands of Fahan ;
The summer was gone, yet it lay
On the gently yellowing leaves
Like a beautiful poem, whose tones
Are mute, whose words are forgot,
But its music sleepeth for ever
Within the music of thought.
The robin sang from the ash,
The sunset's pencils of gold
No longer wrote their great lines
On the boles of the odorous limes,
Or bathed the tree-tops in glory,

But a soft strange radiance there hung
  In splinters of tenderest light.
And those who look'd from Glengollen
  Saw the purple wall of the Scalp,
As if through an old church window
  Stain'd with a marvellous blue.

From the snow-white shell strand of Inch
You could not behold the white horses
  Lifting their glittering backs,
  Tossing their manes on Dunree,
  And the battle boom of Macammish
    Was lull'd in the delicate air.
  As in old pictures the smoke
  Goes up from Abraham's pyre,
So the smoke went up from Rathmullen ;
  And beyond the trail of the smoke
  Was a great deep fiery abyss
    Of molten gold in the sky,
  And it set a far track up the waters
    Ablaze with gold like its own.
  Over the fire of the sea,
  Over the chasm in the sky,
  My spirit as by a bridge
Of wonder went wandering on,
  And lost its way in the heaven.

The ship is out on the lake,
The fisherman stands on the deck.
  Rosy and violet sea ;
  Delicate haze in the distance ;
  Woodlands softer than summers ;
  Great golden eye of intense,
  Concentrated, marvellous light ;

Mysterious suggestions of thought ;
Beautiful yearnings of fancy ;
Wonderful imaginations ;
Throbs of the being immortal
Who, prison'd deep in the heart,
Looks through the bars of the flesh :—
What recketh he of them all ?
So to the reasonless eye
The Master's picture is only
A heap of colouring flat,
A strange confusion of strokes ;
And thought, and study, and books,
And fine traditions of taste,
Are the glasses through which we survey
The beauty of natural things,
Till stars come splendidly out
That our eyes would have never beheld ;
And cultured association
Hangeth to things that we see,
Hints and prophetical types,
Shadows grand and immortal,
Sacraments dim and delightful,
Of the things that the eye hath not seen.

Oh this ship and ocean of life !
I, like the fisherman's boy,
On this awful beautiful sea
Gaze on a glory for ever
That I love not, nor know as I ought—
Sail on a beautiful deep,
Hear the soft washing of waves
That set to the shore of our God—
Look on purpureal hills,

Look on exquisite woods,
Soft, and most solemn and stately—
Sail toward the gate of Heaven,
Yet know it not, nor consider!

Hues more radiant by far
Than the Autumn ever could give
Move round my wondrous existence,
The daily deep of my life;
Prospects of things that shall be
In the country over the waves—
Memories, sorrows, and thoughts—
Noble and beautiful words,
Deeds that darkly reveal
The transparent measureless depth
Of the soul of our nature's Redeemer.
Oh for the day that shall teach me
To know their meaning at last,
Beyond the lake of this life,
Beyond the gate of the sunset
Upon the hyaline sea!

228 *The Birthday Crown*

IF aught of simple song have power to touch
Your silent being, O ye country flowers,
Twisted by tender hands
Into a royal brede,

O hawthorn, tear thou not the soft white brow
Of the small queen upon her rustic throne,
But breathe thy finest scent
Of almond round about.

And thou, laburnum, and what other hue
Tinct deeper gives variety of gold,
    Inwoven lily, and vetch
        Bedropp'd with summer's blood,

I charge you wither not this long June day!
Oh, wither not until the sunset come,
    Until the sunset's shaft
        Slope through the chestnut-tree;

Until she sit, high gloried round about
With the great light above her mimic court—
    Her threads of sunny hair
        Girt sunnily by you.

What other crown that queen may wear one
    day,
What drops may touch her forehead not of balm,
    What thorns, what cruel thorns,
        I will not guess to-day.

Only, before she is discrowned of you,
Ye dying flowers, and thou, O dying light,
    My prayer shall rise—'O Christ!
        Give her the unfading crown.

'The crown of blossoms worn by happy bride,
The thorny crown o'er pale and dying lips,
    I dare not choose for her—
        Give her the unfading crown!'

WILLIAM ALEXANDER

229 *Tenebrae*

SAYEST thou then to all that will to hearken:
'The Saint's star grows not dim,
But still through clouds that climb and deeps that darken
Is visible to him.

'Still when the sunset comes, He taketh order,
To whom the right belongs,
Sending His own away across the border,
Silverly and with songs'?

Nay; God prepares His kings for coronation
Not as might you or I,
And, being wondrous, works His preparation
For kingship wondrously.

Not always is the triumph of the sainting
That which our hearts expect,
Tearfully, roughly, doubtingly, and fainting,
How many souls elect

Pass out to that within the lifted curtain,
Roughly into the smooth,
Doubtful into the for ever certain,
The circumfulgent truth?

Tearfully, tearfully, becoming tearless
When trouble's all but o'er,
Fainting when well they might at last be fearless,
Seeing they touch the shore;

Questioning hard by the school unemulous
    Where half our questions cease,
Scarcely a bow-shot off their beds, and tremulous
    Upon the verge of peace;

Head dropping just before the crown is fitted,
    Eyes dim at break of day,
Feet walking feebly through the meadows wetted
    With April into May.

Thanks if some dying light there be, some sweetness
    To me and mine allow'd;
But if so be that human incompleteness
    Compass us like a cloud,

Softly on me and mine, when that is ended,
    Eternal light let fall,
And, after darkness, be our way attended
    By light perpetual.

230 *Frost-Morning*

THE morn is cold. A whiteness newly brought
    Lightly and loosely powders every place,
The panes among yon trees that eastward face
Flash rosy fire from the opposite dawning caught,—
As the face flashes with a splendid thought,
As the heart flashes with a touch of grace
When heaven's light comes on ways we cannot trace,
Unsought, yet lovelier than we ever sought.
In the blue northern sky is a pale moon,

Through whose thin texture something doth appear
Like the dark shadow of a branchy tree.—
Fit morning for the prayers of one like me,
Whose life is in midwinter, and must soon
Come to the shortest day of all my year!

MARY EVA KELLY

(MRS. O'DOHERTY) (54)

231

To Erin

1825-

O IRELAND! Ireland! proud hearts are breaking
For thee to-day,
And eyes that watched for thy glad awaking
Are turned away.
And voices low and tearful,
Are heard of Hope to sing;
But the voice in our heart so fearful,
Nor comfort nor hope can bring.

O Ireland! Ireland! thy life is closing
In the death of pain;
From thy broken heart is slowly oozing
The shower of crimson rain.
There thou art prostrate lying,
With the age of grief grown grey;
There thou art faintly sighing
The dream of the years away.

MARY EVA KELLY

O Ireland ! Ireland ! it is still unriven,
That clanking chain ;
Yet the countless wealth that for thee was given
Might ransom Cain.
In vain were they gifted and brave and truthful—
Our martyred host ;
Thy cause is woe to the old, or youthful—
All, all are lost !

But another, and yet another,
O'er thy cold bier,
Oh, pallid and lifeless mother,
Are watching near ;
They dream in their grief's wild madness
That thou wilt awake again—
They call thee with frenzied sadness,
Those heart-wrung and stricken men !

O Ireland ! Ireland ! dost hear them blending
That piercing dole,
Through the cloud-wrapt skies ascending,
Like the cry of a ruined soul.
They know not, O blessed Mary !
'Tis flowers o'er a corpse they fling ;
They hear not the *Miserere*
The pitying angels sing.

O Ireland ! Ireland ! no streak of dawning
Is on the sky ;
Still at our feet is the wide gulf yawning,
Where treasures on treasures lie.

Down through the deep, deep darkness
Victim on victim springs,
But the hour of its closing, never,
Or morning or midnight brings!

232 *Remembrance*

From the Irish

HOW my heart aches for you!
How my heart breaks for you,
All the day, all the night, all the year through!
Ah! though I'd sigh for you,
Ev'n till I die for you,
Never a meeting may come for us two!

How my heart craves for you!
How my heart raves for you!
Haunted by thoughts that for ever will cling,
Ah! but no gleam of you,
Only this dream of you,
Daylight, or midnight, or twilight will bring!

Ah! for the vanished years,
Seen through my blinding tears,
Down the black river of life as I go—
Drifting all wearily,
Onward so drearily,
While the rain falls and the wild tempests blow.

MARY EVA KELLY

Burning with love for you,
Looking above for you,
Filled with this longing and sorrow and pain!
Ah! though I'd sigh for you,
Ev'n till I die for you,
Never on earth shall we two meet again!

THOMAS D'ARCY McGEE

233 *The Celts*

1825-1868

LONG, long ago, beyond the misty space
Of twice a thousand years,
In Erin old there dwelt a mighty race,
Taller than Roman spears;
Like oaks and towers they had a giant grace,
Were fleet as deers,
With winds and waves they made their 'biding place,
These western shepherd seers.

Their Ocean-God was Manannan, MacLir, (55)
Whose angry lips,
In their white foam, full often would inter
Whole fleets of ships;
Cromah their Day-god, and their Thunderer
Made morning and eclipse;
Bride was their Queen of song, and unto her
They prayed with fire-touched lips.

Great were their deeds, their passions and their sports;
With clay and stone
They piled on strath and shore those mystic forts,
Not yet o'erthrown;
On cairn-crown'd hills they held their council-courts;
While youths alone,
With giant dogs, explored the elk resorts,
And brought them down.

Of these was Fin, the father of the Bard,
Whose ancient song
Over the clamour of all change is heard,
Sweet-voic'd and strong.
Fin once o'ertook Grania, the golden-hair'd,
The fleet and young;
From her the lovely, and from him the fear'd,
The primal poet sprung.

Ossian! two thousand years of mist and change
Surround thy name—
Thy Finian heroes now no longer range
The hills of fame.
The very name of Fin and Gaul sound strange—
Yet thine the same—
By miscalled lake and desecrated grange—
Remains, and shall remain!

The Druid's altar and the Druid's creed
We scarce can trace,
There is not left an undisputed deed
Of all your race,

Save your majestic song, which hath their speed,
And strength and grace ;
In that sole song, they live and love, and bleed—
It bears them on thro' space.

O, inspir'd giant ! shall we e'er behold,
In our own time,
One fit to speak your spirit on the wold,
Or seize your rhyme ?
One pupil of the past, as mighty soul'd
As in the prime,
Were the fond, fair, and beautiful, and bold—
They, of your song sublime !

234 *Salutation to the Celts*

HAIL to our Celtic brethren, wherever they may be,
In the far woods of Oregon or o'er the Atlantic sea ;
Whether they guard the banner of St. George in Indian vales,
Or spread beneath the nightless North experimental sails—
One in name and in fame
Are the sea-divided Gaels.

Though fallen the state of Erin, and changed the Scottish land,
Though small the power of Mona, though unwaked Lewellyn's band,

Though Ambrose Merlin's prophecies are held as idle
tales,
Though Iona's ruined cloisters are swept by northern
gales:
One in name and in fame
Are the sea-divided Gaels.

In Northern Spain and Italy our brethren also dwell,
And brave are the traditions of their fathers that they
tell:
The Eagle or the Crescent in the dawn of history
pales
Before the advancing banners of the great Rome-
conquering Gaels.
One in name and in fame
Are the sea-divided Gaels.

A greeting and a promise unto them all we send;
Their character our charter is, their glory is our end,—
Their friend shall be our friend, our foe whoe'er assails
The glory or the story of the sea-divided Gaels.
One in name and in fame
Are the sea-divided Gaels.

235 *The Man of the North Countrie*

HE came from the North, and his words were few,
But his voice was kind and his heart was true;
And I knew by his eyes no guile had he,
So I married the man of the North Countrie.

Oh ! Garryowen may be more gay,
Than this quiet street of Ballibay ;
And I know the sun shines softly down
On the river that passes my native town.

But there's not—I say it with joy and pride—
Better man than mine in Munster wide ;
And Limerick town has no happier hearth
Than mine has been with my man of the North.

I wish that in Munster they only knew
The kind, kind neighbours I came unto :
Small hate or scorn would ever be
Between the South and the North Countrie.

236 *Home Thoughts*

IF Will had wings,
  How fast I'd flee,
To the home of my heart
  O'er the seething sea !
If Wishes were power,
  If Words were spells,
I'd be this hour
  Where my own love dwells.

My own love dwells
  In the storied land,
Where the Holy Wells
  Sleep in yellow sand ;

And the emerald lustre
  Of Paradise beams,
Over homes that cluster
  Round singing streams.

I, sighing, alas!
  Exist alone;
My youth is as grass
  On an unsunned stone;
Bright to the eye,
  But unfelt below,
As sunbeams that lie
  Over Arctic snow.

My heart is a lamp
  That love must relight,
Or the world's fire-damp
  Will quench it quite;
In the breast of my dear,
  My life-tide springs—
Oh! I'd hurry home here,
  If Will had wings.

For she never was weary
  Of blessing me,
When morn rose dreary
  On thatch and tree;
She evermore chanted
  Her song of Faith,
When darkness daunted
  On hill and heath.

THOMAS D'ARCY McGEE

If Will had wings,
  How fast I'd flee
To the home of my heart
  O'er the seething sea!
If Wishes were power,
  If Words were spells,
I'd be this hour
  Where my own love dwells.

TIMOTHY DANIEL SULLIVAN

237 *Song from the Backwoods*

1827-

DEEP in Canadian woods we've met,
  From one bright island flown;
Great is the land we tread, but yet
  Our hearts are with our own.
And ere we leave this shanty small,
  While fades the Autumn day,
    We'll toast Old Ireland!
    Dear Old Ireland!
    Ireland, boys, hurrah!

We've heard her faults a hundred times,
  The new ones and the old,
In songs and sermons, rants and rhymes,
  Enlarged some fifty-fold.
But take them all, the great and small,
  And this we've got to say:—
    Here's dear Old Ireland!
    Good Old Ireland!
    Ireland, boys, hurrah!

We know that brave and good men tried
  To snap her rusty chain,
That patriots suffered, martyrs died,
  And all, 'tis said, in vain;
But no, boys, no! a glance will show
  How far they've won their way—
    Here's good Old Ireland!
    Loved Old Ireland!
    Ireland, boys, hurrah!

We've seen the wedding and the wake,
  The patron and the fair;
And lithe young frames at the dear old games
  In the kindly Irish air;
And the loud 'hurroo,' we have heard it too,
  And the thundering 'Clear the way!'
    Here's gay Old Ireland!
    Dear Old Ireland!
    Ireland, boys, hurrah!

And well we know in the cool grey eves,
  When the hard day's work is o'er,
How soft and sweet are the words that greet
  The friends who meet once more;
With 'Mary machree!' 'My Pat! 'tis he!'
  And 'My own heart night and day!'
    Ah, fond Old Ireland!
    Dear Old Ireland!
    Ireland, boys, hurrah!

And happy and bright are the groups that pass
  From their peaceful homes, for miles
O'er fields, and roads, and hills, to Mass,
  When Sunday morning smiles!

And deep the zeal their true hearts feel
  When low they kneel and pray,
    O, dear Old Ireland !
    Blest Old Ireland !
    Ireland, boys, hurrah !

But deep in Canadian woods we've met,
  And we never may see again
The dear old isle where our hearts are set,
  And our first fond hopes remain !
But come, fill up another cup,
  And with every sup let's say—
    'Here's dear Old Ireland !
    Loved Old Ireland !
    Ireland, boys, hurrah !'

238 *A Soldier's Wake* (56)

1856

AND this is all she has to lay
  To-night upon the snowy sheets
Before the friends who come the way,
  And sighing take their humble seats—
This medal, bravely, dearly won,
Poor token of her gallant son.

But over this, as nought beside
  Of him she loved to her remains,
The lights are lit, the keen is cried,
  And women croon their saddest strains,
While men who knew his boyhood well,
Say, foes went down before he fell.

These clasps and medal ; only these !
  For this she nursed and loved him long,
She rocked him softly on her knees,
  And filled his ears with pleasant song,
And saw him with a mother's pride,
Grow up and strengthen by her side.

Till bright with manhood's glowing charms
  He in his turn her nurse became,
He clasped her in his manly arms,
  And fondly propped her drooping frame.
Her step grew weak, her eye grew dim,
But then she lived and moved in him.

He went ; he joined the deadly fight,
  His true heart loved her not the less ;
But these are all she has to-night
  To light and cheer her loneliness—
These silver honours, dearly won,
Poor tokens of her gallant son.

But even these, to-morrow morn
  When lights burn out and friends depart,
Shall round her withered neck be worn,
  Shall lie upon her weary heart
Till death, for his dear memory's sake,
And then—shall deck another wake.

ELLEN MARY PATRICK DOWNING[1]

239 *My Owen*

1828–1869

PROUD of you, fond of you, clinging so near
to you,
Light is my heart now I know I am dear to you!
Glad is my voice now, so free it may sing for you
All the wild love which is burning within for you!
Tell me once more, tell it over and over,
The tale of that eve which first saw you my lover.
Now I need never blush
At my heart's hottest gush—
The wife of my Owen her heart may discover!

Proud of you, fond of you, having all right in you,
Quitting all else through my love and delight in
you!
Glad is my heart since 'tis beating so nigh to you!
Light is my step for it always may fly to you!
Clasped in your arms where no sorrow can reach
to me,
Reading your eyes till new love they shall teach
to me.
Though wild and weak till now,
By that blest marriage vow,
More than the wisest know your heart shall preach
to me.

[1] 'Mary' of the *Nation*.

WILLIAM B. M'BURNEY (57)

240 *The Croppy Boy*

A Ballad of '98

'GOOD men and true! in this house who dwell,
To a stranger bouchal,[1] I pray you tell
Is the priest at home? or may he be seen?
I would speak a word with Father Green.'

'The Priest's at home, boy, and may be seen;
'Tis easy speaking with Father Green;
But you must wait, till I go and see
If the holy father alone may be.'

The youth has entered an empty hall—
What a lonely sound has his light foot-fall!
And the gloomy chamber's chill and bare,
With a vested Priest in a lonely chair.

The youth has knelt to tell his sins;
'*Nomine Dei*,' the youth begins:
At '*mea culpa*' he beats his breast,
And in broken murmurs he speaks the rest.

'At the siege of Ross did my father fall,
And at Gorey my loving brothers all,
I alone am left of my name and race,
I will go to Wexford and take their place.

[1] Boy.

'I cursed three times since last Easter day—
At mass-time once I went to play;
I passed the churchyard one day in haste,
And forgot to pray for my mother's rest.

'I bear no hate against living thing;
But I love my country above my King.
Now, Father! bless me, and let me go
To die, if God has ordained it so.'

The Priest said nought, but a rustling noise
Made the youth look above in wild surprise;
The robes were off, and in scarlet there
Sat a yeoman captain with fiery glare.

With fiery glare and with fury hoarse,
Instead of blessing, he breathed a curse:—
''Twas a good thought, boy, to come here and
shrive,
For one short hour is your time to live.

'Upon yon river three tenders float,
The Priest's in one, if he isn't shot—
We hold his house for our Lord the King,
And, amen, say I, may all traitors swing!'

At Geneva Barrack[1] that young man died,
And at Passage they have his body laid.
Good people who live in peace and joy,
Breathe a prayer and a tear for the Croppy boy.

[1] Then a military station in co. Waterford.

JOHN SAVAGE

241 *Shane's Head* (58)

Scene—Before Dublin Castle. *Night*—A Clansman of Shane O'Neill discovers his Chief's head on a pole.

1828–1888

IS it thus, O Shane the haughty ! Shane the valiant ! that we meet—
Have my eyes been lit by Heaven but to guide me to defeat ?
Have I no chief, or you no clan, to give us both defence,
Or must I, too, be statued here with thy cold eloquence ?
Thy ghastly head grins scorn upon old Dublin's Castle Tower,
Thy shaggy hair is wind-tossed, and thy brow seems rough with power ;
Thy wrathful lips, like sentinels, by foulest treachery stung,
Look rage upon the world of wrong, but chain thy fiery tongue.

That tongue, whose Ulster accent woke the ghost of Columbkill,
Whose warrior words fenced round with spears the oaks of Derry Hill ;
Whose reckless tones gave life and death to vassals and to knaves,
And hunted hordes of Saxons into holy Irish graves.

The Scotch marauders whitened when his war-cry
met their ears,
And the death-bird, like a vengeance, poised above his
stormy cheers;
Ay, Shane, across the thundering sea, out-chanting it,
your tongue
Flung wild un-Saxon war-whoopings the Saxon Court
among.

Just think, O Shane! the same moon shines on Liffey
as on Foyle,
And lights the ruthless knaves on both, our kinsmen
to despoil;
And you the hope, voice, battle-axe, the shield of us
and ours,
A murdered, trunkless, blinding sight above these
Dublin towers!
Thy face is paler than the moon; my heart is paler
still—
My heart? I had no heart—'twas yours—'twas
yours! to keep or kill.
And you kept it safe for Ireland, Chief—your life,
your soul, your pride;
But they sought it in thy bosom, Shane—with proud
O'Neill it died.
You were turbulent and haughty, proud, and keen as
Spanish steel—
But who had right of these, if not our Ulster's Chief,
O'Neill,
Who reared aloft the 'Bloody Hand' until it paled
the sun,
And shed such glory on Tyrone as chief had never
done?

He was 'turbulent' with traitors; he was 'haughty' with the foe;
He was 'cruel,' say ye, Saxons! Ay! he dealt ye blow for blow!
He was 'rough' and 'wild'—and who's not wild to see his hearth-stone razed?
He was 'merciless as fire'—ah, ye kindled him—he blazed!
He was 'proud'—yes, proud of birthright, and because he flung away
Your Saxon stars of princedom, as the rock does mocking spray,
He was wild, insane for vengeance—ay! and preached it till Tyrone
Was ruddy, ready, wild, too, with 'Red hands' to clutch their own.

'The Scots are on the border, Shane!' Ye Saints, he makes no breath:
I remember when that cry would wake him up almost from death.
Art truly dead and cold? O Chief! art thou to Ulster lost?
'Dost hear, dost hear? By Randolph led, the troops the Foyle have crossed!'
He's truly dead! he must be dead! nor is his ghost about—
And yet no tomb could hold his spirit tame to such a shout:
The pale face droopeth northward—ah! his soul must loom up there,
By old Armagh, or Antrim's glynns, Lough Foyle, or Bann the Fair!

I'll speed me Ulster-wards—your ghost must wander
there, proud Shane,
In search of some O'Neill, through whom to throb its
hate again.

242 *The Plaint of the Wild Flower*

I WAS not born for the town,
Where all that's pure and humble's trodden down:
My home is in the woods—
The over-arching, cloistered solitudes;
Where the full-toned psalm
Of Nature at her matin broke the calm
Of cloudy pillowed Night
With calmness made more voluble by light:
And where the Minstrel Noon
Made every young stem spring as to a tune;
Ay, where our joys were led
To suit the fluted measures of the orb o'erhead.
I am forlorn
Here 'mid the waking jargon of the day;
Noon brings no light, no song of birds at play;
My plume is in the dust! I pine and pray
For the old woods, the grand old woods away
Where I was born.

Here I am dying; I want room—
Room for the air of Heaven, for the bloom
Of never-tiring nature; room
For the verdure-freighted clouds, and thunder-boom
That sounds relief to drouthy earth;
Room for the sunlight and th' exhaustless mirth

Of laughing July's breeze,
Untangling the meshes of the branching trees;
Room for cool night and ruddy day,
For peace, for health—aught naturally gay;
Room to take vital breath,
And look on anything not painted death!
I am forlorn—
I, who from my earliest golden age,
Sat by the regal Oak's foot, like a page,
And, mantled in moss, at the close of the day
Slept by my prince, in the woods far away
Where I was born.

Here is no room—no room
For e'en a flower's life; nothing but a tomb.
O forest gods! look down,
And shield your other offspring from the town.
Ah! would that I could die
Where o'er my wreck the forest flowers might sigh,
And clustering shrubs anear
Weave dirges low, like leaves above my bier;
Where kindly chestnut leaves
Would shade the woe of every plant that grieves,
And e'en the great Oak's head
Let fall the tears of dew when this poor page is dead.
I am forlorn:
Night brings no darkness and the day no light;
Noon brings but noise to vary my affright;
I'm dying 'neath the city's loathsome blight,
Far, O my mother Nature, from thy sight,
Far from thy earth, thy heaven, and the woodland bright
Where I was born.

CHARLES JOSEPH KICKHAM

243 *Rory of the Hill*

1828–1882

'THAT rake up near the rafters, why leave it there so long?
The handle, of the best of ash, is smooth, and straight, and strong;
And, mother, will you tell me, why did my father frown,
When to make the hay, in summer-time, I climbed to take it down?'
She looked into her husband's eyes, while her own with light did fill,
'You'll shortly know the reason, boy!' said Rory of the Hill.

The midnight moon is lighting up the slopes of Sliav-na-man,—
Whose foot affrights the startled hares so long before the dawn?
He stopped just where the Anner's stream winds up the woods anear,
Then whistled low and looked around to see the coast was clear.
A sheeling door flew open—in he stepped with right good will—
'God save all here, and bless your work,' said Rory of the Hill.

Right hearty was the welcome that greeted him, I
 ween,
For years gone by he fully proved how well he loved
 the Green ;
And there was one among them who grasped him by
 the hand—
One who through all that weary time roamed on a
 foreign strand ;
He brought them news from gallant friends that made
 their heart-strings thrill—
'My sowl ! I never doubted them !' said Rory of the
 Hill.

They sat around the humble board till dawning of
 the day,
And yet not song nor shout I heard—no revellers
 were they :
Some brows flushed red with gladness, while some
 were grimly pale ;
But pale or red, from out those eyes flashed souls that
 never quail !
'And sing us now about the vow, they swore for to
 fulfil'—
'You'll read it yet in History,' said Rory of the
 Hill.

Next day the ashen handle, he took down from where
 it hung,
The toothed rake, full scornfully, into the fire he
 flung ;
And in its stead a shining blade is gleaming once
 again—

Oh! for a hundred thousand of such weapons and such men!
Right soldierly he wielded it, and, going through his drill,
'Attention!'—'Charge!'—'Front, point!'—'Advance!' cried Rory of the Hill.

She looked at him with woman's pride, with pride and woman's fears;
She flew to him, she clung to him, and dried away her tears;
He feels her pulse beat truly, while her arms around him twine—
'Now God be praised for your stout heart, brave little wife of mine.'
He swung his first-born in the air, while joy his heart did fill—
'You'll be a Freeman yet, my boy,' said Rory of the Hill.

Oh! knowledge is a wondrous power, and stronger than the wind;
And thrones shall fall, and despots bow before the might of mind;
The poet and the orator, the heart of man can sway,
And would to the kind heavens that Wolfe Tone were here to-day!
Yet trust me, friends, dear Ireland's strength, her truest strength, is still,
The rough and ready roving boys, like Rory of the Hill.

CHARLES JOSEPH KICKHAM

244 *The Irish Peasant Girl*

SHE lived beside the Anner,
  At the foot of Sliev-na-man,
A gentle peasant girl,
  With mild eyes like the dawn;
Her lips were dewy rosebuds;
  Her teeth of pearls rare;
And a snow-drift 'neath a beechen bough
  Her neck and nut-brown hair

How pleasant 'twas to meet her
  On Sunday, when the bell
Was filling with its mellow tones
  Lone wood and grassy dell!
And when at eve young maidens
  Strayed the river bank along,
The widow's brown-haired daughter
  Was loveliest of the throng.

O brave, brave Irish girls—
  We well may call you brave!—
Sure the least of all your perils
  Is the stormy ocean wave,
When you leave our quiet valleys,
  And cross the Atlantic's foam,
To hoard your hard-won earnings
  For the helpless ones at home.

'Write word to my own dear mother—
  Say, we'll meet with God above;
And tell my little brothers
  I send them all my love;

May the angels ever guard them,
  Is their dying sister's prayer'—
And folded in the letter
  Was a braid of nut-brown hair.

Ah, cold, and well-nigh callous,
  This weary heart has grown
For thy helpless fate, dear Ireland,
  And for sorrows of my own;
Yet a tear my eye will moisten,
  When by Anner side I stray,
For the lily of the mountain foot
  That withered far away.

ELLEN FORRESTER

245 *The Irish Mother at her Child's Grave*

1828–1883

MY very heart-strings, sure, will burst asunder—
  Oh, woe is me!
Damp is the sod that thou art sleeping under—
  Astór machree.

Narrow and dark the bed where thou art lying,
  All cold and lone;
And the wild winds above thee, shrieking, sighing,
  Machree! Ochone!

ELLEN FORRESTER

The frost is nipping thee, my tender blossom,
In that cold place ;
Mavourneen, come and nestle in my bosom
Thy poor chill face.

Thine empty cradle stands beside the fire,
In the cold cot ;
They would have moved it, but at my desire
They touched it not.

Then come ! I'll clasp my arms so close around thee,
And bear thee home ;
Thy father says he will not live without thee ;
Come, darling, come !

I speak to thee, achora ! Don't you hear me ?
My heart will break ;
Why art thou mute, my babe, and I so near thee ?
Alanna, speak ?

My gentle love-bird, thou art fled for ever ;
Thy song is o'er ;
Thy voice is hushed, and I shall hear thee never—
Oh, never more !

The sunshine of my life has all departed ;
The day is gone ;
The night has come, and I am broken-hearted—
Ochone, ochone !

ELLEN FORRESTER

246 *An Irish Beauty*

DARK eyes softly beaming, and pearly teeth gleaming,
And black rippling tresses, loose, flowing, and free;
A face sweet and simple, and many an arch dimple—
That's Nora, my Nora, sweet Nora Magee.

A small foot, a neat foot, a dainty and fleet foot,
No foot in the dance half so nimble you'd see;
As gay as a fairy, and graceful and airy—
That's Nora, my Nora, sweet Nora Magee.

Now teasing, now vexing, and always perplexing
The heart that adores her to such a degree;
Now frowning, now smiling, bewitching, beguiling—
That's Nora, my Nora, sweet Nora Magee.

Dark eyes softly beaming, and pearly teeth gleaming,
Capricious, and wilful, and charming is she;
In kind mood or cruel, she's always my jewel—
My own darling Nora, sweet Nora Magee.

WHITLEY STOKES

247 *From 'Omar Khayyám'*

1830–1909

I DASHED my clay-cup on the stone hard-by:
The reckless frolic raised my heart on high:
Then said a shard with momentary voice:
'As thou have I been; thou shalt be as I.'

WHITLEY STOKES

Annihilation makes me not to fear :
In truth it seems more sweet than lingering here :
  My life was sent me as a loan unsought :
When pay-day comes I'll pay without a tear.

Has God made profit from my coming ? Nay.
His glory gains not when I go away.
  Mine ear has never heard from mortal man
This coming and this going, why are they ?

I'd not have come, had this been left to me :
Nor would I go, to go if I were free :
  Oh ! best of all, upon this lonely earth
Neither to come nor go, yea, not to be !

Oh ! that there were some place where men could rest,
Some end to look for in this lonely quest,
  Some hope that in a hundred thousand years
Our dust might blossom on the Mother's breast !

Alas for me ! the Book of Youth is read :
The fresh glad Spring is now December dead :
  That bird of joy whose name was Youth is flown :
Ay me, I know not how he came or fled !

Sweet airs are blowing on the rose of May :
Sweet eyes are shining down the garden gay :
  Aught sweet of dead yestreen you cannot say—
No more of it, so sweet is this to-day !

When Death uproots my life-plant, ear and grain,
And flings them forth to moulder on the plain,
  If men shall make a wine-jug of my clay,
And brim with wine, 'twill leap to life again.

This jar was once a lover like to me,
Lost in delight of wooing one like thee;
  And, lo! the handle here upon the neck
Was once the arm that held her neck in fee.

Your love-nets hold my hair-forsaken head:
Therefore my lips in warming wine are red:
  Repentance born of Reason you have wrecked,
And Time has torn the robe that Patience made.

248 *Saving Love*

METHOUGHT I stood before the face of God:
  The cherubim in radiance round me sang:
  Then did the eagle-souls of poets clang
(Soaring to His sun-throne), triumphant laud,
Because high songs result o'er all the broad
  Expanse of earth in noble deeds. Upsprang
  Our triple shout of 'Holy!' heaven outrang:
Aye nearer unto Christ we drew unawed.
'Not faith, O wielder of the worlds, nor light,
Nor lays,' I sang, 'have led my soul to Thee;
  But love for her whom Thou hast made so fair.'
Then chanted those beside the Sovran Might:
'Love-angels, dearest to the Lord are we:
  Our sister makes us dearer than we were' (59).

WHITLEY STOKES

249 *The Viking*

Time—Nightfall in the middle of the ninth century. *Place*—At sea, on the poop of a Norse Viking's galley. *Author*—A Gaelic bard captured by the Viking. *Cause of making*—Orders to praise the Viking and his gods.

'BITTER in sooth is the wind to-night,
Rousing the wrath of the white-haired sea;
But smooth-sea-sailing is no delight
To Norroway's heroes fierce and free.

'Strong and swift are the waves to-night,
Roaring over the reefs a-lee:
Stronger, swifter thy ranks in fight,
Charging thy foes till they break and flee.

'Bright and keen are the stars to-night,
Sending their shafts to pierce the sea:
Brighter thy swords when they flash and smite,
Keener thy darts when they drench the lea.

'Glad are the hearts of thy gods to-night:
Odin, the Father, is fain to see
Eyeballs of fire and arms of might,
Sea-kings sailing in warriors' glee.

'Why do I launch this lay to-night,
I, a singer from Christentie?
Thor is stronger than Christ the White:
Therefore I praise thy gods and thee.

'Little but song have I to-night :
  Guerdon of gold give thou to me :
Laud the singer who sings aright :
  Give him his sword, and set him free !'

250 *King Ailill's Death*

From the 'Book of Leinster'

I KNOW who won the peace of God—
  The old king Ailill of the Bann,
Who fought beyond the Irish sea
  All day against a Connaught clan.

The king was routed. In the flight
  He muttered to his charioteer,
'Look back : the slaughter, is it red ?
  The slayers, are they drawing near ?'

The man looked back. The west-wind blew
  Dead clansmen's hair against his face.
He heard the war-shout of his foes,
  The death-cry of his ruined race.

The foes came darting from the height
  Like pine-trees down a swollen fall.
Like heaps of hay in flood, his clan
  Swept on or sank—he saw it all,

And spake, 'The slaughter is full red,
 But we may still be saved by flight.'
Then groaned the king. 'No sin of theirs
 Falls on my people here to-night.

'No sin of theirs, but sin of mine,
 For I was worst of evil kings,
Unrighteous, wrathful, hurling down
 To death or shame all weaker things.

'Draw rein, and turn the chariot round.
 My face against the foemen bend.
When I am seen and slain, mayhap
 The slaughter of my tribe will end.'

They drew, and turned. Down came the foe.
 The king fell cloven on the sod.
The slaughter then was stayed, and so
 King Ailill won the peace of God.

ROBERT DWYER JOYCE

251 *Finneen O'Driscoll the Rover* (60)

1830–1883

AN old castle towers o'er the billows
 That thunder by Cleena's green land,
And there dwelt as gallant a rover
 As ever grasped hilt in the hand;
Eight stately towers of the waters
 Lie anchored in Baltimore Bay;

And over their twenty score sailors
Bold Finneen the Rover holds sway.
Then O, for Finneen the Rover,
Finneen O'Driscoll the free,
As straight as the mast of his galley,
And strong as a wave of the sea!

The Saxons of Cork and Moyallo,
They harried his coasts with their bands;
He gave them a taste of his cannon
And drove them like wolves from his lands;
The men of Clan London brought over
Their strong fleet to make him a slave;
He met them on Mizen's rough breakers,
And the sharks crunched their bones 'neath the wave.
Then O, for Finneen the Rover,
Finneen O'Driscoll the free,
With step like the red stag of Beara,
And voice like the bold sounding sea!

Long time in that strong island castle,
Or out on the waves with his clan,
He feasted and ventured and conquered,
But ne'er struck his colours to man.
In a fight 'gainst the foes of his country
He died as a brave man should die;
And he sleeps 'neath the waters of Cleena,
Where the waves sing his keen to the sky.
Then O, for Finneen the Rover,
Finneen O'Driscoll the free,
With eye like the osprey's at morning,
And smile like the sun on the sea!

ROBERT DWYER JOYCE

252 *The Drynán Dhun*[1]

BY road and by river the wild birds sing;
O'er mountain and valley the dewy leaves spring;
The gay flowers are shining, gilt o'er by the sun;
And fairest of all shines the Drynán Dhun.

The rath of the fairy, the ruin hoar,
With white silver splendour it decks them all o'er;
And down in the valleys where merry streams run,
How sweet smell the blossoms of the Drynán Dhun.

Ah! well I remember the soft spring day
I sat by my love 'neath its sweet-scented spray;
The day that she told me her heart I had won,
Beneath the white blossoms of the Drynán Dhun.

The streams they were singing their gladsome song,
The soft winds were blowing the wild woods among,
The mountains shone bright in the red setting sun,
As we sat 'neath the blossoms of the Drynán Dhun.

'Tis my prayer in the morning, my dream at night,
To sit thus again by my heart's dear delight,
With her blue eyes of gladness, her hair like the sun,
And her bright pleasant smile 'neath the Drynán
Dhun.

[1] The blackthorn or sloebush.

253 *Mairgréad Bán*[1]

MY wild heart's love, my woodland dove,
The tender and the true,
She dwells beside a blue stream's tide
That bounds through sweet Glenroe;
Through every change her love's the same,—
A long bright summer dawn,
A gentle flame,—and oh, her name
Is lovely Mairgréad bán:
Oh, joy, that on her paths I came,
My lovely Mairgréad bán!

When winter hoar comes freezing o'er
The mountains wild and grey,
Her neck is white as snow-wreaths bright
Upon thy crags, Knockea;
Her lips are red as roses sweet
On Darra's flowery lawn;
Her fairy feet are light and fleet,
My gentle Mairgréad bán;
And oh, her steps I love to meet,
My own dear Mairgréad bán!

When silence creeps o'er Houra's steeps,
As blue eve ends its reign,
Her long locks' fold is like the gold
That gleams o'er sky and main.

[1] Pronounced *Maureed bawn*—fair-haired Margaret.

My heart's dark sorrow fled away
  Like night before the dawn,
When one spring day I went astray,
  And met my Mairgréad bán,
And felt her blue eyes' witching ray,
  My lovely Mairgréad bán.

One summer noon, to hear the tune
  Of wild birds in the wood,
Where murmuring streams flashed back the
    beams,
  All rapt in bliss I stood;
The birds sang from the fairy moat,
  From greenwood, brake, and lawn;
But never throat could chant a note
  So sweet as Mairgréad bán,
As through the vales her wild songs float,
  My lovely Mairgréad bán.

254 *Song of the Forest Fairy*

WHERE the gold moss hangs on the mighty
    oak,
Where never was heard the woodman's stroke,
  In the ancient woods
    Where the wild deer bide—
  Where the heron broods
    By the lakelet's side,
Morn, noon, and eve, in the rosy air,
We dance and sport full merrily there.

ROBERT DWYER JOYCE

At night in a glade of the brightest green,
We meet with glad homage our youthful queen.
  There in revel and feast
    We spend the night,
  Or in balmy rest
    Till the morning light;
Or out on the greensward smooth and fair,
We dance and sport so merrily there.

'Tis glorious to see the globes of dew
By the red beams of morn pierced through and
    through;
  'Tis sweet to peer
    Where the wild-flower gleams,
  And sweeter to hear
    The birds and the streams;
And sweeter than all in the blue, bright air,
To dance and sport so merrily there!

ELLEN O'LEARY

255 *To God and Ireland true*

1831-1889

I SIT beside my darling's grave,
  Who in the prison died,
And though my tears fall thick and fast,
  I think of him with pride:
Ay, softly fall my tears like dew,
For one to God and Ireland true.

'I love my God o'er all,' he said,
 'And then I love my land,
And next I love my Lily sweet,
 Who pledged me her white hand:
To each—to all—I'm ever true,
To God—to Ireland—and to you.'

No tender nurse his hard bed smoothed
 Or softly raised his head;
He fell asleep and woke in Heaven
 Ere I knew he was dead;
Yet why should I my darling rue?
He was to God and Ireland true.

Oh! 'tis a glorious memory;
 I'm prouder than a queen
To sit beside my hero's grave
 And think on what has been:
And oh, my darling, I am true
To God—to Ireland—and to you!

STOPFORD AUGUSTUS BROOKE

256 *The Huldra-Woman*

1832–

WHO walks alone in the red pinewood,
 Under the Norway sky?
Olaf the Dane, and his heart is full
 Of wrath and misery.

Then out of the gloom he came into a glade,
And the moon was bright therein ;
And he saw a maiden in the midst,
As beautiful as sin.

Oh soft and fierce her deep grey eyes,
But her cheek like blood on snow !
And her hair was like the flaming fire
Of war-ships in a low.

And she came daintily over the grass,
And laid her hand on his,
'Olaf,' she said, 'come, dance with me,
And thou shalt know my bliss.'

'Oh, I have no heart,' young Olaf said,
'To dance or kiss with thee !
For I am sick within, and moon and sun
Are both alike to me.'

Then he turned him round and saw her back,
And oh, the sight of dread !
For she was as hollow and dark as a boat,
From the heel unto the head.

'A fiend,' he cried, and her wildwood eyes
Flashed like a harlot's knife !
'I am Huldra,' she said, and softly smiled—
'And thou shalt lose thy life.'

Quoth Olaf, 'That would please me well ;
For the woman I love and hate,
Is hollow as thou from the head to the heart,
And death is a better mate.'

'Oh, is it so?' the Huldra laughed,
  'Then thou art free from me;
Stay, stay with me in the long pinewood
  And I will comfort thee.

'And thou shalt forget the liar thou lov'st
  When my arms are round thee flung:
I can make myself like a maid of the earth,
  And I am always young.'

'Is that better than death?' dark Olaf cried,
  'For damned I then shall be;
But I do not care a ray of the moon
  What happens unto me.

'I thought that Love was God in Heaven,
  But I find it flesh on earth;
Fill up the hollow of thy back,
  And come, and make me mirth.

'But swear the oath that binds thee most
  From me thou wilt not err,
For if I have not thee, I must
  Return again to her.'

'I swear by the forest and by the night
  To cling to thee like flame.'
'Then I'll stay,' he said, 'with thee;
  'Tis less of sorrow and shame.'

Woe, woe in Norway! A soul is lost,
  With Huldra gone to stay;
But joy for the woman, for she can love
  Again, and again betray.

257 *Nature and Love*

WHEN first I gave him all my love
  I took the beauty of the world;
Wild winds, and sunlight, stars above,
  And clouds upon the mountains furled,

The life of waters and of woods,
  The sweetness of the flowers and grass,
Dreams of the sunset, joyous moods
  The spirit of the Summer has;

I filled him with their soft romance,
  I set my heart within its shrine;
He saw the lovely countenance
  Of Nature, and then turned to mine.

All, all I loved was given to him,
  All, all I loved was shown to me;
And then, that evening grey and dim,
  The low moon burning o'er the sea,

He kissed me, I gave back his kiss,
  My arms were round him, warm and fast—
'Is Nature more,' I cried, 'than this?
  Have I not conquered her at last?'

Since then, he has loved, and loves, so much,
  That in the grave men say is sleep,
He shall not lose my sweet wild touch
  Through all the silence of the deep,

But, when the immortal passions move,
  Shall quick arise, and with a cry,
Run to mine arms, and say, 'O Love,
  Thou hast not forgotten!—no, nor I.'

258 *Death*

MY little hour of envied joy is past,
  My Love is dead;
Deep in her grave my passionate arms hold fast
  Her wounded head;
Oh, could I lie beside her!—even there
'Twere better than this earth and living air.

All children wonder that I never smile,
  Not mine their pain;
The green trees and the streams I loved beguile
  In vain, in vain;
Where, where is now my laughter, where her
  voice,
And her bright eyes that bade the woods rejoice?

Oh silent dwelling, homeless world, sad heart,
  Always alone!
How canst thou live and bear thy bitter part
  Now she is gone?
Clasp her cold heart to thine, and rise no more;
Enough of loveless life, shut to the door.

STOPFORD AUGUSTUS BROOKE

259 *Song*

From 'Riquet of the Tuft'

DEEP falls the dark, I cannot sleep, mine eyes
Are filled with night:
Tell me, my maidens, in the eastern skies,
Is there no light?
Cry to the moon to sink her lingering horn
In the dim seas, and let the day be born
When Love and I,
All ecstasy,
Shall see him coming through the gates of morn.

Bid him bring rosemary that ever keeps
Remembrance true:
And myrtles gathered where warm Venus sleeps
In fragrant dew;
And marigolds that wed the burning sun,
And close to tell desire the day is done;
And full-blown roses,
Passion's posies,
To deck the room where we shall be at one.

Scatter the flowers, uplift the hymn, he comes;
O Paradise!
Before him sound the pipes and merry drums,
And in his eyes
The morning breaks, and elfin queens above
Stoop to his smile, and hear, like me, the dove
Brood in his voice
And sing, 'Rejoice,
Come forth, my bride'—'I come, I come, my Love.'

JOHN WALSH

260 *Drimin Donn Dílis*[1]

1835–1881

OH! Drimin donn dílis! the landlord has come,
Like a foul blast of death has he swept o'er our home;
He has withered our roof-tree—beneath the cold sky,
Poor, houseless and homeless, to-night must we lie.

My heart it is cold as the white winter's snow;
My brain is on fire, and my blood's in a glow.
Oh! Drimin donn dílis! 'tis hard to forgive
When a robber denies us the right we should live.

With my health and my strength, with hard labour and toil,
I dried the wet marsh and I tilled the harsh soil;
I moiled the long day through, from morn till even,
And I thought in my heart I'd a foretaste of Heaven.

The Summer shone round us above and below,
The beautiful Summer that makes the flowers blow:
Oh! 'tis hard to forget it, and think I must bear
That strangers shall reap the reward of my care.

[1] The dear brown cow.

JOHN WALSH

Your limbs they were plump then—your coat it was
silk,
And never was wanted the mether of milk;
For freely it came in the calm Summer's noon,
While you munched to the time of the old milking
croon.

How often you left the green side of the hill,
To stretch in the shade, and to drink of the rill!
And often I freed you before the grey dawn,
From your snug little pen at the edge of the bawn.

But they racked and they ground me with tax and
with rent,
Till my heart it was sore, and my life-blood was spent:
To-day they have finished, and on the wide world,
With the mocking of fiends from my home was I
hurled.

I knelt down three times for to utter a prayer,
But my heart it was seared, and the words were not
there;
Oh! wild were the thoughts through my dizzy head
came,
Like the rushing of wind through a forest of flame.

I bid you, old comrade, a long last farewell;
For the gaunt hand of famine has clutched us too
well;
It severed the master and you, my good cow,
With a blight on his life, and a brand on his brow.

JOHN WALSH

261 *To my Promised Wife*

DEAR maiden, when the sun is down,
And darkness creeps above the town,
The woodlands' green is changed to brown,
And the mild light
Melting beneath the tall hills' frown
Steals into night,

I don an honest coat of grey,
And, setting stupid care at bay,
Across the fields of scented hay
I stroll along,
Humming some quaint old Irish lay
Or simple song.

And when, dear maid, I come to you,
A laughing eye of brightest blue,
And flushing cheek of crimson hue,
Tell whom I greet,
And bounds a little heart as true
As ever beat.

The green grass on the river-side,
The full moon dancing on the tide,
The half-blown rose that tries to hide
Her blush in dew,
Are fair, but none, my promised bride,
As fair as you.

And though, dear love, our gathered store
Of gold is small, the brighter ore
Of love's deep mine we'll seek the more,
And truth shall be
The guard beside our cottage-door,
Astór machree!

262 *The Western Winds*

A MAIDEN sat on an ocean-steep;
She gazed on the place where the sun went down,
Her face was mild as an infant's sleep,
Her silken hair was a wavy brown.
She murmured sadly, softly, and low,
As the soothing tone of the gentle dove,
'Of all the winds the heavens can blow,
The West, the West is the one I love.

'Last night I dreamed that a summer eve
Brought back my long-lost love to me;
He clasped me close, and "No longer grieve,"
He whispered me softly, "astór machree."
Alas, alas!' and her voice was low
As the plaintive tone of the gentle dove,
'The sun is gone, and the West winds blow,
Yet where, oh! where is my plighted love?

''Tis a long dark dream, like a funeral hymn;
Will it ever end—will it pass away?
My heart is sad, and my eyes are dim;
Will it ever behold hope's dawning day?'

Her voice sank down to an accent low
  As the soothing tone of the gentle dove—
'How sweet the rush of the West winds blow!
  But where, ah! where is my only love?

'If Eoghan comes, will he bring to me
  The heart that away from Erin he bore?
They say that all in that land are free,
  And perhaps he may love its maidens more.
Oh no, oh no!' she murmured low,
  As soft as the tone of the plaintive dove;
'The Western wind is the one, I know,
  That will bear me homeward the heart I love.

'Sad was the hour that saw him sail—
  'Twas for life, dear life, he was forced to flee;
Dark was the ship when she bent to the gale,
  For she bore my world, my all from me.
Astór!' she murmured, sad and low
  As the soothing tone of the gentle dove,
'Why did not I to that black ship go,
  And be near you for ever, my absent love?'

Weep not, sweet maid; for his face you will see;
  He will clasp that hand to his own once more;
He will tread o'er his native hills as free
  As he does even now on the distant shore;
For their ranks are full, and their hearts are true,
  And their arms are young, and bold, and brave;
We will see their ships when the sun sinks through
  The golden brim of the Western wave.

CHARLES P. O'CONOR

263 *Maura du of Ballyshannon*

1837–

MAURA du[1] of Ballyshannon!
  Maura du, my flower of flowers!
Can you hear me there out seaward,
  Calling back the bygone hours?
Maura du, my own, my honey!
  With wild passion still aglow,
I am singing you the old songs
  That I sung you long ago.
And you mind, love, how it ran on—
      'In your eyes astór machree!
      All my heaven there I see,
      And that's true!
      Maura du!
Maura du of Ballyshannon!'

Maura du of Ballyshannon!
  Maura du, my soul's one queen!
Big with love my heart is flying,
  Where the grass is growing green.
Maura du, my own, my honey!
  That I love you, well you know,
And still sing for you the old song,
  That I sung you long ago.
And you mind, love, how it ran on—
      'In your eyes astór machree!
      All my Heaven there I see,
      And that's true!
      Maura du!
Maura du of Ballyshannon!'

[1] Dark Mary.

CHARLES P. O'CONOR

Maura du of Ballyshannon !
  Maura du, the day is drear,
Ah, the night is long and weary,
  Far away from you, my dear !
Maura du, my own, my honey !
  Still let winds blow high or low,
I must sing to you the old song,
  That I sung you long ago,
And you mind, love, how it ran on—
      'In your eyes astór machree !
      All my Heaven there I see.
      And that's true !
      Maura du !
Maura du of Ballyshannon !'

Maura du of Ballyshannon !
  Maura du, when winds blow south,
I will with the birds fly homeward,
  There to kiss your Irish mouth.
Maura du, my own, my honey !
  When time is no longer foe,
By your side I'll sing the old song,
  That I sung you long ago,
And you mind, love, how it ran on—
      'In your eyes astór machree !
      All my Heaven there I see,
      And that's true !
      Maura du !
Maura du of Ballyshannon !'

JOHN FRANCIS O'DONNELL

264 *A Spinning Song*

1837–1874

MY love to fight the Saxon goes,
And bravely shines his sword of steel,
A heron's feather decks his brows,
And a spur on either heel;
His steed is blacker than a sloe,
And fleeter than the falling star;
Amid the surging ranks he'll go
And shout for joy of war.

Twinkle, twinkle, pretty spindle, let the white wool drift and dwindle,
Oh! we weave a damask doublet for my love's coat of steel.
Hark! the timid, turning treadle, crooning soft old-fashioned ditties
To the low, slow murmur of the brown, round wheel.

My love is pledged to Ireland's fight;
My love would die for Ireland's weal,
To win her back her ancient right,
And make her foemen reel.
Oh, close I'll clasp him to my breast
When homeward from the war he comes;
The fires shall light the mountain's crest,
The valley peal with drums.

JOHN FRANCIS O'DONNELL

Twinkle, twinkle, pretty spindle, let the white wool drift and dwindle,
Oh! we weave a damask doublet for my love's coat of steel.
Hark! the timid, turning treadle, crooning soft old-fashioned ditties
To the low, slow murmur of the brown, round wheel.

WILLIAM EDWARD HARTPOLE LECKY

265 *Old Age*

1838–1903

NOW the solemn shadows lengthen,
Life's long day is well nigh done,
Impulse fails and habits strengthen,
Pleasures vanish one by one.
Feebly o'er the dark'ning dial,
Parting rays their image fling;
Times of triumph, times of trial,
Lose their rapture, lose their sting.

How much now appears unreal
In the past that stirred us so:
Pinings for the high ideal,
Passion's dreams, ambition's glow;
All life's aims grow dimmer, fainter,
With a languid, calm decay,
Fading as the mighty Painter
Shades the scene with twilight grey.

Fancy dies. Illusions follow.
  Love lasts best, but not its bloom;
And the gayest laugh sounds hollow,
  Echoed from an op'ning tomb.
Soon the past holds all our treasure,
  All that childless age loves best.
Young men still may live for pleasure:
  Old men only ask for rest.

266 *Voices of the Evening*

THE sailors were chanting their measured songs
  To the throb of the glittering oar,
And each ripple seemed laden with melody,
  As it broke on the silent shore.

And the sun went down in the burning sky,
  And the western wave grew bright,
As the day, like a dream of loveliness,
  Melted in misty light.

And a spirit within me seemed to say
  Farewell to the paths of toil,
Farewell to the strife of the labouring pen,
  The strife of the barren soil.

I ask not the will that can hew its way
  Where the battles of life are fought,
Or the mind that can melt down the world of dreams
  In the fire of searching thought.

No lovelier light adorns the sky
Than the trembling light of the star,
And the mind that shines with a wavering beam
Is the best and the loveliest far.

I ask not to climb to Wealth's glittering heights,
Or to stand where Fame's sunflush glows,
But the twilight calm and the valley's shade,
And the violet more than the rose.

But the sun sank down, and a keen, fresh breeze
Renerved my spirit again,
And a voice came floating over the waves,
And it told of strife with men.

For life is a struggle and not a dream,
And ambition's power must last,
Till the first fresh strength of the mind be gone,
Till the fire of youth be past.

267 *Love and Sorrow*

LOVE in the country, Sorrow in the town:
Let Love have roots, but Sorrow only wings;
Where life moves slow each feeling deepens down:
A crowded life the quickest solace brings.

But Love from Sorrow never more will part,
She would not heal the wounds her sister made;
She makes more keen each feeling of the heart;
The brightest sunshine casts the darkest shade.

WILLIAM EDWARD HARTPOLE LECKY

268 *Early Thoughts*

OH gather the thoughts of your early years,
Gather them as they flow,
For all unmarked in those thoughts appears
The path where you soon must go.

Full many a dream will wither away,
And Springtide hues are brief,
But the lines are there of the autumn day,
Like the skeleton in the leaf.

The husbandman knows not the worth of his seed
Until the flower be sprung,
And only in age can we rightly read
The thoughts that we thought when young.

GEORGE SIGERSON

269 *Eivlin a Rúin*[1] (61)

Old Form. From the Irish of Carrol O'Daly
(14th Century)

1839-

FAIN would I ride with thee,
Eivlin a rúin;
Fain would I ride with thee,
Eivlin a rúin!

[1] See No. 82.

GEORGE SIGERSON

Fain would I ride with thee,
To Tirauli's tide with thee,
In hope to abide with thee,
        Eivlin a rúin!

I'd spend kine with thee,
        Eivlin a rúin!
Kine upon kine with thee,
        Eivlin a rúin!
I'd walk the world so wide,
To win thee for my bride,
Never to leave thy side,
        Eivlin a rúin!

'Wilt thou come,—wilt thou stay?
        Eivlin a rúin!
Wilt thou come,—wilt thou stay?
        Earth's only boon!'
'I'll come, I will not stay!
I'll come, I will not stay!
I'll come, I will not stay!
        But flee with thee soon!'

Céad mile fáilté, here!
        Eivlin a rúin!
Céad mile fáilté, here!
        Eivlin a rúin!
A hundred thousand welcomes dear,
Nine hundred thousand welcomes here,
O welcomes for ever here!
        Eivlin a rúin!

GEORGE SIGERSON

270 *The Mariner's Hymn*

From the Irish

BARK, bravest in battle of billow and breeze !
True tower in the tempest, dry deck in the seas !
When flash the wild waters, in mountains of might !
You leap through the breakers with bounds of delight !
The high, bright tide ! the high, bright tide !
Queen of my heart, my joy, my pride !
My beautiful bark on the high, bright tide !

With robes from the Indies I've dighted my fair,
How swells her white bosom against the blue air !
Right buoyant the craft below, shapely the sail,
And, O God ! but to see her rise out of the gale !
On the high, bright tide ! the high, bright tide !
Queen of my heart, my joy, my pride !
My beautiful bark on the high, bright tide !

'Grey Deelan, who stands with unchangeable brow,
Behold how the surges race off from her prow,
Behold, and give judgement if ever you've seen
Bark on the waters to peer with my queen.'
On the high, bright tide ! the high, bright tide !
Queen of my heart, my joy, my pride !
My beautiful bark on the high, bright tide !

Then answered grey Deelan : 'Since first I withstood
The roar-rush of ocean's tumultuous flood,
By night and day watch I, but never could mark
From seaward or shoreward, a bark like thy bark !'

On the high, bright tide! the high, bright tide!
Queen of my heart, my joy, my pride!
My beautiful bark on the high, bright tide!

'Lord of the heavens!' the mariners pray,
'Give succour, give shelter, keep, keep her away!
She cleaves the blue billows, she comes like a flash,
And through us and o'er us she'll instantly dash!'
On the high, bright tide! the high, bright tide!
Queen of my heart, my joy, my pride!
My beautiful bark on the high, bright tide!

271 *The Blackbird of Daricarn*

From the Irish

SWEET thy song, in Dari grove,
No sweeter song from east to west;
No music like thy voice of love—
And thou beneath thy nest!

A strain the softest ever heard,
No more shall come its like to men.
O Patrick! list the wondrous bird—
Thou'lt chant thy hymn again.

If thou, as I, but knew the tale
It sings to all the ancient isle,
Thy tears would rise, and thou wouldst fail
To mind thy God awhile.

GEORGE SIGERSON

In Norroway beyond the wave,
  Its forest glades and streams among,
That bird was found by Fionn the brave,
  And still we hear its song.

'Tis Daricarn yon western wood—
  The Fianna huntsmen loved it best,
And there, on stately oak and good,
  Lost Fionn placed its nest.

The tuneful tumult of that bird,
  The belling deer on ferny steep—
This welcome in the dawn he heard,
  These soothed at eve his sleep.

Dear to him the wind-loved heath,
  The whirr of wings, the rustling brake,
Dear the murmuring glens beneath,
  And sob of Droma's lake.

The cry of hounds at early morn,
  The pattering o'er the pebbly creek,
The cuckoo's call, the sounding horn,
  The swooping eagle's shriek.

The mountain, not the cell, they sought
  Great Fionn and the Fianna fleet;
Than tinkle of the bells, they thought
  The blackbird's song more sweet!

GEORGE SIGERSON

272 *A Fair Foe*

From the Irish

THERE'S a shade on my soul,
And my heart is in dole
From pearly day dawning till soft even air,
With love for the white
Fresh Flower of Delight,—
With love for the Maid of the fair-flowing hair.

Her mind is a dove,
And the wit of my love
Is more supple and swift than a bird on the wing;
More sweet is her mouth
Than wine of the South,
Or all the hill honey that Greek poets sing.

To the dew-drops below
Her golden curls flow,
See, the flame of the berry her smooth cheek upon!
In each little ear,
That no picture could peer,
There sparkles a jewel as bright as the sun.

Over earth far and wide,
Could I choose me a bride,
And wed a rich daughter of royalty's line;
Through life she could be
But a sorrow to me—
For the Flower of the World has this poor heart of mine!

JOHN TODHUNTER

273 *The Banshee*

1839–

GREEN, in the wizard arms
  Of the foam-bearded Atlantic,
An isle of old enchantment,
A melancholy isle,
Enchanted and dreaming lies;
And there, by Shannon's flowing,
In the moonlight, spectre-thin,
The spectre Erin sits.

An aged desolation,
She sits by old Shannon's flowing,
A mother of many children,
Of children exiled and dead,
In her home, with bent head, homeless,
Clasping her knees she sits,
Keening, keening!

And at her keen the fairy-grass
Trembles on dun and barrow;
Around the foot of her ancient crosses
The grave-grass shakes and the nettle swings;
In haunted glens the meadow-sweet
Flings to the night wind
Her mystic mournful perfume;
The sad spearmint by holy wells
Breathes melancholy balm.

Sometimes she lifts her head,
With blue eyes tearless,
And gazes athwart the reek of night
Upon things long past,
Upon things to come.

And sometimes, when the moon
Brings tempest upon the deep,
And roused Atlantic thunders from his caverns in the west,
The wolfhound at her feet
Springs up with a mighty bay,
And chords of mystery sound from the wild harp at her side,
Strung from the heart of poets ;
And she flies on the wings of tempest
Around her shuddering isle,
With grey hair streaming :
A meteor of evil omen,
The spectre of hope forlorn,
Keening, keening !

She keens, and the strings of her wild harp shiver
On the gusts of night :
O'er the four waters she keens—over Moyle she keens,
O'er the Sea of Milith, and the Strait of Strongbow,
And the Ocean of Columbus.

And the Fianna hear, and the ghosts of her cloudy hovering heroes ;

And the swan, Fianoula,[1] wails o'er the waters of
Inisfail,
Chanting her song of destiny,
The rune of the weaving Fates.

And the nations hear in the void and quaking time
of night,
Sad unto dawning, dirges,
Solemn dirges,
And snatches of bardic song;
Their souls quake in the void and quaking time of
night,
And they dream of the weird of kings,
And tyrannies moulting, sick
In the dreadful wind of change.

Wail no more, lonely one, mother of exiles, wail no
more,
Banshee of the world—no more!
Thy sorrows are the world's, thou art no more alone;
Thy wrongs, the world's.

274 *Deirdre's Farewell to Alba* (62)

O LAND, Land of my heart,
There sinks my joy in the waters!
O Alba, ne'er would I leave thee,
But now I go with my lover!

[1] See Note 2.

JOHN TODHUNTER

I waft farewell o'er the waters
To you, Dun-finn and Dun-fiagh,
My love to the hills above you,
My love to the isle of Drayno !

O wood of Cone, green wood
Where Ainli roved in the morning,
Too short the days that I sigh for,
No more in Alba with Naisi !

Glen of Laith, Glen of Laith,
Where warm I slept in thy covert,
On badger's brawn and on venison
You feasted me, Glen of Laith !

Glen Masàn, Glen Masàn,
Long grow the leaves of thy hart's-tongues ;
But never more shall ye rock me,
O grassy creeks of Masàn !

But thou, Glen Eta, Glen Eta,
Where first I ordered my homestead,
O happy thou mad'st my rising,
Sweet nook of the sun, Glen Eta !

Glen of the Roes, Glen-da-Rua,
Blest be the man who loves thee !
Sweet shouts over bending branches
The cuckoo in Glen-da-Rua !

O Drayno of sounding shore,
White gleams the sand through thy water,
Dear Drayno, ne'er would I leave thee,
But now I go with my lover !

JOHN TODHUNTER

275 *Deirdre's Great Lamentation for the Sons of Usnach*

OCHONE for the land left lonely,
Without the Three, without the Three!
The warmth of the sun goes with you
To the cold house of the dead!

Without them the Red-Branch House
Is a place of ghosts, of black horror;
The feasts of the mighty mourn them,
The women of Eri weep!

My curse on Fergus, that left them,
My curse on Buiné, that sold them,
My curse on Cathvah, that bound them,
My curse on Maini, that slew them!

And my curse's curse on the King
That snared them with words of honey,
Black hills of hate be above him,
My curse upon Conchobar!

O better than mother's love
Were Naisi's arms around me!
O gentler than loving brothers
Were Ainli and Ardàn!

They fed me with love, they kept me
With spoil in their nest of eagles;
Without them the fields of Eri
Are blasted, and black the skies!

Ochone for the land left lonely
Without the Three, without the Three!
The warmth of the sun goes with you
To the cold house of the dead?

The Closing of the Tomb

In the house without a fire
Heap the black stones over me;
With Naisi where cold he lies
Let the clods cover me!

276 *The Swans' Lament for the Desolation of Lir*[1]

A LOST dream to us now is our home,
Ullagone! Ochone-a-rie!
Gall to our heart! Oh, gall to our heart!
Ullagone! Ochone-a-rie!

A hearthless home, without fire, without joy,
Without a harp, without a hound!
No talk, no laughter, no sound of song,
Ullagone for the halls of Lir!

Where now are the prosperous kings?
Where are the women? Where is the love?
The kiss of welcome warm on our cheeks?
The loving tongue of hounds on our hands?

[1] See Note 2.

Oh! the greatness of our mishap!
Oh! the length of our evil day!
Bitter to toss between sea and sea,
But worse the taste of a loveless home.

Children we left it, swans we return.
To a strange place, strangers. None lives to say:
'These are the Children of Lir.' A dream,
In a dream forgotten are we this night!

Is this the place of music we knew,
Where howls the wolf through the halls of Lir?
Where mirth in the drinking-horn was born,
Chill falls the rain on the hearth of Lir.

Ullagone! Ochone-a-rie!
Gall to our hearts is that sight to-night
Ullagone! Ochone-a-rie!
A lost dream to us now is our home!

277 *The Death-Song of Turann* (63)

LOW lie your heads this day,
My sons! my sons!
The strong in their pride go by me,
Saying: 'Where are thy sons?'

They spit on my grief, they sully
The snows of my age upon me,
Sonless I stand in Tara,
A laughter, a lonely shame.

How shall I walk in strength
In the gathering of the chiefs?
A shaking leaf is my valour,
Wanting your spears about me.

How shall I sit in honour
In the counsel of the kings?
My beard of wisdom the scorner
Shall pluck, with none to defend me.

Happy the dead lie down,
Not knowing the loss of children:
My life in your grave lies dead,
And I go down to my children.

Without you, my hoary age
Is a faltering of the feet.
Without you, my knees that tremble
Go stumbling down to the grave.

Bad is life to the father
In the house without a son,
Fallen is the House of Turann,
And with it I lie low!

278 *The Lament of Aideen for Oscar* (64)

THE sere woods are quailing
  In the wind of their sorrow,
Their keen they might borrow
  From the voice of my wailing.

My bed's the cold stone
By the dark-flowing river :
Ochone-a-rie ! Ochone !
Thou art gone, and for ever !

Ah ! why didst thou love me
But to leave me despairing,
My anguish out-staring
The bleak heavens above me ?
I lie all alone
Where hope's morning comes never :
Ochone-a-rie ! Ochone !
I have lost thee for ever !

The dumb grave mocks my raving.
From the dead comes no token,
Where thy good sword lies broken.
Thou art cold to my craving.
We may lie down and moan,
But our champion wakes never :
Ochone-a-rie ! Ochone !
We are fallen for ever.

279 *The Marseillaise*

WHAT means this mighty chant, wherein the wail
Of some intolerable woe, grown strong
With sense of more intolerable wrong,
Swells to a stern victorious march—a gale
Of vengeful wrath ? What mean the faces pale,
The fierce resolve, the ecstatic pangs along
Life's fiery ways, the demon thoughts which throng
The gates of awe, when these wild notes assail
The sleeping of our souls ? Hear ye no more

Than the mad foam of revolution's leaven,
Than a roused people's throne-o'erwhelming tread?
Hark! 'tis man's spirit thundering on the shore
Of iron fate; the tramp of titans dread,
Sworn to dethrone the gods unjust from heaven.

GEORGE ALEXANDER CHADWICK

280 *The Helper*

1840-

I CANNOT purge my thoughts from sin—
By day my thoughts, my dreams by night:
O, wash me, and I shall be clean:
O, let Thy daylight, streaming in,
Turn darkness bright!

I cannot bring my soul to Thee,
To whom my soul would fain be brought:
O come, O take my heart from me!
Teach me to love: I fain would be
Found, taken, taught.

I cannot reach Thee, O great God,
Nor serve, nor trust, nor pray to Thee:
I faint, I bleed upon the road—
Bind Thou my wounds and staunch my blood,
And rescue me!

So shall I sing upon that road
Made safe, along that journey sweet:
Sing of my Lord who bears my load,
Sing of my tired feet washed by God—
My hands and feet.

GEORGE ALEXANDER CHADWICK

281

Weary

SOME grave is known to God,
  Some green sequestered sod,
Wrapped in whose fragrant fold
I shall no more grow cold.

And God hath Saints who sing,
And holy hands which bring
Offerings and gifts more meet
Than mine, who clasp His feet.

And ask to toil no more,
But, on the golden shore,
To rest, and dream, and be
As God's dead men are, free.

Yet, since He frees me not,
I wait and wonder what
Undreamed-of thing God hath,
Better to give than death.

WILLIAM ALEXANDER CRAIG

282

A Norse War-Song

A.D. 750

From the Saga of 'The Death-Song of Lodbroc'

WE hew'd with our swords,
  We hew'd with our swords.

Our swift galleys ruffled
The face of the fiords.

WILLIAM ALEXANDER CRAIG

When we landed in wrath
On the shores of the Goth,

It was I, Lodbroc, then
Was the leader of men,

Because I had slain
The fierce snake of the plain—

We hew'd with our swords.

The enemy's bands
Met death at our hands.

We carved out a feast,
We carved out a feast,

For the beak of the bird
And the fang of the beast.

The gold-footed king
Of the birds on his wing

Swoop'd down on the shore,
And the ravens drew round
And waded in gore.

And with eyeballs aglare
Came the wolf from his lair.

For he knew we had spread
For his banquet the dead.

WILLIAM ALEXANDER CRAIG

We hew'd with our swords.

We steered by the track,
By the Viking track

Where the spears go out
And the spoils come back.

We sailed on the flood,
We sailed on the flood,

To scatter the homestead
And revel in blood.

With the rise of the sun
Was our battle begun.

We hew'd with our swords.

We hollowed our tracks
With the blows of the axe.

Our keen arrows bit,
And the roar of the spears

As the targes were hit
Sang loud in our ears.

And the hum of the bows
Buzzed out from our hands

As our swift arrows flashed
Through the gleam of the brands,

And rattled like hail
On the close-woven mail.

We hew'd with our swords.

The tempest of blows
Fell fast on our foes,

And the flow of their blood
Came like rivers in flood ;

Then before the red sun
Had sunk over the plain,

The red ground was piled
With the heaps of the slain.

A bountiful day
For the wild birds of prey,

That gathered with shrieks,
As they whetted their beaks

In the flesh of the dead,
In the feast we had spread.—

We hew'd with our swords.

EDMUND JOHN ARMSTRONG

283 *Among the Mountains*

1841–1865

I WANDER on the barren moors
Alone, and thy dear memory lures
My thoughts to anguish, Madeline.
O, would that Time could backward roll,
And flash upon my weary soul
Days that seem never to have been!

Alas, alas, I cannot trace
The perfect outline of thy face!
It fades, it cheats me—as I stray
All aimless on this dismal waste,
And strive with colours of the Past
To gild yon dreary verge of day.

Dark plain, that, like a stagnant sea,
Dost mock my spirit's vacancy;
Still darker hills, that loom behind;
You vex my vision with the sense
Of something lost, an influence
Like wailings of the midnight wind.

I close my sight . . in vain! The hues
Of liquid light are there, as dews
Upon an opening rose; the lines
Are dimmed; they vanish; all is blank . .
Through the tall reeds and rushes dank
The sad cold wind of evening whines!

What dungeon worse than this may be?
A barren plain without a tree,
  And these bleak mountains, underneath
Their canopy of heavy cloud!
The earth is folded in a shroud,
  And breathes the humid air of Death!

284 *Sunset in the Devil's Glen*

Co. Wicklow

WARM the summer wind is blowing;
  From the west the sun is glowing
  Over lake and heath and fen;
Merrily the stream is flowing;
On the hills the kine are lowing;
Dark and long the shadow's growing,
  Purpling o'er the Devil's Glen;
Far away, in light and gloom,
Glendalough's gaunt mountains loom.
The trysting-hour has passed away;
The sweet sad smile o' the dying day
Changes from rosy-red to grey.

285 *A Dedication*

MY land, my Erin, can we sing of thee
  Save in that music ringing through thy vales,
And through thy people's hearts,—how bold and free,

How sadly like a Rachel's piteous wails,
Dying in anguish, faintly, brokenly,
With more of woe than all a poet's tales?

Thy music is thy speech : so half in fear
I link this story now in rhythmic law,
And miss in words that plaintive warble, clear

And dreamful, which first woke my soul with awe,
And thrilled it into motion, as a mere
Is rippled weirdly by the mountain flaw.

286 *A New Birth*

MY fate, my portion in the strife
Of this strange world, my after-life
With all its hopes and fears,
Rest on the issue of To-day !
Spirit of Goodness, chase away
The clouds that gather o'er me now,
The fire that wreathes my aching brow,
The intermitting thrill
That tingles through my frame ; the throb
That heaves my breast ; the thoughts that rob
Mine eyes of sleep ! O, let me bow
Submissive to Thy will !

EDWARD DOWDEN

287 *Awakening*

1843–

WITH brain o'erworn, with heart a summer clod,
With eye so practised in each form around,—
And all forms mean,—to glance above the ground
Irks it, each day of many days we plod,

Tongue-tied and deaf, along life's common road.
But suddenly, we know not how, a sound
Of living streams, an odour, a flower crowned
With dew, a lark upspringing from the sod,
And we awake. O joy and deep amaze!
Beneath the everlasting hills we stand,
We hear the voices of the morning seas,
And vernal prophesyings in the land,
While from the open heaven leans forth at gaze
The encompassing great cloud of witnesses.

288 *Swallows*

WIDE fields of air left luminous,
Though now the uplands comprehend
How the sun's loss is ultimate:
The silence grows; but still to us
From yon air-winnowing breasts elate
The tiny shrieks of glee descend.

Deft wings, each moment is resigned
Some touch of day, some pulse of light,
While yet in poised, delicious curve,
Ecstatic doublings down the wind,
Light dash and dip and sidelong swerve,
You try each dainty trick of flight.

Will not your airy glee relent
At all? The aimless frolic cease?
Know ye no touch of quelling pain,
Nor joy's more strict admonishment,
No tender awe at daylight's wane,
Ye slaves of delicate caprice?

Hush, once again that cry intense!
High-venturing spirits, have your will!
Urge the last freak, prolong your glee,
Keen voyagers, while still the immense
Sea-spaces haunt your memory,
With zests and pangs ineffable.

Not in the sunshine of old woods
Ye won your warrant to be gay
By duteous, sweet observances,
Who dared through darkening solitudes,
And 'mid the hiss of alien seas,
The larger ordinance obey.

289 *Sunsets*

DID your eyes watch the mystic sunset splendours
Through evenings of old summers, slow of parting,—
Wistful while loveliest gains and fair surrenders
Hallow'd the West,—till tremulous tears came starting?

Did your soul wing her way on noiseless pinion
Through lucid fields of air, and penetrated
With light and silence roam the wide dominion
Where Day and Dusk embrace,—serene, unmated?

And they are past the shining hours and tender,
And snows are fallen between, and winds are driven?
Nay, for I find across your face the splendour,
And in your wings the central winds of heaven.

They reach me, those lost Sunsets. Undivining
  Your own high mysteries you pause and ponder;
See, in my eyes the vanished light is shining,
  Feel, through what spaces of clear heaven I wander!

290 *Evening*

LIGHT ebbs from off the Earth; the fields are strange,
  Dusk, trackless, tenantless; now the mute sky
Resigns itself to Night and Memory,
And no wind will yon sunken clouds derange,
No glory enrapture them; from cot or grange
The rare voice ceases; one long-breathèd sigh,
And steeped in summer sleep the world must lie
All things are acquiescing in the change.
Hush! while the vaulted hollow of the night
Deepens, what voice is this the sea sends forth,
Disconsolate iterance, a passionless moan?
Ah! now the Day is gone, and tyrannous Light,
And the calm presence of fruit-bearing Earth;
Cry, Sea! it is thy hour; thou art alone.

291 *An Autumn Song*

LONG Autumn rain;
White mists which choke the vale, and blot the sides
Of the bewildered hills; in all the plain
No field agleam where the gold pageant was,
And silent o'er a tangle of drenched grass
  The blackbird glides.

In the heart,—fire,
Fire and clear air and cries of water-springs,
And large, pure winds; all April's quick desire,
All June's possession; a most fearless Earth
Drinking great ardours; and the rapturous birth
Of wingèd things.

292 *Life's Gain*

'NOW having gained Life's gain, how hold it fast?
The harder task! because the world is still
The world, and days creep slow, and wear the will,
And custom, gendering in the heart's blind waste,
Brings forth a wingèd mist, which with no haste
Upcircling the steep air, and charged with ill,
Blots all our shining heights adorable,
And leaves slain Faith, slain Hope, slain Love the last.'
O shallow lore of life! He who hath won
Life's gain doth hold nought fast, who could hold all,
Holden himself of strong, immortal Powers.
The stars accept him; for his sake the Sun
Has sworn in heaven an oath memorial;
Around his feet stoop the obsequious Hours.

ELIZABETH DICKINSON WEST
(MRS. EDWARD DOWDEN)

293 *Adrift*

UNTO my Faith, as to a spar, I bind
My Love—and Faith and Love adrift I cast
On a dim sea. I know not if at last
They the eternal shore of God shall find.

I only know that neither waves nor wind
  Can sunder them ; the cords are tied so fast
  That Faith shall never—doubts and dangers past—
Come safe to land, and Love be left behind.

294 *'There shall be no more Sea'*

'THERE shall be no more Sea.' Ah, surely this
  Is only for the souls who reach the bliss
Of Paradise ! They need not seek the kiss
Of Earth's great mother, Sea ; nor will they miss,
Whose pulses with new-risen life beat high,
The soothings of the æonian lullaby,
Which now doth win man's weariness to lie
Lapped in its sound and be content to die.

Hearts strong in vigour of their fresh great joy
Will ask no more the leaping waves to buoy
Their moods to kindred laughter, and destroy
Through alien glee their human cares' annoy
A little while. The eyes whereon doth break
The light of Heaven, what need have they to take
Sad pleasure in those ocean gleams that make
Dim lives worth living for their beauty's sake ?

Yet though the Blessed need no more the Sea,
Will not God leave her to the Lost ?—that she,
Who could not save them from their woe, may be
Their nurse to comfort, ever tenderly
With vast and low-voiced hushabies to still
The restlessness of pain incurable,
And with a sense of vague, fair sadness fill
Their hunger for lost good adorable.

ELIZABETH DICKINSON WEST

Men love her, earth's old Sea. She loves them well.
If she may be their mother too in Hell,
Will she not rock them there with lulling swell,
In her deep constancy? Ah, who can tell?
If waters' strength and love's be not in vain,
Some souls who nevermore God's grace might gain
May yet to peace of dreamless sleep attain,
Lost to all gladness, lost alike to pain.

JOHN BOYLE O'REILLY

295

A White Rose

1844-1890

THE red rose whispers of passion,
And the white rose breathes of love;
Oh, the red rose is a falcon,
And the white rose is a dove.

But I send you a cream-white rosebud
With a flush on its petal tips;
For the love that is purest and sweetest
Has a kiss of desire on the lips.

ARTHUR O'SHAUGHNESSY

296

Ode

1844-1881

WE are the music-makers,
And we are the dreamers of dreams,
Wandering by lone sea-breakers,
And sitting by desolate streams;—

World-losers and world-forsakers,
  On whom the pale moon gleams:
Yet we are the movers and shakers
  Of the world for ever, it seems.

With wonderful deathless ditties
We build up the world's great cities,
  And out of a fabulous story
  We fashion an empire's glory:
One man with a dream, at pleasure,
  Shall go forth and conquer a crown;
And three with a new song's measure
  Can trample an empire down.

We, in the ages lying
  In the buried past of the earth,
Built Nineveh with our sighing,
  And Babel itself with our mirth;
And o'erthrew them with prophesying
  To the old of the new world's worth;
For each age is a dream that is dying,
  Or one that is coming to birth.

297

Song

I MADE another garden, yea,
    For my new love;
I left the dead rose where it lay,
    And set the new above.
Why did the summer not begin?
    Why did my heart not haste?
My old love came and walked therein,
    And laid the garden waste.

She entered with her weary smile,
Just as of old;
She looked around a little while,
And shivered at the cold.
Her passing touch was death to all,
Her passing look a blight:
She made the white rose-petals fall,
And turned the red rose white.

Her pale robe, clinging to the grass,
Seemed like a snake
That bit the grass and ground, alas!
And a sad trail did make.
She went slowly up to the gate;
And there, just as of yore,
She turned back at the last to wait,
And say farewell once more.

298

At the Last

BY weary paths and wide
Up many a torn hillside,
Through all the raging strife
And the wandering of life,
Here on the mountain's brow
I find, I know not how,
My long-neglected shrine
Still holy, still mine.

The wall, with leaves o'ergrown,
Is ruined but not o'erthrown;
Surely the door hath been
Guarded by one unseen;

Surely the prayer last prayed
And the dream last dreamed have stayed.
I will enter, and try once more
To dream and pray as of yore.

299 *The Line of Beauty*

WHEN mountains crumble and rivers all run dry,
When every flower has fallen and summer fails
To come again, when the sun's splendour pales,
And earth with lagging footsteps seems well-nigh
Spent in her annual circuit through the sky;
When love is a quenched flame, and nought avails
To save decrepit man, who feebly wails
And lies down lost in the great grave to die;
What is eternal? What escapes decay?
A certain faultless, matchless, deathless line,
Curving consummate. Death, Eternity,
Add nought to it, from it take nought away;
'Twas all God's gift and all man's mastery,
God become human and man grown divine.

GEORGE F. SAVAGE-ARMSTRONG

1845–1906

300 *Glens of Wicklow*

GLENS of Wicklow, o'er the sea
Comes to-night a voice to me,
Bidding faint-winged Memory hie
Backward to the years that lie

'Mid a past so drear and clouded
The sick heart, in sorrow shrouded,
Seldom dares to peer at it,
But where sun-born phantoms flit;
And I roam, a blissful child,
Through your woodland-hollows wild,
Hear your plunging cataracts cry,
Watch the wild-hawks in the sky,
Climb the fraughan-tufted steep,
Down the dizzy gorges peep;
And in boyhood's vision see
The sweet false dreams of days to be.

Glens of Wicklow, forest-crowned,
In your deeps a Spirit I found
Strayed adown the sunbeams golden
'Twixt the bearded branches olden
To the torrent's pools of gold;
And her eyes, beneath the fold
Of bright tresses aureoled,
Held within their azure wells
Magic smiles and wildering spells;
And she chanted down the breeze
Songs that swayed me as swept trees
Tossed i' the whirlwind; till I panted
For the things whereof she chanted,—
Victory's wreath, and Wisdom's dower,
Glory of great deeds, and Power,
Knowledge, Fame for endless days,
The world's worship, the world's praise.

Ah, I think that truer-hearted
Lived I then, or e'er I parted,

Following her wild music's flight
By weird ways through thickest night,
To find bitter her most sweet!
Now anew my pulses beat
To a music old and dear
Dropping dreamily on mine ear—
Sound of rivulets o'er the rocks,
Bleating of the mountain flocks,
Buzz of bees in blooms a-sway,
Laughter of light winds at play,
Blackbird's pipe and robin's trill,
Patter of nuthatch's bill,
Crash of boughs where the squirrel leaps,
Splash of troutlet in still deeps,
Herdsman's cry, and maiden's song,
Sounds that unto you belong,
And whereon my spirit fed
In the purer summers sped,
Finding life and goodliest rest,
Nursed on kindly Nature's breast.

Glens of Wicklow, torrent-cloven,
Round your streams my life was woven ;
Even now as faces fled
Of the dearest droopt and dead
Flashing on the changèd brain,
To revive a soul nigh slain
With the loss of their love's dower
And that withereth hour by hour,
Are ye to my heart left dry
By a drear Philosophy.
What of beauty here remaineth
From your olden influence raineth ;

What of noble in me liveth,
That your far-off impulse giveth;
What of childhood's heart here stays
Is your boon of the olden days,
Folded in your mild caress,
Cared with loving-tenderness.

301 *Lugnaquillia*

GRAND Lugnaquillia! There we lay at peace,
Cooled by the summer wind, and gazed adown
To left and right athwart the rolling hills
To the blue sea and round the cultured plains
Basking to westward in the midday beam.
For many a mile the tawny mountains heaved
In rough confusion. Here amid the heaths
A brown dull tarn reflected the heaven's blue,
Or the slow-moving shadow of a cloud
Darkened a cliff or valley. Northward far
Slieve-Cullinn, dwindled to an arrowy point,
Lifted his rosy peak beyond grey Djouce,
That in a cleft amid the summer woods
Showed, nestling, Luggalà; and near us ran
The Avonbeg by Fananierin's base
Away to mingle with bright Avonmore,
And low amid Ovoca's wooded vale
We traced the wedded waters to the sea;
Then, turning, watched beneath in wide Imahl
Far-winding Slaney glittering in the noon,
And fashioned for our fancies in the haze
Faint in the west the rims of Galteemore.

GEORGE F. SAVAGE-ARMSTRONG

302 *Home-Longings*

GWEEDORE, CO. DONEGAL

I, WANDERING hither listless from afar,
Have drunk within this Vale a two days' bliss.
Dear were the noises of the tempest's war
On the rough beach, and dear the torrent's brawl
Thundering on high, and dear the sunset's kiss
Flushing the peak of pallid Errigal.
Yet, since to lonely men full many a time
God seems far off where human love is small,
And other vales, through Memory sublime,
Await me, and the Sacred Ashes lie
By gentler seas beside a tamer shore—
I leave the wild Atlantic's jubilant roar,
The scarpéd cliffs that scowl against the sky,
The lough, and barren dales, and mountain hoar,
And take farewell of all without a sigh.

303 *Silence*

LOVE dying set his finger on these lips,
And froze them into silence. I may sing
Never again the old glad way! O, bring
My heart a little pleasure in eclipse!
When the morn rises, when the white moon dips
Seaward, or when lithe birds are on the wing,
And with clear music radiant woodlands ring,
And all things find relief,
Let not my mouth be dumb and mine eyes blind
And drowsed mine ear amid the earth's delight.

Hard is this burthen of pent woe to bear,—
The dull faint soul that seeks and cannot find
Life's natural joy, worn with a wordless grief,
Sick with a nameless care.

304 *Summer Rhyme*

LEAF on the bough and fly on the wing,
Birds that sing, winds that swing
Roses thickly clustering,
Woodbine-blooms that clamber and cling,
Ferns that fresh in the woodland spring,
Flowers that sweets to the breezes fling,
Babble of streams and drip of wells,
Golden gleams and balmy smells,
Bees a-buzz in tremulous bells,—
What is the word their gladness tells,
What the bliss they bring?

Summer is loose and Spring's away;
Hearts be gay, pipe and play,
Revel and laugh the livelong day,
Bind the brow with bloom o' the May,
Lave the limbs i' the foam and spray,
Whirl i' the dance at evening grey,
Beat the moss with lightsome feet,
Tumble and toss the hay in the heat,
Stray in the grass, stray in the wheat—
This the bliss of their burden sweet,
These the words they say.

GEORGE F. SAVAGE-ARMSTRONG

305 *Helen's Tower* (65)

BY Love's hand reared, on thine aërial height
Rise, pure Love's witness, and, 'mid storm and flame,
Earthquake and thunder, o'er wide lands proclaim
Death by Love vanquished, and beyond the Night
Eternal splendours of eternal Light;
Hope, born of Love which grief nor time can tame,
Triumphant; Severance but a needless name;
And Joy unending one with sovereign Might!
Yea, thou, through whose firm tissue seems to thrill
Love's message from the Living to the Dead,
With throbbings of some sweet ethereal Will
Responsive through thy stony fibre sped,
Prove blent in one serene Eternity
The world men see not with the earth they see!

JOHN KEEGAN CASEY

306 *Maire my Girl*

1846–1870

OVER the dim blue hills
Strays a wild river,
Over the dim blue hills
Rests my heart ever.
Dearer and brighter than
Jewels and pearl,
Dwells she in beauty there,
Maire my girl.

JOHN KEEGAN CASEY

Down upon Claris heath
  Shines the soft berry,
On the brown harvest tree
  Droops the red cherry.
Sweeter thy honey lips,
  Softer the curl
Straying adown thy cheeks,
  Maire my girl.

'Twas on an April eve
  That I first met her ;
Many an eve shall pass
  Ere I forget her.
Since my young heart has been
  Wrapped in a whirl,
Thinking and dreaming of
  Maire my girl.

She is too kind and fond
  Ever to grieve me,
She has too pure a heart
  E'er to deceive me.
Were I Tyrconnell's chief
  Or Desmond's earl,
Life would be dark, wanting
  Maire my girl.

Over the dim blue hills
  Strays a wild river,
Over the dim blue hills
  Rests my heart ever ;

Dearer and brighter than
  Jewels or pearl,
Dwells she in beauty there,
  Maire my girl.

307 *Donal Kenny*

'COME, piper, play the "Shaskan Reel,"
  Or else the "Lasses on the Heather,"
And, Mary, lay aside your wheel
  Until we dance once more together.
At fair and pattern oft before
  Of reels and jigs we've tripped full many;
But ne'er again this loved old floor
  Will feel the foot of Donal Kenny.'

Softly she rose and took his hand,
  And softly glided through the measure,
While, clustering round the village band
  Looked half in sorrow, half in pleasure.
Warm blessings flowed from every lip
  As ceased the dancers' airy motion:
O Blessed Virgin! guide the ship
  Which bears bold Donal o'er the ocean!

'Now God be with you all!' he sighed,
  Adown his face the bright tears flowing—
'God guard you well, avick,' they cried,
  'Upon the strange path you are going.'
So full his breast, he scarce could speak,
  With burning grasp the stretched hands taking,
He pressed a kiss on every cheek,
  And sobbed as if his heart was breaking.

'Boys, don't forget me when I'm gone,
  For sake of all the days passed over—
The days you spent on heath and bawn,
  With Donal Ruadh, the rattlin' rover.
Mary, agra, your soft brown eye
  Has willed my fate,' he whispered lowly;
'Another holds thy heart: good-bye!
  Heaven grant you both its blessings holy!'

A kiss upon her brow of snow,
  A rush across the moonlit meadow,
Whose broom-clad hazels, trembling slow,
  The mossy boreen wrapped in shadow;
Away o'er Tully's bounding rill,
  And far beyond the Inny river;
One cheer on Carrick's rocky hill,
  And Donal Kenny's gone for ever.

The breezes whistled through the sails,
  O'er Galway Bay the ship was heaving,
And smothered groans and bursting wails
  Told all the grief and pain of leaving.
One form among that exiled band
  Of parting sorrow gave no token,
Still was his breath, and cold his hand:
  For Donal Kenny's heart was broken.

308 *Gracie Og Machree*

I PLACED the silver in her palm
  By Inny's smiling tide,
And vowed, ere summer time came on,
  To claim her as a bride.

But when the summer time came on
  I dwelt beyond the sea ;
Yet still my heart is ever true
  To Gracie og machree.

O bonnie are the woods of Targ,
  And green thy hills, Rathmore,
And soft the sunlight ever falls
  On Darre's sloping shore ;
And there the eyes I love—in tears
  Shine ever mournfully,
While I am far, and far away
  From Gracie og machree.

When battle steeds were neighing loud,
  With bright blades in the air,
Next to my inmost heart I wore
  A bright tress of her hair.
When stirrup-cups were lifted up
  To lips, with soldier glee
One toast I always fondly pledged,
  'Twas Gracie og machree.

Oh ! I may never, never clasp
  Again, her lily hand,
And I may find a soldier's grave
  Upon a foreign strand ;
But when the heart pulse beats the last,
  And death takes hold of me,
One word shall part my dying lips,
  Thy name, astór machree.

ALFRED PERCEVAL GRAVES

309 *Father O'Flynn*

1846–

OF priests we can offer a charmin' variety,
Far renowned for larnin' and piety;
Still, I'd advance ye widout impropriety,
Father O'Flynn as the flower of them all.
Chorus—Here's a health to you, Father O'Flynn,
Slainté, and slainté, and slainté agin;
Powerfulest preacher, and
Tinderest teacher, and
Kindliest creature in ould Donegal.

Don't talk of your Provost and Fellows of Trinity,
Famous for ever at Greek and Latinity,
Faix and the divels and all at Divinity,
Father O'Flynn 'd make hares of them all!
Come, I vinture to give ye my word,
Never the likes of his logic was heard,
Down from mythology
Into thayology,
Troth! and conchology if he'd the call.
Chorus—Here's a health to you, Father O'Flynn, etc.

Och! Father O'Flynn you've the wonderful way
wid you,
All ould sinners are wishful to pray wid you,
All the young childer are wild for to play wid you,

You've such a way wid you, Father avick!
Still for all you've so gentle a soul,
Gad, you've your flock in the grandest control;
Checking the crazy ones,
Coaxin' onaisy ones,
Liftin' the lazy ones on wid the stick.
Chorus—Here's a health to you, Father O'Flynn, etc.

And though quite avoidin' all foolish frivolity,
Still at all seasons of innocent jollity,
Where was the play-boy could claim an equality
At comicality, Father, wid you?
Once the Bishop looked grave at your jest,
Till this remark set him off wid the rest:
'Is it lave gaiety
All to the laity?
Cannot the clargy be Irishmen too?'
Chorus—Here's a health to you, Father O'Flynn, etc.

310 *The Wreck of the 'Aideen'*

IS it cure me, docther, darlin'? an ould boy of sivanty-four,
After soakin' off Berehaven three and thirty hour and more,
Wid no other navigation underneath me but an oar.

God incrase ye, but it's only half myself is livin' still,
An' there's mountin' slow but surely to my heart the dyin' chill;
God incrase ye for your goodness, but I'm past all mortial skill.

But ye'll surely let them lift me, won't you, docther, from below?
Ye'll let them lift me surely—very soft and very slow—
To see my ould ship, *Aideen*, wanst agin before I go?

Lay my head upon your shoulder; thank ye kindly, docther, dear.
Take me now; God bless ye, cap'n! now together! sorra fear!
Have no dread that ye'll distress me—now, agin, ochone! I see her.

Ologone! my Aideen's *Aideen*, christened by her laughin' lips,
Wid a sprinkle from her finger as ye started from the slips,
Thirty year ago come Shrovetide, like a swan among the ships.

And we both were constant to ye till the bitter, bitter day,
Whin the typhus took my darlin', and she pined and pined away,
Till yourself's the only sweetheart that was left me on the say.

So through fair and foul we'd travel, you and I thin, usen't we;
The same ould coorse from Galway Bay, by Limerick and Tralee,
Till this storm it shook me overboard, and murthered you, machree.

But now, agra, the unruly wind has flown into the west,
And the silver moon is shinin' soft upon the ocean's
breast,
Like Aideen's smilin' spirit come to call us to our rest.

Still the sight is growin' darker, and I cannot rightly
hear;
The say's too cold for one so old; O, save me, cap'n,
dear!
Now it's growin' bright and warm agin, and Aideen,
Aideen's here.

311 *The Irish Spinning-Wheel*

SHOW me a sight
Bates for delight
An ould Irish wheel wid a young Irish girl at it.
Oh no!
Nothing you'll show
Aquals her sittin' an' takin' a twirl at it.

Look at her there—
Night in her hair,
The blue ray of day from her eye laughin' out on us!
Faix, an' a foot,
Perfect of cut,
Peepin' to put an end to all doubt in us.

That there's a sight
Bates for delight
An ould Irish wheel wid a young Irish girl at it—
Oh no!
Nothin' you'll show
Aquals her sittin' an' takin' a twirl at it.

See! the lamb's wool
Turns coarse an' dull
By them soft, beautiful weeshy white hands of her.
Down goes her heel,
Roun' runs the wheel,
Purrin' wid pleasure to take the commands of her.

Then show me a sight
Bates for delight
An ould Irish wheel wid a young Irish girl at it.
Oh no!
Nothin' you'll show
Aquals her sittin' an' takin' a twirl at it.

Talk of Three Fates,
Seated on sates,
Spinnin' and shearin' away till they've done for me!
You may want three
For your massacree,
But one Fate for me, boys—and only the one for me!

And isn't that fate
Pictured complate—
An ould Irish wheel with a young Irish girl at it?
Oh no!
Nothin' you'll show
Aquals her sittin' an' takin' a twirl at it.

312 *The White Blossom's off the Bog*

THE white blossom's off the bog, and the leaves are off the trees,
And the singing birds have scattered across the stormy seas;
And oh! 'tis winter,
Wild, wild winter!
With the lonesome wind sighing for ever through the trees.

How green the leaves were springing! how glad the birds were singing!
When I rested in the meadow with my head on Patrick's knees;
And oh! 'twas spring time,
Sweet, sweet spring time!
With the daisies all dancing before in the breeze.

With the spring the fresh leaves they'll laugh upon the trees,
And the birds they'll flutter back with their songs across the seas,
But I'll never rest again with my head on Patrick's knees;
And for me 'twill be winter,
All the year winter,
With the lonesome wind sighing for ever through the trees.

STANDISH JAMES O'GRADY

313 *I give my Heart to Thee*

1846–

I GIVE my heart to thee, O mother-land,
I, if none else, recall the sacred womb.
I, if none else, behold the loving eyes
Bent ever on thy myriad progeny
Who care not nor regard thee as they go,
O tender, sorrowing, weeping, hoping land !
I give my heart to thee, O mother-land.

I give my heart to thee, O father-land,
Fast-anchored on thy own eternal soul,
Rising with cloudy mountains to the skies,
O proud, strong land, unstooping, stern of rule,
Me rule as ever ; let me feel thy might ;
Let me go forth with thee now and for aye.
I give my heart to thee, O father-land.

I give my heart to thee, heroic land,
To thee or in thy morning when the Sun
Flashed on thy giant limbs—thy lurid noon—
Or in thy depth of night, fierce-thoughted one—
Wrestling with phantoms of thy own wild soul,
Or, stone-still, silent, waiting for the dawn,
I give my heart to thee, heroic land.

I give my heart to thee, ideal land,
Far-soaring sister of the starry throng.
O fleet of wing, what journeyings are thine,

What goal, what god attracts thee? What unseen
Glory reflected makes thy face a flame?
Leave me not; where thou goest, let me go.
I give my heart to thee, ideal land.

314 *Lough Bray*

NOW Memory, false, spendthrift Memory,
Disloyal treasure-keeper of the Soul,
This vision change shall never wring from thee
Nor wasteful years effacing as they roll,
O steel-blue lake, high-cradled in the hills!
O sad waves, filled with little sobs and cries!
White glistening shingle, hiss of mountain rills,
And granite-hearted walls blotting the skies,
Shine, sob, gleam, gloom for ever. Oh, in me,
Be what you are in Nature—a recess—
To sadness dedicate and mystery,
Withdrawn, afar, in the soul's wilderness.
Still let my thoughts, leaving the worldly roar
Like pilgrims, wander on thy haunted shore.

WILLIAM LARMINIE

315 *From 'Fand'* (66)

1850–1889

'COME to the summer of my beauty, come!
Leave thou the cold pale spring;
Winter is in its heart;
And, born of chill, to chill will it return:

But I am summer eternal,
That have not ripened, being perfect ever,
And shall not thence decline.

'The raw weak years of youth I have not known;
Therefore there is no part of me,
Whereby can ever age take hold,
To draw me down to death:
With steps reluctant down the deep'ning chill,
To where in ever-during gloom he sits,
And frost, that ne'er is frighted of the sun.

'On full-grown pinions I have for ever soared,
And ne'er have lain unfledged,
Helpless within the nest,
Nor learnt by feeble flutterings to rise:
In the mid heights of air I have been born:
My jewelled wings shall never lose their treasures,
Never to earth descend.

'I am the moon, that having ne'er been crescent,
From fulness ne'er shall wane:
Vainly thou shalt not search for me in heaven:
But over thee the river of my beauty
Shall roll in floods, unstinted and unceasing,
Shedding delight and bliss upon thy being,
As the full moon pours light upon the sea.

'Come to me, come, Cuhoolin!
Open wide have I flung to thee
The gates of the golden land, whose air giveth life
that dies not:
Feelest thou not upon thy cheek the breezes,

Fanning thy flame of mortal to divine?
Feel'st thou not that its bliss floweth round thee, soft
as the waters,
Into thy soul's mid core to the likeness of gods transforming?
Surely into thy being already so deeply the glow divine
hath entered,
Never could'st thou endure the dull sad world again:
The cold dark world of men and death;
Turn from it, once and for ever,
And choose thou immortality and Fand.'

316 *From 'Moytura'* (67)

I HAVE ended, O Lu; have obeyed
Thy call, and have told in my singing,
From the days of the misty beginning,
To the brink of the mighty to-morrow, what
triumphs the gods have gained.

I have sung but in brief: I have flown
From peak unto peak, in a moment
Crossing abysses and oceans
Of deeds, as the waves unnumbered, that now
shall remain untold.

On the peaks of the past, upon all,
As I touched them, a light I enkindled,
And, as if from a sun nigh risen,
Darkness in front of us flies, on the skies of the
future is dawn.

Time is a brand that flames
  At point of the present ;—behind it,
  In region of limitless twilight,
Die the sparks it has kindled, the trail of its
    splendour fails.

But the fuel, flame-feeding, grows,
  As onward it rushes, and warmer
  With sun-like visage and broader,
The brightness endures of its passage, the
    future in front of it glows.

Now do the powers of the night
  In threefold horror assemble,
  To sunder the strand at the present,
That, the past in the dark may be swallowed,
    the future no kindling find.

Tremble, ye powers of the gloom :
  Shudder, ye legions of darkness :
  We have weapons to scatter your armies ;
A sword that shall vex and divide you, a flame
    to pursue and consume.

317 *The Nameless Doon*

WHO were the builders? Question not the silence
    That settles on the lake for evermore,
Save when the sea-bird screams and to the islands
The echo answers from the steep-cliffed shore.
O half-remaining ruin, in the lore
Of human life a gap shall all deplore

Beholding thee ; since thou art like the dead
Found slain, no token to reveal the why,
The name, the story. Some one murderèd
We know, we guess ; and gazing upon thee,
And, filled by thy long silence of reply,
We guess some garnered sheaf of tragedy ;—
Of tribe or nation slain so utterly
That even their ghosts are dead, and on their grave
Springeth no bloom of legend in its wildness ;
And age by age weak washing round the islands
No faintest sigh of story lisps the wave.

318 *Sunset at Malinmore*

QUIET are the treeless hills
Clad with short coarse grass and heather ;
Around them the sky's wide circle
And beneath them the silent sea.

And around the sky's wide circle are clouds of fire,
Towers of flaming snow ;
And the plain of the gleaming sea reflects the glitter
In lonely patches of calm.

Wild, fiery-splendid sky !
Silent protest of day against night's dark domination,
Over thy splendour already hangeth the omen of gloom.
And the sea inscrutable rests, vast level of flickering darkness,
Watching the sunset go :
All day to the sky it has spoken and in brightness answered to brightness,
Now will it speak to the night.

If there is gloom in the heaven
Shall not the gloom of hell be twice intense?
Therefore ye faces rise!
Ye that within the sunless depths have dwellings,
And by the deeper terror of your eyes
Smite the night's heart with trembling.

319 *Consolation*

YES, let us speak; with lips confirming
  The inner pledge that eyes reveal;—
Bright eyes that death shall dim for ever,
  And lips that silence soon shall seal.

Yes, let us make our claim recorded
  Against the powers of earth and sky,
And that cold boon their laws award us—
  Just once to live, and once to die.

Thou say'st that fate is frosty nothing,
  But love the flame of souls that are:—
'Two spirits approach and at their touching
  Behold an everlasting star!'

High thoughts, O love; well!—let us speak them!
  Yet bravely face at least this fate,—
To know the dreams of us that dream them
  On blind unknowing things await.

If years from winters' chill recover,
  If fields are green and rivers run;
If thou and I behold each other,
  Hangs it not all on yonder sun?

So, while that mighty lord is gracious
  With prodigal beam to flood the skies,
Let us be glad that he can spare us
  The light to kindle lovers' eyes.

And die assured should life's new wonder,
  In any world our slumbers break,
These the first words that each will utter,
  'Belovéd, art thou too awake?'

EDWARD HARDING

320 *A Morning Meditation*

WHY should we grieve? The skies above are fair;
  The hills lie green and golden in the sun;
  About our feet the rippling waters run;
A thousand perfumes load the pleasant air.
All things are bright and beautiful and glad—
Why, then, should we be sad?

Is there a need that we should turn aside
  From those sweet springs of happiness and rest,
  And to the burden of a troubled breast
Tie the free thoughts that might be roaming wide?
Our hearts are founts of error and of sin—
Why chain our sight within?

Darkness and doubt are dreams that pass away,
  Beyond the cloud that wraps the lives of men,
  And hides the vast unknown from human ken,
The great sun shineth in eternal day.
Ah, fools! to fret whatever fate befall—
Is God not Lord of all?

EDWARD HARDING

321 *Nightfall*

ON wood and wave the gathering shadows fall,
The trees are whispering in the twilight grey,
As if one last 'good-night' they fain would say
Ere darkness shrouds them in her dusty pall.
Now one by one broad oak and poplar tall
Melt into shade ; the golden-mantled day
Past the hushed lakelet softly steals away,
And solemn night sits silently on all.
But hark ! the night-wind slowly creeping by
With low, dull moan the spreading darkness fills,
And slumbering nature wakes to sympathy,
For one and all the oaks and poplars sigh,
And floating faintly o'er the far-off hills
A deep sad voice comes sobbing from the sea.

WILLIAM WILKINS

322 *The Impassable*

1852-

IN Ovoca valley the wood and water
Are dipt in shimmering haze of light,
On the beach at Arklow the sand and water
Flashes and sparkles in blue and white.
In Ovoca valley the woodbine-clusters
Are hung in the wood like chandeliers,
In Arklow harbour the bright tide lustres
The murmurous darkness under the piers.

WILLIAM WILKINS

In Ovoca valley the cart-boy listens—
  'Cuckoo, cuckoo'—through the brooding heat;
In the surge at Arklow the bather glistens
  A fairy—afloat at the green hill's feet.

The streams come down to Ovoca valley,
  Out of the distance, out of the hills;
From ledge to ledge falling musically,
  To a hundred lakes, in a million rills;
From stony teats of huge Lugnaculliogh's,—
  From Mullacleevaun's enormous mass;
From Croghan and Douce and Carrowstick hollows,
  And purple summits o'er Glenmacnass;
From black Nahanagan, wilder Ouler,
  And Luggelaw, walled with wood and rock;
From bright Lough Dan, spreading broader, fuller,
  And the double darkness in Glendalough:
The streamlets repose and the streamlets rally,
  And narrow and broaden down rapid and reach,
Till they mingle at last in Ovoca valley
  With sound that abides like the scent of a peach.
But they flow in tune down Ovoca valley
  Where miners tunnel the clear cliff's flank;
By coppice and meadow down musically,
  And out in the offing to Arklow Bank.

In Ovoca valley a girl is singing
  With glad thoughts fixed on her sailor frank,
While sand upon sand is the bright tide bringing
  To bury that sailor on Arklow Bank.
The good ship sails and the glad girl singeth,
  And sunshine is bright upon stream and sea,
The high hills gleam and the white wave springeth,
  And stout is the sailor and filled with glee;

But when channel and valley in midnight slumber,
  And rain rinses lawn and landing-place,
That ship shall be manned by a mermaid number
  Whose kisses shall marble the mariner's face.
And the morn will be bright in Ovoca valley
  Though the girl's heart break that her sailor sank,
And the wave will omit not a sparkling sally
  In tossing his corse upon Arklow Bank.

323 *A Late Passer*

DOWN the stormy stream,
  Down the stream to the sea.
Broken—lost like a dream,
  All that was dear to me.
Would God my work in the world were done,
And I forgotten and dead and gone.

Plunge of the water beneath
  As of a soul to its doom ;
Weary, aweary am I of breath,
  Ah ! for the rest of the tomb.
The pine leans over the raging river,
So—my heart longs to be still for ever.

Hangs not the parapet clear
  O'er the darkness that gurgles below ?
Ah ! to blot out year upon year
  In the black pool's eddying flow.
But I would not be false for the ease of the dead,
What hides the Future that I can dread ?

Have I any hope—any faith?
  Have I anything left to lose?—
Have I any trust but in Death,
  Waited for—ah! God knows!
For Death is as God in mercy and might,
And shall not the Judge of the earth do right?

Down the stormy stream,
  Out on the infinite sea,
Deep sleep after this feverish dream,
  With all that is dear to me.
So dying hourly, drag on. Be brave,
It cannot be very far to the grave.

324 *A Storm Song*

TOSS, tight boat, by the foam covered bar;
  Dip deep down in the jaws of the brine.
Fly, dark rack, across moon and star,
  Fly, and fly past.—My love is mine.
Storm-stricken cedars, reel on the height;
  Hurled back, shudder, and pitch to the wind.
Swept by the beam of the moon's pale light,
  Lash, and loom grandly.—My love is kind.

Burst, O sea, on the sands of the shore!
  Scream aloud. Fling up your wild arms white.
Grovel, and shriek to the strong wind's roar;
  Peal up your cry through the pitiless night.
Blow, vast gale, over field and bay;
  Over holt and hill whirl the rain and brine.
Ruin and wreck till returns the day;
  Break, and be broken.—My love is mine.

WILLIAM WILKINS

325 *Dei Gratia*

WHEN hawthorn boughs begin to bud
 In eager green along the way,
And merry songsters toss a flood
 Of melody from spray to spray,
And in the budded branches play
 The little winds, not chill or loud,
 But, softly lifted, softly bowed,
Making the perches rock and sway ;
 Then, gladsome as the lamb and lark,
 I break from grievous thoughts away,—
 Forget what's wrong, forget what's dark,
 And see the whole world good and gay.

When pearly skies break up in blue,
 Raining out milky, misty gold,
And all the sweet land through and through
 Is filled with pleasure manifold
Of growth and light and music bold,
 To close the wound and cure the smart,
 And strengthen all the thankful heart
In joyful praises dawnward rolled ;
 Then meekly as the milkmaids bring
 Their primrose posies pure and cold,
 My soul grows happier—thinking Spring
 The smile of him beneath the mould.

GEORGE ARTHUR GREENE

326

Inisfail

1853-

MY grief on the sword
  For the pain of my heart,
That the dead battles roared
  That have rent us apart!

For the Hosts of the Air
  Come like clouds on the gale,
And the fairy-folk share
  In thy woes, Inisfail.

Oh the music of feet
  Where the Good People pass!
Oh the elfin-song sweet!
  Oh the rings in the grass!

Lissom-winged, many-hued
  Is the tongue of the Gael,
Whose melodies brood
  O'er thy glens, Inisfail!

But the music of souls
  Finds no echoed reply
Where the battle-din rolls,
  And the war-eagles cry.

Let the shanachies cease
  Their monotonous tale:
Be the bird-song of peace
  In thy groves, Inisfail!

GEORGE ARTHUR GREENE

O Isle of the Woods!
  Have thy thrushes no song,
In the dim solitudes
  That are silent so long?

The surges that beat,
  And the storm-winds that rail:
Sound no echoes more sweet
  By thy shores, Inisfail?

Lone Daughter of Kings,
  High-throned o'er the tide,
Wherefore slumber the strings
  Of the harp at thy side?

Stand not silent, apart,
  Lest those discords prevail
That set heart against heart
  Of thy sons, Inisfail.

Where the Danaans be (68)
  In the voice-haunted glen,
Oh the wail of the Shee,[1]
  And the mourning of men!

Our Queen of the West!
  While harsh accents assail,
We pine for thy rest
  And thy songs, Inisfail!

[1] Ir. *Sidhe*—the Fairy Folk.

GEORGE ARTHUR GREENE

327 *Beyond?*

WHAT lies beyond the splendour of the sun,
Beyond his flashing belt of sister-spheres?
What deeps are they whereinto disappears
The visitant comet's sword, of fire fine-spun?

What rests beyond the myriad lights that run
Their nightly race around our human fears?
Hope-signals raised on multitudinous spears
Of armies captained by the Eternal One?

Beyond the sun, and far beyond the stars,
Beyond the weariness of this our day,
Beyond this fretting at the prison-bars,
The urgent soul, divine in soulless clay,
Bids us set forth, through endless avatars,
To seek where God has hidden Himself away.

328 *Mountain Voices*

OVERHEAD the waters falling
Where the hills are riven apart;
Mystic mountain voices calling—
Mountain voices vainly calling:
There is silence in my heart.

Now Before is gone, and After
Drags along with saddened smart;
Echoes rise of children's laughter—
Rise, and fall, of children's laughter:
There is silence in my heart.

Mountain Voice ! now wild and eery,
Now so sweet ! whate'er thou art,
Let me go, for I am weary—
Worn, forlorn, and very weary :
There is silence in my heart.

329 *The Past*

O SPIRIT of the Past ! Who hath not heard—
High on the sacred hills, when no wind blew,
Rising from valleys where no echo stirred—
The murmur of the ages, floating through
The silences of thought ? nor seen
In sleep the swift feet of the dreams flash by,
When each revealing footfall is a light
Thrusting a spear of flame into the night,
Opening eternal doors, and bringing nigh
What shall be, and hath been ?

For who shall call the Past a skein undone,
And not a part of that which shall return ?
Man wheels his circle round a deathless sun,
And with each meeting curve new splendours burn
That shall for ever glow.
For all deeds, all events, are quenchless lights :
All that is done, is gained ; what hath been, is :
Down in the plain are blind uncertainties,
But they who stand upon the mountain heights,
Watching the world, they know.

FRANCIS A. FAHY

330 *The Ould Plaid Shawl*

1854–

NOT far from old Kinvara, in the merry month of May,
When birds were singing cheerily, there came across my way,
As if from out the sky above an angel chanced to fall,
A little Irish cailín in an ould plaid shawl.

She tripped along right joyously, a basket on her arm;
And oh! her face; and oh! her grace, the soul of saint would charm:
Her brown hair rippled o'er her brow, but greatest charm of all
Was her modest blue eyes beaming 'neath her ould plaid shawl.

I courteously saluted her—'God save you, miss,' says I;
'God save you kindly, sir,' said she, and shyly passed me by;
Off went my heart along with her, a captive in her thrall,
Imprisoned in the corner of her ould plaid shawl.

Enchanted with her beauty rare, I gazed in pure delight,
Till round an angle of the road she vanished from my sight;
But ever since I sighing say, as I that scene recall,
'The grace of God about you and your ould plaid shawl.'

FRANCIS A. FAHY

I've heard of highway robbers that with pistols and
with knives,
Make trembling travellers yield them up their money
or their lives,
But think of me that handed out my heart and head
and all
To a simple little cailín in an ould plaid shawl.

Oh! graceful the mantillas that the signorinas wear,
And tasteful are the bonnets of Parisian ladies fair,
But never cloak, or hood, or robe, in palace, bower,
or hall,
Clad half such witching beauty as that ould plaid
shawl.

Oh! some men sigh for riches, and some men live for
fame,
And some on history's pages hope to win a glorious
name:
My aims are not ambitious, and my wishes are but
small—
You might wrap them all together in an ould plaid
shawl.

I'll seek her all through Galway, and I'll seek her all
through Clare,
I'll search for tale or tidings of my traveller every-
where,
For peace of mind I'll never find until my own I call
That little Irish cailín in her ould plaid shawl.

331 *Little Mary Cassidy*

OH! 'tis little Mary Cassidy 's the cause of all my misery,
And the raison that I am not the boy I used to be;
Oh, she bates the beauties all that we read about in history,
And sure half the country-side is as hot for her as me.
Travel Ireland up and down, hill, village, vale and town,
Fairer than the cailín donn, you're looking for in vain;
Oh, I'd rather live in poverty with little Mary Cassidy
Than Emperor, without her, be of Germany or Spain.

'Twas at a dance at Darmody's that first I caught a sight of her,
And heard her sing the 'Droighnean donn,' (69) till tears came in my eyes,
And ever since that blessed hour I'm dreaming day and night of her;
The divil a wink of sleep at all I get from bed to rise.
Cheeks like the rose in June, song like the lark in tune,
Working, resting, night or noon, she never leaves my mind;
Oh! till singing by my cabin fire sits little Mary Cassidy,
'Tis little aise or happiness I'm sure I'll ever find.

What is wealth, what is fame, what is all that people
fight about
To a kind word from her lips or a love-glance from
her eye?
Oh! though troubles throng my breast, sure they'd
soon go to the right about
If I thought the curly head of her would rest there
by and by.
Take all I own to-day, kith, kin, and care away,
Ship them all across the say, or to the frozen zone:
Lave me an orphan bare,—but lave me Mary Cassidy,
I never would feel lonesome with the two of us
alone.

FANNY PARNELL

332 *After Death*

1855–1883

SHALL mine eyes behold thy glory, O my country?
Shall mine eyes behold thy glory?
Or shall the darkness close around them, ere the sun-
blaze break at last upon thy story?

When the nations ope for thee their queenly circle,
as a sweet new sister hail thee,
Shall these lips be sealed in callous death and silence,
that have known but to bewail thee?

Shall the ear be deaf that only loved thy praises, when
all men their tribute bring thee?
Shall the mouth be clay that sang thee in thy squalor,
when all poets' mouths shall sing thee?

Ah ! the harpings and the salvos and the shoutings of
thy exiled sons returning !
I should hear, tho' dead and mouldered, and the grave-
damps should not chill my bosom's burning.

Ah ! the tramp of feet victorious ! I should hear them
'mid the shamrocks and the mosses,
And my heart should toss within the shroud and quiver
as a captive dreamer tosses.

I should turn and rend the cere-clothes round me,
giant sinews I should borrow—
Crying, 'O, my brothers, I have also loved her in
her loneliness and sorrow !

'Let me join with you the jubilant procession : let
me chant with you her story ;
Then contented I shall go back to the shamrocks,
now mine eyes have seen her glory !'

ROSA MULHOLLAND

(LADY GILBERT)

333 *Immortal Morning*

GOLD spears on the hill,
And the dawn flying
After the dark !
The world's drowsy still ;
What is that voice crying
Before the lark ?

ROSA MULHOLLAND

Echo? Of what sound?
An angel blowing
A reed silver-holed?
Seraphs piping around
(There, where the light's flowing)
On pipes of gold?

Shrill, sweet on the wind,
From the gold, riven
Cloud of the morn,
And glory hid behind
Chanticleer in heaven
Cries 'Day is born!'

Out there in the blue,
The world of spirit,
He shakes his wings
Free of immortal dew,
And shrill with joy (you hear it)
His matins sings.

Perched on a long sun-ray,
Gold, o'er the river,
Heaven's chanticleer
Proclaims immortal day,
Forever and forever,
To mortal ear.

Peter, no more, no more
Weep a sin forgiven,
For sin's foregone.
Sorrow is all of yore,
And this is heaven.
Now death is done.

So, the enchanting bird,
Crowing, crowing,
For joyance sings :
Man hath overheard—
Time is halting and slowing,
And life hath wings.

Now, with full eye,
Gazeth upon it
The sun of earth ;
Echoes fade and die.
Heaven and who have won it
Seem little worth.

Crow, cock on the barn,
Sing, wood-throstle,
Stream, leap in the tarn ;
Our mortal day
Is loud with its morning bustle :
Heaven's far away !

334 *Autumn*

UNDER a purple cloud along the west
The great brown mother lies and takes her rest,
A dark cheek on her hand, and in her eyes
The shadow of primeval mysteries.

Her tawny velvets swathe her, manifold,
Her mighty head is coifed in filmy gold,
Her youngest babe, the small, late-blossomed rose
Upon her swarthy bosom feeds and grows.

With her wide darkling gaze the mother sees
Her children in their homes, the reddening trees
Roofing wet lawns, fruit-laden lattices,
Blue mountain domes, and the grey river-seas.

A myriad flower-faces flush the air,
Sun-kindled eyes, the flaming outspread hair,
And vermeil cheeks, the children of her love,
Whose rapid heart-beats all her deep veins move.

The sun's fair children, he whose kisses burned
Upon her wedded lips, and now hath turned
Life-giving ardours upon other spheres,
Leaving their radiant offspring to her tears.

Still laugh they in their joy, with sapphire eyes,
And leafy wings of gold, and singing cries,
Still clap their rosy hands, and on the breeze
Cast fragments of their leafy draperies.

With tranquil heart the mother watcheth them,
Each flower erect upon its fearless stem ;
A wind-tost head hath lost its ruby crown,
A sapphire zone is unaware let down.

There a wing drooped, and here, a love-lit face
Darkens and drops from its irradiate place ;
A swaying of sweet limbs, and then a fall
Bewildering terror seizeth upon all.

They rush with stumbling feet and blinding hair
To her who waiteth in her darkening lair,
Destruction following ; their anguished cry
Rings in her ears, 'O Mother, must we die?'

Then openeth she, the mighty one, her breast,
And folds them all within her arms of rest;
'Ye are immortal, children of my pain;
Sleep unafraid, for ye shall live again.'

335 *The Faery Earl*

OH, who is this comes ridin',
  Ridin' down the glen?
Is it one of our own Red-Branch Knights (70)
  Or one of the King's men?

With feathers on his helmet,
  And gold upon his shield,
His horse is shod with silver shoes,
  He ridin' through the field!

Oh, this is not a Red-Branch
  Nor one of the King's men,
But this is faery Desmond
  Come ridin' back again.

'O lady of the Castle,
  O lady with gold hair,
O lady with eyes of pity,
  Come down the grey tower stair.

'For I may ask a question,
  And you may answer me,
When the sun is red in the forest,
  And the moon is white on the sea.'

Says she, 'Sir, ask your question,
  And I will answer you;
At sunset or at moonrise
  God send that I speak true!

'I know you by your helmet,
  And by your voice so sweet,
And by your coal-black charger
  With silver on his feet.

'God send you, faery Desmond,
  To come back to your own.'
Says he, 'Your answer, lady,
  Before the sun goes down.

'I'm ridin' ever and ever
  Over the land and sea;
My horse's shoes of silver,
  How long will they last me?'

The lady stood and pondered,
  The salt tear in her eye—
'Oh, would that I had magic
  To make a wise reply.

'Oh, will they wear for ever,
  Or will they wear out fast?
Will he ride home this even'
  And stable his horse at last?'

'Sweet lady, quick, your answer!'
  'Now, God, what can I say?—
Those silver shoes will last, sir,
  To ride till Judgement Day.'

He turned, that faery horseman,
  And shook his bridle rein ;
'Now, come the Day of Judgement
  Ere I ride home again.'

The sun went down in the forest,
  The moon shone bright as pearl,
The lady lay in the castle,
  And died for the faery Earl.

And ye will see him ridin',
  Ridin' down the glen,
Over the seas and the rivers,
  Over the hill and the plain.

Ye'll see the plume on his helmet
  Waftin' among the trees,
And the silver shoes of his charger
  Chasin' the moonlit seas.

He's ridin' ever and ever,
  He'll ride till Judgement Day ;
Oh, when that ride is over,
  May he ride home, we pray !

OSCAR WILDE

1856–1900

336 *Endymion*

THE apple trees are hung with gold,
  And birds are loud in Arcady,
The sheep lie bleating in the fold,
The wild goat runs across the wold,
But yesterday his love he told,
  I know he will come back to me.

O rising moon! O Lady moon!
  Be you my lover's sentinel,
  You cannot choose but know him well,
For he is shod with purple shoon,
You cannot choose but know my love,
  For he a shepherd's crook doth bear,
And he is soft as any dove,
  And brown and curly is his hair.

The turtle now has ceased to call
  Upon her crimson-footed groom,
The grey wolf prowls about the stall,
The lily's singing seneschal
Sleeps in the lily-bell, and all
  The violet hills are lost in gloom.
O risen moon! O holy moon!
  Stand on the top of Helice,
  And if my own true love you see,
Ah! if you see the purple shoon,
The hazel crook, the lad's brown hair,
  The goat-skin wrapped about his arm,
Tell him that I am waiting where
  The rushlight glimmers in the Farm.

The falling dew is cold and chill,
  And no bird sings in Arcady,
The little fauns have left the hill,
Even the tired daffodil
Has closed its gilded doors, and still
  My lover comes not back to me.
False moon! False moon! O waning moon!
  Where is my own true lover gone,
  Where are the lips vermilion,
The shepherd's crook, the purple shoon?

Why spread that silver pavilion,
  Why wear that veil of drifting mist?
Ah! thou hast young Endymion,
  Thou hast the lips that should be kissed!

337 *Requiescat*

TREAD lightly, she is near
  Under the snow,
Speak gently, she can hear
  The daisies grow.

All her bright golden hair
  Tarnished with rust,
She that was young and fair
  Fallen to dust.

Lily-like, white as snow,
  She hardly knew
She was a woman, so
  Sweetly she grew.

Coffin-board, heavy stone,
  Lie on her breast,
I vex my heart alone,
  She is at rest.

Peace, Peace, she cannot hear
  Lyre or sonnet,
All my life's buried here,
  Heap earth upon it.

338 *Magdalen Walks*

THE little white clouds are racing over the sky,
And the fields are strewn with the gold of the flower of March,
The daffodil breaks under foot, and the tasselled larch
Sways and swings as the thrush goes hurrying by.

A delicate odour is borne on the wings of the morning breeze,
The odour of deep wet grass, and of brown new-furrowed earth,
The birds are singing for joy of the Spring's glad birth,
Hopping from branch to branch on the rocking trees.

And all the woods are alive with the murmur and sound of Spring,
And the rosebud breaks into pink on the climbing briar,
And the crocus-bed is a quivering moon of fire
Girded round with the belt of an amethyst ring.

And the plane to the pine tree is whispering some tale of love
Till it rustles with laughter and tosses its mantle of green,
And the gloom of the wych-elm's hollow is lit with the iris sheen
Of the burnished rainbow throat and the silver breast of a dove.

See! the lark starts up from his bed in the meadow
there,
Breaking the gossamer threads and the nets of dew,
And flashing a-down the river, a flame of blue!
The kingfisher flies like an arrow, and wounds the air.

339 *Les Silhouettes*

THE sea is flecked with bars of grey,
The dull dead wind is out of tune,
And like a withered leaf the moon
Is blown across the stormy bay.

Etched clear upon the pallid sand
Lies the black boat: a sailor boy
Clambers aboard in careless joy
With laughing face and gleaming hand.

And overhead the curlews cry,
Where through the dusky upland grass
The young brown-throated reapers pass,
Like silhouettes against the sky.

THOMAS WILLIAM ROLLESTON

340 *The Grave of Rury* (71)

1857-

CLEAR as air, the western waters
evermore their sweet, unchanging song
Murmur in their stony channels
round O'Conor's sepulchre in Cong.

THOMAS WILLIAM ROLLESTON

Crownless, hopeless, here he lingered ;
  year on year went by him like a dream,
While the far-off roar of conquest
  murmured faintly like the singing stream.

Here he died, and here they tomb'd him,
  men of Fechin, chanting round his grave.
Did they know, ah ! did they know it,
  what they buried by the babbling wave ?

Now above the sleep of Rury
  holy things and great have passed away ;
Stone by stone the stately Abbey
  falls and fades in passionless decay.

Darkly grows the quiet ivy,
  pale the broken arches glimmer through ;
Dark upon the cloister-garden
  dreams the shadow of the ancient yew.

Through the roofless aisles the verdure
  flows, the meadow-sweet and fox-glove bloom ;
Earth, the mother and consoler,
  winds soft arms about the lonely tomb.

Peace and holy gloom possess him,
  last of Gaelic monarchs of the Gael,
Slumbering by the young, eternal
  river-voices of the western vale.

THOMAS WILLIAM ROLLESTON

341 *The Shannon at Foynes*

INTO the West, where o'er the wide Atlantic
The lights of sunset gleam,
From its high sources in the heart of Erinn
Flows the great stream.

Yet back in stormy cloud or viewless vapour
The wandering waters come,
And faithfully across the trackless heaven
Find their old home.

But ah! the tide of life that flows unceasing
Into the luring West
Returns no more, to swell with kindlier fulness
The Mother's breast.

ROSE KAVANAGH

342 *Lough Bray*

1859–1891

A LITTLE lonely moorland lake,
Its waters brown and cool and deep—
The cliff, the hills behind it, make
A picture for my heart to keep.

For rock and heather, wave and strand,
Wore tints I never saw them wear;
The June sunshine was o'er the land,
Before, 'twas never half so fair!

The amber ripples sang all day,
  And singing spilled their crowns of white
Upon the beach, in thin pale spray,
  That streaked the sober strand with light.

The amber ripples sang their song,
  When suddenly from far o'erhead
A lark's pure voice mixed with the throng
  Of lovely things about us spread.

Some flowers were there, so near the brink
  Their shadows in the wave were thrown ;
While mosses, green and grey and pink,
  Grew thickly round each smooth dark stone.

And over all, the summer sky ;
  Shut out the town we left behind ;
'Twas joy to stand in silence by,
  One bright chain linking mind to mind.

Oh, little lonely mountain spot !
  Your place within my heart will be
Apart from all Life's busy lot
  A true, sweet, solemn memory.

343 *St. Michan's Churchyard* (72)

INSIDE the city's throbbing heart
  One spot I know set well apart
From Life's hard highway, Life's loud mart.

ROSE KAVANAGH

Each Dublin lane, and street, and square
Around might echo ; but in there
The sound stole soft as whispered prayer ;

A little, lonely, green graveyard,
The old church tower its solemn guard,
The gate with nought but sunbeams barred ;

While other sunbeams went and came,
Above the stone which waits the name,
His land must write with Freedom's flame.[1]

The slender elm above that stone
Its summer wreath of leaves had thrown
Around the heart so quiet grown.

A robin, the bare boughs among,
Let loose his little soul in song—
Quick liquid gushes, fresh and strong.

And quiet heart and bird and tree,
Seemed linked in some strange sympathy
Too fine for mortal eye to see—

But full of balm and soothing sweet,
For those who sought that calm retreat,
For aching breast and weary feet.

Each crowded street and thoroughfare
Was echoing round it—yet in there
The peace of Heaven was everywhere.

[1] Robert Emmet.

DOUGLAS HYDE

344 *Death Lament of John O'Mahony*

1860–

IN a foreign land, in a lonesome city,
  With few to pity, to know, or care,
I sleep each night while my heart is burning,
  And wake each morning to new despair.

Let no one venture to ask my story
  Who believes in glory or trusts to fame;
Yes! I have within me such demons in keeping
  As are better sleeping without a name.

For many a day of blood and horror,
  And night of terror, and work of dread,
I have rescued nought but my honour only,
  And this aged, lonely, and whitening head.

Not a single hope have I seen fulfilled
  For the blood we spilled when we cast the die;
And the future I painted in brightness and pride
  Has the present belied, and shall still belie.

In this far-off country, this city dreary,
  I languished weary, and sad, and sore,
Till the flower of youth in glooms o'ershaded
  Grew seared, and faded for evermore.

Oh my land! from thee driven—our old flag furled—
  I renounced the world when I went from thee;
My heart lingers still on its native strand,
  And American land holds nought for me.

Through a long life contriving, hoping, striving,
  Driven and driving, leading and led ;
I have rescued nought but my honour only
  And this aged, lonely, and whitening head.

345 *The Druid*

OUR Colum's bark was in the bay,
    But sore our oarsmen were dismayed,
The Druid Brochan barred our way,
  And shouted to his gods for aid ;
And swore by earth and sea and sun
No Christian hound should sail upon
  The lake that he forbade.

His old grey hairs hung loose and long
  About his shoulders bowed with age,
He poured to heaven the piercing song
  (Men said) of some old Pictish sage.
His eyeballs gleamed unearthly fire,
And, as his song rose ever higher,
  He shook with palsied rage.

I swear his mountain demon heard,
  Who knew not that our Saint was nigh,
Nor that a bearer of the Word
  Was come beneath his own wild sky,
Where, king of all men's hopes and fears,
Himself, they said, a thousand years,
  Had ruled as God on high.

He heard, I swear, his priest's distress,
And launched himself in one black cloud
Upon the bosom of Loch Ness,
While Pict and Scot in terror bowed,
And like a fiery thunder-snake
Came tearing down the long dark lake,
We heard him roar aloud.

Upon the wings of one wild storm,
Rushing with furious haste, he came;
I hardly saw his dragon form,
Through sheets and tongues of forkèd flame.
Unceasing thunder crashed behind
The rushing of the mighty wind,
Men trembled at his name.

But through the howling of the gale
More shrill arose the Druid's cry,
'Now wretched Christian wilt thou sail?
Down on thy knees, adore and die,
And thinkest thou to cope with me?
Ye Picts and Scots, at last ye see
I am his master, I.'

And all men on their faces fell,
Only St. Colum, meek and pale,
Rising against the Druid's spell,
Passed in the teeth of that wild gale,
Down to his bark, nor blenched with fear,
But bade us cross ourselves and rear
His mast and span his sail.

DOUGLAS HYDE

We strained the aching mast on high,
  The raving sail we scarcely reared.
The screaming cordage lashed the sky,
  We trembled while the Pagans jeered,
For there was never human oar
Could push that wind-caught bark from shore,
  When such a tempest neared.

While Colum signed the cross above
  Our floundering boat with outstretched hand,
The howling whirlwind burst and drove
  Enormous breakers roods on land.
Yet, lo, our vessel put about,
And through the storm went up their shout,
  'His boat has left the land!'

There, in the teeth of that great wind,
  Through blinding clouds of driven spray,
They saw us sail and leave behind
  Themselves and their accursèd bay.
Our boat sailed on with even keel,
The billow could not make us reel,
  The tempest could not stay.

Old Brochan cursed his powerless god,
  His starting eyeballs wild with fear,
His demon, like a monstrous clod,
  Dropped in the lake to disappear.
But far and wide the word went forth
That Christ was victor in the north,
  And Colum was his seer.

346

The Breedyeen

From the Irish

'TIS the Breedyeen I love,
All dear ones above,
Like a star from the start
Round my heart she did move.
Her breast like a dove,
Or the foam in the cove,
With her gold locks apart,
In my heart she put love.

'Tis not Venus, I say,
Who grieved me this day,
But the white one, the bright one,
Who slighted my stay.
For her I shall pray—
I confess it—for aye,
She's my sister, I missed her,
When all men were gay.

To the hills let us go
Where the raven and crow
In the dark dismal valleys
Croak death-like and low ;
By this volume I swear,
O bright cúl of fair hair,
That though solitude shrieked
I should seek for thee there !

DOUGLAS HYDE

To the hills let us go,
Where the raven and crow
In the dark dismal valleys
Wing silent and slow.
There's no joy in men's fate
But grief grins in the gate:
There's no fair without foul,
Without crooked no straight.

Her neck like the lime,
And her breath like the thyme,
And her bosom untroubled
By care or by time.
Like a bird in the night
At a great blaze of light,
Astounded and wounded
I swoon at her sight.

Since I gave thee my love,
I gave thee my love,
I gave thee my love,
O thou berry so bright—
The sun in her height
Looked on with delight,
And between thy two arms, may
I die on the night!

And I would that I were
In the glens of the air,
Or in dark dismal valleys
Where the wildwood is bare;

What a kiss from her there
I should coax without care,
From my star of the morning,
My fairer than fair!

347 *Ringleted Youth of my Love*

From the Irish

RINGLETED youth of my love,
With thy locks bound loosely behind thee,
You passed by the road above,
But you never came in to find me;
Where were the harm for you
If you came for a little to see me,
Your kiss is a wakening dew
Were I ever so ill or so dreamy.

If I had golden store
I would make a nice little boreen,
To lead straight up to his door,
The door of the house of my stóreen;
Hoping to God not to miss
The sound of his footfall in it,
I have waited so long for his kiss
That for days I have slept not a minute.

I thought, O my love! you were so—
As the moon is, or sun on a fountain,
And I thought after that you were snow,
The cold snow on the top of the mountain;

And I thought after that, you were more
Like God's lamp shining to find me,
Or the bright star of knowledge before,
And the star of knowledge behind me.

You promised me high-heeled shoes,
And satin and silk, my stóreen,
And to follow me, never to lose,
Though the ocean were round us roaring;
Like a bush in a gap in a wall
I am now left lonely without thee,
And this house I grow dead of, is all
That I see around or about me.

348 *My Love, oh! she is my Love*

From the Irish

SHE casts a spell, oh casts a spell!
Which haunts me more than I can tell.
Dearer, because she makes me ill,
Than who would will to make me well.

She is my store, oh she my store!
Whose grey eye wounded me so sore,
Who will not place in mine her palm,
Nor love, nor calm me any more.

She is my pet, oh she my pet!
Whom I can never more forget;
Who would not lose by me one moan,
Nor stone upon my cairn would set.

DOUGLAS HYDE

She is my roon, oh she my roon !
Who tells me nothing, leaves me soon ;
Who would not lose by me one sigh,
Were death and I within one room.

She is my dear, oh she my dear !
Who cares not whether I be here.
Who will not weep when I am dead,
But makes me shed the silent tear.

Hard my case, oh hard my case !
For in her eye no hope I trace,
She will not hear me any more,
But I adore her silent face.

She is my choice, oh she my choice !
Who never made me to rejoice ;
Who caused my heart to ache so soft,
Who put no softness in her voice.

Great my grief, oh great my grief !
Neglected, scorned beyond belief,
By her who looks at me askance,
By her who grants me no relief.

She's my desire, oh my desire !
She warms me like the bright sun's fire ;
Who were than wild-blown ice more cold,
Were I so bold as to sit by her.

She it is who stole my heart,
And left a void and aching smart ;
But if she soften not her eye,
I know that life and I must part.

DOUGLAS HYDE

349 *Happy it is*

From the Irish

HAPPY 'tis, thou blind, for thee
  That thou seest not our star;
Could'st thou see as we now see
  Thou would'st be as we now are.

God! why was I not made blind
  Ere my mind was set upon her!
Oh, when I behold her eye,
  How can I weigh life or honour?

Once I pitied sightless men,
  I was then unhurt by sight;
Now I envy those who see not,
  They can be not hurt by light.

Woe who once has seen her please
  And then sees her not each hour:
Woe for him her love-mesh traps,
  Woe for him who snaps its power.

Woe for him who sees her not,
  Woe his lot who does, I wis,—
Woe for him is not beside her,
  Woe besides for him who is.

KATHERINE TYNAN-HINKSON

350

In Iona

1861–

OH, 'tis pleasant in Iona
  Whether in shine or snow!
Grand it is in Iona
  When the north winds blow.
The birds sing sweet in Iona,
  Oh very sweet and low!
But sore I miss in Iona
  A voice I used to know.

Iona hath the song-birds
  And the hum of the bees,
The distant bark of house-dogs,
  And the wind in the trees.
She hath the singing-cricket,
  And the moan of the seas,
But never the low of cattle
  My homesick heart to ease.

The wee brown cow of Kerry
  Is docile and kind,
The big-framed cow of Leinster
  Is much to my mind,
The wild little cow of the mountains
  Who shall loose or bind?
Sweet is the call of the milkmaid
  Borne upon the wind.

Columba he hath said it—
  'Wherever a cow shall be,
There shall be found a woman,
  Her wiles and witchery.
And in this Holy Island
  May God forbid that she
Should plague with sore temptation
  My holy men and me.'

And since the kine are banished
  Heavy my heart doth go;
Oh sweet it is in Iona
  Whatever wind will blow!
But I, the farmer-brother,
  My tears are sad and slow
For the low of the kindly cattle,
  The voice I used to know.

351

To Inishkea[1]

I'LL rise and go to Inishkea,
  Where many a one will weep with me—
The bravest boy that sailed the sea
  From Blacksod Bay to Killery.

I'll dress my boat in sails of black,
The widow's cloak I shall not lack,
I'll set my face and ne'er turn back
  Upon the way to Inishkea.

[1] Off the coast of Mayo.

In Arran Island, cold as stone,
I wring my hands and weep my lone
Where never my true love's name was known :
    It were not so in Inishkea.

The friends that knew him there will come
And kiss my cheek so cold and numb.
O comfort is not troublesome
    To kindly friends in Inishkea !

'Tis there the children call your name,
The old men sigh, and sigh the same ;
'Tis all your praise, and none your blame,
    Your love will hear in Inishkea.

But you were dear to beast and bird,
The dogs once followed at your word,
Your feet once pressed the sand and sward—
    My heart is sore for Inishkea.

I'll rise and go to Inishkea
O'er many a mile of tossing sea
That hides your darling face from me.
    I'll live and die in Inishkea !

352 *Love's Bird*

WHEN thrushes rest the weary head,
    And linnets lie in gold and green,
When blackbirds on a downy bed
    Are silvered with a moony sheen,

What voice awakes the emerald house?
  What love incarnate flies on wings?
What passion shakes the trembling boughs?
  It is the Bird of Love that sings.

It is the Bird of Love that sings,
  Stabbing our silence like a sword,
And Love himself that flies on wings.
  God and enchanter and no bird.

Our moon of honey, our marriage moon
  Rides in the heaven for our delight.
The silver world grows golden soon,
  Honey and gold spilled in the night.

The Bird of Love, the Bird of Pain,
  He sings our marriage moon away;
Filling the night with golden rain,
  Betwixt the darkness and the day.

Closer and closer, hold me close,
  For is it Love or Death he sings?
And is it Love or Death that goes
  Through the sweet night with rustling wings?

353 *Love Comfortless*

THE child is in the night and rain
    On whom no tenderest wind might blow,
And out alone in a hurricane.
                                        Ah, no,
The child is safe in Paradise!

The snow is on his gentle head,
His little feet are in the snow,
Oh, very cold is his small bed!
Ah, no,
Lift up your heart, lift up your eyes!

Over the fields and out of sight,
Beside the lonely river's flow,
Lieth the child this bitter night.
Ah, no,
The child sleeps under Mary's eyes!

What wandering lamb cries sore distressed,
Whilst I with fire and comfort go?
Oh, let me warm him in my breast!
Ah, no,
'Tis warm in God's lit nurseries!

354 *St. Francis to the Birds*

LITTLE sisters, the birds,
We must praise God, you and I—
You, with songs that fill the sky;
I, with halting words.

All things tell His praise,
Woods and waters thereof sing,
Summer, Winter, Autumn, Spring
And the nights and days.

Yea, and cold and heat,
  And the sun and stars and moon,
  Sea with her monotonous tune,
Rain and hail and sleet,

And the winds of heaven,
  And the solemn hills of blue,
  And the brown earth and the dew,
And the thunder even,

And the flowers' sweet breath,—
  All things make one glorious voice ;
  Life with fleeting pains and joys,
And our brother, Death.

Little flowers of air,
  With your feathers soft and sleek,
  And your bright brown eyes and meek,
He hath made you fair.

He hath taught to you
  Skill to weave in tree and thatch
  Nests where happy mothers hatch
Speckled eggs of blue.

And hath children given :
  When the soft heads overbrim
  The brown nests, then thank ye Him
In the clouds of heaven.

Also in your lives
  Live His laws who loveth you.
  Husbands, be ye kind and true ;
Be homekeeping, wives—

Love not gossiping ;
Stay at home and keep the nest ;
Fly not here and there in quest
Of the newest thing.

Live as brethren live ;
Love be in each heart and mouth ;
Be not envious, be not wroth,
Be not slow to give.

When ye build the nest,
Quarrel not o'er straw or wool ;
He who hath be bountiful
To the neediest.

Be not puffed or vain
Of your beauty or your worth,
Of your children or your birth,
Or the praise you gain.

Eat not greedily :
Sometimes for sweet mercy's sake,
Worm or insect spare to take ;
Let it crawl or fly.

See ye sing not near
To our church on holy day,
Lest the humble folk should stray
From their prayers to hear.

Now depart in peace :
In God's name I bless each one ;
May your days be long i' the sun
And your joys increase.

And remember me,
  Your poor brother Francis, who
  Loveth you, and thanketh you
For this courtesy.

Sometimes when ye sing,
  Name my name, that He may take
  Pity for the dear song's sake
On my shortcoming.

355 *In the May*

OH, my swallows! hasten up from the South,
  For young May walks knee-deep in the Irish meadows,
And living gold is her hair, and the breath of her mouth
  Is delight, and her eyes are starring the happy shadows;
The honey heart o' the cowslip lies at her feet,
  The faint-flushed buds of the hawthorn trail o'er her bosom,
And the floating gown that covers her, fragrant and sweet,
  Is the drifted rose and snow of the apple-blossom.

Fair are the passionate skies of the southern land,
  Blue beyond dreams, and a great sun hangeth all golden;
Fair are the hills that are sceptred kings, as they stand
  With the gold on their brows and their ermine mantles unfolden,

And the purple robe to their feet, and the death on
their eyes;
And fair the vales where the sunny rivers are singing:
There are the vines, and the olives silver of guise,
And overhead are the white doves wheeling and
winging.

Oh, but our Irish woods are lovely to-day!
The trees are young knights, in whose helms the
proud plumes quiver;
Singing lustily goeth the wind on his way;
The voice of a naiad chants in the reeds by the river;
A young wind bloweth the dancing grasses aside;
On baby leaves at their play is a white sun
streaming;
And down from the hills the rain comes veiled as a bride,
With dripping feet, and her silver mantle all
gleaming.

Surely the nightingale, under a southern moon,
Singeth the deathless tale of her passion divinely;
But oh, the innocent joy of the blackbird's tune,
And the liquid trill of the thrush as she carols finely!
Whistle, my blackbird, out in the orchard croft;
Whistle, my gold-throat, clear as the viols of heaven;
Answer, my thrush, with your silver fluting and soft
Make faint the pale translucent air of the even!

Long of coming! our king-cup meadows are gold,
And the daisies dance in the balmy wind that is
blowing;
I hear the bleating of young lambs free from the fold;
The shadows fly where the spears of the wheat ear
showing;

Soon will the lilac open, waxen and sweet,
 And laburnum's torch flare out in the golden weather;
And oh, the joy of our summer were incomplete
 Wanting the flash and gleam of the swallow's feather.

Hasten, hasten! over the leagues of foam;
 Flee over yeasty seas, over low land and high land,
And answer, swallows, answer true when ye come—
 In all the lands is a land as lovely as my land?
Up from the southward floats with the breast of a dove
 A silver cloud to our misty skies that are summer's,
And lo! the flash of the happy wings that we love,
 The wheel and whir of our swallows, our dear late-comers.

356 *A Song of Summer*

OH, sweet it is in Summer,
 When leaves are fair and long,
To lie amid lush, scented grass,
Where gold and grey the shadows pass,
A swift, unresting throng;
And hear low river voices
Sing o'er the shining sands,
That seem a glory garb to wear
Of emerald and jacinth rare,
The work of fairy hands;
And see afar the mountains, heaven-kissed,
Shine through the white rain's silvery-sheeted mist.
Oh, fair the balmy morning,
When gay the sun doth ride,

And white plumes sail against the blue,
And all the land is fresh with dew,
And sweet the hay-fields wide!
Yet fairer windless evening,
When the pale vesper star
Parts her long veil of dusky hair,
And looks with gentle eyes and fair
From palaces afar,
And sings the nightingale to tranced skies
Of love and pain and all high mysteries.

PATRICK JOSEPH McCALL

357 *The Bonny Light Horseman*

A Jacobite Ballad

1861–

A POOR lonely maiden, I'm now going over
To Shemus, in Flanders, to look for my lover:
Oh Mary, my pity! how shall I discover
My bonnie light horseman, away in the war?

We lived by the banks of the broomy Blackwater,
My father and mother, and I, their one daughter,
Till red grew our valley with burning and slaughter,
By Kirke's Saxon butchers, let loose in the war!

We fled to the cave—to the haunt of the Torie;
And Emun, my lover, for vengeance and glory,
Took sabre and steel—sad, oh Mary, my story!—
A bonnie light horseman, he joined in the war!

I parted from him on the street of Dungannon :
He lost at the Boyne, but won at the Shannon ;
Till Shemus, the craven, left him at Duncannon—
My bonnie light horseman, so brave in the war !

From Limerick, with Sheldon, away he went sailing :
'Forget him, dear Eileen !' my parents cried, wailing :
They're now in the clay, while I sigh, unavailing,
For my bonnie light horseman, afar in the war !

They've told me !—ah, love, shall I never more see you ?
Now, Erin, cold, cold is the hand that would free you !
They have told me at last—'Oh, astórín mo chree hu !'
My bonnie light horseman is slain in the war !

358 *The Bouchaleen Bawn*[1]

A Spinning Duet (73)

MAUREEN

I WENT to the wood when the morning was breaking,
Oró, the Ring o' the Dawn !
The lark a new song for true lovers was making ;
And whom did I meet but my Bouchaleen bawn !

[1] Ir. *Bhuachailín* (pron. *vouchaleen*) *Bán*—The fair-haired little boy.

PATRICK JOSEPH McCALL

Cauth

To meet Shaun O'Farrell you roved thro' the wild-
wood !
Oró, the Ring o' the Dawn !
The love of your prime is the love of your childhood—
So take him and make him your Bouchaleen bawn !

Maureen

'Twas not Shaun O'Farrell I went to meet therein ;
Oró, the Ring o' the Dawn !
With a gad[1] on his back let him plough over Erinn ;
Then find me and bind me my Bouchaleen bawn !

Cauth

Alas, fickle colleen, where can you find better ?
Oró, the Ring o' the Dawn !
He sings a sweet song, and he writes a kind letter—
So take him and make him your Bouchaleen bawn !

Maureen

I like song and letter, not writer or singer ;
Oró, the Ring o' the Dawn !
And so for a better much longer I'd linger—
So find me and bind me my Bouchaleen bawn !

Cauth

You went to the greenwood to meet Mike O'Malley,
Oró, the Ring o' the Dawn !
Who whistles a jig as he rides down the valley—
So take him and make him your Bouchaleen bawn !

[1] A twisted withe of osiers.

PATRICK JOSEPH McCALL

MAUREEN

I'd love him and prove him and hold him for ever ;
  Oró, the Ring o' the Dawn !
But he is too stupid, or I am too clever—
  So find me and bind me my Bouchaleen bawn !

CAUTH

Yet go with the dull if he be but good-hearted ;
  Oró, the Ring o' the Dawn !
By east and by west may you never be parted,
  You'll take him and make him your Bouchaleen bawn !

MAUREEN

The song-bird would pine in the smoke and the smother ;
  Oró, the Ring o' the Dawn !
Go east and go west till you chance on another ;
  And find me and bind me my Bouchaleen bawn !

CAUTH

For Donal O'Falvey you'd roam the world over—
  Oró, the Ring o' the Dawn !
Tho' many his darlings, you may be his lover—
  So take him and make him your Bouchaleen bawn !

MAUREEN

Ah, Sheevaun [1] O'Kelly would tear out my tresses,
  Oró, the Ring o' the Dawn !
If Donal should venture to seek my caresses—
  Come, find me and bind me my Bouchaleen bawn !

[1] Judith.

CAUTH

That jewel is rarest whose finding was hardest!
  Oró, the Ring o' the Dawn!
That cargo is dearest whose journey was farthest,
  So take him and make him your Bouchaleen bawn!

MAUREEN

No tree ever grew but 'twas matched by another;
  Oró, the Ring o' the Dawn!
And the King of the Forest is Brian, your brother!
  Now find me and bind me my Bouchaleen bawn!

359 *Dunlang O'Hartigan* (74)

Lament of Aoibhell, the Fairy Queen

'TIS my bitter grief and sorrow,
  On this awful morrow,
That I cannot win for thee thy breath
Back from Death,
    Dunlang O'Hartigan!

I had given thee in my liosses[1]
My heart's brimming kisses—
I had charmed thee all the evening long
With sweet song,
    Dunlang O'Hartigan!

But when Murrough, Son of Brian,
Called thee, youthful lion!

[1] Fairy forts.

PATRICK JOSEPH McCALL

From my kiss and song of tuneful flow
Thou wouldst go,
    Dunlang O'Hartigan !

Vain my pleading, prayer, and weeping,
To hold thee in keeping !
My own cloak to thee I then did yield
For thy shield,
    Dunlang O'Hartigan !

On Clontarf's red plain I found thee
With that cloak around thee ;
I alone saw thee like lightning go
Through the foe,
    Dunlang O'Hartigan !

It was there at brink of even,
Murrough cried sore driven :
'Where is he that loved me lingering now—
Where art thou,
    Dunlang O'Hartigan ?'

It was there, when foes were flying,
I heard thee replying,
Flinging off the cloak that kept thee clear—
'I am here,
    Dunlang O'Hartigan !'

Through thee, that dear friend caressing,
Winged a dart distressing !
Ah, thou wouldst have known a happier kiss
In my lios,
    Dunlang O'Hartigan !

STEPHEN LUCIUS GWYNN

360 *The Woman of Beare* (75)

From the Irish

1865-

EBBING, the wave of the sea
 Leaves, where it wantoned before
Wan and naked the shore,
Heavy the clotted weed.
And in my heart, woe is me!
Ebbs a wave of the sea.

I am the Woman of Beare.
Foul am I that was fair,
Gold-embroidered smocks I had,
Now in rags am hardly clad.

Arms, now so poor and thin,
Staring bone and shrunken skin,
Once were lustrous, once caressed
Chiefs and warriors to their rest.

Not the sage's power, nor lone
Splendour of an agèd throne,
Wealth I envy not, nor state.
Only women folk I hate.

On your heads, while I am cold,
Shines the sun of living gold.
Flowers shall wreathe your necks in May:
For me, every month is grey.

STEPHEN LUCIUS GWYNN

Yours the bloom : but ours the fire,
Even out of dead desire.
Wealth, not men, ye love ; but when
Life was in us, we loved men.

Fair the men, and wild the manes
Of their coursers on the plains ;
Wild the chariots rocked, when we
Raced by them for mastery.

Lone is Femen : vacant, bare,
Stands in Bregon Ronan's Chair.
And the slow tooth of the sky
Frets the stones where my dead lie.

The wave of the great sea talks :
Through the forest winter walks.
Not to-day by wood and sea
Comes King Diarmuid here to me.

I know what my king does.
Through the shivering reeds, across
Fords no mortal strength may breast,
He rows—to how chill a rest !

Amen ! Time ends all.
Every acorn has to fall.
Bright at feasts the candles were,
Dark is here the house of prayer.

I, that when the hour was mine
Drank with kings the mead and wine,
Drink whey-water now, in rags
Praying among shrivelled hags.

Amen! Let my drink be whey,
Let me do God's will all day—
And, as upon God I call,
Turn my blood to angry gall.

Ebb, flood, and ebb: I know
Well the ebb, and well the flow,
And the second ebb, all three—
Have they not come home to me?

Came the flood that had for waves
Monarchs, mad to be my slaves,
Crested as by foam with bounds
Of wild steeds and leaping hounds.

Comes no more that flooding tide
To my silent dark fireside.
Guests are many in my hall,
But a hand has touched them all.

Well is with the isle that feels
Now the ocean backward steals:
But to me my ebbing blood
Brings again no forward flood.

Ebbing, the wave of the sea
Leaves, where it wantoned before,
Changed past knowing the shore,
Lean and lonely and grey.
And far and farther from me
Ebbs the wave of the sea.

STEPHEN LUCIUS GWYNN

361 *Ireland*

IRELAND, oh Ireland! centre of my longings,
 Country of my fathers, home of my heart!
Overseas you call me: 'Why an exile from me?
 Wherefore sea-severed, long leagues apart?'

As the shining salmon, homeless in the sea depths,
 Hears the river call him, scents out the land,
Leaps and rejoices in the meeting of the waters,
 Breasts weir and torrent, nests in the sand,

Lives there and loves; yet with the year's returning,
 Rusting in the river, pines for the sea,
Sweeps back again to the ripple of the tideway,
 Roamer of the waters, vagabond and free.

Wanderer am I like the salmon of thy rivers;
 London is my ocean, murmurous and deep,
Tossing and vast; yet through the roar of London
 Comes to me thy summons, calls me in sleep.

Pearly are the skies in the country of my fathers,
 Purple are thy mountains, home of my heart.
Mother of my yearning, love of all my longings,
 Keep me in remembrance, long leagues apart.

362 *Out in the Dark*

OH, up the brae, and up and up, beyont the fairy
 thorn,
It's there they hae my baby laid, that died when he
 was born.

Afore the priest could christen him to save his soul, he died ;
'It never lived at all,' they said.—'Twas livin' in my side.

For many a day an' many a night, an' weary night and day,
I kent him livin' at my heart, I carena what they say.
For many a day an' many a night I wearied o' unrest,
But now I'm sore to hae my wean back hidden in my breast.

He'll sure be thinkin' long for me, an' wearyin' his lone
Up in thon corner by the whins wi' neither cross nor stone :
Ay, tho' I'd died wi' him itself, they wouldna let us be—
The corner o' a field for him, the holy ground for me.

Thare many a wean that lies wi' him, and none that got a name,
Thare many a wife, hard put till it, was glad that dead they came,
Ay, many a man that scarcely minds a child o' his lies there :
But och ! 'tis cruel hard to quit the first you'd ever bear.

The graves are all that tiny that they'd hardly raise
a mound,
And couples o' a Sunday do be coortin' on thon
ground,
An' thare none that thinks upon them ; but my heart'll
be there still,
On the sod among the bracken an' the whins upon
the hill.

I'd be feared to come o' night there, for the hill is
fairy ground :
But thare may be more nor fairies dancin' in the fairy
round—
Och, an' if I only thought it ! sure I'd let them do
their worst,
An' I'd go to see my baby, tho' I be to be accursed.

But I'll never reach my wean now, neither here nor
in the sod,
An' I'm better wi' the Christians an' the souls that's
saved for God—
Och, to feel his fingers on me, an' to clasp him when
he smiled !
Sure ye'd think there'd be one heaven for the mother
an' the child.

363 *Cowslips*

COWSLIPS, sweetlips, smelling of the summer,
Coming with the cuckoo, bringing in the May,
Lifting heads in pastures, where the cattle spare you,
Waiting to be gathered when the children come
to play.

STEPHEN LUCIUS GWYNN

Daffodils were golden, nodding in the uplands,
Golden in the marshes flares the marigold :
Softer hued the cowslips, winsomer and sweeter—
Sure the soul of flowers is the odour that they hold.

Faint and soft and honied, fragrant as the kine's breath,
Wafted airs of cowslips gladden London streets ;
Yellow-speckled handfuls, pennyworths of sunshine,
To the dusty passers they are lavish of their sweets.

Not from London barrows came our Irish cowslips,
Tossed and cramped and prisoned all the night they've lain ;
But when morning reddened, lest they should feel strangers,
Cowslips from each cutting kept a-nodding to the train.

Kindly was the thought for children who this May-time
Weave no cowslip necklace, wind no cowslip ball ;
London parks are gay with beds of guarded blossom,
But, to pluck and treasure—not a cowslip in them all.

Cowslips, sweetlips, smelling of the country,
Coming with the cuckoo, bringing in the May,
Straight and tall and slender, springing in the pastures,
Waiting to be gathered when the children come to play.

FRANCES WYNNE

364 *Whisper*

1866–1893

YOU saucy south wind, setting all the budded beech boughs swinging
Above the wood anemones that flutter, flushed and white,
When far across the wide salt waves your quick way you were winging,
Oh! tell me, tell me, did you pass my sweetheart's ship last night?
Ah! let the daisies be,
South wind! and answer me:
Did you my sailor see?
Wind, whisper very low,
For none but you must know
I love my lover so.

You've come by many a gorsy hill, your breath has sweetness in it,
You've ruffled up the high white clouds that fleck the shining blue;
You've rushed and danced and whirled, so now perhaps you'll spare a minute,
To tell me whether you have seen my lover brave and true?
Wind, answer me, I pray;
I'm lonelier every day,
My love is far away;
And, sweet wind, whisper low,
For none but you must know
I love my lover so.

FRANCES WYNNE

365 *Sea-Gulls*

EARLY in the year,
When blustering March was here,
And the clouds seemed always grey,
There came a sudden, sun-bright day,
In the midst of rainy weather,
Shining out of a blue and breezy sky,
Shedding a silver shimmer down on the sea.
Do you remember, my friend, how we
On that morning clear,
Left the town behind us, you and I,
And lay among flower-flecked gorse and heather,
We two together?
Down below us, the glittering bay
In rippling radiance stretched away;
A distant church spire here and there
Flashed in the sunshine, aglint and fair;
And far, far off, all faintly hued
In the flooding light, the mountains stood.
The sea-gulls, with wide white wings outspread,
Passed so close to us overhead,
As they slowly flew,
That, though we spoke gently, I and you,
They might have heard what we said.
Ah! sea-gulls, swooping, slipping
Under the water blue;
Sea-gulls, diving and dipping;
Ah! sea-gulls, softly swaying,
Sea-gulls, poising and playing,
I wonder if you knew
What we were saying?

FRANCES WYNNE

When the heather wore its purplest glory,
  And the gorse gleamed with its rarest gold,
One of us was listening to a story,
  Rapturously new, and yet how old!
    Ah! sea-gulls, restless, roving,
    Sea-gulls, daring and bold,
    There is nought as sweet as loving!

When the wild nights come of storm and raining,
  And the dark waves sweep in with sullen roar,
One of us will still be sobbing, straining,
  After that which tarries evermore.
    Sea-gulls, with tired wings trailing,
    The long black billows o'er,
    Ah! sea-gulls, wandering, wailing,
    On the deserted shore,
    There is nought so sad as failing!

THOMAS EKENHEAD MAYNE

366 *A Dirge for the Deep-sea Trawler*

1866–1899

FROM the mouth of the rolling Humber
  To where Thames' grey waters sweep,
They are laid in their beds to slumber
  Far down in the hoary deep.

From the waves that lash upon Dover
  Across to the Netherlands,
They rest with their toils all over
  And moulder away in the sands.

THOMAS EKENHEAD MAYNE

From Denmark's savage surges
  To the tides that on Orkney beat,
The blasts are singing the dirges
  Of the men of the fishing fleet.

The winds that cut like sabres
  And the bleak and biting wave,
Are lulling them after their labours
  And moaning o'er one wide grave.

The hungry sea that holds them
  Is for ever insatiate,
And down in the weed that infolds them
  The crab and the dog-fish wait.

Where mightily rise the breezes
  And smite the surge aloft,
Where the spray-sheet falls and freezes,
  Where the caps of the waves are doffed,

Where the smack is gulfed in the furrows
  And rises again on the crest,
Where the boom in the roller burrows—
  Death's empire is mightiest.

The sea-birds call to each other
  Far out in the storm-stream wild
Like the scream of a widowed mother,
  Like the cry of an orphaned child.

But where is the heart that falters
  Though the cloud-rack bears the squall,
Or his path o'er the billows alters,
  Or shrinks from his work at the trawl?

To battle against the despoiler,
  And fight in the teeth of the gale,
To the life of the deep-sea toiler,
  And Death shall *he* make him quail?

No!—when the foam-clots dapple
  The face of the threatening flood,
And at length in the last death-grapple
  They are England's dauntless blood.

Ah! vain are the North Sea's pledges
  And earnests of sunlight smile;
They shall find his bones in the dredges
  And know how her vows beguile.

Ah! false are her ways when fairly
  She trembles in wind-borne light,
When the tripping breezes barely
  Tip the azure waves with white.

She is false—for her rages follow
  At the skirts of her moments gay,
And the roar of her wrath is hollow
  As the howl of a beast of prey.

And ever the crests roll over
  While the smacksman lies below,
From the waves that lash upon Dover
  To the sullen Humber's flow.

THOMAS EKENHEAD MAYNE

367 *An Tir-nan-Óg*[1]

IN the land that I love is no wrong done,
 Nor hurt nor evil beneath the fair sun,
The stainless skies ever tremble above
The sweet green plains of the land that I love.

The leaf never falls, the great green leaf
Never droops on the tree in wan winter's grief;
The red rose bloometh the long year long,
The bird never ceases its sweet low song.

The scent of the flowers on the faint wind blown
Reaches the foot of the soul's white throne,
And spirits stand with their pale feet
Bathed in the bloom of the meadows sweet.

The seasons change not, the birds do not die,
Asleep on the flowers the white Hours lie;
It is Beauty's own land, whose sway is so strong
Time's hand is not lifted against her for wrong.

Love's cheeks fade not—there ever glows
The blush of the summer's sweet wild rose;
The light in her eyes is not quenched but is fed
By lustrous light from the pure stars shed.

How shall I reach this land that I love?
Through the way of the wind the high hills above?
Down through the blue wide ways of the sea?
Ah, no! the soul's way mine must be.

[1] The Land of Youth—Hy-Brasail. See Note 8.

THOMAS EKENHEAD MAYNE

368 *Dew*

THE warm winds stealing o'er the grass
Are sweet to the daffodil,
But not till the colder night-winds pass
Will the crystal dews distil;
Fair is the dew on petal and leaf,
Fairer sweet eyes made grave with grief.

When morn is red and winds grow chill
A crown on the rose is set,
Dew-laden drops the daffodil,
Begemmed is the violet;
But sweeter the eyes that the passing years
Have lit with the spirit-light of tears.

369 *Winter Sunshine*

ACROSS the bitter frost and snow
Of this dead and barren time
The sun bursts warm and bright, as though
He dreamt of his summer prime.

Across a chasm wide and black
As the yawning cave of night
The touch of a bygone time comes back
To fill my soul with light;
Ah, God! for the desolated track
Time leaves in his hungry flight.

THOMAS BOYD

370 *To the Leanán Sidhe*[1]

1867–

WHERE is thy lovely perilous abode?
In what strange phantom-land
Glimmer the fairy turrets whereto rode
The ill-starred poet band?

Say, in the Isle of Youth hast thou thy home,
The sweetest singer there,
Stealing on wingéd steed across the foam
Thorough the moonlit air?

And by the gloomy peaks of Erigal,
Haunted by storm and cloud,
Wing past, and to thy lover there let fall
His singing robe and shroud?

Or, where the mists of bluebell float beneath
The red stems of the pine,
And sunbeams strike thro' shadow, dost thou breathe
The word that makes him thine?

Or, is thy palace entered thro' some cliff
When radiant tides are full,
And round thy lover's wandering starlit skiff
Coil in luxurious lull?

[1] Lianhaun Shee—The Fairy Muse.

And would he, entering on the brimming flood,
  See caverns vast in height,
And diamond columns, crowned with leaf and bud,
  Glow in long lanes of light.

And there the pearl of that great glittering shell
  Trembling, behold thee lone,
Now weaving in slow dance an awful spell,
  Now still upon thy throne?

Thy beauty! ah, the eyes that pierce him thro'
  Then melt as in a dream;
The voice that sings the mysteries of the blue
  And all that Be and Seem!

Thy lovely motions answering to the rhyme
  That ancient Nature sings,
That keeps the stars in cadence for all time,
  And echoes through all things!

Whether he sees thee thus, or in his dreams,
  Thy light makes all lights dim;
An aching solitude from henceforth seems
  The world of men to him.

Thy luring song, above the sensuous roar,
  He follows with delight,
Shutting behind him Life's last gloomy door,
  And fares into the Night.

THOMAS BOYD

371 *The Heath*

THROUGH the purple dusk on this pathless heath
Wanders a horse with its rider, Death.
The steed like its master is old and grim,
And the flame in his eye is burning dim.

The crown of the rider is red with gold,
For he is lord of the lea and the wold.
A-tween his ribs, against the sky
Glimmer the stars as he rideth by.

A hungry scythe o'er his shoulder bare
Glints afar through the darkening air,
And the sudden clank of his horse's hoof
Frightens the Wanderer aloof.

372 *Love on the Mountain*

MY love comes down from the mountain
Through the mists of dawn ;
I look, and the star of the morning
From the sky is gone.

My love comes down from the mountain,
At dawn, dewy-sweet ;
Did you step from the star to the mountain,
O little white feet?

THOMAS BOYD

O whence came your twining tresses
  And your shining eyes,
But out of the gold of the morning
  And the blue of the skies ?

The misty mountain is burning
  In the sun's red fire,
And the heart in my breast is burning
  And lost in desire.

I follow you into the valley
  But no word can I say ;
To the East or the West I will follow
  Till the dusk of my day.

'A. E.'

373 *Babylon*

1867–

THE blue dusk ran between the streets : my love was winged within my mind,
It left to-day and yesterday and thrice a thousand years behind.
To-day was past and dead for me, for from to-day my feet had run
Through thrice a thousand years to walk the ways of ancient Babylon.
On temple top and palace roof the burnished gold flung back the rays
Of a red sunset that was dead and lost beyond a million days.

The tower of heaven turns darker blue, a starry sparkle
now begins;
The mystery and magnificence, the myriad beauty and
the sins
Come back to me. I walk beneath the shadowy
multitude of towers;
Within the gloom the fountain jets its pallid mist in
lily flowers.
The waters lull me and the scent of many gardens,
and I hear
Familiar voices, and the voice I love is whispering in
my ear.
Oh real as in dream all this; and then a hand on mine
is laid:
The wave of phantom time withdraws; and that
young Babylonian maid,
One drop of beauty left behind from all the flowing of
that tide,
Is looking with the self-same eyes, and here in Ireland
by my side.
Oh light our life in Babylon, but Babylon has taken
wings,
While we are in the calm and proud procession of
eternal things.

374 *The Winds of Angus*

THE grey road whereupon we trod became as holy
ground:
The eve was all one voice that breathed its message
with no sound:

And burning multitudes pour through my heart, too
bright, too blind,
Too swift and hurried in their flight to leave their
tale behind.
Twin gates unto that living world, dark honey-
coloured eyes
The lifting of whose lashes flushed the face with
paradise—
Beloved, there I saw within their ardent rays unfold
The likeness of enraptured birds that flew from deeps
of gold
To deeps of gold within my breast to rest or there
to be
Transfigured in the light, or find a death to life
in me.
So love, a burning multitude, a seraph wind which
blows
From out the deep of being to the deep of being goes:
And sun and moon and starry fires and earth and
air and sea
Are creatures from the deep let loose who pause
in ecstasy,
Or wing their wild and heavenly way until again
they find
The ancient deep and fade therein, enraptured,
bright and blind.

375 *Reflections*

HOW shallow is this mere that gleams!
Its depth of blue is from the skies;
And from a distant sun the dreams
And lovely light within your eyes.

We deem our love so infinite
Because the Lord is everywhere,
And love awakening is made bright
And bathed in that diviner air.

We go on our enchanted way
And deem our hours immortal hours,
Who are but shadow kings that play
With mirrored majesties and powers.

376 *Creation*

AS one by one the veils took flight,
The day withdrew, the stars came up :
The spirit issued dark and bright,
Filling thy beauty like a cup.

Sacred thy laughter on the air,
Holy thy lightest word that fell,
Proud the innumerable hair
That waved at the enchanter's spell.

Oh Master of the Beautiful,
Creating us from hour to hour,
Give me this vision to the full
To see in lightest things Thy power !

This vision give, no heaven afar,
No throne, and yet I will rejoice,
Knowing beneath my feet a star,
Thy word in every wandering voice.

'A. E.'

377 *The Virgin Mother*

WHO is that goddess to whom men should pray
But her from whom their hearts have turned away,
Out of whose virgin being they were born,
Whose mother nature they have named in scorn
Calling its holy substance common clay.

Yet from this so despised earth was made
The milky whiteness of those queens who swayed
Their generations with a light caress,
And from some image of whose loveliness
The heart built up high heaven when it prayed.

Lover, your heart, the heart on which it lies,
Your eyes that gaze, and those alluring eyes,
Your lips, the lips they kiss, alike had birth
Within this dark divinity of earth,
Within this mother being you despise.

Ah, when I think this earth on which we tread
Hath borne these blossoms of the lovely dead,
And made the living heart I love to beat,
I look with sudden awe beneath my feet
As you with erring reverence overhead.

378 *Reconciliation*

I BEGIN through the grass once again to be bound to the Lord;
I can see, through a face that has faded, the face full of rest
Of the earth, of the mother, my heart with her heart in accord;
As I lie 'mid the cool green tresses that mantle her breast
I begin with the grass once again to be bound to the Lord.

By the hand of a child I am led to the throne of the King,
For a touch that now fevers me not is forgotten and far,
And His infinite sceptred hands that sway us can bring
Me in dreams from the laugh of a child to the song of a star.
On the laugh of a child I am borne to the joy of the King.

379 *The Hermit*

NOW the quietude of earth
Nestles deep my heart within;
Friendships new and strange have birth
Since I left the city's din.

Here the tempest stays its guile,
Like a big kind brother plays,
Romps and pauses here awhile
From its immemorial ways.

Now the silver light of dawn
  Slipping through the leaves that fleck
My one window, hurries on,
  Throws its arms around my neck.

Darkness to my doorway hies,
  Lays her chin upon the roof,
And her burning seraph eyes
  Now no longer keep aloof.

And the ancient mystery
  Holds its hands out day by day,
Takes a chair and croons with me
  By my cabin built of clay.

When the dusky shadow flits
  By the chimney nook I see
Where the old enchanter sits,
  Smiles, and waves, and beckons me.

380 *Illusion*

WHAT is the love of shadowy lips
  That know not what they seek or press,
From whom the lure for ever slips
  And fails their phantom tenderness?

The mystery and light of eyes
  That near to mine grow dim and cold;
They move afar in ancient skies
  'Mid flame and mystic darkness rolled.

O beauty, as thy heart o'erflows
  In tender yielding unto me,
A vast desire awakes and grows
  Unto forgetfulness of thee!

'A. E.'

381 *Immortality*

WE must pass like smoke or live within the spirit's fire ;
For we can no more than smoke unto the flame return :
If our thought has changed to dream, our will unto desire,
As smoke we vanish though the fire may burn.

Lights of infinite pity star the grey dusk of our days :
Surely here is soul : with it we have eternal breath :
In the fire of love we live, or pass by many ways,
By unnumbered ways of dream to death.

JANE BARLOW

382 *A Misunderstanding*

''TIS my bitter grief,' she said.
(The western light ebbed, streaming back
Across the ocean-strand that laid
Its frost of foam and rust of wrack
To rim her doorway square and black.
Beyond the sill a brooding shade,
Unruffled by the sunset's wraith
Where from the hearth it glimmered red,
Thronged all her little house with night.
One day that brought her cureless scathe
Had sorrow touched her comely head
With sudden snow there set in sight,
The seamew's wing and merle's wing mixt

Above kind eyes, and sad and bright,
With folded crease of care betwixt.)
    ''Tis my grief: too young and old
Were they all to understand,
When the hunger came and cold;
Though I told them, oft I told,
How the blight was on the land,
And the people's crops around
Lay black-rotted in the ground,
And the good turf gone to loss
In the summer's teeming rain.
But my talk was all in vain.
God forgive me, I'd be cross,
For the children had me vexed,
When it's asking me they'd keep
From one morning to the next:
Would I give them ne'er a bit?
    'Troth and would I. Deep and steep
I'd have climbed, dear hearts, for it,
Or gone barefoot ten score mile.
But I'd naught, mavrone! I'd naught,
And belike the creatures thought
I had plenty all the while.
    'So I'd bid them go to sleep,
Or I'd bid them run and play,
But, poor souls, the live-long day
They'd do nothing else than sit
Crouching close about the fire
I was pestered keeping lit
With the driftwood off the shore;
For thin branches, light and small,
Are the best I can drag higher
Through this shingle to the door,
Now I've no one any more

To be lending me a hand.
  'But the trouble of my trouble,
Whatsoever may befall,
Day and night I ne'er forget,
Was my mother there, bent double
Till she looked no size at all
In her little old grey shawl,
With her heart, well knew I, set
On her evening cup of tea;
'Deed those times she missed it sore,
When I'd ne'er a grain to wet,
Though a word she wouldn't say.
  'So when sunsetting was past,
She'd come creeping o'er the floor,
And reach down her cup and plate
Dinny brought her from Belfast—
They be shining yonder yet—
And she'd leave them standing ready,
For a sign to show 'twas late.
Then she'd sit again and wait,
Like a lad whose net is cast,
With the little trick she'd planned;
Ah, she'd watch me long and steady,
And I'd dread to stir or speak,
But I'd see her how at last
Very sorrowful she'd take
And fetch back the empty cup,
Making shift to hang it up
With her old hand all ashake;
Maybe thinking in her mind
I'd turned thankless and unkind—
Sure my heart came nigh to break.
  'Many a time I wished to God
Not so much that He'd contrive

For the creatures' bit and sup,
Since the blight's upon the land,
Scarce a spud left, scarce a sod,
Till the folks can hardly live,
And I wouldn't ask Him aught
That He mightn't have to give—
But I wished they would be let
Have the sense to understand,
So that less they'd grieve and fret,
And be sure I grudged them naught.
'"Tis my bitter grief,' she said.
(The listening neighbour duly sought
To speak some witless, kindly word,
That wooeth hope, when hope lies dead.
Perhaps she heeded not nor heard.
So far she looked across the strand,
And past the lone fields of the sea,
Where light down fading paths was fled.)
'"Tis my heart's long grief,' said she,
'For they ne'er could understand.'

383 *A Ruin*

MIRK on clear skies, swept afar,
Swart sail of thunder
Drift with the hid fraughting fire,
Fierce as from heart of a star,
That smiting hath shattered in sunder
A dungeon bale-haunted and dire,
A keep long accursed by the seathe
Of a captive held hope-reft thereunder,
Who here at light's birth, in heaven's breath,
Tastes wonder on wonder.

This prisoner wist not how his harm befell,
Nor recked of fairer lot than ever to dwell
Girt by those walls. Yet was their ampler room
His earliest memory, with its midday gloom
Grey near a casement's blink, high noon for him ;
And Paradise he saw if green and dim
Some shadowy bough swung in and out of sight
Athwart the crevice, his one dull jewel of light,
Soon lost. For doomed he was in that fell tower
To obey the ban of its compelling power,
That led him, loth, to where, more dark and strait,
His chamber with no chink prepared a fate
Full piteous. Yet his griefs but halted there ;
Needs must he follow anon down narrower stair
That nightmare guide, till his groping deaf and blind
Touched fresh despair : the stair begin to wind
He felt : he knew that solid dark and cold
Furled coiling, closing round him fold on fold,
Still, step by step. And ever as down he went
A weight of horror pressed sore on him, and pent
The frenzy, risen up else to end in wrack,
All sense dashed out against those barriers black.
And ever as down he went, foul crawling things
He brushed with hand and foot, of slime or stings
Inevitable aware with shuddering heed.
Then through an age-long pause seemed he a seed
Of anguish, whelmed alone in some vast orb,
That list not loose, nor list his life absorb,
To make the world-great atom of misery naught.
Thus, poised o'er stifling pangs stood Time, and
    circling brought
The same woe's hour.
                                        Whereon a crash, a glare,
A ruin uprooted, glory of limpid air

In eyes joy-wildered. Nay, beyond, around,
What regions marvellous wrought with sight and sound,
Of greeting voice and face what master-bliss,
May ne'er be told, and but surmised amiss
By hearts that seek in dreams such haps as this :—

Mirk on clear skies, swept afar,
Swart sail of thunder
Drift with the hid fraughting fire,
Fierce as from heart of a star,
That smiting hath shattered in sunder
A dungeon bale-haunted and dire,
A keep long accursed by the scathe
Of a captive held hope-reft thereunder,
Who here at light's birth, in heaven's breath,
Tastes wonder on wonder.

384 *On Lisnadara*

ON Lisnadara soft, full soft, falls sleep
Ere dreams begin,
When down the fading hills slow shadows creep
To shut them in,
With all their fields enfolden, hushed and stilled
From steep to steep,
Whose secret, till the east shine amber-silled,
Grey mists shall keep.

For blithe the morn with flower of flame would break,
And radiance spilled,
That round a shimmering shore flushed all the lake
Rose-red, and filled

The glen with latticed lights, while strange soothsay
 The breezes spake :
How sure our morrow young as yesterday
 Should yonder wake,
And, kindling crystal-clear across the dew
 A wonder-way,
Lead forth thereon old joyance wrought anew
 In faëry ray.
Nor need a whit to fear when dusk bereaves
 Of form and hue
The drowsy world, and builds dim walls and eaves
 Our sight to mew,
Bound with most gentle spell, whose magic shed
 White slumber weaves,
Careless as laps a feather-fended head
 Among close leaves.

Yet if the years at last teach bitter lore
 In sweet joy's stead,
Each glad hour grown a pearl, with grudging sore
 Slipped from the thread ;
Yea, when long slopes of fiery-fronded fern
 Thrill to heart's core
Grief for the day whose embers withering burn
 To bloom no more ;
And footsteps, strayed on lonely paths afar,
 No more shall turn,
Beyond the faint blue heights that hope debar
 And patience spurn ;
And streams, sped by with many a chiming leap,
 But silence mar,
Where listeners fain would hear athwart night's deep
 Some echoing star—

So wild the cry that answer ne'er hath won
From Fate's stern keep :
Yet, yet a peace shall be indeed begun
With shadows' sweep,
And rest for hearts worn wearier than to weep
Bring set of sun ;
For soft on Lisnadara, soft falls sleep,
When dreams are done.

385 *Out of Hearing*

NO need to hush the children for her sake,
Or fear their play :
She will not wake, mavrone, she will not wake.
'Tis the long sleep, the deep long sleep she'll take,
Betide what may.
No need to hush the children for her sake ;
Even if their glee could yet again outbreak
So loud and gay,
She will not wake, mavrone, she will not wake.
But sorrow a thought have they of merry-make
This many a day :
No need to hush the children. For her sake
So still they bide and sad, her heart would ache
At their dismay.
She will not wake, mavrone, she will not wake
To bid them laugh, and if some angel spake
Small heed they'd pay.
No need to hush the children for her sake :
She will not wake, mavrone, she will not wake.

EVA GORE-BOOTH

386 *To Maeve* (76)

NOT for thee, oh Maeve, is the song of the wandering harper sung,
 For men have put lies on thy lips, and treason, and shrieking fear,
Because thou wert brave, they say thou wert bitter and false of tongue,
 They mock at thy weakness now—who once fled from thy flaming spear.

Now thou art cold on the mountains—buried and silent and blind—
 Dumb as the hills and the stars, blind as the waves of the sea.
A clatter of treacherous tongues goes railing along the wind
 And many an evil word is spoken in hatred of thee.

Was it Fergus whose envious breath first cast o'er thy shining name
 A poison of venomous words in the midst of the mourning host,
Till thy glory shone before them a wicked and perilous flame,
 And thy beauty seemed but a snare, thy valour an empty boast?

They have buried thy golden deeds under the cairn
on the hill,
And no one shall sing of thy hero soul in the days
to come ;
For the sky is blue with silence, and the stars are very
still,
The sea lies dreaming about thee, even the mountains are dumb.

387 *The Little Waves of Breffny*

THE grand road from the mountain goes shining to
the sea,
And there is traffic in it and many a horse and cart,
But the little roads of Cloonagh are dearer far to me,
And the little roads of Cloonagh go rambling
through my heart.

A great storm from the ocean goes shouting o'er the hill,
And there is glory in it and terror on the wind,
But the haunted air of twilight is very strange and still,
And the little winds of twilight are dearer to my
mind.

The great waves of the Atlantic sweep storming on
their way,
Shining green and silver with the hidden herring
shoal,
But the Little Waves of Breffny have drenched my
heart in spray,
And the Little Waves of Breffny go stumbling
through my soul.

388 *Aspiration*

SOUL of the acorn buried in the sod,
Lord of high trees and sunset haunted hills,
Planter of primroses and Very God
Of the bright daffodils,
Pity the weakness of the growing grain—
And drench our fields with rain.

Soul of the Light and Spirit of the Sword,
Flash one great thought through hosts of huddled years,
God of great deeds and dream-inspired Lord
Of pity and of tears,
Pity the weary ploughman's barren toil—
Cast sunshine on the soil.

Dream of dim lights and twilight-haunted wind,
Spirit that moves upon the waters' face,
Lighten the wave-washed caverns of the mind
With a pale starry grace :
Pity the midnight hours of Death and Birth,
Bring Hope back to the earth.

389 *In the Pinewoods*

HERE the white stars brood high above the austere pines,
And the long pine stems seem to gather up the shadowy stream
Of the earth's beauty, all her flowing curves and rapturous lines,
Folded together and lifted up in a long ecstatic dream.

Here in the silent wood Beauty and Peace join hands
at last,
And all the wars of the world have shrivelled and
fallen away,
For the winds of an Unknown Will are blowing out
of the vast,
And the soul of the world grows one with the lips
that pity and pray.

390 *A Moment's Insight*

BEYOND the smoke there burns a veilèd fire,
Behind the horizon sails a ship of dreams,
Yet in the night of deeds and dull desire
The earth that blinds our eyes our Mother seems.

Lo, now the smoke rolls her thick cloud away,
And white sails gleam on the horizon line;
Fierce Pity whispers in the ears of clay,
And broken gods still know themselves divine.

ETHNA CARBERY
(MRS. SEUMAS MAC MANUS)

391 *Feithfailge*

THE blue lake of Devenish!
I put my thousand blessings there,
(The blue lake of Devenish);
On shadow waters all a-stir,
And on the wind-blown honeysuckle
Beauty of Feithfailge's hair.

ETHNA CARBERY

The blue lake of Devenish!
I pray, if God but grant the grace,
(The blue lake of Devenish),
To win that dear enchanted place,
Where spring bides in the apple-blossom
Beauty of Feithfailge's face.

The blue lake of Devenish!
I vex the purple dark with sighs—
(The blue lake of Devenish)
Across the world my sorrow flies,
A-hunger for the grey and wistful
Beauty of Feithfailge's eyes.

The blue lake of Devenish!
I wander far, yet find no rest—
(The blue lake of Devenish)
Sore-haunted ever, and oppressed
By dreams that pillow on the snow-white
Beauty of Feithfailge's breast.

The blue lake of Devenish!
She walks there in the quiet, meet
(The blue lake of Devenish)
For prayerful thoughts, and visions sweet,
And cool green grasses kiss the lightsome
Beauty of Feithfailge's feet.

The blue lake of Devenish!
I would the red gold were my part,
(The blue lake of Devenish)
Ripe fields, and herds upon Drimart,
That by my fire might shine the lovelit
Beauty of Feithfailge's heart.

ETHNA CARBERY

392 *Hills o' my Heart*

HILLS o' my heart!
I have come to you at calling of my one love and only,
I have left behind the cruel scarlet wind of the east,
The hearth of my fathers wanting me is lonely,
And empty is the place I filled at gathering of the feast.

Hills o' my heart!
You have cradled him I love in your green quiet hollows,
Your wavering winds have hushed him to soft forgetful sleep,
Below dusk boughs where bird-voice after bird-voice follows
In shafts of silver melody that split the hearkening deep.

Hills o' my heart!
Let the herdsman who walks in your high haunted places
Give him strength and courage, and weave his dreams alway:
Let your cairn-heaped hero-dead reveal their grand exultant faces,
And the Gentle Folk be good to him betwixt the dark and day.

Hills o' my heart!
And I would the Green Harper might wake his soul to singing,
With music of the golden wires heard when the world was new,
That from his lips an echo of its sweetness may come ringing,
A song of pure and noble hopes—a song of all things true.

Hills o' my heart!
For sake of the yellow head that drew me wandering over
Your misty crests from my own home where sorrow bided then,
I set my seven blessings on your kindly heather cover,
On every starry moorland loch, and every shadowy glen.
Hills o' my heart!

393 *Mo Craoibhín Cno*[1]

A SWORD of Light hath pierced the dark, our eyes have seen the Star:
Oh Eiré, leave the ways of sleep now days of promise are:
The rusty spears upon your walls are stirring to and fro,
In dreams they front uplifted shields—then wake,
Mo Craoibhín Cno!

[1] Pronounced *mŭ chreeveen nō*. My cluster of nuts—My brown-haired girl—Ireland.

ETHNA CARBERY

The little waves creep whispering where sedges fold
you in,
And round you are the barrows of your buried kith
and kin ;
Oh ! famine-wasted, fever-burnt, they faded like the
snow
Or set their hearts to meet the steel—for you,
Mo Craoibhín Cno !

Their names are blest, their caoine sung, our bitter
tears are dried ;
We bury Sorrow in their graves, Patience we cast
aside ;
Within the gloom we hear a voice that once was ours
to know—
'Tis Freedom—Freedom calling loud, Arise !
Mo Craoibhín Cno !

Afar beyond that empty sea, on many a battle-place,
Your sons have stretched brave hands to Death before
the foeman's face—
Down the sad silence of your rest their war-notes
faintly blow,
And bear an echo of your name—of yours,
Mo Craoibhín Cno !

Then wake, agrá ! We yet shall win a gold crown
for your head,
Strong wine to make a royal feast—the white wine
and the red—
And in your oaken mether the yellow mead shall flow,
What day you rise, in all men's eyes—a Queen,
Mo Craoibhín Cno !

The silver speech our fathers knew shall once again
be heard ;
The fire-lit story, crooning song, sweeter than lilt of
bird ;
Your quicken-tree shall break in flower, its ruddy
fruit shall glow,
And the Gentle People dance beneath its shade—
Mo Craoibhín Cno !

There shall be peace and plenty, the kindly open door,
Blessings on all who come and go—the prosperous and
the poor—
The misty glens and purple hills a fairer tint shall show,
When your splendid Sun shall ride the skies again—
Mo Craoibhín Cno !

394 *Moorloch Mary*

LIKE swords of battle the scythes were plying,
The corn lay low in a yellow rout,
When down the stubble, dew-wet and glinting,
A golden shaft of the sun came out :
It was Moorloch Mary, the slender blossom,
Who smiled on me in the misty morn,
And since that hour I am lost with grieving,
Through sleepless nights, and through days forlorn.

Oh ! Moorloch lies in a world of heather
Where Mary's little brown feet go bare,
And many a shadowy peak divides us,
Yet I will journey to find her there :
I will climb the mountains and swim the rivers,
I will travel the crests of the heath, wind-blown ;
Her face in my heart like a star I carry,
And it shall guide me unto my own.

ETHNA CARBERY

When I come at last to my Moorloch Mary,
I will take her little brown hands in mine,
And kiss her lips where the rowans tarry,
And kiss her hair where the sun-rays shine,
And whisper, 'Astórin, my heart was haunted
By wistful eyes of the sweetest grey,
That drew it over the hills of Derry—
O Moorloch Mary, bid the wanderer stay!'

PADRAIC COLUM

395 *The Plougher*

SUNSET and silence! A man: around him earth savage, earth broken;
Beside him two horses—a plough!

Earth savage, earth broken, the brutes, the dawn-man there in the sunset,
And the Plough that is twin to the Sword, that is founder of cities!

'Brute-tamer, plough-maker, earth-breaker! Canst hear? There are ages between us.
Is it praying you are as you stand there alone in the sunset?

'Surely our sky-born gods can be naught to you, earth child and earth master?
Surely your thoughts are of Pan, or of Wotan, or Dana?

'Yet, why give thought to the gods? Has Pan led your brutes where they stumble?
Has Dana numbed pain of the child-bed, or Wotan put hands to your plough?

'What matter your foolish reply! O man, standing lone and bowed earthward,
Your task is a day near its close. Give thanks to the night-giving God.'

Slowly the darkness falls, the broken lands blend with the savage;
The brute-tamer stands by the brutes, a head's breadth only above them.

A head's breadth? Ay, but therein is hell's depth, and the height up to heaven,
And the thrones of the gods and their halls, their chariots, purples and splendours.

396 *A Drover*

TO Meath of the pastures,
From wet hills by the sea,
Through Leitrim and Longford
Go my cattle and me.

I hear in the darkness
Their slipping and breathing.
I name them the bye-ways
They're to pass without heeding.

Then the wet, winding roads,
  Brown bogs with black water;
And my thoughts on white ships
  And the King o' Spain's daughter.

O farmer, strong farmer!
  You can spend at the fair,
But your face you must turn
  To your crops and your care.

And soldiers, red soldiers!
  You've seen many lands;
But you walk two and two,
  And by captain's commands.

O the smell of the beasts,
  The wet wind in the morn,
And the proud and hard earth
  Never broken for corn!

And the crowds at the fair,
  The herds loosened and blind,
Loud words and dark faces
  And the wild blood behind.

(O strong men with your best
I would strive breast to breast
I could quiet your herds
With my words, with my words!)

I will bring you, my kine,
  Where there's grass to the knee;
But you'll think of scant croppings
  Harsh with salt of the sea.

PADRAIC COLUM

397 *An Old Woman of the Roads*

OH to have a little house,
 To own the hearth and stool and all—
The heaped-up sods upon the fire,
 The pile of turf against the wall!

To have a clock with weights and chains,
 And pendulum swinging up and down!
A dresser filled with shining delph,
 Speckled and white and blue and brown!

I could be busy all the day
 Clearing and sweeping hearth and floor,
And fixing on their shelf again
 My white and blue and speckled store.

I could be quiet there at night
 Beside the fire and by myself,
Sure of a bed, and loth to leave
 The ticking clock and shining delph.

Och! but I'm weary of mist and dark,
 And roads where there's never a house or bush,
And tired I am of bog and road,
 And the crying wind and the lonesome hush!

And I am praying to God on high,
 And I am praying Him night and day,
For a little house—a house of my own—
 Out of the wind's and the rain's way.

PADRAIC COLUM

398 *A Cradle Song*

O MEN from the fields!
  Come softly within.
Tread softly, softly,
  O men coming in!

Mavourneen is going
  From me and from you,
Where Mary will fold him
  With mantle of blue.

From reek of the smoke
  And cold of the floor,
And the peering of things
  Across the half-door.

O men from the fields!
  Soft, softly come thro'.
Mary puts round him
  Her mantle of blue.

JAMES H. COUSINS

399 *The Coming of Niamh* (77)

SOFTLY, as comes a wind across the sea
  That thrills the waves to music on the beach,
And stirs the trees to whisperings each to each,
And bids the birds pipe low sweet song of glee;

So, like a summer morning, came to me
My Queen, my Niamh ; and her gentle speech
Spake regal lineage longer than the reach
Of memory, older than the thrones that be.

And thro' the tumults that around me rise,
She speaks of hidden and tremendous things—
Grails yet unwon, and Quests that never cease ;
And calls me forth to where, with quenchless eyes,
She with the deathless dwells, and folds her wings
Enthroned in vast, unutterable Peace.

400 *The Bell-branch*

SHOHEEN, sho-lo :
Birds are homeward winging.
Shoheen, sho-lo :
Herdsmen on the hills are singing :
'Short the night, and long the day,
Come, ye weary flocks away :
Folded in deep shadows drowse,
And on long sweet grasses browse
Where the murmuring waters flow.'

Shoheen, sho-lo :
Hark, the Bell-branch ringing.
Shoheen, sho-lo :
Danaans from the hills are singing :
'Time is old, and earth is grey—
Come, ye weary ones, away,
Where, with white, untroubled brows
The Immortals dream and drowse,
And the streams of quiet flow.'

401 *Behind the Plough*

BLACK wings and white in the hollow
Follow the track of the team,
While the sun from the noon declining
Is shining on toil-wet brows.
Birds of the mountain and sea-birds
Circle and swoop and scream,
Searching for spoils of the furrow
Where slowly the ploughman ploughs.

Make me room, O birds! I am sweeping
From the Boughs of Sleeping afar;
I have winged thro' the mists of the ages,
Where sages drone and drowse;
I follow the feet of the Horses
That drag the Morning Star,
To search in the spoils of the furrow,
Where God the Ploughman ploughs.

402 *The Awakening*

IN this enchanted hour 'twixt light and light
Of sinking moon and widening morn, mine ear
Gathers from quivering leaf, and river clear,
Sounds sweetened by the touch of passing Night;
While on a leafy platform, shut from sight,
But to the heart, by hearing, doubly near,
A songbird, throbbing with the opening year,
Outsoars in joy his wing's supremest flight.

JAMES H. COUSINS

New day, new birth, new hope, new power have given
Wings to the soul to soar, and leave behind
Life's inessentials. What majestic sky
Is this where, unamazed, from some old heaven,
I hear the Harp of Angus on the wind,
And mark Cuchullin's Shade speed singing by?

'WILLIAM DARA'

(WILLIAM A. BYRNE)

403 *The Last Voyage*

I FLED between the clanging gates and stood
  Alone amid the chestnut's bee-lulled sleep,
Tasting the pangless quiet as a food,
  For I had suffered deep.

It was too late to sing or laugh again.
  All, all was changed, and I had probed too far
In nightlong meditations stabbed with pain,
  To know what pleasures are.

Away I went among the wistful leaves
  Sick with the brooding pain of blossoming,
Through by-ways where the brick-red spider weaves,
  Through lanes of whispering.

Heavy with love of all forgetfulness
  Among the unknown flowers I knelt and prayed:
'Make me like these or just a little less.'
  That was the prayer I said.

'WILLIAM DARA'

I lifted up dead flowers with all my hands,
The unknown wild things, till their dying scent
Spread like a white breath o'er the winterlands,
And hid me as I went.

So drift my feet where man has reaped in vain,
Where sleep is dead, thought droops its wounded
wings,
A shipwreck on the sleepless sea of pain
Among the shipwrecked things.

But ever to those waves I bend mine eyes,
Which Christ has crossed with lonely, lonely feet.
And hear the uncomplaining waters rise
With voices, oh, how sweet!

Sweet, sweeter far than all the coreless joys
Youth plucks amid the branches of the mind,
Or fame that dies within its own sweet noise,
Leaving no sweet behind.

So may I pass forgotten and unknown
O'er these unsleeping waters to the grave,
And taste the lonely bliss of pain alone
Crossing the last, long wave.

404 *Song of a Turf-sod*

DRAW in your stools, good folk, for heating
And gaze into mine eyes,
And see what sets the kind hearts beating,
Where the lonesome cricket cries.

‘WILLIAM DARA’

I was the broom and crookèd heather,
I was the moss that grew,
But time has moulded us together
Beneath the years of dew.

I kissed the elk’s feet in my branches
And trembled at his tramp
Ages before my purple ranches
Were cut to make a clamp.

I heard the wild-ducks and the wild-geese
Cackling about the lakes,
Where nothing now disturbs the mild peace
The bog-rush meadow makes.

I show that winsome past is dying :
Time hid it in my heart
Where, by a small stream’s endless crying,
I heard my youth depart.

I hold that past, but I will show it
To the Irish faces only.
Folk, if you light me, you will know it,
When the cricket makes you lonely !

Draw near, when round you chills are creeping
From winds among the broom,
And shadows, from your shoulders leaping,
Dance jigs about the room.

I have surprises, hid for showing,
  When by my light you start,
Watching the old, queer faces going
  Across my burning heart.

And while I doze in ashes piling,
  Perhaps yourself you'll see,
Through some old Gaelic gateway smiling
  In my antiquity.

405 *Faces in the Night*

I SEE them through the night,
  Those still, but speaking faces,
    Faces full of dreams,
  Like lonely forest places,
Fringed with glooming light,
And fraught with hush of leaves and withered
    streams.

Who look along the night
  With such dream-laden eyes,
    Eyelids drooped and sad?
  Ah, days that will not rise,
Plumed for no new flight,
Look rather with the eyes that once ye had!

'HAL D'ARCY'

406 *An Erris Fairy*

BABY was lonely with mother away
Reaping the yellow corn all the long day.
Now the cows have come home, and the clouds they lie deep
On the crags of Slievemore like wool of the sheep.
Hush, little one; the turf burns bright,
And the Good People bring you sweet dreams to-night.

See, a fairy of fortune is waiting for thee:
He sits on the hearth with a hand on each knee;
On his thumb is a ring as varied in hue
As sunlight entrapped in a bright drop of dew.
He can point out the place where the dark mountains hold
Their treasures of silver, of copper, and gold.

His hair is bog-cotton, his eyes black as sloes;
He's a turf-sod in height from his head to his toes;
His coat it is dyed in the fuchsia's soft red,
And he wears a wee cap on the top of his head.
He has two little shoes with buckles so bright,
And he dances by hidden streams all through the night.

Hush, where the bright waves laugh and moan,
The mermaid of Erris is sitting alone;

She is singing a song so wild and loud
To men buried with never a candle or shroud.
Hush, little one, if you hear that sound,
The ocean will be thy burying-ground.

407 *A Turf-Carrier*

WHERE is your home, woman dear?
The hills are grey and lone;
The fields are full of stone;
There's hardly space for summer flowers to bloom;
There's nothing 'live in view,
Except myself and you,
And your donkey with the cleaves full of turf.

What waits you in your cabin, woman dear?
For comfort is but spare
On these stony hills of Clare,
When your lonely way has come unto an end.
Is there any one to greet you,
Is there any one to meet you,
And the donkey with the cleaves full of turf.

What's in your heart, woman dear?
'A dream of little faces
That soon will take their places
In the crackle of the fire's red glow;
And so I cheer my day,
On my long and windy way,
With my donkey and the cleaves full of turf.'

WILLIAM MACNEILE DIXON

408 *Ad Animam*

(*Infelix Loq.*)

WEARY not, Soul, because the world is shaken
 With frets and fevers, and bemoans its ills,
Because with each new sun the people waken
 Only to feed their still unsated wills :

Because the slave sits high in Fortune's favour,
 And still the fool is dandled at her breast,
Because the lord of life, Love, cannot save her
 From all the Furies that invade her rest.

Weary not, Soul, because the wisest sages
 Mingle no weeping with their last farewells,
Since to their ears across earth's vanish'd ages
 Comes sadder music than of funeral bells.

I will not in the weakling's tones that flatter,
 Whisper to thee, O Soul, a lover's tales,
That the four winds of Heaven blow to scatter
 For thee the perfumes of Elysian vales.

That sun and moon keep their unwearied courses
 Only to find thee guidance on thy ways,
That the seas roll, and earth deploys her forces
 To give thee pleasance, and make sweet thy days.

Nor when the thunder wakes and the skies darken
  Shall I unveil thee any sheltered shrine,
Nor to the tempest's voices bid thee hearken
  To catch the safe assurance of a sign.

Earth is no garden in a Summer season,
  Nor is the care of roses thine employ ;
Thou art the slave of no self-flattering reason
  To twine thee wreaths of an infatuate joy.

Set store, O Soul, by that thou hast unborrow'd,
  Strength, that time's wheels can neither break nor bring,
Here in the space where thou hast joyed and sorrow'd
  To lift an indefatigable wing.

Put forth thy bark, though lone and unbefriended,
  All winds that blow will spread thy resolute sails ;
No skill but thine can steer thee where are ended
  The shifting surges and the roaring gales.

Better than calm the storm to speed and friend thee,
  Flight on swift seas that greet thee with their foam ;
Stars that but smile in calm, in storm will lend thee
  Heart to endure and light to lead thee home.

409 *Væ Victis*

THE mists of morning scaled the rocks
    Where climbed the mountain-nurtured flocks
  Beneath the northern sun,
The dews were on the heather bloom
That edged the precipice's gloom
  Where streams unnumbered run.

WILLIAM MACNEILE DIXON

They said, 'The mountain furrow yields
But scanty happy harvest fields
  To greet the harvest moon,
To follow where the swallow flies
Where gentler stars make gentler skies
  Were not unwisely done.'

They said, 'The winter tempests rave,
The hungry ocean-travelling wave
  Makes here its ceaseless cry,
We are grown weary of the wind,
The hill-paths and the mists that blind
  The shepherd suddenly.

'The snow-drift sweeps the mountain wall
To spread its white funereal pall,
  A frozen drapery;
The torrent through its gloomy rifts
Is wild with yellow foam and lifts
  A voice of dynasty.'

They said, 'No more, no more of these
Tumultuous combatants of ease!
  The fabled islands lure,
Where in no season of the year
The glory of the woods is sere,
  But all glad things endure.'

They built and launched a stately bark,
And when the morn rose and the dark
  Fled far into the hills,
They left the land and loosed the sheet,
And steered beyond the Cape to meet
  The glebe that no man tills.

And sworn in league forlornly free,
In calm or storm, on every sea,
  Thro' night to seek, and day,
Some right fair land of corn and wine,
And ease and carelessness divine,
  Where care is done away;

They followed ocean's fleeting rim
When sun or stars shone bright or dim,
  In merry mood or grave,
Nor heeded days nor hours that fled
Fleeter than ever white wings spread
  Bore bark upon a wave.

But fleet or far howe'er they sailed
The season's crescents grew and paled,
  Nor saw in any clime
Cross harbour-bar or ship or crew
To port that every seaman knew
  In this or former time.

The mists of morning scale the rocks
Where climb the mountain-nurtured flocks
  Beneath the northern sun,
The dews are on the heather bloom
Edging the precipice's gloom,
  Where streams unnumbered run.

410 *Monserrate Adieu!*

SO fades the vision and so flit the shades,
  To the dim underworld of memory,—
The palms, the woody terraces, the glades,
  The shining plain, Collares and the sea.

Below the margin of the world extreme
  The starry hours dip from the wheeling pole,
And Bella Vista, Penha Verde seem
  But fairy pictures of the dreaming soul.

Wide are the seas, and with new friends you may
  To many shores and many havens come,
But we alone can to each other say,
  'Once we took ship and found Elysium.'

411 *Exsequiæ*

WHEN the house is haunted by death,
  The spectre unseen and unheard,
And the living are scant of their breath,
  Though the sleeper hears never a word:

When the grave-sward is trampled to clay,
  And the drip of the world-blotting rain
From skies of a passionless grey
  Beats true to the pulses of pain;

O Father and Maker and God!
  How falters the heart of thy child,
How breathless and cold is the sod,
  How lonely the infinite wild!

'JOHN EGLINTON'

412 *The Winds*

'WHO are the winds? Who are the winds?'
—The storm was blowing wild—
'Who are the winds? Who are the winds?'
—So question'd me the wild-eyed child.

'They are the souls, O child,' I said,
'Of men who long since ceased to hope;
And lastly, wishing to be dead,
They lay down on the mountain-slope,
And sigh'd their wills away;
And nature taking them hath made
Round and about the world to stray.
Yet oft is waked the fitful pain,
Which causes them to blow,
And still the passion stirs again
Which vex'd them long ago;
And then no longer linger they,
But with a wild shriek sweep away,
And the green waves whiten to the moon,
And ships are wreck'd, and shores are strewn.'

413 *The Omen*

FROM out its chamber, green and high,
A bird leap'd forth at break of day,
And speeding o'er the wood, came nigh
Where two great glittering armies lay.

It swoop'd aside, and clamour stirred
The pale grey region where it flew ;
And wavering down the plain, the bird
Reach'd the calm river-nook it knew.

But either army paused nor spoke,
And one read foul and one read fair;
And straight the storm of battle broke,
With ruin here and triumph there.

At eve the bird flew back again,
The plain beneath now bare and wide ;
Stars throng'd, the skies were fleec'd, in pain
The stricken warrior turn'd and died.

From cape to mountain beacons gleam'd,
And cities waked with peal and blare.
Head under wing it slept, nor dream'd
Of that wild symbol traced in air.

414 *Acceptation*

ESTABLISH in some better way
My life, thou Godhead ! that I may
Know whether it as virtue ranks
To scorn Thy gifts, or give Thee thanks.

For now I feel Thee near, unsought.
But why, when I seemed worth Thy thought,
High-soul'd, impatient for a task—
Why not have called me then, I ask ?

'JOHN EGLINTON'

No mountings of the spirit please ;
Thou dost accept our dregs and lees ;
The wise are they that feel Thy rod,
And grief alone is near to God.

ALICE FURLONG

415 *Messages*

GOD loosed His shining flock at even,
And every little, gold bird came winging
Into the dim, grey heaven,
Sailing and singing.
Swift and eager in luminous flight
Through the breathing dark of the summer night.
Ah, little birds,
With gold wings palpitating over the blue,
Whither go you,
Journeying by airy hill and hollow ?
I fain would follow
Through the ways of heaven.
I, the man bereaven,
In whose heart is a wound as of a thousand swords.

On your heavenly road
You are so high, so high,
Can you see my sweetheart's face
By the crystal lattices,
When the gates of the House of God
You go faring by ?
Her hair is a mist of light,
Her eyes are the eyes of a dove,
Her vesture is maiden-white,
She is my beautiful love !

ALICE FURLONG

I know you will find her, for sure,
Walking by Mary's side,
My lady lily-pure!
My saint, all sanctified!
Tell her I bring a daffodil in March
To her grave under the larch;
A lily in Summer's prime,
A golden leaf in the harvest-time,
And red, red berries in the rime,
When desolate and chill,
The winds moan on the purple hill.

Tell her no maiden's face doth pleasure me
Save in its dear resembling of hers,
For any maiden's voice on land or sea
My sad heart never stirs.
No rose may blossom on her dead, young cheek,
Out from her grave no voice shall ever speak.
O birds of God!
Tell her I am with nor hope or succour
Since the day He took her
Into His rest.
Yea, the wolf of pain hath gnawed
To the very quivering core of the living heart in
my breast!

Hie away!
Blue i' the east is the dawn o' the day.
And the eagle of the Sun
Would reign alone.
Out of his road!
Little star-birds, fly home to God!

ALICE FURLONG

416 *A Caoine for Owen Roe* (78)

HEAVY the housings about his bed,
  Cold the clay that will hide his head.
 The sun was red in the sky at noon,
The crescent moon was dim with dread.

Through the blind night the banshee cried,
The death-watch beat in the wall by his side,
 The priest had untied his bonds of sin,
And every window was open wide.

Over and done are the warrior's wars,
There is martyr's balm for the martyr's scars;
 Brake the prison-bars, and on soaring wing,
His soul went singing among the stars.

Sing, O Angels, 'twixt stars and space!
Weep, O Lady, your love's dead face!
 To the keening-place come the women of grief,
Keening the Chief of Hy-Nial's race.

We bear his body by road and rath,
We bear his body by glen and path;
 Thrice hath the magpie cursed in his flight,
Black is the blight on the aftermath.

Weird and wild is the wail of woman,
Humbled the head of the haughty Roman.
 Dark the omen and dark the vision,
In deep derision outlaughs the foeman.

Chant the death-chant, O friars grey!
House the Chief in the holy clay!
  Moon, hide away! Be blind, O Sun!
Christ and country are slain to-day!

417 *A March Song*

DEAD is the dark Winter
  (Oh, the primrose on the hill!)
March bloweth his fanfare
  I' the horn o' the daffodil.

Rain water in the dykes
  Is clear as amber glass;
It feedeth the tall spikes
  Of the high green grass.

Earthward dancing sunbeams
  Wave their wizard wands,
Flaggers into green flames
  Flicker by the ponds.

Oh but March is kind!
  At every road's edge
Sways on the warm wind
  A budding thorn hedge.

And the crows have built their nest
  I' the highest bough of the larch.
When the wind is from the west
  Mild and kind is March!

PAUL GREGAN

418 *Mother of Mothers*

WEARY of carking thought and sick of hoping,
  Mother of Mothers, unto thee I come,
Blinded with too much light, and darkly groping,
  Silent, for words are only for the dumb.
Unto thine ancient bosom, Mother, take me,
  Wrap me about with arms of dusky night,
Soothe me with ocean sounds pulsative, make me,
  Even as thou art, a burning stillness quite.

Here, in thy broad, green lap of verdure lying,
  Drop from thy myriad eyes of pity down
Some tears of comfort ; hear me wildly crying—
  Let thy sweet song my fretful murmurs drown.
Mother, thy son who left thine arms at morning
  Radiant with hope, high courage, and with trust,
Night, from her sable windows, sees returning
  Trailing his broken banners in the dust.

Mother of ages ; mother, foe, and lover,
  Stretch out thine arms and circle me about ;
Open thy heart, thy heart enraptured, cover
  Me in its core, nor ever let me out.
Oh, the fierce gladness of thy touch magnetic,
  Oh, the cool life that soothes the fire of mine,
Oh, the rich breath inspiring song prophetic,
  Oh, the full silence, joy's electric wine.

Fill me with light from out thy heart's recesses,
Pour through my being all thy flood of fire ;
Oh, how I faint beneath thy wild caresses—
Nature grown feeble with too vast desire!
Into the deepest, stillest of thy water
Deep let me dive, oh, far and still and deep,
Far from the sounds of toil and rage and slaughter,
There for a calm infinitude to sleep!

419 *Nature and Man*

ALL of Nature and her wonders,
Pomp of earth and air and sea,
And the glorious wealth she squanders,
Came of old from me.

I—the mountains and the rivers,
And the sun's surpassing glow,
All the woodland's leafy quivers—
Made them long ago.

I, eternal, I, undying,
Bade the stars and planets shine—
World on world through space outflying—
With a song divine.

And the day and night divided,
Set and ruled the seasons four,
And the teeming waters guided
Round the fertile shore.

Made the waters of the ocean,
And the clouds that sail aloft ;
Gave the wind their mighty motion
And their murmur soft.

PAUL GREGAN

We, my brothers, built the heaven—
  You and I, the One and All—
Forged the deadly lightning-levin,
  And the thunder-call.

Earth and sea can but restore us
  What we gave them ages gone;
Earth and sea and sky adore us—
  We, the All, the One.

CAHIR HEALY

420 *In the Lap o' the Bog*

WEARY was I of the clamour and rush of the town,
Of its lies and its sins and seductions, its walls of brown,
    And its squalid dreams;
And my soul was athirst for the gold-starred brae,
The cabin, rose-grown. and the whins in the May,
    The glint of wine-dark streams.

Strained were my ears for the swish of the wind in the grass,
The rapture of fiddling, the songs of the Sidhe [1] that pass,
    On their steeds of fog,
And the tales by the fire, and the laugh and the tear,
Where reigneth nor gold nor the devil—out here,
    In the lap o' the bog.

[1] Fairies.

CAHIR HEALY

421 *Th' Song o' th' Say*

NIGHT an' morn it's on me, this wearyin' for th' say
An' th' swish o' breakers an' th' clank o' oars in Inver Bay;
'Tis a sin to be grievin', they tell me, but sure 'twas God above,
That put in my heart th' song that fills it with longin' an' love.

Many's th' year since I left it, th' home so purty, so poor,
An' took th' windin' casaun[1] that led to th' worl' across th' moor,
But first I went down th' beach to kiss th' ledge by th' shore,
Ah, God! I can feel th' salt on my lips th' day an' evermore.

A 'kerchief o' spotted red held all my store, an a' shell,
An' a song o' th' say within it, th' music I loved so well;
Now when th' childre are weary I take them up on my breast,
An' th' song that th' shell keeps singin' soothes each weeshy head to rest.

'Tis many's th' year, an' I'm thinkin' will th' longin' ever be stilled?
For I'm here in th' lonely city yet, an' my dream is unfulfilled.
But though 'tis years since it sang to me, my heart knows that some day,
When life is over, as th' voice of a lover, I'll hear th' song o' th' say.

[1] Path.

EMILY H. HICKEY

422 *To One Stricken and Smitten*

DOES not thy door stand open free,
Ever day by day and night to me?—
I will come in and sing to thee.

Come, with the tears scarce dry on my cheek,
Come to thy heart, beloved, and speak
Of love the strong, in my words the weak.

Rough is the way thy feet have trod;
Ah, and thy blood hath stained the sod;
Who shall entreat for thee to God?

Lo, but the earth at rest doth lie,
Drinking in dew abundantly—
Why should thy soul be parched and dry?

Lo, but the earth laughs laughter free,
Girt with the sunbeams' grace and glee—
Thou art bedrenched in thine agony.

Shall I not sing for thee soft and low,
That which I sang for thee long ago?
O my darling, I love thee so!

Dear, while thy fretted spirit curbs
Hunger with life's most bitter herbs,
And while the rush and noise disturbs,

And while the thorns yet pierce thy feet,—
Yea, to the end of peace complete,
I will come in and love thee, sweet.

423 *Per Te Ad Lucem*

WHEN I pass out to the light,
From dark to exceeding bright,
From cold to the warmth of the sun,
How shall that good be won?
What is the way for me,
Master, how shall it be?

How if the longed-for way
Which I hunger for to-day,
Which I pray for with eager breath,
Should be the way called death?
Were this the way for me,
Master, how would it be?

How if the way I seek
With footsteps weary and weak,
Scarcely able to move,
Should be the way called love?
Were this the way for me,
Master, how would it be?

How if the way I desire
Should lie through the heart of the fire,

And glowing bonds amain
Clasped me in utter pain?
  Were this the way for me,
  Master, how would it be?

I know not, dear my Lord;
Humbly I wait Thy word;
Through death, love, pain, I need
Only Thy hand to lead;
  And the one true way for me,
  Master, is trusting Thee.

424 *A Gift*

WHAT can I give, O well-beloved, to thee,
  Whose clear, firm knock at my heart's door I heard;
  I, reading o'er my life's old pages, blurred
Where bitter tears had fallen fast and free?
For thou didst enter in and comfort me
  Whose soul was passion-tost and tempest-stirred,
  Till I grew patient as a brooding bird,
And rest came down upon me, verily.

What can I give thee for a guerdon meet?
  The utter depths and heights of love's sublime
  I cannot fathom, dear, I cannot climb,
For sacred things to lay before thy feet:
I kneel thy suppliant, and I give thee, Sweet,
  The right to go on giving for all time.

NORA HOPPER

(NORA CHESSON)

425 *Dirge for Aoine*[1]

WHITE and golden here she lies;
 Mouth-of-Rose was she.
Violets hide her sleeping eyes;
 Leaves of rosemary
Keep her from the rainy skies,
Winter's cold or spring's surprise,
 Brawling summer bee.

White and golden flowers we bring,
 Gipsy-rose and bloom:
Spider shall not snare her wing,
Yellow wasp not dare to sting
What we cover, while we sing,
 Under drifts of bloom;
But bees bring her, murmuring,
 Honey and perfume.

Oh my grief! her yellow hair
 Tempts no wind to-day.
Folded round her forehead fair
 All her tresses stay,
Stealing from the summer air
 Half its gold away.
Suddenly the woods are bare—
Beechwoods that so shining were
 In the moon of May.

[1] A fairy queen, dwelling at Knockainy, co. Limerick.

She will never rise again,
  Woman o' the Shee.
In the moonlight fair and fain
  She will never be.
Poppies red and bearded grain,
Bending, bowing in the rain,
Sunrise-gold and sunset-stain
  She will never see.
For her ears all songs are vain,
  Tossed from tree to tree.

'Tis my grief that we must go
  (Thus our doom is said),
Dancing lightly as the snow,
Or as autumn leaves that blow
Lightly, lightly to and fro,
  With no tears to shed,
  Though we loved her yellow head,
Though her yellow head is low
Where the tattered ragweeds grow,
Though the very squirrels know
  Aoine's dead.

426 *The Dark Man*

ROSE o' the World, she came to my bed
  And changed the dreams of my heart and head;
For joy of mine she left grief of hers,
And garlanded me with a crown of furze.

Rose o' the World, they go out and in,
And watch me dream and my mother spin;
And they pity the tears on my sleeping face
While my soul's away in a fairy place.

Rose o' the World, they have words galore,
And wide's the swing of my mother's door:
And soft they speak of my darkened eyes—
But what do they know, who are all so wise?

Rose o' the World, the pain you give
Is worth all days that a man may live—
Worth all shy prayers that the colleens say
On the night that darkens the wedding-day.

Rose o' the World, what man would wed
When he might dream of your face instead?
Might go to his grave with the blessed pain
Of hungering after your face again?

Rose o' the World, they may talk their fill,
For dreams are good, and my life stands still
While their lives' red ashes the gossips stir;
But my fiddle knows—and I talk to her.

427 *The Fairy Music*[1]

THERE'S many feet on the moor to-night, and they fall so light as they turn and pass,
So light and true that they shake no dew from the featherfew and the hungry grass.
I drank no sup and I broke no crumb of their food, but dumb at their feast sat I;
For their dancing feet and their piping sweet, now I sit and greet till I'm like to die.

[1] Ir. *Ceol-Sidhe.*

Oh kind, kind folk, to the words you spoke I shut my
ears and I would not hear!
And now all day what my own kin say falls sad and
strange on my careless ear;
For I'm listening, listening, all day long to a fairy
song that is blown to me,
Over the broom and the canna's bloom, and I know
the doom of the Ceol-Sidhe.

I take no care now for bee or bird, for a voice I've
heard that is sweeter yet.
My wheel stands idle: at death or bridal apart I
stand and my prayers forget.
When Ulick speaks of my wild-rose cheeks, and his
kind love seeks out my heart that's cold,
I take no care though he speaks me fair, for the new
love casts out the love that's cold.

I take no care for the blessed prayer, for my mother's
hand or my mother's call.
There ever rings in my ear and sings, a voice more
dear and more sweet than all.
Cold, cold's my breast, and broke's my rest, and oh it's
blest to be dead I'd be,
Held safe and fast from the fairy blast, and deaf at
last to the Ceol-Sidhe!

428 *Mo Bouchaleen Bwee*[1]

MO Bouchaleen bwee, and mo Bouchaleen bwee,
It's I would go with you wherever you be:
I'd climb the high hills and I'd sail the salt sea
If I might go with you, mo Bouchaleen bwee.

[1] Ir. *Mo Bhuachailín* (pron. *vouchaleen*) *Buidhe*, My yellow-haired lad.

Most dear and most green are the fair hills of Eri,
But on steeper hillsides my feet would not weary :
My feet on the ice and the snowfield might be
If you climbed beside me, mo Bouchaleen bwee.

If you were in exile, whatever winds blew,
It's I would be houseless and homeless with you :
My breast for your fair head a pillow should be,
And my heart for your castle, mo Bouchaleen bwee !

With sorrow before and with danger behind,
I'd follow you, heeding nor weather nor wind :
So kind and so faithful and patient I'd be,
If I might go with you, mo Bouchaleen bwee.

429 *The Cold Wind*

A COLD wind entered the lamp-lit room,
  As winter never enters the street.
I shut my book on a rose in bloom,
  And gathered my strength my doom to meet ;
  There never was rose so dark and sweet.

The door was shut and the window barred ;
  The air was full of the rose's breath,
And close at my side my love kept guard,
  And tried to hold me away from Death,
But touched him not, though he held me hard.

The cold wind blew on my weary brows,
  The cold wind crept on the soles of my feet ;
In the deep of night, in the sleeping house,
  I heard in my bosom the trapped heart beat,
And lifted my eyes my doom to meet.

Death and my love by me stood so close,
The cold wind lifted their yellow hair.
My love was as pale as a Christmas rose;
Death was as tall and twice as fair,
With the patient eyes of a wayfarer.

I took my hands from my dear love's hold:
Back I fell from my dear love's kiss.
Is it Love or Death, then, whose breast feels cold
Against my heart, where the red rose is?
Will Death's white rose match herself with this?

430 *Gold Song*

'GOLD of butterflies, gold of bees,
Gold of ragweeds and golden seas;
Gold on gorses for kissing's sake,
Which of these will you touch and take,
Moirín, Moirín?'

Golden butterfly's not for me,
I'll ha' none o' the golden bee:
My heart of gold shall not beat or break,
Though I love the gorses for kissing's sake,
Mother, Mother!

'Then rest you merry, through heat and cold,
Sweet lips of cherry, sweet heart of gold;
Yet Gold-Heart surely shall come some day
To cry for grey wings to fly away,
Moirín, Moirín!'

S. CHARLES JELLICOE

431 *Laudator Temporis Acti*

WHEN we lament the light of other days
In some dark hour of passionate despair,
The temple, that of ruined joys we rear,
Is such as never met our living gaze.
The hand of mem'ry tenderly that strays
Amid the dead leaves where the blossoms were—
As some lone mother sees the little chair,
And her dead darling crowns with heavenly rays—
The scattered petals lovingly doth range,
But all the stinging thorn-pricks doth forget,
And paints a picture all of flowers and green.
So when we ponder on some mournful change,
'Tis not what was our secret thoughts regret,
But what we fancy haply might have been.

432 *The Destiny of Dreams*

I DREAMED that heaven was builded
Of fair thoughts gleaned on earth
To be new cast and gilded
In the mould of another birth.
And each bright hope we win here
Will find its true life there,
But every thought of sin here
Will make that heaven less fair.
O God, keep ever from us
All thoughts not bright and true,
That so the Land of Promise
May be of Beauty too!

433

Advice to a Lover

OH! if you love her,
 Show her the best of you;
So will you move her
 To bear with the rest of you.
Coldness and jealousy
 Cannot but seem to her
Signs that a tempest lurks
 Where was sunbeam to her.
Patience and tenderness
 Still will awake in her
Hopes of new sunshine,
 Tho' the storm break for her;
Love, she will know, for her,
 Like the blue firmament,
Under the tempest lies
 Gentle and permanent.
Nor will she ever
 Gentleness find the less,
When the storm overblown
 Leaveth clear kindliness.
Deal with her tenderly,
 Skylike above her,
Smile on her waywardness,
 Oh! if you love her.

434

Erin's Plea

OH! England, thou now art but learning
 What the tale of thine annals well shows,
That the land where the shamrock is native
 Can bear richest blooms of the rose.

Oh ! England, where'er the rose flourish
  In lands over ocean's wide flood,
The soil where its roots strike the deepest
  Enriched was with Erin's best blood.

Oh ! England, where'er in full splendour
  The glory of rose-blooms is seen,
Remember the men whose loved emblem
  Is one humble leaflet of green.

435 *Can you give Gladness to Me*

CAN you gather the sparks of the fire that is dead ?
  Can you catch the sweet notes of the song that is fled ?
Can you follow the flight of the bird that has sped ?
  And can you give gladness to me ?

You may kindle new flames on the hearth that is chill ;
The lute with new melody haply may thrill ;
You may cage a new songster to sing, an you will ;
  But you cannot give gladness to me.

The spirit's that's cold can be warmed ne'er again ;
The heart that is broken can sing no sweet strain ;
The youth that is fled comes not back ; it is vain :
  You cannot give gladness to me.

LIONEL JOHNSON

436

Saint Columba

DEAD is Columba: the world's arch
  Gleams with a lighting of strange fires,
They flash and run, they leap and march,
  Signs of a Saint's fulfilled desires.

Live is Columba: golden crowned,
  Sceptred with Mary lilies, shod
With angel flames, and girded round
  With white of snow, he goes to God.

No more the grey eyes long to see
  The oakwoods of their Inisfail;
Where the white angels hovering be:
  And ah, the birds in every vale!

No more for him thy fierce winds blow,
  Iona of the angry sea!
Gone, the white glories of thy snow,
  And white spray flying over thee!

Now, far from the grey sea, and far
  From sea-worn rocks and sea-birds' cries,
Columba hails the morning star,
  That shines in never nighted skies.

High in the perfect Land of Morn,
  He listens to the chaunting air:
The Land, where music is not born,
  For music is eternal there.

There, bent before the burning Throne,
He lauds the lover of the Gael :
Sweet Christ ! whom Patrick's children own :
Glory be Thine from Inisfail !

437

The Red Wind

RED Wind from out the East :
Red Wind of blight and blood !
Ah, when wilt thou have ceased
Thy bitter, stormy flood ?

Red Wind from over sea,
Scourging our lonely land !
What Angel loosened thee
Out of his iron hand ?

Red Wind ! whose word of might
Winged thee with wings of flame ?
O fire of mournful night,
What is thy master's name ?

Red Wind ! who bade thee burn,
Branding our hearts ? who bade
Thee on and never turn,
Till waste our souls were laid ?

Red Wind ! from out the West
Pour Winds of Paradise :
Winds of eternal rest,
That weary souls entice.

Wind of the East! Red Wind!
  Thou witherest the soft breath
Of Paradise the kind:
  Red Wind of burning death!

O Red Wind! hear God's voice:
  Hear thou, and fall, and cease.
Let Inisfail rejoice
  In her Hesperian peace.

438 *Enthusiasts*

LET your swords flash, and wound the golden air of God:
  Bright steel, to meet and cleave the splendour of His sun!
  Now is a war of wars in majesty begun:
Red shall the cornfields ripen, where our horses trod,
Where scythe nor sickle swept, but smote war's iron rod:
  Where the stars rose and set, and saw the blood still run.
  So shall men tell of us, and dread our deeds, though done:
New annals yet shall praise time's fiercest period.

Let your swords flash, and wound the glowing air: now play
  A glorious dance of death, with clash and gleam of sword.
Did Syrian sun and moon stand still on Israel's day?
  Those orbs halt over Ajalon at Joshua's word?

Of us, who ride for God, shall Christian children say:
To battle, see! flash by armed angels of the Lord.

439 *The Last Music*

CALMLY, breathe calmly all your music, maids!
Breathe a calm music over my dead queen,
All your lives long, you have nor heard, nor seen,
Fairer than she, whose hair in sombre braids
With beauty overshades
Her brow, broad and serene.

Surely she hath lain so an hundred years:
Peace is upon her, old as the world's heart.
Breathe gently, music! Music done, depart:
And leave me in her presence to my tears,
With music in mine ears;
For sorrow hath its art.

Music, more music, sad and slow! she lies
Dead: and more beautiful than early morn.
Discrowned am I, and of her looks forlorn:
Alone vain memories immortalise
The way of her soft eyes,
Her musical voice low-borne.

The balm of gracious death now laps her round,
As once life gave her grace beyond her peers.
Strange! that I loved this lady of the spheres.
To sleep by her at last in common ground:
When kindly sleep hath bound
Mine eyes, and sealed mine ears.

Maidens! make a low music: merely make
  Silence a melody, no more. This day,
  She travels down a pale and lonely way:
Now, for a gentle comfort, let her take
    Such music, for her sake,
      As mourning love can play.

Holy my queen lies in the arms of death:
  Music moves over her still face, and I
  Lean breathing love over her. She will lie
In earth thus calmly, under the wind's breath:
    The twilight wind, that saith:
      Rest! worthy found, to die.

440 *'To Weep Irish'*

LONG Irish melancholy of lament!
  Voice of the sorrow, that is on the sea:
Voice of that ancient mourning music sent
  From Rama childless: the world wails in thee.

The sadness of all beauty at the heart,
  The appealing of all souls unto the skies,
The longing locked in each man's breast apart,
  Weep in the melody of thine old cries.

Mother of tears! sweet Mother of sad sighs!
  All mourners of the world weep Irish, weep
Ever with thee: while burdened time still runs,
  Sorrows reach God through thee, and ask for sleep.

And though thine own unsleeping sorrow yet
 Live to the end of burdened time, in pain:
Still sing the song of sorrow! and forget
 The sorrow, in the solace, of the strain.

JAMES JOYCE

441 *Strings in the Earth and Air*

STRINGS in the earth and air
 Make music sweet;
Strings by the river where
 The willows meet.

There's music along the river,
 For Love wanders there,
Pale flowers on his mantle,
 Dark leaves on his hair.

All softly playing,
 With head to the music bent,
And fingers straying
 Upon an instrument.

442 *Bid Adieu to Girlish Days*

BID adieu, adieu, adieu,
 Bid adieu to girlish days,
Happy Love is come to woo
 Thee and woo thy girlish ways—
The zone that doth become thee fair,
 The snood upon thy yellow hair.

JAMES JOYCE

When thou hast heard his name upon
  The bugles of the cherubim
Begin thou softly to unzone
  Thy girlish bosom unto him.
And softly to undo the snood
  That is the sign of maidenhood.

443 *What Counsel has the Hooded Moon*

WHAT counsel has the hooded moon
  Put in thy heart, my shyly sweet,
Of Love in ancient plenilune,
  Glory and stars beneath his feet—
A sage that is but kith and kin
With the comedian Capuchin ?

Believe me rather than am wise
  In disregard of the divine,
A glory kindles in those eyes,
  Trembles to starlight. Mine, O Mine !
No more be tears in moon or mist
For thee, sweet sentimentalist.

THOMAS KEOHLER

444 *Song*

I WOULD swathe thee in hues of the orient,Queen,
  Or sun-dancing sheen of the waves,
I would build thee a palace of ivory, Queen,
  With heroes and gods for slaves.

I would give thee all these and a thousandfold more
  If I were but free as of old,
But my will is adrift on the sea of desire,
  And Love is a tale untold.

445 *Supplication*

A MURMURED sound of ecstasy
  Is on the hills to-night,
A joy that cannot hide its head
  In wonder and delight.

The trees stand silent as I pass,
  Arms raised as if to bless.
The very grass beneath my feet
  Sheds fragrant holiness.

But on I go with restless feet,
  And heart oppressed with care,
Seeking some shrine where I may lay
  A fragile gift of prayer.

O priestess of the silent hills,
  Whereon the light of day
Clings, and the shadows of the night
  Are half afraid to stay,—

Lead me unto thy secret place,
  Where I may weep and pray,
So may the passion of the night
  Absolve the sin of day!

THOMAS KEOHLER

446 *The Town beyond the Trees*

I STOOD within the quiet woodland ways,
  Listening for Love's forgotten melodies.
I heard them not, for all the earth was filled
  With murmurings from the town beyond the trees.

And so I prayed unto the bright-winged Lord
  To send His music down the shining breeze,
That I might sing to those who toiled amidst
  The murmurings of the town beyond the trees.

No answer came, for oh ! I only brought
  A heart half-haunted by Love's mysteries,
And all my ears were heavy with the sound
  Of murmurings from the town beyond the trees.

447 *Wind and Sea*

O FIERCE and rushing sea ! O clamorous wind !
  Speak to my rebel heart, speak and be kind,
For I am near to thee by closest ties
Of kinship, and by love that never dies.

Give me, impetuous sea, thy wild strong heart !
Give me, O surging wind, thy furious art !—
Eternal warriors on the passionless sky,
Whom death dare touch not, nor decay come nigh.

And yet I know, O wind ! O shuddering sea !
I have one boon which God denies to thee ;
Ye must rage on eternally, nor cease,
For me, for me alone is death's glad peace.

EMILY LAWLESS

448 *An Exile's Mother*

THERE'S famine in the land, its grip is tightening still,
There's trouble, black and bitter, on every side I glance,
There are dead upon the roadside, and dead upon the hill,
But my Jamie's safe and well away in France,
Happy France,
In the far-off, gay and gallant land of France.

The sea sobs to the grey shore, the grey shore to the sea.
Men meet and greet, and part again as in some evil trance,
There's a bitter blight upon us, as plain as plain can be,
But my Jamie's safe and well away in France,
Happy France,
In the far-off, gay and gallant land of France.

Oh not for all the coinèd gold that ever I could name
Would I bring you back, my Jamie, from your song, and feast, and dance,
Would I bring you to the hunger, the weariness and shame,
Would I bring you back to Clare out of France!
Happy France,
From the far-off, gay and gallant land of France.

I'm no great sleeper now, for the nights are cruel cold,
And if there be a bit or sup 'tis by some friendly
chance,
But I keep my old heart warm, and I keep my courage
bold
By thinking of my Jamie safe in France,
Happy France,
In the far-off, gay and gallant land of France.

449 *Fontenoy*, 1745

I.—Before the Battle: Night

OH bad the march, the weary march, beneath these
alien skies!—
But good the night, the friendly night, that soothes
our tired eyes.
And bad the war, the tedious war, that keeps us
sweltering here;
But good the hour, the friendly hour, that brings the
battle near,
That brings us on the battle, that summons to their
share
The homeless troops, the banished men, the exiled
sons of Clare.

Oh little Corca Bascinn, the wild, the bleak, the fair!
Oh little stony pastures, whose flowers are sweet, if
rare!
Oh rough and rude Atlantic, the thunderous, the wide,
Whose kiss is like a soldier's kiss which will not be
denied!

The whole night long we dream of you, and waking
think we're there,—
Vain dream, and foolish waking, we never shall see
Clare.

The wind is wild to-night, there's battle in the air ;
The wind is from the west, and it seems to blow from
Clare.
Have you nothing, nothing for us, loud brawler of the
night ?
No news to warm our heart-strings, to speed us
through the fight ?
In this hollow, star-pricked darkness, as in the sun's
hot glare,
In sun-tide, moon-tide, star-tide, we thirst, we starve
for Clare !

Hark ! yonder through the darkness one distant rat-
tat-tat !
The old foe stirs out there, God bless his soul for that !
The old foe musters strongly, he's coming on at last,
And Clare's Brigade may claim its own wherever
blows fall fast.
Send us, ye western breezes, our full, our rightful
share,
For Faith, and Fame, and Honour, and the ruined
hearths of Clare.

II.—After the Battle : Early Dawn, Clare Coast

'Mary mother, shield us ! Say, what men are ye,
Sweeping past so swiftly on this morning sea ?'

'Without sails or rowlocks merrily we glide
Home to Corca Bascinn on the brimming tide.'

'Jesus save you, gentry! why are ye so white,
Sitting all so straight and still in this misty light?'
'Nothing ails us, brother; joyous souls are we
Sailing home together, on the morning sea.'

'Cousins, friends, and kinsfolk, children of the land,
Here we come together, a merry, rousing band;
Sailing home together from the last great fight,
Home to Clare from Fontenoy, in the morning light.

'Men of Corca Bascinn, men of Clare's Brigade,
Hearken, stony hills of Clare, hear the charge we made;
See us come together, singing from the fight,
Home to Corca Bascinn, in the morning light.'

450 *The Stranger's Grave* (79)

LITTLE feet too young and soft to walk,
Little lips too young and pure to talk,
Little faded grass-tufts, root and stalk.

I lie alone here, utterly alone,
Amid pure ashes my wild ashes mingle;
A drownèd man, with a name, unknown,
A drifting waif, flung by the drifting shingle.
Oh, plotting brain, and restless heart of mine,
What strange fate brought you to so strange a shrine?

Sometimes a woman comes across the grass,
Bare-footed, with pit-patterings scarcely heard,
Sometimes the grazing cattle slowly pass,
Or on my turf sings loud some mating bird.
Oh, plotting brain, and restless heart of mine,
What strange fate brought you to so strange a shrine?

Little feet too young and soft to walk,
Little lips too young and pure to talk,
Little faded grass-tufts, root and stalk.

451 *A Retort*

NOT hers your vast imperial mart,
Where myriad hopes on fears are hurled,
Where furious rivals meet and part
To woo a world.

Not hers your vast imperial town,
Your mighty mammoth piles of gain,
Your loaded vessels sweeping down
To glut the main.

Unused, unseen, her rivers flow,
From mountain tarn to ocean tide;
Wide vacant leagues the sunbeams show,
The rain-clouds hide.

You swept them vacant! Your decree
Bid all her budding commerce cease;
You drove her from your subject sea,
To starve in peace!

EMILY LAWLESS

Well, be it peace ! Resigned they flow,
No laden fleet adown them glides,
But wheeling salmon sometimes show
Their silvered sides.

And sometimes through the long still day
The breeding herons slowly rise,
Lifting grey tranquil wings away
To tranquil skies.

Stud all your shores with prosperous towns !
Blacken your hill-sides, mile on mile !
Redden with bricks your patient downs !
And proudly smile !

A day will come before you guess,
A day when men, with clearer light,
Will rue that deed beyond redress,
Will loathe that sight.

And, loathing, fly the hateful place,
And, shuddering, quit the hideous thing,
For where unblackened rivers race,
And skylarks sing.

For where, remote from smoke and noise,
Old leisure sits knee-deep in grass ;
Where simple days bring simple joys,
And lovers pass.

I see her in those coming days,
Still young, still gay ; her unbound hair
Crowned with a crown of starlike rays,
Serenely fair.

EMILY LAWLESS

I see an envied haunt of peace,
Calm and untouched ; remote from roar,
Where wearied men may from their burdens cease
On a still shore.

SHANE LESLIE

452 *Ireland To-day*

SHE moves most sad and beautiful
Amid her hills of green ;
She weeps the brave, the dutiful,
Who owned her once for queen.

Of all her fighting men bereft,
Of bard and feaster's throng,
She keepeth sweet the love they left,
The memory of their song.

Ah ! well the clans in distant time,
Who met a glorious doom ;
And well the clans whom foreign clime
Hath laid in purple tomb :

For now they seek another's fame,
And some have learnt to hate ;
And some who bear the ancient name
Have passed the traitor's gate.

The poor alone, the peasant-born,
In ardour lawless set,
Is staunch amid his fellows' scorn,
And finds her flawless yet.

Beside her moves the dreamers' band,
  Their hearts a-flaming fast ;
For old-world songs their dreams have fanned
  With whispers from the past.

Around her many lovers sigh,
  The courtiers of her woe,
And now her rainbow heart climbs high,
  And now it melteth low.

And now she speaks her holy tongue,
  And to the Gaelic heard
A thousand hearts have echoed strong,
  And distant lands are stirred.

She moves most sad and beautiful
  Amid her hills of green ;
She seeks the brave, the dutiful,
  To own her yet as queen.

453 *The Exiles Speak to Ireland*

ART not dead, O mother, leaping
  Thus toward the fight ?
Wounded, thou wert only sleeping
  In thy armoured might ;
They had never killed the weeping
  On thy branded sight.

We were building towns, and sowing
  Corn and tree and vine ;
We had gleaned the gold-dust flowing
  On the southern line,
We who thought to own the lowing
  Herds of Argentine.

SHANE LESLIE

Didst thou watch us how we scattered,
  How we fought and cried ?
Didst thou see the foreign tattered
  Banners at our side ?
All the gates of war we battered,
  Every cause we tried.

Is there better store in 'Derry
  Than the garnered south ;
Honey on the rocks of Kerry,
  Silver under Howth,
And the gold the fairies bury
  At each river mouth ?

Thou, O Ireland ! art and wast in
  All our dreaming low,
And thy spirit everlasting
  Makes this seeming so,
Thro' our sad remembrance casting
  Rays of gleaming woe.

In our mirth and in our dirges
  Thou hast ever part,
While thy restless loving urges
  On the Gaelic heart ;
Children born beyond the surges
  Whisper what thou art.

Thou art heart-sick, calling, Ireland,
  In the foreign breeze ;
Thou art stricken, holy sireland,
  In our wealth and ease,
Thou art still the beckoning fireland
  On a hundred seas.

SHANE LESLIE

454 *Requiem*

IN sweet Irish clay may I lie
  Heart clasped to my race,
O brothers and sisters of mine,
  Give me of your space!
For mine was the life that you lived,
  The fight that you fought,
And bright in the gloom of mine own
  Were deeds you had wrought.
So let the dear dust of your dead
  Drift over my face,
And this be the dirge that you sing
  And song that you trace.
A pebble is thrown to the beach
  From whence it was brought,
A leaf has dropped weary for rest
  To those it had sought.

455 *Rebel Mother's Lullaby*

AH, rest to the morrow, for many the sorrow
  That waking will brew;
    Gone is thy brother,
  Long must I rue;
    Hark not thy mother
  Rocking thee to,
Rocking thee fro, Lennavan mo,
  Ireland's own woe
Never must keep children from sleep,
  Lennavan mo.

SHANE LESLIE

The clouds are fast creeping, and Mary is
 weeping
 Her tears down the sky;
 Grey is the evening
 When Irishmen die;
 Hark not the keening,
 Rest thee and lie,
Lennavan mo, Lennavan mo,
 Far be the foe,
Ours is the strife, yours is dear life,
 Lennavan mo.

Earl Garrat is hiding, Lord Edward is riding,
 And fast is his rein;
 The horses are stamping
 Over the plain;
 Hark not the tramping,
 Turn thee again,
Lennavan mo, Lennavan mo,
 Nestle down low,
Others may ride, you must abide,
 Lennavan mo.

ELIZABETH MARY LITTLE

456 *A Whisper*

WHEN the grip of the black frost tightened
 And hurricane winds held strife,
So weary was I of the winter
 I almost wearied of life.

ELIZABETH MARY LITTLE

No sun on the level horizon,
  No glimmer of blue, or green,
Only the winds' wild pinions
  Grey sky and grim earth between.

Then low in my ear a whisper
  Rejoiced me exceedingly,
So dear in its dream of beauty
  It dropped out of faërie.

'Sweeter than horns of elfland
  You'll hear down a whitethorn lane,
In exquisite April weather,
  The cuckoo calling again.'

Ah! some of us children of summer
  So steadfastly mourn the sun,
Our eyes are fixed on the zenith
  Where yearly his race is run.

'What of the gold of his arrows,
  What of the light?'—we say,
'What of the tarrying seconds
  Should bear to us back the day?'

He is well on his wondrous journey,
  His progress of royal state,
With banners and woodland music
  Earth moves to meet him elate:

With music and woodland banners
  Of ever-belovèd green,
And the opening eyes of the snowdrops
  Each tremulous tress between.

But now 'tis my heart that whispers
  Pulsing a glad refrain :
'Soon, soon, not in dreams but daylight
  I shall hear it close and plain.'

Yes, sweeter than horns of elfland,
  Hard by, in a whitethorn lane,
By the gold-crowned Hill of Killiney
  The cuckoo calling again !

457 *Life*

AH Life ! that mystery that no man knows,
  And all men ask, the Arab from his sands,
The Cæsar's self, lifting imperial hands,
And the lone dweller where the lotus blows ;
O'er trackless tropics and o'er silent snows
She dumbly broods, that Sphinx of all the lands,
And if she answers no man understands,
And no cry breaks the blank of her repose.

But a new form dawned once upon my pain
With grave sad lips, but in the eyes a smile
Of deepest meaning dawning sweet and slow,

Lighting to service, and no more in vain
I ask of Life 'What art thou ?' as erewhile,
For since Love holds my hand I seem to know.

SIDNEY ROYSE LYSAGHT

458 *The Unexplored*

OUT of lonely seas we sailed
After dusk and crossed the bar
Ere the darkness wholly veiled
Haven shores and lands afar;
Ere the path of wild-rose light
O'er the hills had faded quite,
Or the shore-lights' golden rays
Glowed across the water-ways.

Wonderlands of which we dreamed
Over the unventured seas
Never more enchanted seemed,
Never lovelier than these;
These that, hidden till the dawn
Now no boundary confines,
Save where starry skies have drawn
Silvery horizon lines.

There, between the veiled and shown,
Wonders hidden are our own;
Forest voices whisper there
Lore of days that never were;
Secrets vision hides we find
Written in the undefined;
Revelations in the guessed,
Treasures in the unpossessed.

Darker, over waters dark,
  Loom the shores ; and still remains,
Here and there, a light to mark
  Ships along the haven lanes.
Softer, over ripples soft,
  Far away the sea-winds blow ;
Fairer than the stars aloft
  Shine the stars in depths below.

Ah ! what seek we ? Even now,
While we wonder, we endow
All things near us and afar
With the dreams that nowhere are :
Reading into the unknown
Hopes that we have long outgrown,
Weaving into the unseen
Tidings of the might-have-been.

Soon along the eastern rim
  Light shall steal, and silver mist
Flash to rose, and uplands dim
  Wake in folds of amethyst.
Soon shall tidings twilight told,
  Soon shall pathways starlight drew
Vanish in the morning's gold,
  Hide behind the noonday's blue.

Now, till morn, remain our own
  Magic shores of old surmise,
Peaks no morning can dethrone,
  Lands that know no boundaries.

There the unfulfilled abides ;
There the touch of night unbars
Gates of ways that noonday hides,
Paths that reach beyond the stars.

459 *The Penalty of Love*

IF Love should count you worthy, and should deign
One day to seek your door and be your guest,
Pause ! ere you draw the bolt and bid him rest,
If in your old content you would remain.
For not alone he enters : in his train
Are angels of the mists, the lonely quest,
Dreams of the unfulfilled and unpossessed.
And sorrow, and Life's immemorial pain.

He wakes desires you never may forget,
He shows you stars you never saw before,
He makes you share with him, for evermore,
The burden of the world's divine regret.
How wise were you to open not !—and yet,
How poor if you should turn him from the door.

460 *To my Comrades*

YOU, who once dreamed on earth to make your mark
And kindle beacons where its ways were dark ;
To whom, for the world that had no need of you,
It once had seemed a little thing to die ;
Who gave the world your best, and in return
No honour won, and no reward could earn !
Sad Comrade ! we were shipmates in one crew,—
Somewhere we sailed together, you and I.

SIDNEY ROYSE LYSAGHT

O you of little faith, the promised heir
Of life eternal, mourning days that were;
  You, who to lift up one belovèd head
    Out of the dust and feel one presence nigh,—
To make again one vanished summer live,
Your birthright of eternal life would give!
  I also murmur, 'Give me back my dead!'
    The comrade of your unbelief am I.

You, against whom all fates have been arrayed;
Who heard the voice of God and disobeyed;
  Who, reckless and with all your battles lost,
    Went forth again another chance to try;
Who, fighting desperate odds yet fought to win,
And sinning bore the burden of your sin!
  We have been on the same rough ocean tossed,
    And served the same wild captain, you and I.

You, who desired no laurel of the race
But the approval of one absent face;
  For whom has earth no home, no place of rest
    Save in the bosom where you may not lie;
Beggared of all but Love's immortal right,
Still for the sake of one you lost to fight!
  Oh, we have met upon the unknown quest
    And watched the stars together, you and I.

O wanderer, if at last your ship should find
Home, and the sheltered havens left behind,
  I shall be with you in that merry crew
    Under the same old flag we used to fly;
But, if at last, of every promise shorn,
With leaking timbers and with canvas torn,
  Still for the pride of seamanship sail you,—
    There also, in your chartless ship, sail I.

SEOSAMH MAC CATHMHAOIL
(JOSEPH CAMPBELL)

461 *The Herb-Leech*

I HAVE gathered luss
At the wane of the moon,
And supped its sap
With a yewen spoon.
I have sat a spell
By the carn of Medb,
And smelt the mould
Of the red queen's grave.
I have dreamed a dearth
In the darkened sun,
And felt the hand
Of the Evil One.
I have fathomed war
In the comet's tail,
And heard the crying
Of Gall and Gael.
I have seen the spume
On the dead priest's lips,
And the 'holy fire'
On the spars of ships;
And the shooting stars
On Barthelmy's Night,
Blanching the dark
With ghostly light;
And the corpse candle
Of the seer's dream,
Bigger in girth

Than a weaver's beam ;
And the shy hearth-fairies
About the grate,
Blowing the turves
To a whiter heat.
All things on earth
To me are known,
For I have the gift
Of the Murrain Stone !

462 *The Silence of Unlaboured Fields*

THE silence of unlaboured fields
Lies like a judgement on the air :
A human voice is never heard :
The sighing grass is everywhere—
The sighing grass, the shadowed sky,
The cattle crying wearily !

Where are the lowland people gone ?
Where are the sun-dark faces now ?
The love that kept the quiet hearth,
The strength that held the speeding plough ?
Grasslands and lowing herds are good,
But better human flesh and blood !

463 *As I came over the Grey, Grey Hills*

AS I came over the grey, grey hills
And over the grey, grey water,
I saw the gilly leading on,
And the white Christ following after.

Where and where does the gilly lead?
  And where is the white Christ faring?
They've travelled the four grey sounds of Orc,
  And the four grey seas of Eirinn.

The moon is set and the wind's away,
  And the song in the grass is dying,
And a silver cloud on the silent sea
  Like a shrouding-sheet is lying.

But Christ and the gilly will follow on
  Till the ring in the east is showing,
And the awny corn is red on the hills,
  And the golden light is glowing!

464 *Go, Ploughman, Plough*

GO, ploughman, plough
  The mearing lands,
The meadow lands,
The mountain lands:
All life is bare
Beneath your share,
All love is in your lusty hands.

Up, horses, now!
And straight and true
Let every broken furrow run:
The strength you sweat
Shall blossom yet
In golden glory to the sun.

THOMAS MAC DONAGH

465 *Two Songs from the Irish*

I

THE stars stand up in the air,
  The sun and the moon are gone,
The strand of its waters is bare,
  And her sway is swept from the swan.

The cuckoo was calling all day,
  Hid in the branches above,
How my stóirín is fled far away—
  'Tis my grief that I gave her my love!

Three things through love I see—
  Sorrow and sin and death—
And my mind reminding me
  That this doom I breathe with my breath.

But sweeter than violin or lute
  Is my love—and she left me behind!
I wish that all music were mute,
  And I to all beauty were blind.

She's more shapely than swan by the strand,
  She's more radiant than grass after dew,
She's more fair than the stars where they stand—
  'Tis my grief that her ever I knew!

II

'Tis a pity I'm not in England
  Or with one from Erin thither bound,
Or out in the midst of the ocean
  Where the thousands of ships are drowned.

From wave to wave of the ocean
  To be guided on with the wind and the rain—
And O King! that Thou mightst guide me
  Back to my love again!

466 *Litany of Beauty*

O BEAUTY, perfect child of Light!
  Sempiternal soul of all delight!—
White, and prankt with gold like the gold of the night,
The gold of the stars in quiet weather,—
White and shapely and pure,
Like the lily-flower from stain secure,
With life and virginity dying together!

One Lily there is I know
That liveth forever, unstained, immortal, a mystic
    flower;
Perfectly wrought its frame,
Gold-bedecked and eternal white—
White, more white than cold of the snow;—
For never, never, near it came,
Never shall come till the end of all,
Hurtful thing in wind or shower,
Worm or stain or blight;

But ever, ever, gently fall
The dews elysian of years that flow
Where it doth live secure,
In flawless comeliness mature,
Golden and white and pure,—
In the fair far-shining glow
Of eternal and holy Light.

O shapely Flower that must for aye endure!
O Voice of God that every heart must hear!
O Hymn of purest souls that dost unsphere
The ravished soul that lists! O white, white Gem!
O Rose that dost the senses drown in bliss!
No thing can stay, no thing can stem,
No thing can lure the heart to miss
Thy love, thy joy, thy rapture divine—
O Beauty, Beauty, ever thine
The soul, the heart, the brain,
To hymn thee in a loud perpetual strain,
Shriller and sweeter than song of wine,
Than lay of sorrow or love or war—
Beauty of heaven and sun and day,
Beauty of water and frost and star,
Beauty of dusk-tide, narrowing, grey . . .
Beauty of silver light,
Beauty of purple night,
Beauty of solemn breath,
Beauty of closèd eye, and sleep, and death . . .
Beauty of dawn and dew,
Beauty of morning peace
Ever ancient and ever new,
Ever renewed till waking cease
Or sleep forever, when loud the angel's word

Through all the world is heard . . .
Beauty of brute and bird,
Beauty of earthly creatures
Whose hearts by the hand of God are stirred . . .
Beauty of the soul,
Beauty informing forms and features,
Fairest to God's eye,
Beauty that cannot fade or die
Till eternal atoms to ruin roll!

Beauty of blinded Trust,
Led by the hand of God
To a heaven where cherub hath never trod . . .
Austere Beauty of Truth,
Lighting the way of the Just . . .
Splendid Beauty of Youth,
Staying when Youth is fled,
Living when Life is dead,
Burning in funeral dust!

The glory of form doth pale and pall,
Beauty endures to the end of all.

467 *Death in the Woods*

WHEN I am gone and you alone are living here still,
You'll think of me when splendid the storm is on the hill,

Trampling and militant here—what of their village
 street?—
For the baying of winds in the woods to me was
 music sweet.

Oh, for the storms again, and youth in my heart
 again!
My spirit to glory strained, wild in this wild wood
 then,
That now shall never strain—though I think if the
 tempest should roll
I could rise and strive with Death, and smite him
 back from my soul.

But no wind stirs a leaf, and no cloud hurries the
 moon;
I know that to-night our lake with stars and shadows
 is strewn—
A night for a villager's death, who will shudder in
 his grave
To hear—alas, how long!—the winds above him
 rave.

How long! Ah Death, what art thou, a thing of
 calm or of storms?
Or twain—their peace to them, to me thy valiant
 alarms?
Gladly I'd leave them this corpse in their churchyard
 to lay at rest
If my wind-swept spirit could fare on the hurricane's
 kingly quest.

And sure 'tis the fools of knowledge who feign that
the winds of the world
Are but troubles of little calms, by the greater Calm
enfurled !—
I know them for symbols of glory, and echoes of one
Voice dread,
Sounding where spacious tempests house the great-
hearted Dead.

And what but a fool was I, crying defiancc to Death,
Who shall lead my soul from this calm to mingle
with God's very breath !—
Who shall lead me hither perchance while you are
waiting here still,
Sighing for thought of me when the winds are out on
the hill.

468 *Song*

LOVE is cruel, love is sweet,
Cruel, sweet :
Lovers sigh till lovers meet,
Sigh and meet—
Sigh and meet, and sigh again—
Cruel sweet ! O sweetest pain !

Love is blind, but love is sly,
Blind and sly :
Thoughts are bold, but words are shy,
Bold and shy—
Bold and shy, and bold again—
Sweet is boldness, shyness pain.

SEUMAS MAC MANUS

469 *Shane O'Neill* (80)

IN thy wild and windy upland, Tornamona,
  High above the tossing Moyle,
Lies in slumber, deep and dreamless now, a warrior
  Weary worn with battle-toil.
On his mighty breast the little canna[1] blossoms,
  And the scented bog-bines trail;
While the winds from Lurigaiden whisper hush-songs
  Round the bed of Shane O'Neill.

Time was once, O haughty warrior! when you slept not
  To the crooning of the wind;
There was once a Shane whom daisies could not smother,
  And whom bog-weeds could not bind—
Once a Shane with death-shafts from his fierce eyes flashing,
  With dismay in fist of mail—
Shane, whose throbbing pulses sang with singing lightning—
  Shane, our Shane, proud Shane O'Neill!

Him the hungry Scot knew, and the thieving Saxon,
  Traitorous Eireannach as well;
For their mailed throats often gurgled in his grasping
  As he hurled their souls to hell.

[1] Bog-cotton.

Sassenach, now, and flouting Scot, and Irish traitor,
Breathe his name and turn not pale,
Set their heel upon the warrior's breast, nor tremble—
God ! the breast of Shane O'Neill !

Will you never, O our Chieftain, snap the sleep-cords ?
Never rise in thunderous wrath—
Through the knaves and slaves that bring a blight on Uladh,
Sweeping far a dread red swath ?
O'er the surges shout, O you on Tornamona,
Hark, the soul-shout of the Gael !
Rise, O Chief, and lead us from our bitter bondage—
Rise, in God's name, Shane O'Neill !

470 *The Path across the Moor*

ONE harvest evening as I took the road from Glenties fair,
I o'ertook a fresh-lipped cailín of modest mien and air ;
So pleasant our discoursing was, it grieved me, to be sure,
When she said at length 'Good-bye, kind sir, my path's across the moor.'

I looked upon her wistfully—her gaze fell on the grass.
'It's lonesome walking is the moor,' I said, 'mo chailín dheas,[1]

[1] My pretty little girl.

And the path is not so narrow, but there's room for
two, I'm sure ;
If you don't object I'll take with you the path across
the moor ?'

'The moon is up, the path is straight,' she answered
courteouslie,
'And I never do feel lonesome when crossing of
Tiree :
I thank you very kindly, sir, but to my father's door
I've always took the path alone,' she said, 'across
the moor.'

'That the path's both safe and pleasant for one, I'm
sure is true ;
But you guess not its delights,' I said, 'when jogged
along by two.'
'A kind good-bye, pray, gentle sir ! My father he is
poor,
And I, a humble maid, have never been beyont the
moor.'

'You do your father wrong,' I said, 'for his is
wealth untold,
The King of royal Spain is not so rich, for all his
gold,
And, rank and worldly riches for me have little lure—
I'd barter both, with you to walk henceforth across
the moor.'

I looked into her tender eyes, she blushed and cast
them down ;
I touched my lips upon her hand ; still Rosie did not
frown ;

I took her hands in both of mine, and prisoned them
secure,
While she murmured, 'You may join me on the
path across the moor.'

ALICE MILLIGAN

471 *The Dark Palace*

THERE beams no light from thy hall to-night,
Oh House of Fame;
No mead-vat seethes and no smoke upwreathes
O'er the hearth's red flame;
No high bard sings for the joy of thy kings,
And no harpers play;
No hostage moans at thy dungeon rings
As in Muircherteach's day.

Fallen! fallen! to ruin all in
The covering mould;
The painted yew, and the curtains blue,
And the cups of gold;
The linen, yellow as the corn when mellow,
That the princes wore;
And the mirrors brazen for your queens to gaze in,
They are here no more.

The sea-bird's pinion thatched Gormlai's grianan;[1]
And through windows clear,
Without crystal pane, in her Ard-righ's[2] reign
She looked forth from here.

[1] Palace. [2] High king.

There were quilts of eider on her couch of cedar ;
And her silken shoon
Were as green and soft as the leaves aloft
On a bough in June.

Ah, woe unbounded ! where the harp once sounded
The wind now sings ;
The grey grass shivers where the mead in rivers
Was outpoured for kings ;
The min [1] and the mether [2] are lost together
With the spoil of the spears ;
The strong dún only has stood dark and lonely
Through a thousand years.

But I am not in woe for the wine-cup's flow,
For the banquet's cheer,
For tall princesses with their trailing tresses
And their broidered gear ;
My grief and my trouble for this palace noble
With no chief to lead
'Gainst the Saxon stranger on the day of danger
Out of Aileach Neid.

472 *A Nocturne*

ON a night of sorrow I cried aloud her name.
God, who heard, said : 'Hasten,' and in my dream she came.
She stood ; I saw her clearly by the moon's white flame ;
Her eyes were sweet as ever ; her voice was yet the same.

[1] Gold crescent-shaped ornament. [2] Wooden cup.

ALICE MILLIGAN

No illumining radiance lit her girlish brow—
As in life I loved her, I beheld her now ;
I smiled in joy to greet her ; nor did I think it
strange
That death had wrought no change.

She bore with her no blossoms unknown to earthly
land,
No tall white flowers of paradise, stately and grand ;
There were violets on her breast—blue violets—
And a red rose in her hand.

'How have you gathered ?' I asked my gentle one,
'In that unchanging region of never-ceasing sun,
Where the March winds blow never, and no rain-
shower ever wets
Those little violets ?'

'I have had them long,' she said : 'I have loved
them much,
They were the last flowers given my living hands to
touch,
And in the fevered night of pain before my death,
Sweet was the fragrance of their breath.'

'But surely you have gathered in the celestial land
That other flower which lovingly is kept in your
hand ?
For there is not growing here on the mountain in the
snows
Any such crimson rose.'

With looks of tenderest reproach my words were met.
'Dear, I have remembered! Dear, can you forget?
Seaward north of Derry, it fed on sun and dew;
It was a gift from you.'

And I shall always treasure it as priceless in worth,
God has made nothing fairer than the little flowers of
earth,
As He has no more to give in His heaven above
Than your own heart's gift of never-changing love.

473 *A Benediction*

DEAR little boy,
Soft-handed, playing with white daisies now
Playing above tree shadows on the grass
Where sorrowful I pass,
A gloom upon the sunlight of your joy
Seems to fall down whilst I am laying now
A kiss upon the brightness of your brow,
For with that kiss I did not wish you joy,
Dear little boy.

But this I wish for you,
Not fortune, not much ease, not blissful days,
Not overmuch of even well-won praise.
Not even at end of life your labours due—
But that beneath those little faltering feet,
In sacrifice complete,
A hard path may be chosen, the upward way,
On which I pause to-day—
Pause, helpless, weary, and can walk no more,
Whose work in life is o'er.

And I bequeath,
When I must rest my share of earth beneath,
My days of toil being done,
The hope of this so nearly hopeless heart
To you, weak little one,
To be cherished and held apart,
Perhaps by failure to be tried and shaken,
Yet not by you forsaken ;
But kept, as I have kept it, handed on
Till, when you too are dust beneath the flowers,
Triumph at last is ours,
When darkness yields to dawn ;
And may it be our best of heaven to know
That God has made it so.

Now you may run,
White-pinafored, into the spreading sun ;
Mid shadows racing as the clouds pass by,
Go, play, as thoughtless as the butterfly,
The white, gay thing that you are chasing after,
With ringing childish laughter ;
And I, whose innocent days of mirth are o'er,
Seeing you look to me and laugh again,
Feel hope steal back into my heart once more—
Hope, with this thought of pain,
That, oh ! you would be frightened if you knew
All I have wished for you.

474 *A Song of Freedom*

IN Cavan of little lakes,
As I was walking with the wind,
And no one seen beside me there,
There came a song into my mind :

ALICE MILLIGAN

It came as if the whispered voice
  Of one, but none of human kind,
Who walked with me in Cavan then,
  And he as invisible as wind.

On Urris of Inish-Owen,
  As I went up the mountain side,
The brook that came leaping down
  Cried to me—for joy it cried ;
And when from off the summit far
  I looked o'er land and water wide,
I was more joyous than the brook
  That met me on the mountain side.

To Ara of Connacht's isles,
  As I went sailing o'er the sea,
The wind's word, the brook's word,
  The wave's word, was plain to me—
'As we are, though she is not
  As we are, shall Banba be—
There is no king can rule the wind,
  There is no fetter for the sea.'

SUSAN L. MITCHELL

475 *Immortality*

AGE cannot reach me where the veils of God
    Have shut me in,
For me the myriad births of stars and suns
    Do but begin,

And here how fragrantly there blows to me
        The holy breath,
Sweet from the flowers and stars and hearts of men,
        From life and death.

We are not old, O heart! we are not old,
        The breath that blows
The soul aflame is still a wandering wind
        That comes and goes;
And the stirred heart with sudden raptured life
        A moment glows.

A moment here—a bulrush's brown head
        In the grey rain,
A moment there—a child drowned and a heart
        Quickened with pain;
The name of Death, the blue deep heaven, the scent
        Of the salt sea,
The spicy grass, the honey robbed
        From the wild bee.

Awhile we walk the world on its wide roads
        And narrow ways,
And they pass by, the countless shadowy groups
        Of nights and days;
We know them not, O happy heart!
        For you and I
Watch where within a slow dawn lightens up
        Another sky.

476 *Amergin* (81)

I BUZZ in the dizzy fly, I crawl in the creeping things.
I croak in the frog's throat and fly on the bird's wings.

I play on the keys of the brain, a thought goes here,
goes there ;
Bird or beast it has bounds, but I am everywhere.

I dip in the pools of the rocks and the minnow plays
with me.
Finned I am like a fish, and merry children are we.

At the dumb call of darkness I go to the ocean's side,
I stand on the docile beach and bridle the eager tide.

The fretted waters I hold in the hollow of my hand.
From my heart go fire and dew and the green and
the brown land.

477 *Homeless*

I ASKED for sunlight and a long, long day
To build my little home,
Setting an altar where my heart might lay
Fire 'ere the god should come.

I built my walls with patient carefulness,
Secure and small, nor knew
A wild wind straying from the wilderness
Had sought their shelter too.

My heart woke up in storms, my shelter sweet
In ruins fell apart.
Once more I go by cruel ways to meet
The ordeal of the heart.

SUSAN L. MITCHELL

478 *Exile*

MY wild will spreads its wings and flies
  To reach your heart, my dove.
The winds of love on which I rise
  Gather in storms above,
  And drift me from my love.

Love's self I sought and in thy heart
  I thought his home must be,
Though all his storms sweep us apart,
  My homing wings to thee
  Flutter continually.

Where shall I find thee? To and fro
  Thy homeless bird is driven.
For ever lonely must I go
  From every shelter riven,
  Wing-weary under heaven.

CHARLOTTE GRACE O'BRIEN

479 *Sonnet*

WHEN the heart presses hard against its bars
  And all the aching senses seek to reach
Through some determinate sweet form of speech
A rest and outcome from their inward jars,
The sonnet then amid our brain's mad wars
Draws near to us, as some soft-handed leech,
Giving our thoughts deliverance, setting each
Firm and alone—self-centred as the stars.

Then to this newborn thing new beauties come,
And earth and air and all the sky and sea
Bring tribute to it of sweet minstrelsy,
—So sweet, the cry within the heart is dumb
And where our life held pain and cruel drought
Is now a font we scarce can live without.

480 *The River*

POOR Mick was trotting on to the town,
The side car under him going;
He looked on the water swollen and brown,
He looked on the river flowing.

The day was drear and heavy and dank,
A sleety wind was blowing,
And the river creeping up over the bank
Was in to the roadside going.

Now all that day till the night drew near,
For the wind was bitterly blowing,
Poor Mick sat gossiping here and there,
While the river was steadily flowing.

'And why would ye lave? 'tis a cruel night;
Oh, why should ye be going?
Bide ye here till the morning light,
For the blackest wind is blowing!'

'The wife will be wanting her bread and tay
And oil for to light her sewing—
Myself never minded the roughest day
Or the blackest black wind blowing.

CHARLOTTE GRACE O'BRIEN

'Gi' alang, old mare! get up out of that!
  For sure 'tis home we're going!'
He buttoned his coat and settled his hat,
  Nor thought of the river flowing.

But cold and drear and dark was the night,
  The sleety wind was blowing,
And where the road that morning was right
  The river's edge was flowing.

Mavrone! for the childer, mavrone! for the wife,
  They listen the north winds blowing.
Mavrone! for the gasping struggling life,
  Mavrone! for the river flowing.

The morrow's morn saw the trembling mare,
  Saw the river muddily flowing,
Saw boys and men seeking here and there,
  Though the soft south winds were blowing.

Oh! the early sun is fair to see
  And the winter 'll soon be going,
But deep and dank and dark lies he,
  Though the sweet south winds are blowing.

CATHAL O'BYRNE

481 *Grainne* (82)

After the Death of Diarmuid

FORTH from the twilight of a wood she came,
  Where blossoming isles of purple harebells gleamed,
Set in a shimmering, sunflecked sea of green.

Fair was her face as the deep rose of the dawn,
And lithe her form as the lake grasses tall,
That whispered of her beauty to the breeze.
Tear-stained her cheeks—rock roses washed with spray,
Great haunting memories dwelt of happier days
Deep in the shadowy depths of her sad eyes.
Her hair flowed down, a gleaming golden wave,
O'er snowy fold and fold of her white robe.
Like sun-kissed water on a silver strand,
Its ripples streaming on a soft west wind,
Were mirrored in the wide, weed-laden lake
Where she passed by. The silent, sleepy birds,
Thinking the sun had backward from the west
Turned in his course, and with his shafts of gold
Had stabbed the heart of the dim, silent pool,
Burst into music, and a shower of song
Fell through the leaves to greet this new day-star.
Twin dew-wet quickenberries were her lips, one word
Came through their rosy portals, 'Diarmuid.'
It rang adown the dusky, flower-strewn glades,
Through aisles of forest trees, of mighty oaks,
Of quivering aspen, and of silver larch,
And stately giant pines, and hazel groves;
The melody of murmuring waters caught the sound,
And chaunted 'Diarmuid' to the mossy stones.
Down to the depths of the calm woods it sank,
And up through arching green to the broad sky,
Through traceries of bronze and blue above,
And far beneath of glimmering gold and green,
The nightingale caught up the new, sweet sound,
And for an instant held it in her throat,
Then flung it on the silence of her bower,
Where as it fell it burst in silver rain,
And scattered to the winds its sparks of song.

The myriad songsters caught the glittering drops,
And flying with the gems throughout the wood,
Sang 'Diarmuid' in silver syllables, till the notes,
Forming one grand, sweet chord, went echoing
Through the vast aisles and gold-green garden ways,
And all the wood rang sweet with 'Diarmuid.'
Until the hills in pity sent the name
Back to the forest fringe whereat she stood.
And it at length found its true resting-place
Deep in the inmost core of her lone heart.

482 *Eiré's Awakening*

SAW you the wraith-light flicker and fail,
  Men of the glens, through the blinding sleet?
Saw you a cloud o'er the grey sky sail,
  And wrap the day in its winding-sheet?
Heard you the roar of the tempest's breath,
  Lashing the waves in its passionate scorning?
Felt you the stillness as deep as death?
  'Twas but the hour of our Eiré's mourning.

Heard you the woe of the caoiner's tale,
  Men of the glens, in your eerie shieling?
Heard you the sound of the banshee's wail,
  You of the hills, o'er the upland stealing?
Saw you the wan light grey and cold
  Break in the east, at the day-star's peeping?
Saw you his glory of crimson and gold?
  'Twas but the hour of our Eiré's sleeping.

CATHAL O'BYRNE

Heard you a song by a siren sung,
  Men of the glens, through the woodland ringing,
In the liquid tones of the Gaelic tongue,
  Sweet as the sunlit streamlet's singing ?
See you a myriad stern-brow'd men,
  The very earth 'neath their grand tread shaking,
Seeking the singer through brake and fen ?
  This, this is the hour of our Eiré's waking.

'MOIRA O'NEILL'

483 *Birds*

SURE maybe ye've heard the storm-thrush
    Whistlin' bould in March,
Before there's a primrose peepin' out,
  Or a wee red cone on the larch ;
Whistlin' the sun to come out o' the cloud,
  An' the wind to come over the sea,
But for all he can whistle so clear an' loud,
  He's never the bird for me.

Sure maybe ye've seen the song-thrush
  After an April rain
Slip from in-undher the drippin' leaves,
  Wishful to sing again ;
An' low wi' love when he's near the nest,
  An' loud from the top o' the tree,
But for all he can flutter the heart in your breast,
  He's never the bird for me

Sure maybe ye've heard the cushadoo
  Callin' his mate in May,
When one sweet thought is the whole of his life,
  An' he tells it the one sweet way.
But my heart is sore at the cushadoo
  Filled with his own soft glee,
Over an' over his 'me an' you!'
  He's never the bird for me.

Sure maybe ye've heard the red-breast
  Singin' his lone on a thorn,
Mindin' himself o' the dear days lost,
  Brave wid his heart forlorn.
The time is in dark November,
  An' no spring hopes has he:
'Remember,' he sings, 'remember!'
  Ay, thon's the wee bird for me.

484 *'Cuttin' Rushes'*

OH, maybe it was yesterday, or fifty years ago!
  Meself was risin' early on a day for cuttin' rushes,
Walkin' up the Brabla' burn, still the sun was low,
  Now I'd hear the burn run an' then I'd hear the thrushes.
Young, still young!—an' drenchin' wet the grass,
  Wet the golden honeysuckle hangin' sweetly down;
Here, lad, here! will ye follow where I pass,
  An' find me cuttin' rushes on the mountain.

Then was it only yesterday, or fifty years or so?
  Rippin' round the bog pools high among the heather,
The hook it made me hand sore, I had to leave it go,
  'Twas he that cut the rushes then for me to bind
    together.
Come, dear, come!—an' back along the burn
  See the darlin' honeysuckle hangin' like a crown.
Quick, one kiss,—sure, there's some one at the turn!
  'Oh, we're after cuttin' rushes on the mountain.'

Yesterday, yesterday, or fifty years ago. . . .
  I waken out o' dreams when I hear the summer
    thrushes,
Oh, that's the Brabla' burn, I can hear it sing an' flow,
  For all that's fair, I'd sooner see a bunch o' green
    rushes.
Run, burn, run! can ye mind when we were young?
  The honeysuckle hangs above, the pool is dark an'
    brown:
Sing, burn, sing! can ye mind the song ye sung
  The day we cut the rushes on the mountain?

VINCENT O'SULLIVAN

485 *Norman Cradle-song*

WHEN the moon is afloat,
    And the ocean at rest,
The sea-elf goes forth
    To the town he loves best:

Up from his cave, over the wave,
With joy in his breast.
Singing : Sleep, little baby,
And dream on the sea,
That lulls round thy cradle,
And murmurs to thee.

The stars are a-shine,
And the waves are at play—
Rushing in to the shore
From the wind-stricken bay;
And the sea-elf is there, with the brine in his hair,
As merry as they.
Singing : The soft fleecy moon
Is laughing with glee,
And soothing, my baby,
A dream-song to thee.

The sea-elf goes roving
When the moon waxes bright,
And plays in the churchyard
Till fadeth the light :
His morrice he paces, then deftly retraces
His steps through the night.
Singing : Alack, it is gone !
The silvery moon,
With its great holy face
It waneth too soon :

Ere it passes, my baby,
A hymn it will croon,
Of the splendour of God
And the Heavenly moon.

486 *By the Sea-wall*

WING thy race when the night comes down,
  My cream-white bird with the scarlet mouth,
Fly to my dear in the sea-walled town,
  Where she dreams her life in the soundless south :
Nestle thee close to her yearning breast
  With a flutter of wings and a frightened stare,
And all the love-notes she loveth best
    Breathe there ! Breathe there !
  My cream-white bird with the scarlet mouth.

Out from the fog on the cold sea-wall,
  The death-witch comes with her ruined hands ;
The thread of her voice is thin and small,
  Yet it whines afar over goodly lands !
God have thee in keeping, my cream-white bird,
  My gentle queen lulled in love's mysteries,—
God help thee ! the tune of thy voice she has heard :
    She sees ! She sees !
  The gaunt death-witch with the ruined hands.

She is weaving and weaving thy winding-sheet,
  My beautiful love with the dreaming eyes ;
Her red tears fall and shall snare thy feet,
  My passionate bird with the soft milk cries.
Her arm round thy musk-rose body she slips,
  On thy face the grey sorrow of age is thrown ;
Her leering mouth brushes the dew from thy lips :
    My own ! My own !
  My beautiful love with the dreaming eyes.

VINCENT O'SULLIVAN

487 *Lake Glamour*

WHEN night-birds leave their nests
Sweet dews to sup,
From the lake's sheeny breast
Moon-waves splash up,
And raindrops rock to rest
In lily's cup;
While from the stars comes dripping scented light:
Oh, good night!

When the hair of the water-maid
Clings to the oar,
Till the dreaming moon, half afraid,
Basketh no more;
When kelpies lurk in the shade,
Craved by the shore;
And even the low twangling harp-notes sound white:
My love, good night!

488 *Spring*

LEAVES of the lilac mingle with the flowers
And silvery drops of rain sprent o'er the sod:
I dream away the soundless, soothing hours,
'Mid breezes straying from the Court of God.

'SEUMAS O'SULLIVAN'

489 *The Grey Dusk*

I

TREMULOUS grey of dusk,
Deepening into the blue,
It is the path that leads
Ever to you.

Child of the dusk, your eyes
Quietly light my way,
Quiet as evening stars,
Quiet and grey.

All the magic of dusk,
Tremulous, grey and blue,
Gathers into my heart,
Quiet for you.

II

Child, I thought that we two by some grey sea
Went walking very quietly, hand in hand,
By a grey sea along a silent strand,
And you had turned your eyes away from me
To where grey clouds, uplifted mightily,
Made on the far horizon a silver land,
And I would not recall your eyes to me,
Because I knew from your shy clasping hand
How joy within your heart, a wanderer long,
Outwearied now had come, a nesting bird,
And folded there his wings, too glad for song;
And so I knew at last that you had heard

Through the long miles of grey sea-folding mist,
Soft as the breast of some glad nesting dove,
From grey lips grown articulate, twilight-kissed,
All the secret of my unuttered love.

490 *Envy*

PINE-TREE swaying, swaying softly,
Envy not my Lady so,
Though she moves with lovelier motion
Than your swaying boughs can show.

Sigh not, little breeze, O, sigh not
In the tree-tops everywhere;
Though you have no sound more joyous
Than her laughter on the air!

Pout not so your lips, red rosebud,
Red lips green-engarlanded;
Though her mouth has lovelier moulding
Round her soft lips' lovelier red.

Envy not, O, wild red rosebud,
Sighing breeze, and pine-tree tall,
One whose beauty makes the world you
Live in, lovelier for you all!

491 *The Sedges*

I WHISPERED my great sorrow
To every listening sedge;
And they bent, bowed with my sorrow,
Down to the water's edge.

But she stands and laughs lightly
To see me sorrow so,
Like the light winds that laughing
Across the water go.

If I could tell the bright ones
That quiet-hearted move,
They would bend down like the sedges
With the sorrow of love.

But she stands laughing lightly,
Who all my sorrow knows,
Like the little wind that laughing
Across the water blows.

492 *The Twilight People*

IT is a whisper among the hazel bushes;
It is a long, low, whispering voice that fills
With a sad music the bending and swaying rushes;
It is a heart beat deep in the quiet hills.

Twilight people, why will you still be crying,
Crying and calling to me out of the trees?
For under the quiet grass the wise are lying,
And all the strong ones are gone over the seas.

And I am old, and in my heart at your calling
Only the old dead dreams a-fluttering go;
As the wind, the forest wind, in its falling
Sets the withered leaves fluttering to and fro.

GEORGE ROBERTS

493 *A Lark singing in the City*

EARTH-nested bird, when you were free
  To soar and sing exultingly,
Your day was a revel in sun and light
And your rest was so close to the earth at night,
That now in your cage on a fourth-floor sill
Your song is as blithe as o'er meadow or hill.
Though beneath you surges the crowd in the street,
Though your sky is a space of fifty feet
You can still have sight of the sun your god,
And have still six inches of clover-sod.
Your song of rejoicing to be is strong
To rise over the noise of the city throng.
It falls upon our dusty hearts
Like the glittering spray from water-carts,
And tells us if we drink but deep
Of earth and sun our joy we keep.

494 *The Convent Bell*

O CONVENT bell! long, long ago
  Your peal was refuge for my heart;
The homeward path you seemed to show
  Lay from the world's ways far apart.

But now you hammer prison bars—
  I hear the passing children's mirth—
Above the walls mad dancing stars
  Mingle their music with the earth.

What though night-long aspiring prayer
And adoration in my soul
Ascend as incense through the air
To weave for me an angel's stole—

The mother's heart is still more blest,
When stirring in her arms she feels
Her baby's hand grope for the breast,
For heaven her own soul reveals.

O, sad and far, O convent bell!
Your call to prayer on this May eve;
For unborn babes your funeral knell
Makes Mary mother weep and grieve.

495 *Your Question*

YOU ask me, sweetheart, to avow
What charm in you I most adore,
But how can I discriminate
From your innumerable store.

Yet 'tis not all you really are,
Nor yet what I might wish to see,
But an ideal far above
I worship—what you wish to be.

'Then pray,' you answer, 'tell me now
What 'tis I most desire to be.'
Dear heart, your fondest dreams aspire
To be—just what you are to me.

MATTHEW RUSSELL

496 *The Little Flower Strewers* (83)

DEAR children, kiss your flowers, and fling them
at His feet;
He comes, the Lord of flowers, of all things fair and
sweet.
His glory all is hidden, but who He is you know:
Then throw your flowers before Him, and kiss them
as you throw.

Yet envy not the flowers, that die so sweet a death—
One heart's fond sigh is sweeter than rose's perfumed
breath;
More sweet than sweetest incense the tears of love
that flow,
The thrill of faith that mingles with every flower you
throw.

Yes, let your flowers be emblems of holy thoughts
and prayers
That from your hearts are springing—for hearts alone
He cares.
Oh! may your hearts before Him with loving wor-
ship glow,
While thus you throw your flowers and kiss them
as you throw.

With lips unstained and rosy, kiss all the roses fair—
But thorns lurk 'mid the roses, and life is full of care.

Accept its thorns and roses—both come from God, you know :
So bear your crosses gaily, and kiss them as you go.

Not all your path, dear children, can smile, like this, with flowers :
For lifetimes would be fruitless, if all were sunny hours.
The rain and snow in season must make the roses grow :
So throw your flowers, dear children, and kiss them as you throw.

Ah ! soon the rose-leaves wither—we, too, like flowers must die,
But in the heavenly springtime shall bloom again on high,
That God unveiled beholding whom 'neath these veils we know,
And at whose feet, dear children, our flowers, our hearts, we throw.

PATRICK A. SHEEHAN

497 *A Prophecy*

O IRELAND, dark-hooded in sea-fog and mist
And thy feet lapped around by the pitiless sea,
And thy harpstrings, broken and trailed in the wind,
And thy fangless watch-hound, looking afar ;
The white of thy forehead is smitten with signs,

PATRICK A. SHEEHAN

Not the seals of the quick, as thy father Phœnicians
bore,
But dark cicatrized with the time wounds and pain,
Which fester, but gleam with a light and a hope,
Who speaketh of thee?

Flotsam and waif on Time's eternal sea,
In faded gold the mariners read afar
Thy name, and think of old-time legendaries,
But deem thee unworthy to pick up or save;
Derelict of Ocean; its tumultuous throngs,
Shuttles that weave betwixt the old and new,
Wind in the warp and woof of mighty emperies,
Thou alone untouched, as plague-stricken,
Who careth for thee?

Grey, dead hands point from out thy well-filled graves,
Stately thy turrets, that tremble not, nor break;
Though lichened crosses lean with weight of years
And stretch them listless through the dust-strewn
grass;
And thou a leaf from the black-lettered past
Of vanished chivalry, swiftly vanished faiths?
But, for it hurts the eye to study thee,
The soul to watch thy illustrations dread,
Men turn from thee.

Wizards in valleys, ghosts in lofty towers,
Grey keeps o'erhanging lonely, inky lakes;
Spirits clank up the green and granite stairs
That lead from sea-wash to enchanted moat.
Art thou enchanted? Smitten into stone

By some fell wizard in a far-off time?
And the puissant word that melts or wakes
From gloomy trance and staring impotence,
Who'll speak to thee?

Are thy transgressions wreathen round thy head?
Do they come up, and fall upon thy neck?
Hath God poured out His fury like to fire?
And set thee in dark places, like the dead?
Wounded to death, like some poor, timorous thing,
Seekest thou sepulchres of slime and dust
To hide thy head, and nurse thy mortal hurt,
And let thy memory pass from living men,
Who shudder at thee?

And yet one child of thine will prophesy,
Not smitten with a pythoness's rage,
But watching the unrolling of the scroll,
That Time, God's child, is stealing from God's hand;—
Thou, the Elect, for thou hast passed through fire;
Thou, the encrowned, for Thou hast tasted woe;
Thou shalt yet speak, and all the world will hear;
And all with foreheads drooped and downcast eyes,
Shall haste to thy beck, O Sybil of the Seas,
And worship thee!

498 *The Soul-bell*

NIGHT, and its noon, and a far to-morrow,
Grey with the fears
Of a Future that leans to a Past to borrow
Its meed of tears.

PATRICK A. SHEEHAN

White are the drifts outside; and hither,
Around her bed,
White comes the face, that asks, oh, whither
Fares forth my dead?

White is the taper clasped in her fingers!
Her lips are white;
Recall Thy judgement, O God! that lingers
This weary night!

Hark! from the ivy across the river
Moaneth the bell;
Death! fling thy arrow back to its quiver;
There! it is well!

Still as the marble and cold she seemeth,
Looking afar;
Round the wide orb of her future gleameth
Her life's lone star.

Frail, how the garments of Life still hold her
From the far flight
Through the trail of the stars, whose eyes enfold her
Beyond the night.

Hark! how again the soul-bell splinters
The granite gloom,
Thick with the murk of a thousand winters,
And a halting doom.

Come, O ye Spirits, that float and hover
Above the soul!
Is there no gleam of bliss to cover
Grey death and dole?

There, once again, like a bolt from heaven
(Why always three ?)
Thunders the soul-bell till earth is riven
'Twixt you and me.

A flash of crimson; in some far bourn
A star hath bled ;
Earth and the sky have met to mourn
Ismene, dead !

DORA SIGERSON SHORTER

499 *A Ballad of Marjorie*

'WHAT ails you that you look so pale,
O fisher of the sea ?'
''Tis for a mournful tale I own,
Fair maiden Marjorie.'

'What is the dreary tale to tell,
O toiler of the sea ?'
'I cast my net into the waves,
Sweet maiden Marjorie.

'I cast my net into the tide,
Before I made for home ;
Too heavy for my hands to raise,
I drew it through the foam.'

'What saw you that you look so pale,
Sad searcher of the sea ?'
'A dead man's body from the deep
My haul had brought to me !'

'And was he young, and was he fair?'
'Oh, cruel to behold!
In his white face the joy of life
Not yet was grown a-cold.'

'Oh, pale you are, and full of prayer
For one who sails the sea!'
'Because the dead looked up and spoke,
Poor maiden Marjorie.'

'What said he, that you seem so sad,
O fisher of the sea?
(Alack! I know it was my love,
Who fain would speak to me!')

'He said, "Beware a woman's mouth—
A rose that bears a thorn."'
'Ah, me! these lips shall smile no more
That gave my lover scorn.'

'He said, "Beware a woman's eyes,
They pierce you with their death."'
'Then falling tears shall make them blind
That robbed my dear of breath.'

'He said, "Beware a woman's hair—
A serpent's coil of gold."'
'Then will I shear the cruel locks
That crushed him in their fold.'

'He said, "Beware a woman's heart
As you would shun the reef."'
'So let it break within my breast,
And perish of my grief.'

'He raised his hands : a woman's name
  Thrice bitterly he cried :
My net had parted with the strain ;
  He vanished in the tide.'

'A woman's name! What name but mine,
  O fisher of the sea?'
'A woman's name, but not your name,
  Poor maiden Marjorie.'

500 *Ireland*

'TWAS the dream of a God,
    And the mould of His hand,
That you shook 'neath His stroke,
That you trembled and broke,
  To this beautiful land.

Here He loosed from His hold
  A brown tumult of wings,
Till the wind on the sea
Bore the strange melody
  Of an island that sings.

He made you all fair,
  You in purple and gold,
You in silver and green,
Till no eye that has seen
  Without love can behold.

I have left you behind
  In the path of the past,
With the white breath of flowers,
With the best of God's hours,
  I have left you at last.

501 *Last Eve*

LAST eve as I leaned from my lattice, looked out at the night
  Where the grey of the sea misted into the grey of the skies,
  Came with quick beating of wings and long, sorrowful cries
Beautiful birds, and I wept, being blind with their white.

How the wind's strong invisible hands beat on doorway and pane,
  And the sea seemed to writhe and roar in an anguish of thought !
  How the moon's frightened face looking down seemed to shun what she sought,
Hid so pale in cloud fingers to weep in a passion of rain !

They had come in the night and the storm, winging back to my breast,
  These hopes that were hopeless, these dreams that were ever as dreams ;
  Rending my heart with sharp beaks and their passionate screams,
Leashing my soul with the storm from its haven of rest.

Night long did I put them away, did they turn again,
Till the tumultuous waves bore them out in their creepy recess,
Tossed them back on the reef with a deadly pretence of caress;
Flung up by the hand of the sea, beaten back by the lash of the rain.

White birds, it is over and done, your last passion has paled;
The world has no place for your flight nor my heart for your screams.
O hopes that were hopeless, sweet dreams that were ever as dreams,
Let go! get back to your graves, you have fought and have failed.

502 *The Kine of my Father*

THE kine of my father, they are straying from my keeping;
The young goat's at mischief, but little can I do:
For all through the night did I hear the banshee keening;
O youth of my loving, and is it well with you?

All through the night sat my mother with my sorrow;
'Whisht, it is the storm, O one childeen of my heart!'
My hair with the wind, and my two hands clasped in anguish;
Black head of my darling! too long are we apart.

Were your grave at my feet, I would think it half a blessing ;
I could herd then the cattle, and drive the goats away ;
Many a Paternoster I would say for your safe keeping ;
I could sleep above your heart until the dawn of day.

I see you on the prairie, hot with thirst and faint with hunger ;
The head that I love lying low upon the sand.
The vultures shriek impatient, and the coyote dogs are howling,
Till the blood is pulsing cold within your clenching hand.

I see you on the waters, so white, so still, forsaken,
Your dear eyes unclosing beneath a foreign rain :
A plaything of the winds, you turn and drift unceasing;
No grave for your resting ; oh mine the bitter pain!

All through the night did I hear the banshee keening:
Somewhere you are dying, and nothing can I do ;
My hair with the wind, and my two hands clasped in anguish ;
Bitter is your trouble—and I am far from you.

503 *The Watcher in the Wood*

DEEP in the wood's recesses cool
I see the fairy dancers glide,
In cloth of gold, in gown of green,
My lord and lady side by side.

But who has hung from leaf to leaf,
From flower to flower, a silken twine—
A cloud of grey that holds the dew
In globes of clear enchanted wine?

Or stretches far from branch to branch,
From thorn to thorn, in diamond rain,
Who caught the cup of crystal pure
And hung so fair the shining chain?

'Tis death, the spider, in his net,
Who lures the dancers as they glide,
In cloth of gold, in gown of green,
My lord and lady side by side.

504 *The Heart of a Maid*

IN the heart of a rose
Lies the heart of a maid;
If you be not afraid
You will wear it. Who knows?

In the pink of its bloom,
Lay your lips to her cheek;
Since a rose cannot speak,
And you gain the perfume.

If the dews on the leaf
Are the tears from her eyes;
If she withers and dies,
Why, you have the belief,

That a rose cannot speak,
Though the heart of a maid
In its bosom must fade,
And with fading must break.

DORA SIGERSON SHORTER

505 *Clouds*

LAUGHTER and song for my cheer,
  Life is so fair.
None so happy as I
  Anywhere ;
Birds in the woods carol clear,
White clouds in the sky.

Song silent and brow with a frown,
  Why is this so ?
Guiltless am I
  Would you know,
The lark from the heavens drops down ;
Grey clouds in the sky.

Sighing and tears for my sorrow,
  Life is so drear,
None so weary as I,
  'Tis a mere
Waste of love, and a wish for to-morrow—
Black night in the sky.

506 *Love in my Arms lies Sleeping*

ROSES red for the fair young head to weave a crown,
  Let them be half blown,
For a rose in June it will fade too soon to gold and brown.
For thee my own
The fairest blossoms in all love's land, for that small hot hand,

And a bird to sing all the sweet day through,
Lest fear should wake in the heart of you,
And I hear my own heart's beating;
Wild roses red for the fair gold head,
Love in my arms lies sleeping.

Lilies fair for the wind-blown hair,
It were better so
Than a blossom dead,
And a rose's thorn; but the fresh glad morn brings
breath of snow.
Hath summer fled?
Hath winter come when I dreamt it spring?
Is my sweet bird dead that he does not sing?
I hear but my heart's sad weeping.
Loose and cold is thy soft hands' hold;
Love in my arms lies sleeping.

507 *The Enemies*

I COULD have sung as sweet as any lark
Who in unfettered skies doth find him blest,
And sings to leaning angels prayer and praise,
For in God's garden the most lowly nest.

But came the cares—a grey and stinging throng
Of liliputian foes, whose thrust and dart
Did blind my eyes and hush my song in tears;
Their brushing wings flung poison to my heart.

I could have fought, in truth, a goodly fight,
Braved death, nor feared defeat before one foe;
Against these puny cares I strive in vain,
They sting my soul unto its overthrow.

JAMES STEPHENS

508 *The Whisperer*

THE moon was round,
  And as I walked along
There was no sound,
Save where the wind with long
Low hushes whispered to the ground
  A snatch of song.

No thought had I
Save that the moon was fair,
And fair the sky,
And God was everywhere.
I chanted as the wind went by
  A poet's prayer.

Then came a voice—
'Why is it that you praise
And thus rejoice,
O stranger to the ways
Of Providence ? God has no choice
  In this sad maze.

'His law He laid
Down at the dread beginning,
When He made
The world and set it spinning,
And His casual hand betrayed
  Us into sinning.

'I fashion you,
And then for weal and woe,
My business through,
I care not how ye go,
Or struggle, win or lose, nor do
  I want to know.

'Is no appeal,
For I am far from sight,
And cannot feel
The rigour of your plight;
And if ye faint just when ye kneel,
  That, too, is right.

'Then do not sing,
O poet in the night,
That everything
Is beautiful and right.
What if some wind come now and fling
  At thee in spite?'

All in amaze
I listened to the tone
Mocking my praise:
And then I heard the groan
That old tormented nature did upraise
  From tree and stone.

And as I went
I heard it once again,
That harsh lament:
And fire came to my brain;
Deep anger unto me was lent
  To write this strain.

JAMES STEPHENS

509 *The Shell*

AND then I pressed the shell
Close to my ear
And listened well,
And straightway like a bell
Came low and clear
The slow, sad murmur of far distant seas,
Whipped by an icy breeze
Upon a shore
Wind-swept and desolate.
It was a sunless strand that never bore
The footprint of a man,
Nor felt the weight
Since time began
Of any human quality or stir
Save what the dreary winds and waves incur.
And in the hush of waters was the sound
Of pebbles rolling round,
For ever rolling with a hollow sound.
And bubbling sea-weeds as the waters go
Swish to and fro
Their long, cold tentacles of slimy grey.
There was no day,
Nor ever came a night
Setting the stars alight
To wonder at the moon:
Was twilight only and the frightened croon,
Smitten to whimpers, of the dreary wind
And waves that journeyed blind—
And then I loosed my ear—oh, it was sweet
To hear a cart go jolting down the street!

ELINOR SWEETMAN

510 *The House Desolate*

ROOF of our fathers, belovèd, behold we return to thee
Joyful, remembering our mutual anguish at parting:
How thy doors drawn apart like the lips of a desolate woman,
Dumb, let us forth; how thy windows appealed to the heavens:
'Restore them, O God!' and thy stairway, with hollows introdden
By the feet of our fathers at rest and their burden of honours,
Clung to our feet; yea the stones in the walls cried: 'Stay with us!'
Stones many-witnessing, worn as the bed of a stream is
Worn with the life of the waters it holds in its bosom;
Stones that have cradled us, stones that shall coffin us, hail to ye!

Mother unchilded, our Niobe, lo! we return to thee!
Daughter of sorrows, have comfort, behold we return to thee!
Where is thy welcome?
What is this thing?—art thou deaf, art thou blind, O our Mother?
Behold, our hounds in thy halls, and our doves in thy laurel
Call to thee, cry as of yore, and in laughter and music
Voices of children ascend with thy chorister-starlings;

Where is thine answer of old ?—yea, what hath gone out of thee !
What lieth dead in thee ?—how art thou altered and alien !
We are not changed, we are loyal ; as waves of an ocean
Yearn to the shore, so we yearn to thee, home of our fathers ;
Now we behold thee, thou seemest not shrunken or dwindled,
Shell of our race, and its tomb, we revere thee for ever !

But thou, O desired and belov'd—O thou bourne of our wishes !—
Lone hast thou stood over-long, over-long hast thou waited,
Sealed are thy senses of stone, and thy being dis-humanised
Owns us no more, or at best with a dim recognition ;
As the hound by his masters forsaken, in piteous expectancy
Waiteth the voice and the touch that are music and balm to him,
Broken by loneliness waiteth—they in their season
Eager of welcome return through the years, and caress him.
Lo ! he is dulled and confused : with a blunted remembrance
Vaguely he greets them at first, and remaineth despondent.
Thus we return to thee, roof of our fathers, belovèd,
Eager of welcome, rejoicing ;—but thou, O most faithful,
Thou hast forgotten us !

ELINOR SWEETMAN

511 *Pastoral of the Orchard*

COLIN

HOW looked your love, sweet Shepherd, yestereven,
When under apple-boughs ye stole a tryst,
While Hesper held the glowing gates of heaven
Ere colder stars besprent its amethyst?
Ah! happy one, how looked those lids ye kissed,
And seemed her blush of half its rose bereaven
By wan green glimmer and by meadow mist,
From grassy floor, with leaves enshadowed o'er,
Dim filtering through the seven-score trees and seven
Of the orchard by the shore?

SHEPHERD

Colin, the grass was grey and wet the sod
O'er which I heard her velvet footfall come;
But heaven, where yet no pallid crescent rode,
Flowered in fire behind the bloomless plum;
There stirred no wing nor wind, the wood was dumb,
Only blown roses shook their leaves abroad
On stems more tender than an infant's thumb—
Soft leaves, soft hued, and curled like Cupid's lip;
And each dim tree shed sweetness over me,
From honey-dews that breathless boughs let slip
In the orchard by the sea.

COLIN

Yea, Shepherd, I have seen how blossoms fold,
And waded deep, where deep an orchard grows;
But what of her whose sweet ye leave untold,
Whose step fell softer than a south-wind blows?

ELINOR SWEETMAN

What of her beauty?—saw ye not unrolled
O'er little ears and throat a twine of gold?
And wore her lip the blown or budded rose?
O did she reach through balmy pear and peach,
White arms for greeting—did ye heaven hold
In the orchard by the beach?

Shepherd

Nay, Colin, but I heard through walls of laurel
A tide impassioned brimming silent spaces,
Guessed its soft weight, and knew its hoarded coral
Given and withdrawn to shyer farther places;
Methought each wave shook loose in long embraces
Wild trees and tangle over shells auroral,
And never wave but held all heaven's faces,
And seemed to sweep a mirrored moon asleep,
To break and blanch among the wet wood-sorrel,
In the orchard by the deep.

Colin

O Shepherd, leave to speak of ocean-brede,
And crescents gliding o'er the cold sea-floor;
All men may watch a risen tide recede,
And scarlet secrets of the deep explore.
Were not your nymph's fair face and footstep more
Than foam and flake within a garden weed?
More sweet than hymning seas her sweet love-lore?
Her hair, her hand, more soft than feathers fanned
From sleeping doves, by small winds newly freed
In the orchard by the strand?

ELINOR SWEETMAN

Shepherd

O dull of soul and senseless! get thee gone!
What though the lyre of him who loves be strung
To deep of heaven and deep of sea—alone
The deep of love is ever more unsung!
Such music lieth hush upon the tongue.
No, by the gods! not thou, nor anyone
Shall force these stammering lips to do it wrong,
Nor babble o'er from common door to door
What I, by favour of my gods, have known
In the orchard by the shore!

512 *To a Nightingale*

MINSTREL unseen, who singest to the skies,
Hope not to make the vestal night pulsate
To such wild strains of music passionate;
For she on Heaven hath fixed her virgin eyes,
And, deaf to thine entrancing melodies,
Doth quiring angels, silent, contemplate,
While, hid in shadow, thou may'st sing and wait,
To thine own longing making sad replies.

He is thy love! O see, at Heaven's edge
Where trees expectant stand along the ridge,
Thy song is crowned ere yet its ardour sinks;—
Dawn leans her down through golden window-bars
And flings with shining hands her wreathed pinks
Among the silver lilies of the stars.

ELINOR SWEETMAN

513 *Fairy Song*

WHEN daisies close and poppies nod,
  And meadow grass to earth is laid,
And fairies dance on moonlit sod,
  Or quaff of dewdrops in the shade,
Come ! gentle dreams, in velvet shod,
  And foot it round each sleeping maid.

Come softly hither, dove-winged flock,
  And on their pillows make your nest,
And light as down from puff-ball clock
  Let kisses on their eyes be prest,
Then sit upon the couch and rock
  Each tender little heart to rest.

JOHN M. SYNGE

514 *Beg-Innish*

BRING Kateen-beug and Maurya Jude
  To dance in Beg-Innish,
And when the lads (they're in Dunquin)
  Have sold their crabs and fish,
Wave fawny shawls and call them in,
And call the little girls who spin,
And seven weavers from Dunquin,
  To dance in Beg-Innish.

JOHN M. SYNGE

I'll play you jigs, and Maurice Kean,
  Where nets are laid to dry,
I've silken strings would draw a dance
  From girls are lame or shy;
Four strings I've brought from Spain and France
To make your long men skip and prance,
Till stars look out to see the dance
  Where nets are laid to dry.

We'll have no priest or peeler in
  To dance in Beg-Innish;
But we'll have drink from M'riarty Jim
  Rowed round while gannets fish,
A keg with porter to the brim,
That every lad may have his whim,
Till we up sails with M'riarty Jim
  And sail from Beg-Innish.

HERBERT TRENCH

515 *From 'Deirdre Wedded'* (84)

VOICE OF CIR

out of a century more remote, but unknown

AS a horseman breaks on a sea-gulf enwomb'd in
  the amber woods
Where tide is at ebb, and out on the airy brim,
Glass'd upon cloud and azure, stand multitudes
Of the flame-white people of gulls—to the sky-line dim

All breast to the sun—and his hoofs expand the
desolate strait
Into fevers of snows and ocean-wandering cries:
Even so, chanters divine, in some woman's fate
At coming of him to be loved do her dreams arise.

And Deirdre the exquisite virgin pale as the coat of
swans
Took the flame of love in her heart at the time of dew
And clad her in ragged wool from a coffer of bronze
And walked in the chill of night, for her soul was new.

'Why thick with the berries of sweetness, ye barren
thorns of the spring?
I could drink up this tempest cold, as a burning wine.
Why laugh, my grief, for art thou not bride of a king,
And the drinkers drink to a couch array'd to be thine?'

Where the wounded toss without sleep in the warrior's
hive of stones—
The house Bron Bhearg—she laid her cheek to the
wall
And bless'd them by stealth, with no pang at the
sound of groans,
Having that in her rich heart which could heal
them all.

To the fortress-gate on the steep that looketh toward
Creeve Roe
She fled, and spied not a sling-cast off the flare
Of a torch, and the skull fixed over the gate. And lo,
To the right-hand watchmen paced by the water
there.

And the shag-hair'd guard, with a mock, laid spears
in their passage-house
Athwart, for who was this phantom over the
grass
Like a filcher of food? And Deirdre uncover'd her
brows
And cried: 'I am Deirdre!' And sullen they gave
her the pass.

And towards Creeve Roe the dip of the cuckoo's vale
was dark
To blindness. She pluck'd her steps on that miry
road
Through copses alive with storm, till at length a
spark
Show'd the forge where the smith on the heroes' way
abode.

Now Culann the smith was wise; and leaping her
spirit stirr'd
With the soft roar of his hide-wing'd fire as it
soar'd:
'Has the son of Usnach pass'd?' 'Yea, gone back!'
With the word
He smote on a ribbon of iron to make him a sword.

And the argentine din of anvils behind her steadily
dwindling
The woman fled to the wastes, till she came to a
Thorn
Black, by the well of a God, with stars therein
kindling
And over it rags fluttering from boughs forlorn.

And she knelt and shore with a knife a lock of her deathless hair,
And leash'd the black-shuddering branch with that tress, and pray'd :
'Sloe-tree, thou snow of the darkness, O hear my prayer,
And thou, black Depth, bubble-breather, vouchsafe thine aid ;

'From Connachar's eyes of love let me hide as a grey mole,
Sons of the Earth's profound, that no weeper spurn !
I have look'd on a face, and its kindness ravish't my soul,
But deliverance pass'd ; unto you for escape I turn !'

And loud as the sloven starlings in winter whistle and swarm
Came the banish'd of Usnach nigh, thrice fifty strong
As they drove Eman away on that night of storm
And Naois spoke with his brothers behind the throng :

'O, Aillean, O, Ardan, hark ! What cry was that ? For some cry
Rang on my soul's shield ; hark ! hear ye it now ?'
But they rein'd not their weary chariots, shouting reply
'It was fate, 'twas the curs'd hag that is crouch'd on a bough !'

Tossing they drove out of sight, Naois the last, and his hood
Rain-dripping mantled the wind. One ran like a roe,
And call'd on that great name from the night-bound wood,
'Stay, long-awaited, stay ! for with thee I go !'

And his brothers cried, 'Halt not! the host of the air makes moan
Or a gang of the wild geese, going back to the lake.'
But Naois rear'd up the deep-ribb'd Sron, 'Good Sron,
Thou and I needs must turn for our fame's sake.'

And he heard a voice: 'Son of Usnach, take me to be thy wife!'
He bent from the withers, the blaze of her trembling drew
The breath from his lips and the beat from his heart's life;
And he said, 'Who art thou, Queen?' But himself knew,

And mutter'd 'Return, return, unto him that I hate. For know
Him least of all I rob, least of all that live!'
But she cried: 'Am I then a colt, that ye snare from a foe
With a bridle's shaking? I am mine own to give.'

'Thy beauty would crumble away in the spate of my wild nights,
And famine rake out thine embers, the lean paw
Of jeopardy find thee. He is not rich in delights
Whose harp is the grey fell in the winter's flaw.'

And she laid her arm round the neck of Sron: 'Hast heard
Horse swollen-vein'd from battle, insulter of death—
Whose back is only a perch for the desert bird—
Whose fore-hooves fight—whose passage is torn with teeth,

'And dost thou not shudder off the knees of a master deaf
To the grief of the weak?' And the lad, deeply-moved, rejoins:
'Mount then, O woman, behind me,'—and light as a leaf
Drawing her up from his foot to the smoking loins

Shook loose the ox-hide bridle. Even as the great gull dives
From Muilréa's moon-glittering peak when the sky is bare,
Scraped naked by nine days' wind, and sweepingly drives
Over night-blurr'd gulfs and the long glens of the air,

And feels up-tossing his breast an exhaustless breath bear on
Spouted from isleless ocean to aid his flight—
So fiercely, so steadily gallop'd the sinewy Sron,
Braced by that double burden to more delight.

Though his mane wrapp'd a wounded bridle-hand, fast, fast
As giddy foam-weltering waters dash'd by the hoof
Flee away from the weirs of Callan, even so pass'd
Dark plains away to the world's edge behind and aloof. . . .

516 *Maurya's Song*

RUSHES that grow by the black water
When will I see you more?
When will the sorrowful heart forget you,

Land of the green, green shore?
When will the fields and the small cabin
See us more
In the old country?

What is to me all the gold yonder?
She that bore me is gone.
Knees that dandled and hands that blessed me
Colder than any stone;
Stranger to me than the face of strangers
Are my own
In the old country.

Vein o' my heart, from the lone mountain
The smoke of the turf will die
And the stream that sang to the young childer
Run down alone from the sky:
On the door-stone, grass,—and the cloud lying
Where they lie
In the old country.

CHARLES WEEKES

517

Titan

WHAT matters where the great God flings
Down on earth's floor thy thinking clay,
If thou canst rise and live to-day
The life of emperors and kings!

So take thy soul and keep it sane;
And, treading firm the green earth-sod,
Look upward from that place to God,
That He shall see thy soul again.

There undejected, there unhurled
Asunder—sick with mortal change;
Self-held from star to star to range,
Or one with all the working world.

O king of kings and emperors!
Though vagabond of night and morn—
Some dusty quarry-fellow born
To walk beside a tattered horse.

518 *Think*

THINK, the ragged turf-boy urges
O'er the dusty road his asses;
Think, on the sea-shore far the lonely
Heron wings along the sand;
Think, in woodland under oak-boughs
Now the streaming sunbeam passes:
And bethink thee thou art servant
To the same all-moving hand.

WILLIAM BUTLER YEATS

519 *The Song of Wandering Ængus*

I WENT out to the hazel wood,
Because a fire was in my head,
And cut and peeled a hazel wand,
And hooked a berry to a thread;
And when white moths were on the wing,
And moth-like stars were flickering out,
I dropped the berry in a stream
And caught a little silver trout.

When I had laid it on the floor
  I went to blow the fire a-flame,
But something rustled on the floor,
  And someone called me by my name:
It had become a glimmering girl
  With apple blossom in her hair
Who called me by my name and ran
  And faded through the brightening air.

Though I am old with wandering
  Through hollow lands and hilly lands,
I will find out where she has gone,
  And kiss her lips and take her hands;
And walk among long dappled grass,
  And pluck till time and times are done
The silver apples of the moon,
  The golden apples of the sun.

520 *The Lake Isle of Innisfree*

I WILL arise and go now, and go to Innisfree,
  And a small cabin build there, of clay and wattles made;
Nine bean rows will I have there, a hive for the honey bee,
And live alone in the bee-loud glade.

And I shall have some peace there, for peace comes dropping slow,
Dropping from the veils of the morning to where the cricket sings;
There midnight's all a glimmer, and noon a purple glow,
And evening full of the linnet's wings.

I will arise and go now, for always night and
day
I hear lake water lapping with low sounds by the
shore;
While I stand on the roadway, or on the pavements
grey,
I hear it in the deep heart's core.

521 *The Happy Townland*

THERE'S many a strong farmer
Whose heart would break in two,
If he could see the townland
That we are riding to;
Boughs have their fruit and blossom
At all times of the year;
Rivers are running over
With red beer and brown beer.
An old man plays the bagpipes
In a golden and silver wood;
Queens, their eyes blue like the ice,
Are dancing in a crowd.

The little fox he murmured,
'O what of the world's bane?'
The sun was laughing sweetly,
The moon plucked at my rein;
But the little red fox murmured,
'O do not pluck at his rein,
He is riding to the townland
That is the world's bane.'

When their hearts are so high
  That they would come to blows,
They unhook their heavy swords
  From golden and silver boughs;
But all that are killed in battle
  Awaken to life again:
It is lucky that their story
  Is not known among men.
For O, the strong farmers
  That would let the spade lie,
Their hearts would be like a cup
  That somebody had drunk dry.

The little fox he murmured,
  'O what of the world's bane?'
The sun was laughing sweetly,
  The moon plucked at my rein;
But the little red fox murmured,
  'O do not pluck at his rein,
He is riding to the townland
  That is the world's bane.'

Michael will unhook his trumpet
  From a bough overhead,
And blow a little noise
  When the supper has been spread.
Gabriel will come from the water
  With a fish-tail, and talk
Of wonders that have happened
  On wet roads where men walk,
And lift up an old horn
  Of hammered silver, and drink
Till he has fallen asleep
  Upon the starry brink.

The little fox he murmured,
  'O what of the world's bane?'
The sun was laughing sweetly,
  The moon plucked at my rein;
But the little red fox murmured,
  'O do not pluck at his rein,
He is riding to the townland
  That is the world's bane.'

522 *The Withering of the Boughs*

I CRIED when the moon was murmuring to the birds,
'Let peewit call and curlew cry where they will,
I long for your merry and tender and pitiful words,
For the roads are unending, and there is no place to my mind.'
The honey-pale moon lay low on the sleepy hill,
And I fell asleep upon lonely Echtge of streams.
No boughs have withered because of the wintry wind;
The boughs have withered because I have told them my dreams.

I know of the leafy paths that the witches take,
Who come with their crowns of pearl and their spindles of wool,
And their secret smile, out of the depths of the lake;
I know where a dim moon drifts, where the Danaan kind
Wind and unwind their dances when the light grows cool

On the island lawns, their feet where the pale foam
gleams.
No boughs have withered because of the wintry wind;
The boughs have withered because I have told them
my dreams.

I know of the sleepy country, where swans fly round
Coupled with golden chains, and sing as they fly.
A king and a queen are wandering there, and the
sound
Has made them so happy and hopeless, so deaf and so
blind
With wisdom, they wander till all the years have
gone by;
I know, and the curlew and peewit on Echtge of
streams.
No boughs have withered because of the wintry wind;
The boughs have withered because I have told them
my dreams.

ELLA YOUNG

523 *Cleena* (85)

PALE, in the twilight, the crested waves are falling
On a lone shore where never a sea-bird strays;
Softly the twilight wind is calling, calling,
Calling for Cleena of the olden days.

Once a thousand lovers sang her praises,
Wove her name in chant and storied rann;
Cleena, for whose sake the sea-god raises,
Wave on wave, his crested foam-white clan.

Gods and heroes once the battle-gear uplifted
  All for Cleena of the curling, golden head;
O'er her beauty now the dust has drifted,
  The songs are silent, and her lovers dead.

Only where waves in shadowy foam are falling,
  Falling, falling ever, with a sound of tears,
Earth and sea a vanished joy recalling,
  Mourn for Cleena and the long-forgotten years.

Mournful wind, your grief cannot avail her.
  Sea-foam drifting, drifting through the night—
She has peace and silence, why bewail her?
  Cleena! Cleena! dead, forgotten quite!

524 *The Wind from the West*

BLOW high, blow low,
  O wind from the west:
You come from the country
  I love the best.

O say have the lilies
  Yet lifted their heads
Above the lake-water
  That ripples and spreads?

Do the little sedges
  Still shake with delight
And whisper together
  All through the night?

Have the mountains the purple
  I used to love,
And peace about them,
  Around and above?

O wind from the west,
  Blow high, blow low,
You come from the country
  I loved long ago!

525 *My Lady of Dreams*

ONE night the beauty of the stars
  Made magic for me white and still:
I climbed the road above the hill,
The road no waking footstep mars.

I met my Lady in the wood,
  The black pine wood above the hill,
  Dream-fair her beauty, white and still;
I knelt as one before the Rood.

White Dream that makes my life a war
  Of wild desire and baffled will,
  Once more my soul with beauty fill,
Rise through the darkness, O my Star!

526 *A Dream-garden*

WILL you come one day to see me
  In my House of Dream?
I'll light the way before you
  With a rainbow gleam.

ELLA YOUNG

You'll see the cloud-walled garden
  Where my lilies grow,
And count the sunflowers swaying
  In a golden row.

The south wind blows the rose leaves
  Before the sun,
In a cloud of crimson sweetness
  When day is done.

And the stars come out a-flutter
  Like moths white-winged
Among my apple branches
  All flame be-ringed.

Flame-fair the apples shimmer
  And change and glow,
And nowhere but in cloud-land
  Such apples grow.

O come and see my garden
  And my House of Dream,
I'll light the way before you
  With a rainbow-gleam!

ANONYMOUS

527 *The Boyne Water* (86)

JULY the First, of a morning clear, one thousand six hundred and ninety,
King William did his men prepare, of thousands he had thirty ;
To fight King James and all his foes, encamped near the Boyne Water,
He little fear'd though two to one, their multitudes to scatter.

King William call'd his officers, saying : 'Gentlemen, mind your station,
And let your valour here be shown before this Irish nation ;
My brazen walls let no man break, and your subtle foes you'll scatter,
Be sure you show them good English play as you go over the water.'

Both foot and horse they marched on, intending them to batter,
But the brave Duke Schomberg he was shot as he cross'd over the water.
When that King William did observe the brave Duke Schomberg falling,
He rein'd his horse with a heavy heart, on the Enniskilleners calling :

'What will you do for me, brave boys—see yonder
men retreating?
Our enemies encourag'd are and English drums are
beating;'
He says, 'My boys, feel no dismay at the losing of
one commander,
For God shall be our king this day, and I'll be general
under.'

Within four yards of our fore-front, before a shot was
fired,
A sudden snuff they got that day, which little they
desired;
For horse and man fell to the ground, and some hung
in their saddle;
Others turn'd up their forked ends, which we call
'coup de ladle.'

Prince Eugene's regiment was the next, on our right
hand advanced,
Into a field of standing wheat, where Irish horses
pranced—
But the brandy ran so in their heads, their senses all
did scatter,
They little thought to leave their bones that day at
the Boyne Water.

Both men and horse lay on the ground, and many
there lay bleeding;
I saw no sickles there that day—but, sure, there was
sharp shearing.

Now, praise God, all true Protestants, and heaven's
and earth's Creator,
For the deliverance that He sent our enemies to scatter.

The Church's foes will pine away, like churlish-
hearted Nabal,
For our deliverer came this day like the great
Zorobabel.

So praise God, all true Protestants, and I will say no
further,
But had the Papists gain'd the day there would have
been open murder.
Although King James and many more were ne'er
that way inclined,
It was not in their power to stop what the rabble
they designed.

528 *Shule Aroon* (87)

I WISH I were on yonder hill,
'Tis there I'd sit and cry my fill,
Till every tear would turn a mill,
Is go dee tu mavourneen slaun!
Shule, shule, shule aroon,
Shule go suckir, agus shule go cuin,
Shule go deen durrus augus eiligh lume,
Is go dee tu mavourneen slaun!

I'll sell my rock, I'll sell my reel,
I'll sell my only spinning-wheel,
To buy for my love a sword of steel,
Is go dee tu mavourneen slaun!
Chorus—Shule, shule, shule aroon, etc.

I'll dye my petticoats, I'll dye them red,
And round the world I'll beg my bread,
Until my parents shall wish me dead,
Is go dee tu mavourneen slaun !
Chorus—Shule, shule, shule aroon, etc.

I wish, I wish, I wish in vain,
I wish I had my heart again,
And vainly think I'd not complain,
Is go dee tu mavourneen slaun !
Chorus—Shule, shule, shule aroon, etc.

But now my love has gone to France,
To try his fortune to advance ;
If he e'er come back 'tis but a chance,
Is go dee tu mavourneen slaun !
Chorus—Shule, shule, shule aroon, etc.

529 *The Cruiskeen Lawn* (88)

LET the farmer praise his grounds,
Let the huntsman praise his hounds,
The shepherd his dew-scented lawn ;
But I, more blest than they,
Spend each happy night and day
With my charming little cruiskeen lawn,[1] lawn, lawn,
My charming little cruiskeen lawn.
Gra ma chree ma cruiskeen,
Slainté geal mavourneen,
's gra machree a cooleen bawn.

[1] Ir. *An Cruscín Lán*—The little full jug.

Gra machree ma cruiskeen,
Slainté geal mavourneen,
Gra machree a cooleen bawn, bawn, bawn,
's gra machree a cooleen bawn.

Immortal and divine,
Great Bacchus, god of wine,
Create me by adoption your son ;
In hope that you'll comply
My glass shall ne'er run dry,
Nor my smiling little cruiskeen lawn, etc.

And when grim death appears,
In a few but pleasant years,
To tell me that my glass has run ;
I'll say, Begone, you knave,
For bold Bacchus gave me leave,
To take another cruiskeen lawn, etc.

Then fill your glasses high,
Let's not part with lips a-dry,
Though the lark now proclaims it is
dawn ;
And since we can't remain,
May we shortly meet again,
To fill another cruiskeen lawn, etc.

530 *The Wearin' o' the Green* (89)

O PADDY dear, an' did ye hear the news that's
goin' round ?
The shamrock is by law forbid to grow on Irish
ground !

No more St. Patrick's Day we'll keep, his colour can't
be seen,
For there's a cruel law agin the wearin' o' the Green!
I met wid Napper Tandy, and he took me by the hand,
And he said, 'How's poor ould Ireland, and how does
she stand?'
She's the most disthressful country that iver yet was seen,
For they're hangin' men an' women there for the
wearin' o' the Green.

And if the colour we must wear is England's cruel Red,
Let it remind us of the blood that Ireland has shed;
Then pull the shamrock from your hat, and throw it
on the sod,
And never fear, 'twill take root there, tho' under foot
'tis trod!
When law can stop the blades of grass from growin'
as they grow,
And when the leaves in summer-time their colour
dare not show,
Then I will change the colour, too, I wear in my
caubeen,
But till that day, plase God, I'll stick to wearin' o' the
Green.

531 *The Shan Van Vocht* (90)

OH! the French are on the sea,
Says the Shan Van Vocht;[1]
The French are on the sea,
Says the Shan Van Vocht;
Oh! the French are in the Bay,

[1] Ir. *Sean Bhean Bhocht*, The poor old woman—Ireland.

They'll be here without delay,
And the Orange will decay,
  Says the Shan Van Vocht.
    Oh ! the French are in the Bay,
    They'll be here by break of day,
    And the Orange will decay,
      Says the Shan Van Vocht.

And where will they have their camp ?
  Says the Shan Van Vocht ;
Where will they have their camp ?
  Says the Shan Van Vocht ;
On the Curragh of Kildare,
The boys they will be there,
With their pikes in good repair,
  Says the Shan Van Vocht.
    To the Curragh of Kildare
    The boys they will repair,
    And Lord Edward will be there,
      Says the Shan Van Vocht.

Then what will the yeomen do?
  Says the Shan Van Vocht ;
What will the yeomen do ?
  Says the Shan Van Vocht ;
What should the yeomen do
But throw off the Red and Blue,
And swear that they'll be true
  To the Shan Van Vocht ?
    What should the yeomen do
    But throw off the red and blue,
    And swear that they'll be true
      To the Shan Van Vocht ?

And what colour will they wear?
  Says the Shan Van Vocht;
What colour will they wear?
  Says the Shan Van Vocht;
What colour should be seen
Where our fathers' homes have been,
But our own immortal Green?
  Says the Shan Van Vocht.
    What colour should be seen
    Where our fathers' homes have been,
    But our own immortal Green?
      Says the Shan Van Vocht.

And will Ireland then be free?
  Says the Shan Van Vocht;
Will Ireland then be free?
  Says the Shan Van Vocht;
Yes! Ireland shall be free,
From the centre to the sea;
Then hurrah for Liberty!
  Says the Shan Van Vocht.
    Yes! Ireland shall be free,
    From the centre to the sea;
    Then hurrah for Liberty!
      Says the Shan Van Vocht.

532 *Rory O'Moore* (91)

ON the green hills of Ulster the white cross waves
  high,
And the beacon of war throws its flames to the sky;
Now the taunt and the threat let the coward endure,
Our hope is in God and in Rory O'Moore!

Do you ask why the beacon and banner of war
On the mountains of Ulster are seen from afar!
'Tis the signal our rights to regain and secure,
Through God and our Lady and Rory O'Moore!

For the merciless Scots, with their creed and their
swords,
With war in their bosoms, and peace in their words,
Have sworn the bright light of our faith to obscure,
But our hope is in God and Rory O'Moore.

Oh! lives there a traitor who'd shrink from the strife,
Who, to add to the length of a forfeited life,
His country, his kindred, his faith would abjure?
No! we'll strike for our God and for Rory O'Moore.

533 *The Lamentation of Hugh Reynolds* (92)

MY name it is Hugh Reynolds, I come of honest
parents,
Near Cavan I was born, as plainly you may see;
By loving of a maid, one Catherine MacCabe,
My life has been betrayed; she's a dear maid to
me.[1]

The country were bewailing my doleful situation,
But still I'd expectation this maid would set me
free;
But, oh! she was ungrateful, her parents proved
deceitful,
And though I loved her faithful, she's a dear maid
to me.

[1] An Irish idiom, meaning—cost him dearly.

ANONYMOUS

Young men and tender maidens, throughout this
Irish nation,
Who hear my lamentation, I hope you'll pray for
me ;
The truth I will unfold, that my precious blood she
sold,
In the grave I must lie cold ; she's a dear maid to
me.

For now my glass is run, and the hour it is
come,
And I must die for love and the height of loyalty :
I thought it was no harm to embrace her in my
arms,
Or take her from her parents ; but she's a dear maid
to me.

Adieu, my loving father, and you, my tender mother,
Farewell, my dearest brother, who has suffered sore
for me ;
With irons I'm surrounded, in grief I lie confounded,
By perjury unbounded ! she's a dear maid to
me.

Now, I can say no more ; to the Law-board[1] I must
go,
There to take the last farewell of my friends and
counterie ;
May the angels, shining bright, receive my soul this
night,
And convey me into heaven to the blessed Trinity.

[1] Gallows.

ANONYMOUS

534 *My Connor*

OH ! weary's on money—and weary's on wealth,
And sure we don't want them while we have our health ;
'Twas they tempted Connor over the sea,
And I lost my lover, my cushla machree.
Smiling—beguiling—cheering—endearing—
Oh ! dearly I lov'd him, and he loved me.
By each other delighted—and fondly united—
My heart's in the grave with my cushla machree.

My Connor was handsome, good-humoured, and tall,
At hurling and dancing the best of them all ;
But when he came courting beneath our old tree,
His voice was like music—my cushla machree.
Smiling, etc.

So true was his heart and so artless his mind,
He could not think ill of the worst of mankind,
He went bail for his cousin who ran beyond sea,
And all his debts fell on my cushla machree.
Smiling, etc.

Yet still I told Connor that I'd be his bride,—
In sorrow or death not to stir from his side.
He said he could ne'er bring misfortune on me,
But sure I'd be rich with my cushla machree.
Smiling, etc.

The morning he left us I ne'er will forget,
Not an eye in our village but with crying was wet.
'Don't cry any more, mavourneen,' said he,
'For I will return to my cushla machree.'
Smiling, etc.

Sad as I felt then, hope mixed with my care,
Alas! I have nothing left now but despair.
His ship—it went down in the midst of the sea,
And its wild waves roll over my cushla machree.
  Smiling—beguiling—cheering—endearing—
  Oh! dearly I lov'd him and he loved me.
  By each other delighted—and fondly united—
  My heart's in the grave with my cushla machree.

535 *The Geraldine's Daughter*

SPEAK low!—speak low—the banshee is crying;
  Hark! hark to the echo!—she's dying! 'she's dying!'
What shadow flits dark'ning the face of the water?
'Tis the swan of the lake—'Tis the Geraldine's Daughter.

Hush, hush! have you heard what the banshee said?
Oh! list to the echo! she's dead! 'she's dead!'
No shadow now dims the face of the water;
Gone, gone is the wraith of the Geraldine's Daughter.

The step of yon train is heavy and slow,
There's wringing of hands, there's breathing of woe;
What melody rolls over mountain and water?
'Tis the funeral chant for the Geraldine's Daughter.

The requiem sounds like the plaintive moan
Which the wind makes over the sepulchre's stone;
'Oh, why did she die? our heart's blood had bought her!
Oh, why did she die, the Geraldine's Daughter?'

The thistle-beard floats—the wild roses wave
With the blast that sweeps over the newly-made grave;
The stars dimly twinkle, and hoarse falls the water,
While night-birds are wailing the Geraldine's Daughter.

536 *The Drynán Dhun*[1]

MY love he is fairer than a soft summer's day,
And his breath is far sweeter than new-mown hay,
And his hair shines like gold when revived by the sun,
And the name that they give him's the Drynán Dhun.

My boy he is gone to cross over the main,
May God send him safe to his true love again,
For I wander all day, until night-time comes on,
And I sleep on the leaves of the Drynán Dhun.

If I had a small cot on the ocean to row
I would follow my darling wherever he'd go;
I'd rather have my true love to sport and to play,
Than all the gold treasures on the land and the sea.

My love he is handsome and fair to be seen,
With his red rosy cheeks he is fit for a queen,
With his two sparkling eyes as bright as the sun,
And he is fair as the blossom of the Drynán Dhun.

Impatient I wait for my love to return,
And for his long absence I never cease to mourn,
I will join with the small birds when the summer comes on,
For to welcome the blossom of the Drynán Dhun.

[1] The Sloe-tree: metaphorically—a small dark Man.

ANONYMOUS

537 *Lament of Morian Shehone for Miss Mary Bourke*

From the Irish

'THERE'S darkness in thy dwelling-place and silence reigns above,
And Mary's voice is heard no more, like the soft voice of love,
Yes! thou art gone, my Mary dear! and Morian Shehone
Is left to sing his song of woe, and wail for thee alone.
Oh snow-white were thy virtues!—the beautiful, young,
The old with pleasure bent to hear the music of thy tongue:
The young with rapture gazed on thee, and their hearts in love were bound,
For thou wast brighter than the sun that sheds its light around.
My soul is dark, O Mary dear! thy sun of beauty's set;
The sorrowful are dumb for thee—the grieved their tears forget;
And I am left to pour my woe above thy grave alone;
For dear wert thou to the fond heart of Morian Shehone.

'Fast-flowing tears above the grave of the rich man are shed,
But they are dried when the cold stone shuts in his narrow bed;

Not so with my heart's faithful love—the dark
grave cannot hide
From Morian's eyes thy form of grace, of loveliness,
and pride.
Thou didst not fall like the sere leaf, when autumn's
chill winds blow—
'Twas a tempest and a storm-blast that has laid my
Mary low.
Hadst thou not friends that loved thee well? hadst
thou not garments rare?
Wast thou not happy, Mary? wast thou not young
and fair?
Then why should the dread spoiler come, my heart's
peace to destroy,
Or the grim tyrant tear from me my all of earthly
joy?
Oh, am I left to pour my woes above thy grave
alone?
Thou idol of the faithful heart of Morian
Shehone!

'Sweet were thy looks and sweet thy smiles, and
kind wast thou to all;
The withering scowl of envy on thy fortunes dared
not fall;
For thee thy friends lament and mourn, and never
cease to weep—
Oh, that their lamentations could awake thee from
thy sleep!
Oh, that thy peerless form again could meet my
loving clasp!
Oh, that the cold damp hand of Death could loose
his iron grasp!

Yet, when the valley's daughters meet beneath the
tall elm tree,
And talk of Mary as a dream that never more
shall be,
Then may thy spirit float around, like music in the
air,
And pour upon their virgin souls a blessing and a
prayer.
Oh, am I left to pour my wail above thy grave
alone?'
Thus sinks in silence the lament of Morian Shehone.

538 *Kitty of Coleraine*

AS beautiful Kitty one morning was tripping
With a pitcher of milk from the fair of Coleraine,
When she saw me she stumbled, the pitcher down
tumbled,
And all the sweet butter-milk watered the plain.
'Oh! what shall I do now? 'twas looking at you, now;
Sure, sure, such a pitcher I'll ne'er meet again;
'Twas the pride of my dairy! O Barney MacCleary,
You're sent as a plague to the girls of Coleraine!'

I sat down beside her, and gently did chide her,
That such a misfortune should give her such pain;
A kiss then I gave her, and, ere I did leave her,
She vowed for such pleasure she'd break it again.
'Twas hay-making season—I can't tell the reason—
Misfortunes will never come single, 'tis plain;
For very soon after poor Kitty's disaster
The devil a pitcher was whole in Coleraine.

539 *By Memory Inspired*

BY Memory inspired,
And love of country fired,
The deeds of men I love to dwell upon ;
And the patriotic glow
Of my spirit must bestow
A tribute to O'Connell that is gone, boys—gone :
Here's a memory to the friends that are gone !

In October Ninety-seven—
May his soul find rest in Heaven !—
William Orr to execution was led on :
The jury, drunk, agreed
That Irish was his creed ;
For perjury and threats drove them on, boys—on :
Here's the memory of John Mitchell that is gone !

In Ninety-eight—the month July—
The informer's pay was high ;
When Reynolds gave the gallows brave MacCann ;
But MacCann was Reynolds' first—
One could not allay his thirst ;
So he brought up Bond and Byrne, that are gone, boys—gone :
Here's the memory of the friends that are gone !

We saw a nation's tears
Shed for John and Henry Shears ;
Betrayed by Judas, Captain Armstrong ;
We may forgive, but yet
We never can forget
The poisoning of Maguire that is gone, boys—gone :
Our high Star and true Apostle that is gone !

How did Lord Edward die?
Like a man, without a sigh;
But he left his handiwork on Major Swan!
But Sirr, with steel-clad breast,
And coward heart at best,
Left us cause to mourn Lord Edward that is gone, boys—gone:
Here's the memory of our friends that are gone!

September, Eighteen-three,
Closed this cruel history,
When Emmett's blood the scaffold flowed upon:
Oh, had their spirits been wise,
They might then realise
Their freedom! but we drink to Mitchell that is gone, boys—gone:
Here's the memory of the friends that are gone!

540 *Music in the Street* (93)

IT rose upon the sordid street,
A cadence sweet and lone;
Through all the vulgar din it pierced,
That low melodious tone.
It thrilled on my awakened ear
Amid the noisy mart,
Its music over every sound
Vibrated in my heart.

I've heard full oft a grander strain
Through lofty arches roll,
That bore on the triumphant tide
The rapt and captive soul.

ANONYMOUS

In this the breath of my own hills
  Blew o'er me soft and warm,
And shook my spirit, as the leaves
  Are shaken by the storm.

As sounds the distant ocean wave
  Within a hollow shell,
I heard within this far-off strain
  The gentle waters swell
Around my distant island shore,
  And glancing through the rocks,
While o'er their full and gliding wave
  The sea-birds wheeled in flocks.

There, through the long delicious eves
  Of that old haunted land
The Naiads, in their floating hair,
  Yet dance upon the strand ;
Till near and nearer came the sound,
  And swelled upon the air,
And still strange echoes trembled through
  The magic music there.

It rose above the ceaseless din,
  It filled the dusky street,
As some cool breeze of freshness blows
  Across the desert's heat.
It shook their squalid attic homes—
  Pale exiles of our race—
And drew to dingy window panes
  Full many a faded face.

And eyes whose deep and lustrous light
  Flashed strangely, lonely there,
And many a young and wistful brow
  Beneath its soft brown hair;
And other eyes of fiercer fire,
  And faces rough and dark—
Brave souls! that bore thro' all their lives
  The tempests on their bark.

In through the narrow rooms it poured,
  That music sweeping on,
And perfumed all their heavy air
  With flowers of summers gone,
With water sparkling to the lips,
  With many a summer breeze,
That woke into one rippling song
  The shaken summer trees.

In it, along the sloping hills,
  The blue flax blossoms bent;
In it, above the shining stream,
  The 'Fairy Fingers' leant;
In it, upon the soft green rath,
  There bloomed the Fairy Thorn;
In their tired feet they felt the dew
  Of many a harvest morn.

In it, the ripe and golden corn
  Bent down its heavy head;
In it, the grass waved long and sweet
  Above their kindred dead;

In it, the voices of the loved,
They might no more behold,
Came back and spoke the tender words
And sang the songs of old.

Sometimes there trembled through the strain
A song like falling tears,
And then it rose and burst again
Like sudden clashing spears ;
And still the faces in the street,
And at the window panes,
Would cloud or lighten, gloom or flash,
With all its changing strains.

But, ah ! too soon it swept away,
That pageantry of sound,
Again the parted tide of life
Closed darkly all around.
As in the wake of some white bark,
In sunshine speeding on,
Close in the dark and sullen waves,
The darker where it shone.

The faces faded from my view,
Like faces in a dream ;
To its dull channel back again
Crept the subsiding stream.
And I, too, starting like the rest,
Cast all the spell aside,
And let the fading music go—
A blossom down the tide.

NOTES

1. *Oliver's Advice* (p. 29).

This ballad is based on a generally accepted anecdote of Cromwell. It is said that on one occasion, when he and his troops were about to ford a river to make an attack upon the enemy, he delivered the usual stimulating address, closing with the words, 'Put your trust in God; but mind to keep your powder dry.'

2. *Fionnuala* (p. 36).

Fionnuala was the daughter of Lir; she and her brothers were turned into swans by the enchantments of her step-mother Aoife, and condemned for centuries to dwell on several Irish waters. One of these was Moyle, the channel lying between the north-east corner of Ireland and Scotland. They were compelled to roam the waters until the sound of St. Patrick's bell should be heard in the land; when this occurred they resumed their shape, but were then old and decrepid creatures, and they immediately died. The legend of the Children of Lir makes one of the 'Three Sorrows of Story-telling.'

3. *Róisín Dubh* (p. 58).

'"Róisín Dubh" (Little Black Rose) is an allegorical ballad, in which strong political feelings are conveyed as a personal address from a lover to his fair one. The allegorical meaning has been long since forgotten, and the verses are now remembered and sung as a plaintive love ditty. It was composed in the reign of Elizabeth of England, to celebrate an Irish hero, Hugh Ruad O'Donnell of Tyrconnell. By Rôisín Dubh, supposed to be a beloved female, is meant Ireland. The toils and sufferings of the patriot soldier are throughout described as the cares and feelings of an anxious lover addressing the object of his affections. The song concludes with a bold declaration of the dreadful struggle which would be made, before the country should be surrendered to the embraces of our hero's hated and implacable rival. The air is a good specimen of the characteristic melancholy which pervades Irish music.'—*Hardiman's 'Irish Minstrelsy.'*

4. *John O'Dwyer of the Glen* (p. 59).

The plaintive note of this song has reference to the destruction of the forest trees in Ireland during the centuries of conquest and confiscation, done both for profit and safety.

5. *Killeevy* (p. 61).

'In the churchyard of Erigle Truagh, in the barony of Truagh, county Monaghan, there is said to be a spirit which appears to persons whose families are there interred. Its appearance, which is generally made in the following manner, is uniformly fatal, being an omen of death to those who are so unhappy as to meet with it. When a funeral takes place, it watches the person who remains last in the graveyard, over whom it possesses a fascinating influence. If the loiterer be a young man it takes the shape of a beautiful female, inspires him with a charmed passion, and extracts a promise to meet in the churchyard in a month from that day; this promise is sealed by a kiss, which communicates a deadly taint to the individual who receives it. It then disappears, and no sooner does the young man quit the churchyard than he remembers the history of the spectre—which is well known in the parish—sinks into despair, dies, and is buried in the place of appointment on the day when the promise was to have been fulfilled. If, on the contrary, it appears to a female, it assumes the form of a young man of exceeding elegance and beauty.'—***Author's Note.***

NOTES

6. *O'Sullivan Bear* (p. 68).

'One of the Sullivans of Bearhaven, who went by the name of Morty Oge, fell under the vengeance of the law. He had long been a very popular character in the wild district which he inhabited, and was particularly obnoxious to the local authorities, who had good reason to suspect him of enlisting men for the Irish Brigade in the French service, in which it was said he held a captain's commission. Information of his raising these "Wild Geese" (the name by which such recruits were known) was given by a Mr. Puxley, on whom, in consequence, O'Sullivan vowed revenge, which he executed by shooting him on Sunday while on his way to church. This called for the interposition of the higher powers, and accordingly a party of military was sent round from Cork to attack O'Sullivan's house. He was daring and well armed; and the house was fortified, so that he made an obstinate defence. At last a confidential servant of his, named Scully, was bribed to wet the powder in the guns and pistols prepared for his defence, which rendered him powerless. He attempted to escape, but while springing over a high wall in the rear of his house he received a mortal wound in the back. They tied his body to a boat, and dragged it in that manner through the sea from Bearhaven to Cork, where his head was cut off, and fixed on the county jail, where it remained for several years. Such is the story current among the people of Bearhaven. In the version given of it in the rude chronicle of the local occurrences of Cork, there is no mention made of Scully's perfidy; and perhaps that circumstance might have been added by those to whom O'Sullivan was deemed a hero, in order to save his credit as much as possible. The dirge was composed by his nurse, who has made no sparing use of the peculiar energy of cursing, which the Irish language is by all allowed to possess.'—*Author's Note.*

Froude has skilfully blended fact and fiction in treating of these incidents, and the struggles of the time in this remote district, in his *Two Chiefs of Dunboy.*

NOTES

7. *Gougaune Barra* (p. 70).

This is a lonely mountain lake about ten miles beyond Inchigeelagh, on the road from Macroom to Glengarriff. It is shut in on all sides by precipitous mountains except the east, where the infant river Lee makes an outlet. Here St. Finbar, founder of the church in Cork, dwelt as a recluse, and to this day the place is frequented by numbers of devotees. The spot has his holy well, and a number of cells in which prayers are said. It has also a cross raised to the memory of Callanan; and a small stone-roofed chapel has been erected here in recent years.

8. *Hy-Brasail* (p. 107).

It has been a popular belief from a very early period, in the Aran Islands and elsewhere on the western coast, that every seven years a shadowy island appears above the horizon, far away out at sea. Ancient tradition tells that a large part of Ireland was sunk beneath the sea, and that this was what rose on the horizon at intervals of time. It was believed to be a very Eden of beauty—the Land of Youth—but, like that earthly paradise, it too was shut out from mankind. Many sailed to find it, never to return, as tradition tells.

8*a*. *The Bridal of Malahide* (p. 116).

'The story of this ballad is historically true, and receives additional interest from the fact that the armour in which the hero of the ballad was slain is still shown in Malahide Castle, and the monument of the heroine in the neighbouring chapel. Speaking of the latter, Mr. D'Alton says: "Of the monuments, the most worthy of notice is an altar tomb surmounted with the effigy, in bold relief, of a female habited in the costume of the fourteenth century, and representing the Honourable Maud Plunket, wife of Sir Richard Talbot. She had been previously married to Mr. Hussey, son to the Baron of Galtrim, who was slain on the day of her nuptials, leaving her the singular celebrity of having been 'a maid, wife, and widow on the same day.'" In a description of the castle, Mr. Petrie refers to the adventure: "On Whitsun-eve, in the year 1329 (as is recorded by Ware), John de Birmingham, Earl of Louth, Richard Talbot, styled Lord of Malahide, and many of their kindred, together with sixty of their English followers, were slain in a pitched battle at Balbriggan [Ballybragan], in this neighbourhood, by the Anglo-Norman faction of the De Verdons, De Gernons, and Savages—the cause of animosity being the election of the earl to the palatinate dignity of Louth, the county of the latter party."'—C. G. D.

9. *Woman of the Piercing Wail* (p. 124).

'The poem is the production of O'Donnell's bard, Owen Roe Mac an Bháird, or Ward, who accompanied the family in their flight (1607), and is addressed to Nuala, O'Donnell's sister, who was also one of the fugitives. The cause of the flight of the Northern Earls that led to the subsequent confiscation of the six Ulster counties by James I. was the discovery of a letter directed to Sir William Ussher, Clerk of the Council, which was dropped in the Council Chamber on the 7th of May, and which accused the Northern chieftains generally of a conspiracy to overthrow the Government. Whether this charge was founded in truth or not, it is not necessary for us to express any opinion; but as in some degree necessary to the illustration of the poem, we extract the following account of the flight of the Northern Earls, as recorded in the *Annals of the Four Masters*:—

'"Maguire (Cuconnaught) and Donogh, son of Mahon, who was son of the Bishop O'Brien, sailed in a ship to Ireland, and put in at the harbour of Swilly. They then took with them from Ireland the Earl O'Neill (Hugh, son of Ferdoragh) and the Earl O'Donnell (Rory, son of Hugh, who was son of Magnus), and many others of the nobles of the province of Ulster. These are the persons who went with O'Neill, namely, his Countess, Catherina, daughter of Magennis, and her three sons; Hugh, the Baron, John and Brian; Art Oge, son of Cormac, who was son of the Baron; Ferdoragh, son of Con, who was son of O'Neill; Hugh Oge, son of Brian, who was son of Art O'Neill; and many others of his most intimate friends. These were they who went with the Earl O'Donnell, namely, Caffer, his brother, with his sister Nuala; Hugh, the Earl's child, wanting three weeks of being one year old; Rose, daughter of O'Doherty and wife of Caffer, with her son Hugh, aged two years and three months; his (Rory's) brother son Donnell Oge, son of Donnell, Naghtan son of Calvach, who was son of Donogh Cairbreach O'Donnell, and many others of his intimate friends."'—*Author's Note* (condensed).

The bard addresses Nuala on finding her weeping at the grave of her brother (Rory O'Donnell), who was buried in the church of S. Pietro Montorio (1608). Eight years later Hugh O'Neill, Earl of Tyrone, was buried near his brother exile, the Earl of Tyrconnell, in the same church.

10. *Martyr-saint* (p. 126).

'St. Peter. This passage is not exactly a blunder, though at first it may seem one: the poet supposes the grave itself to be transferred to Ireland, and he naturally includes in the transference the whole of the immediate locality around the grave.'—*Author's Note.*

11. *Dark Rosaleen* (p. 134).

This is another rendering of 'Róisín Dubh' (see Note 3), Red Hugh O'Donnell's allegorical address to Ireland. The figurative allusions 'wine from the Royal Pope' and 'Spanish ale' are obvious.

12. *Kincora* (p. 138).

This is a rendering of an Irish poem attributed to Mac Liag of the Court of Brian Boru, on the death of the latter at the battle of Clontarf (1014). The lamentation refers to the fallen greatness of Kincora, the chief residence of that monarch, which stood on the right bank of the Shannon, above the bridge of Killaloe.

13. *Mairgréad ni Chealleadh* (p. 158).

'This ballad is founded on the story of Daniel O'Keefe, an outlaw famous in the traditions of the county of Cork, where his name is still associated with several localities. It is related that O'Keefe's beautiful mistress, Margaret Kelly ('Mairgréad ni Chealleadh'), tempted by a large reward, undertook to deliver him into the hands of the English soldiers; but O'Keefe, having discovered in her possession a document revealing her perfidy, in a frenzy of indignation stabbed her to the heart with his skian. He lived in the time of William III., and is represented to have been a gentleman and a poet.'—*Author's Note.*

14. *Keen* (p. 161).

The Irish is 'Caoine.' 'The keener alone sings the extempore death-song; the burden of the ullagone, or chorus, is taken up by all the females present.'—*Author's Note.*

15. *Brighidín bán mo Stór* (p. 166).

'"Brighidín bán mo Stór" is, in English, "Fair young Bride," or "Bridget my treasure." The proper sound of this phrase is not easily found by the mere English-speaking Irish. The following is the best help I can afford them in the case: "Bree-dheen-bawn-mu-sthore." The proper name Brighit, or Bride, signifies a fiery dart, and was the name of the goddess of poetry in the pagan days of Ireland.'—*Author's Note.*

16. *The Woods of Kylinoe* (p. 172).

'The Woods of Caillino' is an old air, and 'Caillino' an old and favourite burden to songs.

17. *The 'Dark Girl' by the 'Holy Well'* (p. 187).

This poem is founded on an incident at St. John's Well, near Kilkenny, to which the author was himself a pilgrim (1832). He says: 'It is believed that when Heaven wills the performance of cures, the sky opens above the well, at the hour of midnight, and Christ, the Virgin Mother, and

St. John descend in the form of three snow-white doves, and descend with the rapidity of lightning into the depths of the fountain. No person but those destined to be cured can *see* this miraculous phenomenon, but everybody can *hear* the musical sound of their wings as they rush into the well and agitate the waters.' The girl in the poem was not healed, but died on her way home.

18. *Bouchalleen Bawn* (p. 188).

Knockawn is a celebrated fairy-haunted rath, and Kilvawn a well-known churchyard in county Kilkenny. Bawn, in the north of the county, is noted for its fair.

19. *Crom Cruach—King Cormac* (p. 203).

Crom Cruach was the principal idol of the pagan Irish, and was destroyed by St. Patrick. It and the 'sub-gods' stood on the plain of Moy Slaught, which was identified by O'Donovan with the district round the village of Ballymacgouran, in the county Cavan.

'Cormac, son of Art, son of Conn Cead-Catha (Conn of the Hundred Battles), enjoyed the sovereignty of Ireland through the prolonged period of forty years, commencing A.D. 213. During the latter part of his reign he resided at Sletty, on the Boyne, being, it is said, disqualified for the occupation of Tara by the personal blemish he had sustained in the loss of an eye by the hand of Angus, "Dread-Spear," chief of the Desi, a tribe whose original seats were in the barony of Deece, in the county Meath. . . . Cormac had obtained the reputation of wisdom and learning, and appears justly entitled to the honour of having provoked the enmity of the pagan priesthood, by declaring his faith in a God not made by hands of men.'—*Author's Note.*

20. *Maledictive Stones* (p. 204).

This was an old pagan custom, and it descended down to modern times. When curses were invoked the stones were turned, and the malediction was not to be made lightly or without good cause, lest the curse should fall on the head of the person who made it. In the island of Inismurray, off the coast of Sligo, the stones may still be seen on an altar within the cashel, or stone fortification.

21. *Brugh* (p. 204).

The series of great tumuli lying on the north bank of the Boyne, between Slane and Drogheda, are considered to be Brugh, one of the chief burial-places of the ancient kings of Ireland. The megalithic chambers of Newgrange and Dowth are of especial interest as survivals of the burial customs of the Bronze Age.

22. *Aideen's Grave* (p. 208).

'Aideen, daughter of Angus of Ben-Edar (now the Hill of Howth), died of grief for the loss of her husband, Oscar, son of Ossian, who was slain at the battle of Gavra (Gowra, near Tara in Meath) A.D. 284. Oscar was entombed in the rath or earthen fortress that occupied part of the field of battle, the rest of the slain being cast into a pit outside. Aideen is said to have been buried on Howth, near the mansion of her father, and poetical tradition represents the Fenian heroes as present at her obsequies. The cromlech in Howth Park has been supposed to be her sepulchre.'—*Author's Note.*

23. *The Tuatha De Danaan* (p. 208).

These were a race of Scythian origin who invaded Ireland and overthrew the Firbolgs at the great battle of Moytura Cong. They were a tall, red or fair haired people, and were great workers in metals and magic; and to this day they are supposed, in popular superstition, to inhabit the raths and rath-chambers that are scattered over the plains and hills of Ireland. They also destroyed the Fomorians—a northern race of pirates who had long harassed the country—on the plains of northern Moytura, twenty-seven years after the defeat of the Firbolgs.

24. *Sand-Bull's roar* (p. 209).

The sandbanks on the shores of Dublin Bay, at the mouth of the Liffey, are called the North Bull and South Bull respectively, from the dull boom of the breaking waves when driven in by strong easterly winds. Clontarf ('Cluain Tarbh') is the Meadow of the Bulls.

25. *Atharna* (p. 212).

Atharna was a bard at the Court of Conor Mac Nessa. He was vindictive and covetous, and had the power—generally attributed to bards—of blighting and destroying the person on whom his curse fell; this power he used for his own ends.

26. *The Sons of Usnach* (p. 214).

The Sons of Usnach were amongst the famous band of Red Branch Knights at the court of Conor Mac Nessa; they were Naisi, Ardan, and Ainle. Conor had Deirdre brought up, intending to make her his wife; but, nearing the time, she happened to see Naisi, loved him, and asked him to marry her. By the rules of the order no knight could refuse a maiden's request, so they fled to Scotland with his brothers and followers. They were persuaded to return home, and the Sons of Usnach were treacherously slain. This is one of the 'Three Sorrows of Story-telling.' (See Note 42.)

27. *Pastheen Finn* (p. 233).

This means 'Fair little child.' The poem is supposed to have a political meaning, and to refer to the Old Pretender. The original is an ancient Connaught song of a melancholy strain and a sweet air.

28. *The County of Mayo* (p. 235).

'This specimen of our ancient Irish literature is one of the most popular songs of the peasantry of the counties of Mayo and Galway, and is evidently a composition of the seventeenth century. The original Irish, which is the composition of one Thomas Lavelle, has been published, without a translation, by Mr. Hardiman, in his *Irish Minstrelsy;* but a very able translation of it was published by Mr. Ferguson, in a review of that work in the *University Magazine* for June 1834.—C. G. D.

Little is known of George Fox. He was a friend of Sir Samuel Ferguson, who dedicated his poems to him in 1880. Lady Ferguson, in the *Life* of her husband, says that he was the author of the poem, but allowed it to be attributed to Fox from the share the latter had in it.

29. *Lament for Owen Roe* (p. 248).

'This striking and dramatic ballad was the *first* written by Thomas Davis. Before the publication of the first number of the *Nation,* Davis, Dillon, and Duffy agreed to attempt political ballads, on which they had great reliance for raising the spirit of the country; to their next meeting Davis brought the "Lament for Owen Roe," and "The Men of Tipperary."'—C. G. D. See Note 9.

Owen Roe O'Neill was nephew of Hugh, Earl of Tyrone (see Note 9), and figured in the Irish wars of 1641–9. A popular suspicion, which still exists, arose at the time that he was poisoned by wearing a pair of russet slippers presented to him by one of the Plunkets of Louth. He died in Lough Oughter Castle, and was buried in the Franciscan Abbey of Cavan, of which there is now no trace.

30. *Sack of Baltimore* (p. 252).

'Baltimore is a small seaport in the barony of Carbery, in South Munster. It grew up round a castle of O'Driscoll's, and was, after his ruin, colonised by the English. On the 20th of June 1631 the crew of two Algerine galleys landed in the dead of the night, sacked the town, and bore off into slavery all who were not too old, or too young, or too fierce for that purpose. The pirates were steered up the intricate channel by one Hackett, a Dungarvan fisherman, whom they had taken at sea for the purpose. Two years after, he was convicted and executed for the crime. Baltimore never recovered this.'—C. G. D.

NOTES

31. *O'Donnell's Answer* (p. 260).

'Maurice Fitz Gerald, Lord Justice, marched to the north-west, and a furious battle was fought between him and Godfrey O'Donnell, Prince of Tirconnell, at Creadran-Killa, north of Sligo, A.D. 1257. The two leaders met in single combat, and severely wounded each other. It was of the wound he then received that O'Donnell died, after triumphantly defeating his great rival in Ulster, O'Neill. The latter, hearing that O'Donnell was dying, demanded hostages from the Kinel Connell. The messengers who brought this insolent message fled in terror the moment they had delivered it; and the answer to it was brought by O'Donnell on his bier. Maurice Fitz Gerald finally retired to the Franciscan monastery which he had founded at Youghal, and died peacefully in the habit of that Order.'—*Author's Note.*

32. *Rory O'More* (p. 263).

Rory O'More of Leix took a leading part in the Irish war of 1641. He was a man of striking personality, and remains a hero in popular tradition. (See Note 91.)

33. *The Dirge of Desmond* (p. 264).

John, Earl of Desmond, was the central figure in the Geraldine Rebellion in Elizabeth's reign. He and his clan owned the greater part of the province of Munster; the land was laid waste by war and famine, his followers slain and scattered, and he, driven into the mountain fastnesses of Kerry, was finally taken in a wild glen beyond Tralee where he was hiding in a wretched hut. His head was cut off, sent to London, and was spiked on London Bridge (1583). The Desmond territory to the extent of about 580,000 acres was confiscated by the Crown.

34. *The Grave of MacCaura* (p. 282).

'At Callan, a pass on an unfrequented road leading from Glanerought (the vale of the Roughty) to Bantry, the country people point out a flat stone by the pathway, which they name as the burial-place of Daniel MacCarthy, who fell there in an engagement with the Fitzgeralds in 1261. The stone still preserves the traces of characters, which are, however, illegible. From the scanty records of the period it would appear that this battle was no inconsiderable one. The Geraldines were defeated, and their leader, Thomas Fitzgerald, and his son, eighteen barons, fifteen knights, and many others of his adherents slain. But the honour and advantage of victory were dearly purchased by the exulting natives, owing to the death of their brave and noble chieftain.'—*Author's Note.*

35. *Fag an Bealagh* (p. 284).

'To make the general tone and some of the allusions in this song intelligible, we should, perhaps, mention that it was written in October 1842, when the hope and spirits of the people were low; and published in the third number of the *Nation*, as the Charter-song of the contributors. It was supposed to be first sung, as it actually was, at one of their weekly suppers.

'"Fag an Bealach" (Clear the road), or, as it is vulgarly spelt, "Faugh a Ballagh," was the cry with which the clans of Connaught and Munster used in faction fights to come through a fair with high hearts and smashing shillelahs. The regiments raised in the South and West took their old shout with them to the Continent. The 87th, or Royal Irish Fusileers, from their use of it, went generally by the name of "The Faugh a Ballagh Boys." "Nothing," says Napier in his *History of the Peninsular War*, "so startled the French soldiery as the wild yell with which the Irish regiments sprang to the charge;" and never was that haughty and intolerant shout raised in battle, but a charge swift as thought, and fatal as flame, came with it, like a rushing incarnation of "Fag an Bealach!"'—*Author's Note.*

36. *Inishowen* (p. 288).

'Inis-Eoghain (commonly written Innishowen, and pronounced Innishone) is a wild and picturesque district in the county Donegal, inhabited chiefly by the descendants of the Irish clans permitted to remain in Ulster after the plantation of James I. The native language and the old songs and legends of the country are as universal as the people. One of the most familiar of these legends is that a troop of Hugh O'Neill's horse lies in magic sleep in a cave under the hill of Aileach, where the princes of the country were formerly installed. These bold troopers only wait to have the spell removed to rush to the aid of their country; and a man (says the legend) who wandered accidentally into the cave found them lying beside their horses, fully armed, and holding the bridles in their hands. One of them lifted his head, and asked, "Is the time come?" but receiving no answer—for the intruder was too much frightened to reply—dropped back into his lethargy. Some of the old folk consider the story an allegory, and interpret it as they desire.'—*Author's Note.*

37. *The Irish Rapparees* (p. 290).

'When Limerick was surrendered, and the bulk of the Irish army took service with Louis XIV., a multitude of the old soldiers of the Boyne, Aughrim, and Limerick preferred remaining in the country at the risk of fighting for their daily bread; and with them some gentlemen, loth to part from their estates or their sweethearts, among whom Redmond O'Hanlon is, perhaps, the most memorable. The English army and the English law drove them by degrees to the hills, where they were long a terror to the new and old settlers from England, and a secret pride and comfort to the trampled peasantry, who loved them even for their excesses. It was all they had left to take pride in.'—*Author's Note.*

38. *Lord Lucan* (p. 290).

'After the Treaty of Limerick, Patrick Sarsfield, Lord Lucan, sailed with the brigade to France, and was killed whilst leading his countrymen to victory at the battle of Landen, in the Low Countries, on July 29, 1693, saying, as he drew his hand, covered with his heart's blood, from his bosom, and looking at it, "Would that this were for my native land."'—*Author's Note.*

39. *Wild Geese* (p. 299).

The recruits raised for service in France, in the ranks of the Irish Brigade, were conveyed thence by the smuggling vessels which brought wines and brandy to the west coast of Ireland. They were entered in the ship's books as 'Wild Geese,' and their name as such became generally known among the peasantry. The 'Wild Geese' have been from that time until now a favourite theme with verse-writers.

40. *The Clan of MacCaura* (p. 300).

'MacCartha (the correct way of spelling the name in Roman characters) is pronounced in Irish MacCaura, the *th* having, in that language, the soft sound of *h.* The MacCarthys trace their origin to Heber Fionn, the eldest son of Milesius, King of Spain, through Oilioll Olium, King of Munster, in the third century.'—*Author's Note.*

41. *Miodchuart* (p. 301).

This was the great hall at Tara, the remains of which now consist of two parallel lines of earth about 760 feet long. Once every three years the great national convention or Feis was held, when the hall was the scene of great banquets. It was divided into sections, and the openings or entrances on each side may still be traced.

42. *The Red Branch Knights* (p. 301).

These were a famous military order at the court of Conor Mac Nessa, King of the Ultonians, whose palace was Emania, the great fort near Armagh. They attended here yearly under their respective leaders, to be trained in feats of arms and the art of war. One of the most noted of the order was Cuchullain, and round him and his knights a whole cycle of tales has been woven. (See Note 26).

NOTES

43. *Dathy* (p. 302).

'Dathy was killed at the foot of the Alps by lightning, and Niall (his uncle and predecessor) by an arrow fired from the opposite side of the river by one of his own generals, as he sat in his tent on the banks of the Loire, in France.'—*Author's Note.*

44. *Diarmid MacCarthy* (p. 302).

'Diarmid MacCarthy, King of Desmond, and Daniel O'Brien, King of Thomond, were the first of the Irish princes to swear fealty to Henry II.'—*Author's Note.*

45. *Arigideen* (p. 303).

'The Arigideen means "The little silver stream," and Allo "The echoing river." By these rivers and many others in the south of Ireland, castles were erected and monasteries founded by the MacCarthys.'—*Author's Note.*

46. *Lady Wilde* (p. 324).

Jane Francesca Wilde was an early contributor to the *Nation*, and wrote under the name 'Speranza.'

47. *John OHagan* (p. 335).

John O'Hagan was another early contributor to the *Nation*, and wrote under the name 'Sliabh Cuilinn' (Slieve Gullion), a mountain in county Armagh, near Newry.

48. *Ourselves Alone* (p. 337).

The sentiments of this poem anticipate those of the Sinn Fein party of the present day. Both titles, too, are practically identical.

NOTES

49. *A Munster War-Song* (p. 341).

'This ballad relates to the time when the Irish began to rally and unite against their invaders. The union was, alas! brief, but its effects were great. The troops of Connaught and Ulster, under Cathal Croibhdearg (Cathal O'Connor of the Red Hand), defeated and slew Armoric St. Lawrence, and stripped De Courcy of half his conquests. But the ballad relates to Munster; and an extract from Moore's book will show that there was solid ground for triumph: "Among the chiefs who agreed at this crisis to postpone their mutual feuds, and act in concert against the enemy, were O'Brian of Thomond, and MacCarthy of Desmond, hereditary rulers of North and South Munster, and chiefs respectively of the two rival tribes, the Dalcassians and Eoganians. By a truce now formed between those princes, O'Brian was left free to direct his arms against the English; and having attacked their forces at Thurles, in Fogarty's country, gave them a complete overthrow, putting to the sword, adds the Munster annals, a great number of knights."'—C. G. D.

50. *The Wearing of the Green* (p. 351).

This version of the famous ballad occurs in one of Boucicault's plays, and is that usually adopted. The original, which is given among the anonymous poems in this collection (No. 530), dates from 1798, and the author is unknown. (See Note 89.)

51. *A Peasant Woman's Song* (p. 352).

'A few days ago I stood on the North Wall and watched the emigrants embarking for the Far West, as I have often stood on the quays of New York to see them arrive in America. While chewing the cud of many sweet and bitter fancies over this sad review, and picturing to myself the fate of each group as it passed, a chord in the old harp, which every Irishman wears in his breast, twanged in a minor key, and I heard a young Irish wife in the backwoods of Ohio singing this strain.'—*Author's Note.*

NOTES

52. *The Memory of the Dead* (p. 353).

This famous lyric was contributed to the *Nation* in April 1843, when the writer was in his twentieth year. He was never a member of the Young Ireland party, and this was his only contribution to its literature.

53. *The Coolun* (p. 362).

This is justly considered one of the finest of the ancient Irish melodies. The 'Coolun' came to mean 'The youth with the flowing locks.' Statutes were once enforced against wearing the 'Coolun' or long lock of hair, and the bards put in verse the preference of a maiden for a lover who wore it, and so kept alive national sentiment. It thus became a sign of patriotism to wear the 'Coolun,' as in later times the short hair became the sign of a rebel or 'Croppy.' The same idea was embodied in the flowing locks of the Cavalier and the short hair of the Roundhead.

54. *Mary Eva O'Doherty* (p. 391).

Mrs. O'Doherty (Mary Eva Kelly) became a contributor to the *Nation* when quite a young girl, and wrote her 'Lament for Davis' under the signature 'Eva,' the name by which she has since been universally known.

55. *Ocean God* (p. 394).

Manannan, Mac Lir (Son of the Sea), was the god of waters—the Neptune in ancient Irish mythology. Crom was the god of fire, the sun. Bride, or Brighid, was the daughter of the sun, and goddess of wisdom and poetry.

56. *A Soldier's Wake* (p. 402).

'A young soldier of the 18th Royal Irish, named Mac Donnell, was blown to atoms before Sebastopol. A few days since our young hero's widowed mother had his medal with four clasps presented to her, the only relic of her son.

In the course of the evening the poor woman "laid out" the medal on the kitchen table, and having procured four mould candles, she collected her neighbours and kept up the "wake" until an early hour the following morning' (*Tralee Paper*).—*Author's Note.*

57. *William B. M'Burney* (p. 405).

This is the supposed author who contributed to the *Nation* under the signature of 'Carroll Malone' and 'Pontiac.' Who he was is unknown, and even his Christian name and the spelling of his surname are uncertain.

58. *Shane O'Neill* (p. 407).

Shane O'Neill, known as 'Shane-an-Diomais' (John the Proud), was the son of Conn Bacach O'Neill, Earl of Tyrone. He was in constant rebellion against the English power in Ireland; but he was massacred, with fifty of his followers, by the Scots of Antrim at Cushendun in 1567.

59. *Love-angels* (p. 420).

'According to a Rabbinical tradition, the Seraphim, or Angels of Love, are dearer to Jehovah, and stand nearer to His throne, than the Cherubim, or Angels of Light and Intellect.'—*Author's Note.*

60. *Fineen O'Driscoll* (p. 423).

'The O'Driscolls owned Baltimore on the south Cork coast, with the adjacent territory and islands, where the ruins of several of their castles are still to be seen: they were noted sailors and sea-rovers. The hero of this ballad was Sir Finneen O'Driscoll, who flourished in the sixteenth century; and the ruins of his castle at Dunnalong—the "old castle" of the first line of the ballad—still stand on the shore of Sherkin Island, near Cape Clear. His exploits as a bold sea champion are well remembered in history.'—*Author's Note.*

NOTES

61. *Eivlin a Ruin* (p. 446).

'The story of this song anticipates and possibly suggested that of the "Young Lochinvar." The youthful poet-chief O'Daly had been plighted to Eivlin Kavanagh, of the princely house of Leinster, who loved him. In his absence, her parents forced another suitor on her. Carrol O'Daly, however, disguised as a harper, appeared at the feast and won her to fly with him. Handel highly admired the beauty of the air, to which the words of "Robin Adair" and "Erin, the Smile," have been set.'—*Author's Note.*

The source of the air has been the subject of much controversy, being claimed by Scotland and Ireland alike, but there is now no doubt of its Irish origin. It was popular in Elizabethan times, and in the eighteenth century it was a general favourite on the stage. A well-known Irish drinking-song, 'Welcome to Puckstown,' addressed to Robin Adair of Holybrooke, county Wicklow (d. 1737), was set to the air, and it became generally known by his name. It was not until the middle of the eighteenth century that it appeared in a Scotch collection of song. In 1811 the air was adapted to the well-known song, 'What's this dull town to me, Robin Adair,' founded on the romantic love-affair between Lady Caroline Keppell and Robin Adair, a noted surgeon and friend of George III.

62. *Deirdre's Farewell to Alba* (p. 454).

On the elopement of Deirdre with Naisi, the Sons of Usnach and she fled to Alba (Scotland), where they remained for a time. They were induced to return by Fergus, who went over at the request of Conor, and who promised a safe-conduct; but Deirdre had a premonition of their fate, and it is sounded in the melancholy note of the 'Farewell.' (See Note 26.)

63. *Turann* (p. 458).

The fate of the sons of Turann (Tuireann) makes one of the 'Three Sorrows of Story-telling.' Cian, father of Lugh, was wantonly slain by the sons of Turann in a revolt of the

De Danaan against the Fomorians, who exacted a heavy tribute from them. The sons were condemned to pay the eric or blood-fine, and a ninefold task of great difficulty was placed upon them. Through many terrible trials and sufferings the punishment was gone through, and the sons reach Erin wounded, and sick unto death. The unhappy father vainly appealed to Lugh to let one of their spoils—the magic skin of the sow of Túis — be cast upon them and heal them. But the revenge which he nursed for his father's death had in no way cooled, and he refused the request. Turann recites the death-song, and expires on the bodies of his sons.

64. *Lament of Aideen* (p. 459).

Aideen was wife of Oscar, the grandson of Finn Mac Cumhaill. (See Note 21.)

65. *Helen's Tower* (p. 483).

This tower was built on the summit of a hill in the demesne of Clandeboye, to enshrine verses by Helen, Lady Dufferin, on the coming of age of her son, the late Marquis of Dufferin, in 1847. The verses are in an octagonal oak-panelled chamber in the tower, with others by Tennyson and Browning.

66. *Fand* (p. 495).

Cuchullain, prince of the Red Branch Knights, is wooed by the beautiful goddess Fand, who had been the bride of the sea-god Manannan, but was abandoned by him. Emer, wife of Cuchullain, appears and pleads with her husband not to forsake her; and he is finally restored to Emer by the interference of Manannan, and the magic of the Druids, who give to him and his wife drinks of forgetfulness.

67. *Moytura* (p. 497).

On the eve of the battle of Northern Moytura, when the Fomorians were defeated by the De Danaan, the gods of the latter are supposed to be assembled on the summit of Knocknarea. Lu, the sun-god, calls upon Dagda, their bard, to sing of their past achievements, and the lines here quoted are the close of his recital.

68. *De Danaan* (p. 508).

A race of invaders who succeeded the Firbolgs. (See Note 23.)

69. *Droighnean Donn* (p. 513).

The Irish 'Droigheanán donn' ('Drynán dhun') is the sloebush or blackthorn, and is figuratively applied to a lover—a dark-complexioned young man. The song (see No. 536) and air are old, and the former has often been published as a street ballad. There are several variations of the air; the last printed is that by Dr. Joyce in his *Old Irish Folk Music and Songs*, published for the Royal Society of Antiquaries (1909).

70. *The Red Branch Knights* (p. 519).

A great military order in Ulster in the first century. (See Note 42.)

71. *The Grave of Rury* (p. 525).

'Ruraidh O'Conchobhar, last High King of Ireland, died and was buried in the monastery of St. Fechin at Cong, where his grave is still shown in that most beautiful and pathetic of Irish ruins. All the accounts agree in this, but some have it that his remains were afterwards transferred to Clonmacnois by the Shannon.'—*Author's Note.*

72. *St. Michan's Churchyard* (p. 528).

St. Michan's Churchyard, Dublin, is one of the reputed burial-places of Robert Emmet; but the exact spot where his body was laid to rest has never yet been ascertained. Dr. Emmet, an American relative, visited the city a few years ago and conducted a careful inquiry, making an examination of the several places claimed, but with no satisfactory results.

73. *A Spinning Duet* (p. 551).

Dr. Sigerson, quoting O'Curry (*Ancient Music of Ireland*), says that it 'was the custom of peasant girls, when engaged in preparing wool or flax, to assemble. Sometimes the daughter of the house, and some helpers; sometimes the girls of two or three neighbouring families, formed the group. They sang whilst they worked. Now, each sang in turn a popular song; again, and more frequently, two sang alternately extemporaneous verses to peculiar airs, reserved for this kind of song. One girl starts the song by saying she had wandered in a wood; her companion supplies a motive, and with quiet irony suggests a name which she knows will be rejected, whilst she affects to commend its owner. The jest goes on until a favourite is found, when a benison is pronounced.'—*Bards of the Gael and Gall.*

74. *Dunlang O'Hartigan* (p. 554).

'When the Dalcassian hero, Dunlang O'Hartigan, the friend and companion of Murrough, Brian Baroimhe's eldest son, was on his way to the Battle of Clontarf, Aoibhell, the Fairy Queen, met him and tried to dissuade him from fighting that day. For she told him that he would fall with Murrough, and she offered him the delights and the immortality of Fairyland if he would remain away. But he replied that nothing would induce him to abandon Murrough on the day of the battle, and that he was resolved to go, even to certain death. She then threw a magical cloak around him, which made him invisible, warning him that he would certainly be slain if he threw it off. He rushed into the midst of the battle and fought for some time by the side of Murrough, making fearful havoc among the Danes. Murrough looked round him on every side, and at last cried out, 'I hear the sound of the blows of Dunlang O'Hartigan, but I cannot see him!' Then Dunlang could no longer bear to be hidden from the eyes of Murrough, and he threw off the cloak, and was soon after slain, according to the Fairy's prediction.'—*Author's Note.*

75. *Woman of Beare* (p. 556).

'This is an adaptation of a literal rendering of an ancient Irish poem published by Professor Kuno Meyer in *Otia Merseina*. . . . The woman of Beare figures, I believe, in more than one legend. She appears to have been one of these creatures, neither wholly divine nor human, but of more than mortal powers, whom the first Christians found in Ireland. To some, as to the mermaid of Lough Neagh, on their conversion the choice was offered, whether to die at once and go to heaven, or to receive another span of life. It seems as if the woman of Beare made the second choice (unlike S. Liban's convert): and in any case she is the female counterpart to Ossian, and expresses for her sex, as he for the men, a sense of all that is lost by acceptance of the Christian ideal.'—*Author's Note.*

76. *Maeve.*

Maeve was the daughter of Eochy, Ard-Righ, or Head King of Ireland, at the time of the Red Branch Knights; she became Queen of Connaught. The capture of the great brown bull from the Ultonians, who were headed by Cuchullain, and in which foray Maeve led her forces in person, forms the subject of the epic—'Táin bó Cuailgne,' the Cattle-raid of Cooley. She caused the death of her husband Ailill, a Leinster prince, and Maeve herself was slain by a son of Conor Mac Nessa, with a sling-stone cast from the Leinster side of Lough Ree, as she was bathing in its waters. Her reputed burial-place is in the great cairn on Knocknarea, five miles from Sligo. It is an immense pile of loose stones, nearly 600 feet in circumference, and 34 feet high, and is known as Mioscán Maeve. There is evidence, however, to show that she was buried at Rath Croghan, in Roscommon, where she reigned as queen.

77. *Niamh* (p. 601).

Niamh was a wise woman in old Celtic mythology and typical of spiritual beauty. At her request Ossian went in search of Tir-nan-Óg, the Land of Youth.

78. *A Caoine for Owen Roe* (p. 619).

Owen Roe O'Neill was the ablest Irish general in the war of 1641. (See Note 29.)

NOTES

79. *The Stranger's Grave* (p. 649).

'In a graveyard upon Inishmaan,[1] dedicated to unbaptized babies, an unknown drowned man lies buried.'—*Author's Note.*

80. *Shane O'Neill* (p. 672).

On coming of age he took the title of Baron of Dungannore, which was granted to his reputed brother Matthew, and openly rebelled. (See Note 58.)

81. *Amergin* (p. 681).

Amergin, brehon and poet, was one of the Milesian princes who colonised Ireland in pre-Christian times. Some fragments of his verses, generally considered the earliest in the language, have come down to us through ancient manuscripts, of which modern renderings have been made by Dr. Sigerson and Dr. Douglas Hyde.

82. *Grania* (p. 685).

Grania was daughter of Cormac Mac Art, Ard-Righ of Ireland, and was affianced to Finn Mac Cumhaill, Chief of the Fianna, the militia of Erin. But she fell in love with Diarmuid, a lieutenant under Finn, and prevailed on him to carry her away from her hated union with that hero. Popular tradition points to the cromlechs scattered over Ireland as having been erected by Diarmuid for their nightly shelter, during the long pursuit of the lovers by Finn and his followers. Diarmuid met his death at Benbulbin, a conspicuous mountain in Sligo, by a wild boar. Finn appeared on the scene, and refused to save the life of the wounded warrior, by giving him a drink with his hand which was gifted with miraculous powers of healing. Notwithstanding the anger of Grania at this act, she was, according to tradition, afterwards reconciled to Finn, and became his wife.

[1] Aran Islands.

NOTES

83. *The Little Flower Strewers* (p. 699).

'These verses, which borrow their name from one of the prettiest stories ever written—*The Little Flower Seekers*, by Lady Gilbert (Rosa Mulholland)—was suggested by seeing the children kiss each handful of the flowers with which they strewed the corridors of the Convent of Mercy, Baggot Street, Dublin, during the procession of the *Quarant' Ore*, June 24, 1879.'—*Author's Note.*

84. *Deirdre Wed* (p. 722).

The elopement led to the tragic death of the Sons of Usnach, and Deirdre did not long survive their fate. (See Notes 26 and 62.)

85. *Cleena* (p. 734).

Cleena was the Queen of the Fairies of South Munster, and her palace was Carrig-Cleena, near Mallow. Tradition tells how she, a stranger and wanderer from Fairyland, came to Ireland and landed on the shore of Glandore Harbour, co. Cork. Tired and weary she lay down to sleep on the strand, but was drowned by the tide. She survived, however, in the kingdom of the Wee Folk. From the earliest times the sound of the ocean billows breaking on the caverned cliffs of Glandore has been known as 'Tonn-Cleena,' or Cleena's waves.

86. *The Boyne Water* (p. 738).

This version of the famous Orange song is fragmentary. It is that published by Sir Charles Gavan Duffy, and is the oldest. It is more stirring and spirited than the song by Colonel Blacker, which is that usually sung at Orange gatherings.

87. *Shule Aroon* (p. 740).

'The date of this ballad is not positively known, but it appears to be early in the eighteenth century, when the flower of the Catholic youth of Ireland were drawn away to recruit the ranks of the Brigade. The inexpressible tenderness of the air, and the deep feeling and simplicity of the words, have made the ballad a popular favourite, notwithstanding its meagreness and poverty.'—C. G. D.

The version in the text is that given by Dr. Joyce in his *Old Irish Folk Music.* The Irish spelling runs—

'Is go d-téidh tu, a mhúirnín, slán !
Siubhail, siubhail, siubhail, a rúin !
Siubhail go socair, agus siubhail go ciúin
Siubhail go d-ti an doras agus eulaigh liom,
Is go d-téidh tu, a mhúirnín, slán !'

which is literally translated in Mr. Halliday Sparling's collection—

'Move, move, move, O treasure !
Move quietly, and move gently,
Move to the door, and elope with me,
And mayst thou go, O darling, safe !'

88. *The Cruiskeen Lawn* (p. 741).

This inimitable bacchanalian ditty was probably founded on some Gaelic original, of which there are several with the same title and refrain. It belongs to the eighteenth century, when conviviality was universal in Ireland, and has been a general favourite in drinking circles since then. It has been attributed to John O'Keefe the dramatist, but the author is unknown. The striking feature of the song is the clever combination of the two tongues in the same strain. The Irish refrain runs—

'Grádh mo chroidhe mo crúiscín,
Slainté geal mo mhúirnín,
Is grádh mo chroidhe a cúilín bán.
Grádh mo chroidhe mo crúiscín,
Slainté geal mo mhúirnín,
Is grádh mo chroidhe a cúilín, bán, bán, bán,
Is grádh mo chroidhe a cúilín bán.'

The English is—

'The love of my heart is my little jug,—
Bright health to my darling !
The love of my heart is her fair hair,' etc.

NOTES

89. *The Wearin' o' the Green* (p. 742).

This is the old version of the famous street ballad, which was slightly altered by Boucicault, and to which he added a third stanza (see No. 208). The lines referring to Napper Tandy seem to have been adapted from 'The Green upon the Cape,' another ninety-eight ballad. The tune dates probably from the beginning of the eighteenth century, and was printed in 1756. It was a favourite volunteer and rebel marching tune at the close of the century; in the next it became very popular from having been sung by Madame Vestris. (See Note 50.)

90. *The Shan Van Vocht* (p. 743).

This song was written on the occasion of the French fleet starting for Ireland in 1796. A storm scattered the ships, and but a few entered Bantry Bay. The versions of the song are numerous, and on occasions of political excitement, ever since it originated, the title and refrain have been adapted to the popular sentiment of the hour. There are several excellent modern adaptations, notably by Dr. Todhunter, Charles J. Kickham, and Michael Doheny; the last is printed in this volume, No. 110.

91. *Rory O'Moore* (p. 745).

'Roger, or Rory O'Moore, is one of the most honoured and stainless names in Irish history. Writers, who concur in nothing else, agree in representing him as a man of the loftiest motives and the most passionate patriotism. In 1640, when Ireland was weakened by defeat and confiscation, and guarded with a jealous care constantly increasing in strictness and severity, O'Moore, then a private gentleman, with no resources beyond his intellect and his courage, conceived the vast design of rescuing her from England, and accomplished it. In three years England did not retain a city in the island but Dublin and Drogheda. For eight years her power was barely nominal; the land was possessed and the supreme authority exercised by the Confederation created by O'Moore. History contains no stricter instance of the influence of an individual mind. Before the insurrection broke out, the people had learned to know and expect their deliverer, and it became a popular proverb and the burden of national songs, that the hope of Ireland was in "God, the Virgin, and Rory O'Moore." It is remarkable that O'Moore, in whose courage and resources this great insurrection had its birth, was a descendant of the chieftains of Leix, massacred by English troops at Mullaghmast, a century before. But if he took a great revenge, it was a magnanimous one; none of the excesses which stained the first rising in Ulster are charged upon him. On the contrary, when he joined the Northern Army, the excesses ceased, and strict discipline was established, as far as it was possible, among men unaccustomed to control, and wild with wrongs and sufferings.'—C. G. D.

92. *The Lamentation of Hugh Reynolds* (p. 746)

'This ballad has, I understand, been popular in some districts of Ulster for forty years; and two correspondents have sent me details connected with the case out of which it arose. One of them, writing from Cavan, says:—

'"On reading in the 'Ballad Poetry of Ireland' the 'Lament of Hugh Reynolds,' I remembered well when a child going to see him in his condemned cell, on a Good Friday. He was executed the following Tuesday; and as it excited an interest in my mind, I applied to the governor of the prison, Mr. Galloghly, who gave me the date of his execution, the 28th March 1826. He told me that Catherine MacCabe was a very reluctant witness, and was remanded to prison to force her to give evidence against him. He was invited into Cavan by her friends in order to get married. When he came to town, instead of acting according to promise, they handed him over to the police, and he was convicted of housebreaking and abduction. His brother and a man named O'Hara were committed as accomplices, but admitted out on bail. Before the assizes O'Hara left for America. Some of his friends, knowing the consequences, urged the brother John to leave also; but he declared his perfect innocence, and relied on that as sufficient : poor fellow ! he was convicted, and sentenced to die with his brother. However, by the incessant entreaties of his friends to the grand jury and Colonel Sanderson (a great local potentate), a memorial was forwarded to the Castle, and his sentence was commuted; he was finally released after a few months' imprisonment."

'A second correspondent says :—

'"The Reynolds and MacCabe families were both county Cavan people and Catholics. There had been a standing quarrel between them, originating in a 'bit of land.' Both were respectable, but the Reynolds were 'reduced.' Catherine MacCabe swore that Reynolds took her off by force; he, in his dying speech, declared that she went with him freely. The girl's uncle was the person universally believed to be the instigator of the prosecution. I remember him well; his hair was white as snow, and his dress semi-clerical. There was universal sympathy for Reynolds. Catherine MacCabe left Cavan immediately after the execution, and soon died, it was said, of a broken heart. The ballad of 'Hugh Reynolds' is still sung here; and it was a popular belief that a judgement of God pursued the MacCabe family."'—C. G. D. (1866).

93. *Music in the Street* (p. 755).

This poem was written in America. It was published in the collection of *Popular Poetry of Ireland* by 'Duncathail' (Ralph Varian) in 1865, who says that it was suggested by hearing 'Patrick's Day' and 'Garryowen' played on the 4th of July by the band of the 69th Regiment in the streets of New York.

INDEX OF AUTHORS

The figures refer to the numbered selection, not to the pages

INDEX OF AUTHORS

INDEX OF AUTHORS

INDEX OF FIRST LINES

The figures refer to the pages

INDEX OF FIRST LINES

INDEX OF FIRST LINES

INDEX OF FIRST LINES

INDEX OF FIRST LINES

INDEX OF FIRST LINES

INDEX OF FIRST LINES

INDEX OF FIRST LINES

INDEX OF FIRST LINES

INDEX OF FIRST LINES

INDEX OF FIRST LINES

INDEX OF FIRST LINES